PEACE, WAR, AND TRADE ALONG THE GREAT WALL

PEACE, WAR, AND TRADE ALONG THE GREAT WALL

Nomadic-Chinese Interaction
through Two Millennia

SECHIN JAGCHID

AND

VAN JAY SYMONS

INDIANA UNIVERSITY PRESS
Bloomington and Indianapolis

© 1989 by Sechin Jagchid and Van Jay Symons
All rights reserved

No part of this book may be reproduced or utilized in any form or by any means, electronic or mechanical, including photocopying and recording, or by any information storage and retrieval system, without permission in writing from the publisher. The Association of American University Presses' Resolution on Permissions constitutes the only exception to this prohibition.

Manufactured in the United States of America

Library of Congress Cataloging-in-Publication Data

Jagchid, Sechin
[Pei Ya yu mu min tsu yü chung yüan nung yeh min tsu chien ti ho p' ing, chan cheng, yü mao i chih kuan hsi. English]
Peace, war, and trade along the Great Wall : Nomadic-Chinese interaction through two millennia / Sechin Jagchid, Van Jay Symons.
p. cm.
Translation of: Pei Ya yu mu min tsu yü chung yüan nung yeh min tsu chien ti ho p' ing, chan cheng, yü mao i chih kuan hsi.
Bibliography: p.
Includes index.
ISBN 0-253-33187-0
1. Asia, Central—Relations—China. 2. China—Relations—Asia, Central. 3. Nomads. I. Symons, Van Jay. II. Title.
DS329.4.J3413 1989
303.4'8258'051—dc19
88-46020
CIP

1 2 3 4 5 93 92 91 90 89

All battle is well said to be misunderstanding.
—Carlyle

To the myriads of people who, because of misunderstanding, suffered and died along nomadic-sedentarist frontiers

CONTENTS

PREFACE		ix
INTRODUCTION		1
Chapter I.	Trade or Raid	24
Chapter II.	Peace or War	52
Chapter III.	Frontier Markets	79
Chapter IV.	Tribute and Bestowals	114
Chapter V.	Intermarriage	141
Chapter VI.	Conflict or Calm	165
NOTES		189
BIBLIOGRAPHY		224
GLOSSARY		233
INDEX		259

PREFACE

This study began over twenty years ago in 1967 while Sechin Jagchid was a professor of history and Mongolian literature at National Chengchi University and National Taiwan University. It was prompted by Jagchid's concern that historians give inadequate attention to the recurrent conflict between agrarian and nomadic peoples along the Great Wall of China. Initial inquiry led to the Chinese publication in 1972 of *Peace, War and Trade Relationships between the Northern Asian Nomadic People and the Agricultural Chinese*. Joseph Fletcher of Harvard University and Henry Serruys, CICM, then encouraged Jagchid to translate the work and publish it in English. In 1982, Jagchid approached Van Jay Symons and asked him to collaborate on revising and preparing the Chinese work for publication in English.

The challenge in preparing this manuscript for Indiana University Press has been to condense the Chinese work to less than half its original length, give it greater focus, and consider similar studies completed in the West. The Chinese publisher of Jagchid's original work, Cheng-chung Book Company, Ltd., has graciously consented to our publishing this book in English.

During its preparation, we benefited from the editing of our work by our wives, Oyongerel Jagchid and Ruth Thomson Symons. The calligraphy in the glossary and bibliography was done by Oyongerel Jagchid. We are also grateful to Brigham Young University and Augustana College, where we teach, for providing an environment conducive to research. Augustana College also provided travel money to enable us to meet to work on the final drafts.

PEACE, WAR, AND TRADE ALONG THE GREAT WALL

CHRONOLOGICAL TABLE

NOMADIC STEPPE REALM · AGRARIAN CHINESE REALM

NOMADIC PARTICIPANTS	WEST	EAST	NORTH	SOUTH	CHINESE PARTICIPANTS
	Yüeh-chih		Chou Dynasty 1122-256		Shih Huang-ti (r.246-210)
Mao-tun (r.209-174)	Hsiung-nu 200s B.C.-220s A.D.	Tung-hu	Ch'in 221-207		Kao-ti (r.206-195)
Chun-ch'en (r.161-126)			Former Han 206 B.C.-A.D. 8		Wu-ti (r.140-87)
					Wang Hui
Hu-han-yeh (r.58-31)					Han An-kuo
					Hsüan-ti (r.73-49)
			Hsin A.D. 9-23		Wang Mang (r.9-22)
		Wu-huan			Yen Yu
		Hsien-pei	Later Han 25-220		Kuang-wu-ti (r.25-56)
T'an-shih-huai (d.181)		Hsien-pei			
K'o-pi-neng (d.229)			Three Kingdoms 222-280		Ts'ao Ts'ao (d.220)
			Western Chin 265-316		
			Sixteen Kingdoms 304-439	Eastern Chin 317-420	
	T'o-pa		Wei (T'o-pa) 386-557	Sung 420-479	
Jou-jan (Juan-juan) 400-550				Ch'i 479-502	
A-na-k'ui (r.518-552)			Ch'i 550-77	Liang 502-557	
Ishbara Khan (r.581-587)	Turks (T'u-chüeh) 552-744	K	Chou 557-81	Ch'en 557-589	Princess Ch'ien-chin
Shih-pi Khan (r.609-618)			Sui 581-618		Yang-ti (r.605-618)
					Kao-tsu

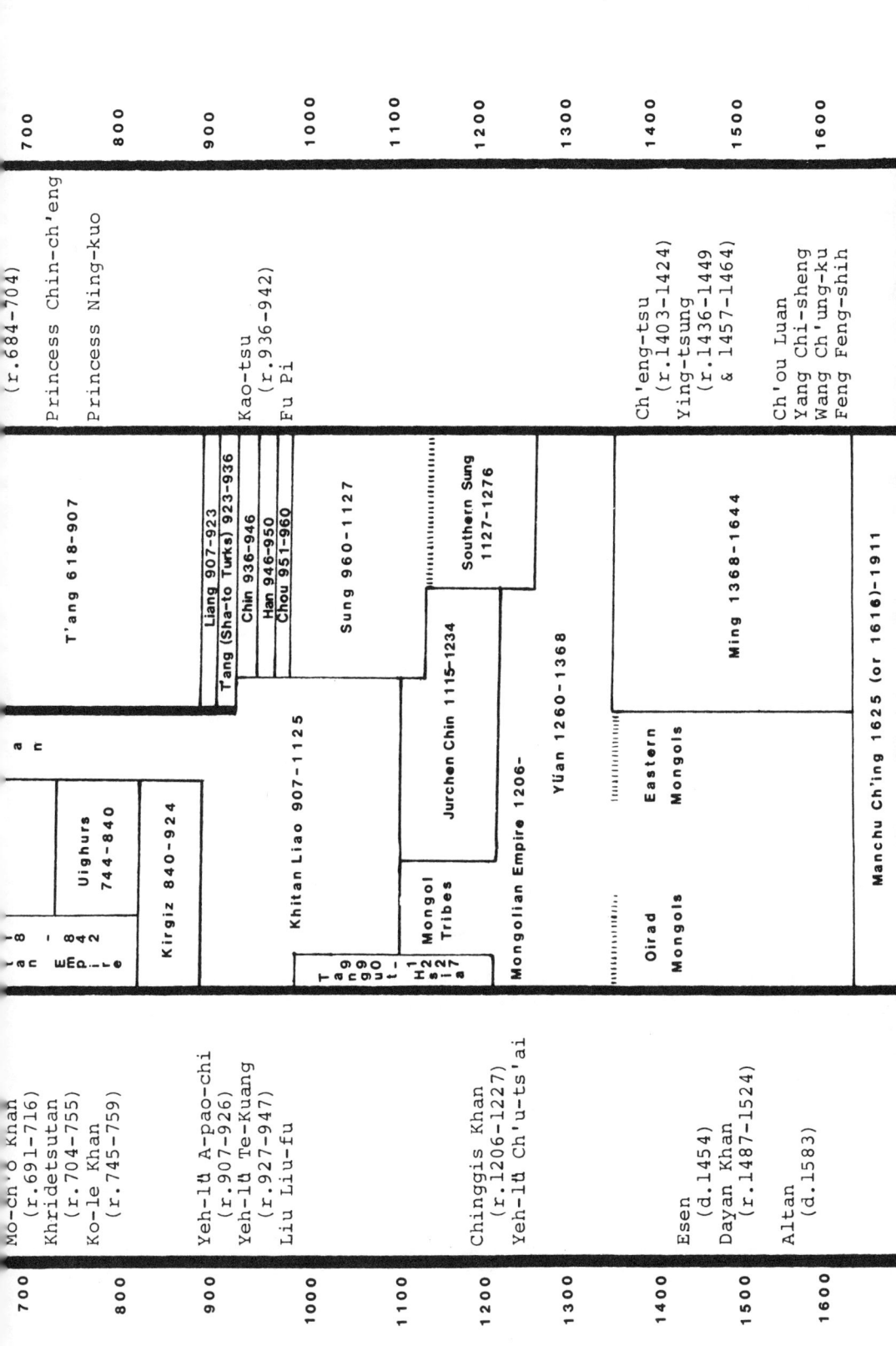

INTRODUCTION

For more than two millennia, trade was the essential element that determined whether peace or war existed along China's northern frontier. Although nomadic peoples derived from their animals transportation, food, clothing, and shelter, they still depended upon the richer and more settled Chinese for grain to supplement their diets; for silk and cotton cloth to provide the beauty, fineness, and comfort their animal skins and wool lacked; and for manufactured goods such as plows to break up the soil or transform into battle weapons. In exchange for the coveted Chinese commodities, nomads offered furs, hides and wool; exotic goods such as jade or precious metals; or domestic animals, particularly horses. Sturdy horses from the steppes played a key role in China's defense of its northern borders, and as a consequence, were the most valuable trade item of the nomadic peoples.[1] When grain, cloth, and manufactured goods could be obtained easily by nomadic peoples, peace was possible, but when exchange mechanisms were closed, war often occurred.

With the exception of a few dynastic periods, this book examines relations between China and her northern nomadic neighbors from the second century B.C. until the middle of the seventeenth century A.D. It focuses on three important institutions created as early as the Han period to facilitate the transfer of goods between China and the nomads. They were frontier markets, the presentation of tribute in exchange for bestowals, and intermarriage. Because nomads depended on goods acquired from their sedentary neighbors and also frequently possessed military forces superior to those of China, they sometimes raided the frontier or waged war on China to gain essential commodities or to force Chinese dynasties to expand the above-mentioned institutions. Nomads carefully and continually gauged whether existing frontier markets, tributary exchange, or intermarriage arrangements were more advantageous to them than raiding China. In turn, Chinese dynasts constantly weighed the costs of maintaining these exchange mechanisms against the expense of warring with nomads. When the nomads felt they were getting too little or the Chinese felt they were giving too much compared to the relative power of each participant in the exchange process, war broke out. This book suggests that trade was the key issue which determined whether peace or war existed along the constantly changing Sino-nomadic frontiers.

Trade was important to pastoral nomads because they depended upon ruminant animals. Nomadic herds utilized natural grasses as fodder, which dictated that non-pastoral activities be accommodated to the need of the animals to move to new grazing land.[2] As a consequence, nomads preferred to trade for the grain essential to their diet because those who attempted to grow their own were forced to break the sod, sow the seed, irrigate the fields, and harvest the crop as a sideline to their primary activity of raising livestock. Because of the numerous obstacles they faced agricultural pursuits were more precarious than herding. The soil was often poor, the tools used for cultivation were primitive, weather conditions were uncertain, and travel to and from one's herds to the fields was often tortuous. During times of unrest or war, it was difficult to tend the fields.

The Soviet anthropologist Sevyan Vainshtein suggests that his studies of pastoral nomads in Tuva show that cultivation was practiced by only the most "barbaric" nomads, those who lived great distances from China, which made trading for grain almost impossible. Wealthy pastoralists who were affluent enough to acquire draft animals, agricultural tools, and seed shunned agriculture. They preferred to trade for or let client households produce grain for them, because animal husbandry was more profitable and involved less risk than farming.[3]

Vainshtein's study also suggests that "the technology of nomad craftsmen was sufficient to make virtually everything required in the economy, even guns and gunpowder copied early on from the Chinese, but the peoples living near settled populations came to acquire high-quality and luxury goods by trade."[4] Some essential objects unique to the nomad, such as pack-carriers, felt, bows, and saddles, were produced only by nomad craftsmen, although they sought other items from sedentary neighbors.[5]

Few early works recognized trade as the determining factor that prevented the outbreak of hostilities along China's northern frontier. During the past two decades, however, research on the importance of trade to frontier stability has increased. Before examining studies on the significance of trade, it is important to consider other explanations for the frequent conflict between nomad and sedentarist. One plausible cause is cultural misunderstanding and incompatibility.[6]

Traditionally, Chinese historians suggested that it was the nature of nomads to be greedy, and this greed made them aggressive. In the *Shih chi*, the Chinese historian Ssu-ma Ch'ien insists that "The Hsiung-nu people are against the Heavenly Way. [They] take robbing and stealing as their business."⁷ And again he states: "The reason that they carry out robbing and looting is because their nature is so."⁸ Chinese were often critical and condescending toward the nomads. They were chauvinistic and considered nomadic peoples barbarous and uncivilized, and, at the same time, they regarded their country, the Middle Kingdom, as endowed with a superior culture.

By suggesting that nomads were barbarians, Chinese historians provided an explanation for frontier conflict, but is it not possible that a second, little studied explanation for nomadic-Chinese discord was nomadic indignation toward Chinese ethnocentrism and arrogance? What nomadic leader would not have found intolerable the formula developed at the end of the sixteenth century by the Ming statesman Chang Chü-cheng advocating that the Ming court work with the Mongols as a master would his vicious dog: "The important principle is for the officials in charge to deal with them in a flexible manner: Just like dogs, if they wag their tails, bones will be thrown to them; if they bark wildly, they will be beaten with sticks; after the beating, if they submit again, bones will be thrown to them again; after the bones, if they bark again, then more beating. How can one argue with them about being crooked or straight or about the observation of law?"⁹

China was often willing to allow less civilized neighbors access to their culture and coveted products, but whenever possible it made the exchange of goods contingent upon nomadic acceptance of Chinese superiority. However, as evidenced by Pan Ku's essay on the Hsiung-nu in the *Han shu*, even when nomads submitted, the Chinese government generally sought to limit nomadic-Chinese interaction. There were several reasons why trade with the nomads was restrained. First, Chinese insisted that they possessed everything (*ti ta wu po*), and in reality, there were only a few goods which nomads could successfully exchange with Chinese. Second, with the exception of a few periods, the dynasties drew most of their income from the countryside by taxing the peasantry. Because they relied little on the income from trade and customs duties to finance government, trade seldom received the dynastic attention given agrarian concerns. Third, there was an intellectual bias against trade. The Confucian philosophy of the Chinese state relegated merchants to the bottom rung on the social ladder on the grounds that merchants did not produce essential goods, such as the grain provided by peasants, or secondary products, like those provided by artisans. It was suggested that merchants enriched themselves at the expense of others and independently produced little of value to the state. As a consequence, trade and merchant activities were often not encouraged by the government. Fourth, sometimes the dynasties did not provide the goods solicited by nomads because they reasoned that trading with nomadic peoples would only enhance nomadic strength and deny the Chinese essential commodities, which could further weaken China. Chinese unwillingness to exchange goods with nomads was also fostered by a realization that nomadic demands for Chinese goods might become excessive and by a fear that nomadic peoples might use trade as a mechanism to spy on China and plan future attacks.

Chinese scholars reasoned that frontier markets and tributary institutions were opened to exchange goods only because of the beneficence of the Chinese court to the nomads. They assumed that the frequency and size of exchange missions were determined by the Middle Kingdom and accepted the assertions found in Chinese documents of Chinese superiority and the premise that nomads quite freely abandoned their own culture in favor of an imitation Chinese one. Historians also suggested that Chinese military actions were basically defensive, thereby casting the Chinese as pacifist and the nomad as the aggressor.

In reality exchange mechanisms established to enable nomads to secure essential goods were often inadequate. Furthermore, despite Chinese rhetoric to the contrary, market and tribute exchanges were frequently dictated to the Chinese by nomadic neighbors who found Chinese assumptions of superiority galling and disruptive to peaceful intercourse. Nomadic military prowess often left the Chinese with no alternative but to meet the nomads' demand for Chinese goods. Furthermore, most nomads exchanged goods with the Chinese and avoided being assimilated by them. As suggested by Yü Ying-shih, there was often as much barbarization of frontier Chinese as Sinicization of the nomad.[10] The chasm between Chinese and nomadic perceptions of themselves and each other, coupled with the abyss between the Chinese rhetoric and the reality of what determined frontier policy, both of which are tied to cultural misconceptions and incompatibility, contributed to the continuing discord between the two sides.

Nineteenth- and early twentieth-century Western scholarship on Sinonomadic relations was limited and generally accepted Chinese assertions of the centrality of the Middle Kingdom, the barbarous nature of nomads, and the willingness of nomads to recognize Chinese preeminence. When

Western historians conducted research on the tributary system, they focused on Sino-Western rivalry along the Southeast China coast.[11] They studied the implications of China's assertions of superiority and China's insistence that Western merchants work within the constraints of a highly regimented trading system to the stabilization of relations with Portugal, Holland, England, and other European nations. During the first opium war (1840–42), the English, restive with the constraints posed by the frontier marketing system at Canton, made war with China and forced it to abandon the tributary system. England secured for itself, and other Western nations that followed its lead, unequal treaties guaranteeing Western access to the trading markets which they coveted. Many of the problems faced by the Western "barbarians" seeking trade with China were identical to those traditionally faced by nomadic "barbarians," yet few Western historians of China effectively saw the link. When conflict occurred between sedentarist and nomad, early Western scholars ignored the factors which led to Anglo-Chinese rivalry, and like the traditional Chinese historians, generally attributed it solely to the rapaciousness of barbarians.[11]

However, beginning with the studies of Ellsworth Huntington and Arnold Toynbee, Western scholars offered a second explanation for Chinese-nomadic conflict. They suggested that physical nature as well as human nature dictated Chinese-nomadic interaction. Arnold Toynbee recognized that Chinese and other sedentarists were inclined to attribute eruptions along their borders to "a demonic force of will and strength of purpose . . ." possessed by evil nomads.[12] However, Toynbee insisted that nomadic invasions were produced mechanically. For example, when a sedentary government fell or declined, a vacuum might be created that would pull its nomadic neighbors toward its relatively unguarded riches. He also recognized that the harsh climate of the steppes could push nomads toward sedentary states.

Drawing from the earlier work of Huntington,[13] who analyzed rainfall patterns by studying tree rings and sediment deposits on lake and river beds, Toynbee asserted that there had been periodic shifts in the location of the climatic zones that encircle the earth latitudinally. As these zones shifted, the arid subtropical zones inhabited by nomadic peoples, which lie between the humid tropical zone and the temperate zone occupied by more sedentary people, had been the most dramatically affected. Increased aridity forced nomads to search for new pasture lands, which led them into conflict with other nomadic peoples. As weaker tribes were driven off their pastures, they in turn contested with other nomads and eventually internal disruption erupted into aggressive actions against sedentarist neighbors. In periods of climatic change, if the arid zone shifted northward, sedentarists south of the nomadic zone were tempted to push north and cultivate land which now received sufficient moisture, although previously it was suitable only for pasture. This, of course, accentuated nomadic-sedentarist conflict.

To verify that climatic change pushed the nomads into violent struggle with the sedentarists, Toynbee attempted to tabulate as many historic eruptions of nomads as possible and correlate them to changes in climate. He claimed that the massive Mongol eruption of the thirteenth-century correlated with a severe period of desiccation in the Central Eurasian[14] steppes and that their fourteenth-century retreat back to their native steppes was made possible by a climatic rebound toward humidity.

Toynbee's findings also suggested that nomadic eruptions were sometimes synchronistic, occurring simultaneously in different regions. For example, during the era when the Cimmarians and Scythians were pushing through the passage between the Pamirs and the Caspian, the Arabs were pressing upon the upper Euphrates from the opposite direction. Additionally, he noted that the expansion of nomads into zones occupied by sedentarists and the eventual retreat of nomads back to the steppe was cyclical and regular with periods of maximum effervescence every six hundred years.

Toynbee believed that both the existence of simultaneous incursions and their cyclical nature argued strongly for climatic influence. However, he recognized that not all nomadic incursions correlated with his climatic tables. He attributed those that did not correspond to climatic variation to the rush of nomads into the vacuums created when there was an absence of effective governmental and military powers in neighboring sedentarist states.[15]

Some scholars, notably G. F. Hudson and Owen Lattimore, challenge Toynbee's concept that increased desiccation inevitably led to the contraction of grazing areas available for nomadic herds, forcing nomads to attack sedentarist neighbors. They suggest that, although a south-to-north shift in aridity would increase the amount of desert in the south, it would also extend the amount of grassland northward at the expense of forested areas. The nomads' domain would shift northward, but the amount of pastureland available for grazing would not notably change.[16]

A more recent study by Gareth Jenkins also suggests that climatic changes may have contributed to nomadic expansion. Jenkins is less deterministic than Toynbee and Huntington but believes that his study of cyclical variations in mean annual temperatures rather than desiccation patterns shows that there may have been a steep decline in the temperatures in Mongolia in the years 1175–1260. This sharp deterioration of weather conditions would adversely affect the extent and height of steppe grasses crucial for domestic and wild animals and extend and make the winters in Central Eurasia more severe, thereby threatening the nomadic livelihood and encouraging Mongol expansion.[17]

The efforts of Huntington, Toynbee, and others, suggesting that the long and tragic history of Chinese-nomadic conflict was dictated by climatic changes, provided an explanation other than nomadic greed or the unwillingness of nomads to accept the Chinese premise of superiority to account for the frequent hostility between nomad and Chinese. Although natural disasters did deprive nomads of food, clothing, and shelter which sometimes caused them in desperation to raid and pillage along Chinese borders, it must be recognized, however, that even during times of climatic stability, nomads relied on Chinese grain, cloth, and manufactured goods and struggled to secure them. Conflict between nomad and sedentarist was not always precipitated by climatic disaster.

In 1982, Joseph Fletcher completed an essay in which he proposed to provide some partial answers to a number of fundamental questions frequently raised about the Mongols during the twelfth to fourteenth centuries. The question of most relevance to this study is what set the Mongols under Chinggis Khan in motion. Fletcher cites an article published in 1972 by Hsiao Ch'i-ch'ing, which summarizes seven basic reasons suggested by scholars for nomadic-Chinese conflict: (1) the greediness and predatory nature of nomads; (2) desiccation of the steppe; (3) overpopulation of the steppe; (4) trade interruptions on the part of the Chinese which prevented nomads from selling surplus goods; (5) the need of nomads to supplement their low-level productivity with the surpluses of the more settled agrarian economy; (6) the desire of nomadic leaders to build a supratribal polity; and (7) the drive of nomads to feel equal to the Chinese and affirm their belief in divine destiny.

Fletcher suggests that any or all of these factors working together may have contributed to the outbreak of Mongol expansion. However, he pays little attention to the premise of traditional Chinese historians who blame warfare on the predatory nature of nomads (number one above). He also downplays arguments which attribute conflict to natural or physical disruptions (number two above), which, in turn, may have set in motion the third and fifth factors. Rather, Fletcher provides a third explanation for war between China and the nomads by suggesting that Chinggis Khan believed he was divinely destined (number seven above) and that the rise of Mongol power in the twelfth century was due to the charismatic leadership of Chinggis Khan and his drive to build a nomadic state (number six above).[18]

Frederick J. Teggart completed a study a short time after Toynbee's in which he observed that billiard balls ricochet off one another like one uprooted nomadic tribe against another, a process which could spread westward from the easternmost edge of the Asian land mass. He asserted that his study of historical developments between 58 B.C. to 107 A.D. shows that there is a correlation between events occurring in Han dynastic China and Europe. "Within these decades every barbarian uprising in Europe followed the outbreak of war either on the eastern frontiers of the Roman empire or in the 'Western Regions' of the Chinese."[19] The study claims that twenty-seven of the forty outbreaks in Europe during this period are traceable to policy changes initiated by the Han government, which disrupted nomadic-sedentarist trade.[20]

Teggart cites classical explanations given to explain barbarian outbreaks. Caesar attributed the migrations of Germanic peoples to ". . . the number of the people and the lack of land."[21] Other scholars thought that barbaric invasions were due to the "martial spirit,"[22] "the longing for adventure,"[23] and "the thirst of rapine"[24] of the nomads. He also notes the extensive debate which has emerged focused on the "climatic pulsations" and desiccation theories of Huntington and Toynbee. However, Teggart suggests that during the period of his study, wars to the west of the Pamirs were primarily due to struggles between the Han and Hsiung-nu to gain control of the silk route trade to the east in the Tarim basin. He believes that trade was essential to stability along the Chinese-nomadic frontier and asserts that a disruption of trade in the East ultimately led to the outbreak of conflict in the West because layers of tribes traded with the Hsiung-nu to obtain the goods they secured from China. When the Hsiung-nu were denied essential goods, all those who, in turn, traded with the Hsiung-nu suffered.[25]

Teggart's observations about the pivotal nature of events in the Tarim Basin to subsequent developments great distances from Central Eurasia have recently been reaffirmed by Christopher I. Beckwith. Beckwith's work is a thorough attempt to chronicle the struggle to build empires among Tibetans, Turks, Arabs, and the Chinese. Although his research deals with the early middle ages, spanning the seventh through the ninth centuries rather than the earlier Han-Hsiung-nu rivalry studied by Teggart, he shows that the focal point of this struggle was again the vast region of Central Eurasia upon which all these great powers bordered. Like Teggart, Beckwith suggests that there was a correlation of events between these countries and even those more distant, most strikingly evidenced by political revolts of great significance which occurred in the Carolingian, Abbisid, Uighur Turkic, and T'ang Chinese realms from 742 to 755. Significantly, all these revolts have been connected to Central Eurasia.[26]

Beckwith's book is primarily a narrative history and, as such, does not thoroughly examine the multiple causes underlying conflict. However, the author does insist that "the importance of the international trade routes through Central Eurasia cannot be overemphasized."[27] Because our work is a study of the Chinese-nomadic frontier, it does not address the broader struggle that, in Beckwith's opinion, dominated Central Eurasia. However, it is clear that the control of the transfer of goods through Central Eurasia has been contested by great powers throughout history. The nomads to the north of China came to regard these goods as essential to their livelihood. In turn, they transferred surplus Chinese silks and luxury items or exchanged these items with traders who carried them westward and realized huge profits by selling them to distant neighbors. Empires sought to control the oases and trade routes of Central Eurasia because they realized they could derive vast profits by either extorting monies from traders or by directly involving themselves in marketing activities.

Recent studies by Thomas J. Barfield and Henry Serruys; edited works of collected essays such as *The Chinese World Order* and *China Among Equals*; and, equally important, the investigations of anthropologists best summarized by A. M. Khazanov have begun to challenge some of the views wed to the traditional Chinese analysis of history, the position of Toynbee, and others. Of particular interest to the thesis of this study is the increasing focus evident in these recent works on the nomads' economic dependence on neighboring sedentarists and the growing recognition of the active role played by nomads to secure essential commodities, themes addressed as early as 1972 in Sechin Jagchid's *Pei-Ya yu-mu min-tsu yü Chung-yüan nung-yeh min-tsu chien ti ho-p'ing chan-cheng yü mao-i chih kuan-hsi* [Peace, War, and Trade Relationships between the Northern Asian Nomadic People and the Agricultural Chinese]. As a consequence, a fourth category, focused on nomadic efforts to secure Chinese goods, is emerging as an explanation for the frequent conflict along China's northern frontiers.

In an essay published in 1981 on "The Hsiung-nu Imperial Confederacy," Thomas J. Barfield suggests that the development of a nomadic state, or "supratribal polity," to use Fletcher's terminology, occurred when nomads were forced to deal more effectively with larger and more highly organized sedentary neighbors.[28] Barfield believes that Han tribute and trade mechanisms seldom provided adequate amounts of grain and other goods to sustain the growing appetites of the Hsiung-nu. As a consequence, Hsiung-nu leaders effectively devised a "predatory strategy of extortion aimed at impressing the Han court with their power"[29] in order to extract even more advantageous trade privileges and subsidies for their people. According to Barfield, the Hsiung-nu state arose to organize military campaigns and conduct foreign affairs with China. It succeeded because the Hsiung-nu chose not to conquer and occupy China but rather to exploit it from a distance. Such policies enabled the Hsiung-nu elite to maintain themselves at the expense of China without exploiting their nomadic subjects.

Barfield cites Egami to show that the economy of the Hsiung-nu empire "was relatively complex, depending on trade, gifts or subsidies from China, and taxes from conquered areas, in addition to their own pastoral production."[30] Barfield asserts that continued Hsiung-nu domination of the imperial confederacy depended on their ability to remain the intermediary between China and the tribes of the steppe. "In time of war the *Shan-yü* [Khan] organized raids that provided loot for both his followers and the Hsiung-nu state.[31] In time of peace the *Shan-yü* acted as sole intermediary between China and the steppe, bringing trade and subsidies that could be redistributed throughout the state hierarchy. By drawing on resources from outside the steppe, the Hsiung-nu state gained a stability it could not otherwise achieve."[32]

Barfield suggests that the Hsiung-nu manipulated the Chinese to enhance their power within the confederacy. They signed treaties with China which guaranteed that the Han and the Hsiung-nu were to be ranked as coequal states, that Chinese princesses would be given in marriage to Hsiung-nu *Shan-yü*, and that tribute would be presented the

Introduction

Hsiung-nu for merely promising to refrain from raiding the frontier. Tributary goods and Chinese subsidies were then distributed among the tribal elite to secure their continued support. Hsiung-nu leaders also demanded that frontier markets be opened to allow ordinary nomads to trade for the goods they desired.[33]

Whereas the focus of Fletcher's essay was the growth of Mongol power in the twelfth century and Barfield's study deals with Hsiung-nu relations with the Han some two thousand years ago, Henry Surreys devoted his life to studying Mongol relations with China during the Ming era (1368–1644). His research is frequently cited in this study because he focused on the trade and tribute institutions of the Ming period, institutions which this study examines through a longer time frame. Serruy's works suggest, as does this study, that peace was possible when a Chinese state was willing to maintain institutions which enabled nomads to obtain essential goods.

Some essays in the edited works *The Chinese World Order* and *China Among Equals* further examine and challenge previous assumptions about the dynamic between nomad and sedentarist. The essays of Chusei Suzuki and Joseph Fletcher in *The Chinese World Order* show that China's claim to cultural superiority was rejected by the more powerful Hsiung-nu during the Han and by Islamic potentates during the Ming. David Farquhar also suggests that the Mongols were initially recognized essentially as equals by the Manchus, who ruled China during the Ch'ing period (1644–1912). Han, Ming, and Ch'ing courts lavished gifts and trade opportunities on these northern neighbors to entice them to enroll as tributaries. The combination of military power to provide stability along the frontier and financial strength to insure tributary exchange was needed to deter nomadic aggression by meeting the demands of border peoples for Chinese goods.[34]

China Among Equals is a compilation of essays about Chinese relations with its nomadic and sedentary neighbors from the tenth through the fourteenth centuries. Essays in this work challenge the traditional view that the foreign relations of China were uniformly applied throughout her history. They make it clear that when nomads required grain, craft or manufactured articles, and textiles from China, they raided the frontier if trading possibilities were unavailable. Because, from the tenth through the fourteenth centuries, nomadic power was on the ascendance, Chinese dynasties, such as the Sung, adopted pragmatic and flexible policies to placate them. Ofttimes northern neighbors demanded and received tribute from the Chinese states and conducted relations with them as diplomatic equals.[35] The actual rhetoric of Sino-nomadic relations varied, depending on the relative strength of each party, but generally during this period, official communications suggested diplomatic equality. However, official records not to be read by barbarians were critical of them and, privately, Chinese intellectuals still held condescending views toward the nomads.[36]

The aforementioned scholars have begun to effectively challenge old assumptions regarding the tributary system and Chinese-nomadic relations. Many argue, as does this work, that trade and other exchange mechanisms were essential to sustain peace along the frontiers between nomad and sedentarist. Increasingly, anthropologists are also reconsidering traditional scholarship about nomads and coming to the same conclusions. An excellent summary of recent anthropological studies on the nomad is provided by A. M. Khazanov in *Nomads and the Outside World*.

Khazanov's work, though comparative and general in focus, primarily deals with nomadic-sedentarist relations in Central Eurasia. He insists that all nomads have had a multifarious influence on sedentary neighbors. Khazanov also suggests that "nomads could never exist on their own without the outside world and its non-nomadic societies. . . ."[37] He agrees with Mahmud Kashgari, who said: "There is no Turk [i.e., nomad—Khazonov] without a Tadjik [sedentary], there is no hat without a head."[38] Khazanov next seeks to discover laws which govern the interrelations between nomads and the outside world.[39] His observations are pertinent to our thesis.

Khazonov observes that nomads generally did not trade for profit "but [for] the elementary means of existence."[40] "Agriculturalists could, in principle, get by without trading with nomads,"[41] however, ". . . for nomads, trade with agriculturalists was a necessary and vital concern, particularly when they were unable to secure for themselves supplies of agricultural and handicraft products by other methods."[42] As a consequence, nomads played the active role in the exchange, driving their herds to the frontiers of China without waiting for traders to enter the steppes.[43] Because the nomads were dependent on Chinese goods, and China frequently sought to stop or limit trade, they were left with little alternative but to resort to arms to gain trade concessions.[44]

Khazanov attempts to explain the origin of nomadic states by suggesting, as did Barfield in his study of the Hsiung-nu, that a major factor leading to the emergence of nomadic states was the need to maintain ". . . regular and uninterrupted trade between the nomads and the sedentary population."[45] He believes that Temüjin's emergence on the eve of the twelfth century was fostered by the instability in Central Eurasia. He also suggests that, once Temüjin was proclaimed Chinggis Khan in 1206, the future of the nascent Mongolian state depended on successful external expansion because the nomadic confederation could only be held together by guaranteeing participants loot, trade, and subsidies.[46]

Khazonov notes that despite the immense extractive abilities of nomadic states, they were, for the following reasons, inherently unstable and generally short-lived. First, nomadism is comparatively labor unintensive and dictates that herdsman travel in small bands to insure adequate water and grazing areas for their animals. Consequently, large nomadic groups could band together for only short periods of time. Second, the livestock-breeding economy of nomadic peoples is constantly threatened by jute, droughts, epidemics, and enemy raids.[47] Vainshtein suggests that it was not uncommon for the pastoral nomads of Tuva to lose one quarter or even one half of their livestock in any one year to disease, predators, or a severe winter.[48] "Decentralization was the most common state of nomadic societies, with central authority appearing only when there was an opportunity for regular military exploitation of other communities."[49]

This book confirms that stable trading relations were essential to insure peace along China's northern frontier. Because nomads acquired essential grain, cloth, and manufactured goods from their sedentary neighbors, the nomad, not the Chinese, was the initiator of most nomadic-Chinese dialogs. It was the nomad, generally through force of arms, who insured that the frontier market and tributary exchange system continued. The pattern of trade and diplomatic relations was most often dictated by nomadic—not Chinese—courts, and nomads were less interested in emulating the Chinese than they were in securing prized goods.

When nomadic peoples approached the frontiers of China, seeking trade with the often unsympathetic and frequently hostile Chinese, they had three options. First, they could clandestinely conduct trade with Chinese and other people from inside the Great Wall who ignored government prohibitions against the private exchange of goods in order to enrich themselves. Second, they could humble themselves, recognize the Chinese assertion of political and cultural superiority, and enroll themselves as tributaries to China. Having shown proper submissiveness, they might then be allowed limited access to the Chinese marketplace. Finally, they could deny China's claim to superiority, attack the frontiers, and seize the goods they desired.

Established trade and tributary exchange was particularly advantageous to nomadic leaders because the Chinese court presented treasures directly to the leaders rather than to their subjects, and they were not obligated to share this wealth with those beneath them. On the other hand, nomadic raids were more beneficial to the rank and file nomadic soldier because custom dictated that booty acquired in war was to be equitably distributed among all participants.[50] Because border defenses were generally quite strong and war with the Chinese was often costly, peace was generally preferred by nomadic peoples to war. However, if the Chinese closed markets and managed to limit the amount of goods surreptitiously exchanged, nomadic rulers were left with little choice but to raid China to acquire the grains and cloth they needed.

For the nomadic peoples north of China, the decision to submit and accept tributary status or attack and renounce Chinese superiority depended on a number of factors, including the relative strength of each party, the impact of weather or disease upon their flocks or herds, the internal dynamics within both the Chinese and their own courts, political and psychological motives affecting the actions of each party, the nature of the often fluid and chaotic frontier zones, and whether or not the Chinese bureaucracy was functioning effectively. This last factor was vital if the frontier markets were to remain open and in the maintenance of the elaborate institutional network needed to uphold the trade and tributary system, which was essential in the keeping of the peace.

As a rule, when the power of a nomadic people and a Chinese state was nearly equal, there was a better chance for peace. When a Chinese court was uncertain of its ability to destroy a nomadic state, it was more willing to establish markets and maintain intermarriage and bestowal mechanisms. When functioning properly, these institutions enabled required goods to reach the hands of China's northern neighbors and negated the need for war. However, when either a nomadic state or a Chinese one became notably stronger than the other, it became less concerned with maintaining an effective dialog, less reliant upon peaceful trading mechanisms, and more prone to rely upon military solutions. Nevertheless, for nomadic states, the opportunity to trade depended upon military power, and the quantity and quality of goods traded was determined by the ratio of power between the nomadic and sedentary peoples. Relative power also determined the rhetoric used in the exchange of court-to-court documents between nomadic and Chinese rulers. For example, powerful Hsiung-nu rulers addressed the Han court on a brother-to-brother basis, and the northern rulers of the Liao and Chin dynasties addressed the Sung court on an uncle-to-nephew basis,[51] whereas some Mongols of the Ming period accepted a vassal-to-lord relationship.

Economically, tribute exchange between two agrarian states was not very important. As a rule, tribute relations between China and the sedentary peoples of Korea and Vietnam were forced upon those countries by the Chinese. Tribute presentation was demanded of these neighboring countries for political reasons, as a visible recognition of Chinese superiority. On the other hand, tribute relations with northern nomadic states were basically a form of economic exchange, having less political significance. Nomadic people generally imposed tribute relations upon the Chinese. Powerful nomadic states simply demanded that Chinese courts accept their "tribute" and, in return, received larger and more valuable bestowals from the Middle Kingdom. Thus, in reality, it was the Chinese who offered "tribute" to nomadic rulers.

Chinese emperors who were inclined to limit court sponsored exchange between China and its northern neighbors ignored the fact that denying nomadic leaders the goods essential to their well-being often forced them to raid the frontiers and make war against China. Nomadic incursions were generally calamitous for China, and pursuing nomadic armies into the vast expanses of Central Eurasia to destroy them was often futile. Nomadic people possessed formidable and generally superior military abilities. In addition, it was immensely difficult to provision Chinese armies with adequate food and fuel supplies during their distant campaigns. Logistical problems were so great that no single Han expedition against the Hsiung-nu lasted even one hundred days.[52] Conducting war against nomadic armies was costly and ineffective.

The failure of the court to open regular channels for trade also encouraged widespread clandestine exchange. Because the frontiers of China were highly fluid and inhabited by Chinese ruffians, vagabonds, exiles, and military personnel, smuggling of every sort took place, rampantly whenever an officially sponsored exchange system was not established and moderately even when it was, despite decrees that smugglers would be executed. Through illegal trading activities, smugglers derived substantial profits that otherwise might have flowed to the court.

Faced with the dual threat of nomadic incursion and clandestine trading activities, while at the same time realizing the futility and enormous expense occasioned by war, Chinese courts sometimes acquiesced to the demands of nomadic leaders and created trade institutions for them which were both costly and humiliating for the Chinese to maintain. Many Chinese emperors recognized that allowing nomadic peoples the opportunity to trade was preferable to provoking them to raid. They admitted, as did one T'ang ruler, that "If we wish to take from them we have to give to them."[53] By regularizing trade with nomadic peoples the government also hoped to curtail illicit trading activities and funnel revenues derived from the exchange into court rather than private coffers.

Although relations between nomadic and Chinese courts were in reality based on power politics, Chinese rulers suggested that paternalistic and virtuous motives lay behind decisions to exchange goods with their northern neighbors. In fact, they sought to utilize trade to strengthen their political, diplomatic, and cultural well-being. However, nomadic people were frequently unwilling to accept the Chinese assertion of superiority or the concept of a Sino-centric world, based upon the premise that the Chinese emperor was the "Son of Heaven" dutifully acting as an intermediary between Heaven and earth for not just the Chinese people but for all peoples within the realm of Chinese influence.[54] Still, continued Chinese insistence on the centrality of their kingdom softened the blow sustained by the Chinese psyche when nomadic military superiority forced them to meet the economic demands of nomadic states. The myth of Sino-centrality aided Chinese emperors to maintain their dynastic power.

The institutional mechanisms ultimately created by nomadic and Chinese courts to facilitate the peaceful exchange of goods were frontier markets, tribute and bestowal, and intermarriage. When these institutions functioned effectively, the borders between China and nomadic states were relatively stable, but the peace was constantly disrupted by outbreaks of war, which was the fault of both the Chinese and the nomad. The chauvinistic Chinese were sometimes unreceptive to people of another culture and unwilling to accommodate the needs of their northern neighbors, and nomadic peoples were equally critical of Chinese culture. Frequently, nomads asked for more than they needed, which placed great strains on Chinese courts, and often their behavior at frontier markets or when journeying to a Chinese capital to present tribute was atrocious.[55] Although a wide range of factors might contribute to nomadic-Chinese discord, trade was nevertheless the primary issue in the continuing dialog between sedentarist and nomad.

This work will survey approximately two thousand years of history, beginning with the earliest well-documented interaction between the Hsiung-nu and the Chinese Han dynasty and continuing to the Mongol-Ming confrontations of the seventeenth century. Because of the space constraints imposed upon writers publishing in English, this book is less than half the length of Jagchid's original Chinese publication. As a consequence, our chief aim has been to retain the spirit of the initial work and make available the Chinese documentation supporting Jagchid's thesis. However, our reliance on the primary Chinese sources has, unfortunately, made it necessary to limit our examination of secondary Western materials.

The focus of our study is primarily the Turkic and Mongolian nomads north of China because their relations with the Chinese were of longer duration and of more significance in determining whether there would be war or peace. The study also focuses on the steppe nomad, rather than the Tibetan,[56] Jurchen, or Manchus,[57] who relied more upon agriculture for a livelihood. The distinction between the steppe nomad and his sedentary Chinese neighbor provides a clearer picture of the dynamic between herding and agrarian peoples than is possible when studying peoples originating north and west of China who also maintained an agricultural base and in the case of the Jurchen and Manchus were more susceptible to Sinicization.

Although this study surveys almost two millennia of history, its main focus is on developments of the Han (202 B.C.–220 A.D.) and Ming (1368–1644) periods of Chinese history. The Ming dynasty is a particularly rich era for studying Mongol-Chinese relations because of the daily court records provided by the *Ming shih-lu* and the private histories of contemporary scholars. No other era provides as full a record. Similarly, the Han dynasty records of Ssu-ma Ch'ien and Pan Ku and additional materials such as Huan K'uan's *Yen-t'ieh lun* provide a rich repository of information on Han-Hsiung-nu interaction.

It is difficult to ascertain why T'ang (618–907) and Sung (960–1279) records regarding nomadic affairs are so sparse. However, Sui and T'ang records provide us with the fullest account of intermarriage as a vehicle for promoting peace and exchange on the northern frontier of China.[58] It is also clear that a dynamic horse trade existed between the Uighur and T'ang courts. This trade developed because of the balanced strength of both participants and the desire of the T'ang to foster good relations with the Uighur as they sought to make them allies in their struggle against the powerful Tibetan state west of China.[59] Sung records relating to her northern neighbors are concerned primarily with the Khitan Liao and the Jurchen Chin states which occupied North China during this period. Sung-Khitan and Sung-Jurchen diplomatic activity was colored by the fact that the Khitan and Jurchen people occupied agricultural North China and therefore they possessed not only native but also sedentary power.

The interaction of three non-Chinese dynasties of conquest with their northern nomadic neighbors and with China are seldom mentioned in this discussion for several reasons. The Jurchen Chin period, established in the early twelfth century, quickly adopted Chinese institutions of government and minutely followed traditional Chinese patterns for conducting international relations. The Jurchen erected a lengthy wall along their northern frontier to delineate their border and that of the steppe nomad, and they also established trading centers to exchange goods with herdsmen to their north. Jurchen-Sung relations basically followed the pattern of relations developed earlier between the Sung and the Khitan Liao. As a consequence, the study of the Chin period offers little new insight into the dynamics of nomadic-Chinese exchange activities.

The Mongol Yüan dynasty so dominated China and the steppes north of China that they did not rely upon the frontier market, tribute and bestowal, and intermarriage institutions. As a consequence the Yüan period is not very helpful to our study of traditional institutions created to promote exchange. However, at this juncture, a few observations about the rise of Mongol power might contribute to efforts to understand the dynamic of peace and war along nomadic-sedentarist borders.

A number of plausible explanations for the growth of Mongol power have been suggested. Some focus on sudden climatic changes which forced the Mongols to abandon seasonal pastures and contest with others. Some stress the ferociousness of the Mongols and their disposition to rape and plunder, whereas others emphasize the charismatic leadership of Chinggis Khan and the need, once a nomad state begins to emerge, to consolidate even greater tracts of land and secure still larger quantities of plunder to retain the allegiance of followers who would otherwise abandon the enterprise and revert to herding. Seldom in the arguments of Toynbee and Jenkins, or those who follow the traditional Chinese view of the nomads, or even in the assessments of Fletcher, are frontier trading policies or the formal exchange of goods considered. Inasmuch as the Mongols of Chinggis Khan's time also depended on trade with China, it seems warranted to suggest that the disruption of trade between the Mongols and their sedentary neighbors may, in part, have contributed to the rise of Mongol power under Chinggis Khan.

The studies of Toyama Gunji show that conflict between the Chin dynasty, occupying North China, and Mongol steppe nomads is evident as early as the second quarter of the twelfth century. The frequency and level of conflict grew until a full-scale war erupted in 1198 between the Chin and the three Mongol tribes of the Onggirad, Khatagin and Salji'ud. Toyama does not explore the relationship of the conflict to the Chin's building of a wall which delimited Chin and nomadic boundaries and could be used to restrict trade. Nonetheless, it is possible that the Chin-Mongol struggle at the end of the twelfth century was related to a disruption of trade.

Chinggis Khan, the future consolidator of the Mongol nomadic state, was directly linked to these Chin-Mongol frontier conflicts. Chinggis's emergence to power was dramatically enhanced by his marriage to Börte, the daughter of an Onggirad leader. Naturally, he could not ignore the earlier tensions between his father-in-law's tribe and the Chin along Chin-Mongolian borders. Moreover, as his power grew, Chinggis sought and failed to sustain trade and tribute arrangements with the Chin which would have enabled him to obtain essential goods from China. Once exchange institutions were closed to him, Chinggis's only alternative was war.[60] The *Yüan shih* suggests:

> Previously, the Emperor [Chinggis Khan] presented yearly tribute to the Chin. The Lord (*chu*) of Chin sent the Prince of Wei (Wei *wang*), Yün-chi to accept the tribute at Ching-chu. Seeing Yün-chi, the Emperor did not show due respect. [Consequently], Yün-chi returned and requested [that the Chin Emperor levy] troops to attack [the Mongols]. Just then the Lord of Chin, Ching, died and Yün-chi ascended the throne. [He] sent a decree to the Country [Mongolia] saying: "Bow and accept this [decree]." The Emperor asked the envoy: "Who is the new Lord (*chün*)." The envoy answered: "The Prince of Wei." Then the Emperor spit toward the south and said: "I thought that the throne of the Emperor of Chung-yüan [the Central Kingdom] is only for a man of Heaven [to occupy]. Now that such a foolish and cowardous [man] occupies it [the throne], why should [I] bow?" [He] mounted his horse and galloped north. The Chin envoy reported to Yün-chi. Yün-chi was very angry. [He] plotted that, when the Emperor came again to enter the enclosure to present tribute, he would be killed. The Emperor knowing [of the scheme] severed [Mongol] relations with the Chin and strengthened the military to prepare [for war].[61]

The initial conflict between Chinggis Khan and the Chin may have been partially due to a breakdown in trade and tribute relations which denied the nomads essential goods. The interest of Chinggis in securing goods rather than territory or political power is apparent by his activities in 1213 when he entered the North China plain and besieged Chung-tu (Peking). After receiving bounteous gifts from the court and plundering the countryside, he returned home. To this point in his career, Chinggis had no designs to occupy land, but rather sought booty to reward his followers.

After the Mongol conquest of northern China in 1234, the Mongolian leaders again regarded China primarily as an area from which to obtain plunder. Chinese land was divided among Mongolian nobles and meritorious officials who were allowed to pillage it for their own advantage. However, as early as 1236, as evidenced by the following dialogue between the Khitan scholar-advisor to the Mongolian court, Yeh-lü Ch'u-ts'ai and Ögödei Khan, the policy began to change. Yeh-lü Ch'u-ts'ai admonished Ögödei Khan:

> "If the land and people remain divided this will creat conflict. It would be better to grant them [the nobles and meritorious officials] more gold and silk [rather than land and people to exploit]." The Emperor said: "It has already been promised. What should I do?" Ch'u-ts'ai said: "The court should appoint officials to collect the tax and distribute it to [the nobles] by the end of the year, and not allow them [the nobles] to freely extort from the people." The Emperor agreed to his plan and set the taxes for the realm under Heaven. The tax was two households were to remit one catty (*chin*) of silk to the state, and five households were to remit one catty of silk as an income of their fiefs (*t'ang-mu*) to the princes and meritorious vassals as the income of the fief.[62]

A third non-Chinese dynasty is also seldom discussed in this work. The Manchu Ch'ing dynasty, like the Yüan, dominated all of China. Even though Ch'ing rulers utilized intermarriage and tributary institutions to promote stability with their northern neighbors, they also adopted new techniques to control the nomads which deserve thorough investigation but cannot adequately be covered here. Three were of special significance. First, the Manchus allowed Chinese merchants to enter Mongolia and Mongols to travel throughout China to exchange goods. The court realized that this would undermine traditional frontier marketing mechanisms. However, Chinese merchants in Mongolia would, it was hoped, provide the nomads with freer access to grain, cloth, and other essential commodities and thereby negate the need for the nomads to secure goods through violence. Still, a serious problem emerged. Trade at frontier markets had been carefully regulated to deter unscrupulous merchants from exploiting the nomads. Unfortunately, the Ch'ing rulers failed to effectively regulate the activities of traveling merchants who cheated both rich and poor nomads. Chinese merchant activities north of the frontier diminished the financial resources of Mongol leaders and weakened their ability to organize resistance to sedentary power. However, the continued unchecked exploitation by Chinese merchants was a catalyst for nomadic resistance to sedentarist domination.[63]

A second policy developed by the Manchus which undermined nomadic power was to fragment Mongol rule by adopting a quasi-feudal system of rewarding Mongol leaders with rank and territorial domains based on their nobility, prestige, and how well they might serve Ch'ing causes. Manchu policy fragmented the steppe by carefully delineating land holdings. As boundaries became demarcated, the mobility of the nomads, which had always been a key to their power, was impeded. The Ch'ing presentation of rank and concomitant stipends created a new hierarchy among the nomads and pitted one nomadic leader and his people against another as they sought greater influence and rewards from Peking.[64]

A third development occurred during the Ch'ing which also diminished Mongol power. As the Manchus consolidated their rule over China, they were highly dependent upon Mongol auxiliaries to supplement their military forces. Consequently, every able-bodied Mongol male between the age of eighteen and sixty was registered for military service. Military registers were carefully kept and few Mongol men were allowed to become monks and enter Lamaist monasteries. However, during the later Ch'ing period, as the Manchus became less reliant on Mongol military power, the registration of Mongols for military service and governmental policies towards the Tibetan Buddhist church grew lax. As the popularity of Buddhism spread, almost half of the male Mongols renounced secular concerns to become lamas and join monasteries. This massive exodus of Mongols from nomadic life diminished the potential for a resurgent Mongol military threat to China because monks produced no offspring and they themselves were unprepared for battle. In addition, Mongols gave freely of their wealth to support Buddhism, which weakened them financially.[65]

This work is embodied in six chapters. Chapters one and two set the context for later discussion because they each use a chronological framework to summarize the interaction between various nomadic states and the Chinese from about 200 B.C. until the early seventeenth century. The first chapter suggests that nomadic aggression was primarily precipitated to secure grain, cloth, and other essential commodities otherwise unavailable to nomadic peoples. Whenever trade was denied them, they waged war, but violence was abandoned if the nomadic peoples could obtain valued products peacefully. Chapter two assesses the ongoing debate in Chinese court circles on how to respond to the continuous demand by the rulers of the nomads for essential Chinese goods. Some dynasties adopted what was basically an activist or warlike approach to deal with nomadic neighbors, whereas others were more pacifistic and created markets and other exchange mechanisms to bring stability to the borders. During some dynasties both strategies or a combination of the two were adopted. Generally, the Chinese sought to utilize the nomadic dependence on Chinese grain and cloth for political advantage. Whereas nomadic leaders were primarily concerned with economic issues, their Chinese counterparts were basically concerned with politics.

Chapters three, four, and five are careful studies of the key institutions developed to promote peace along the frontier. Chapter three examines frontier markets during the Ming period and shows that markets were opened to the Mongolian leaders Esen, in the mid-fifteenth century, and Altan Khan, a century later, but only after they continually warred with China and forced the Chinese to trade with them. Court debate over whether or not to create markets for the Mongols was intense. Once the markets were established, however, relative peace and a degree of prosperity returned to the frontier areas. Although the demands made by Esen and Altan Khan for the riches of China were almost limitless, peace derived from the marketing mechanism was much less expensive than war.

Chapter four focuses on the nomadic presentation of tribute and the concomitant Chinese offers of bestowals and yearly payments. Although many scholars maintain that nomadic peoples enrolled as tributaries to embrace Chinese culture, in reality, they did so more frequently to secure coveted Chinese goods. The tributary status of nomadic leaders was generally determined by the power they possessed. The size and frequency of the exchange of goods was often dictated by the nomadic leaders which was highly advantageous for themselves, and might better be regarded as Chinese tribute presentation to the nomads. The study of nomadic-Chinese relations along the Great Wall might best be assessed as a response by the Chinese to nomadic pressures, not as the conscious coming of the nomads to offer their submission to China.

Chapter five investigates the institution of court-to-court intermarriage. It is tempting to suggest that the brides exchanged between courts were simply another form of exchange. For nomadic rulers, intermarriage meant dowries, wedding gifts, and more ready access to the Chinese marketplace. For the Chinese, intermarriage could quiet a particularly dangerous nomadic leader and bring peace to the country's northern frontiers, enable the Chinese court to drive a wedge between two nomadic groups, or accomplish a number of other important political tasks.

When frontier markets, tribute and bestowals, and intermarriage were functioning effectively, the northern frontiers of China were relatively peaceful. Why then were these mechanisms so readily abandoned to the pursuit of war? In chapter six it is suggested that a wide range of factors contributed to the destabilization of the frontier and the outbreak of war. They include: (1) the prejudice and mistrust felt by nomad and sedentarist toward each other, (2) the ineffectiveness of Chinese dynasties in implementing frontier trading policies and regulating unscrupulous frontier officials, and (3) the chaotic nature of the frontier, rife with unsavory characters and illicit trading activities. Still, it is important to note that throughout history the key element in nomadic-Chinese relations was the dependence of the nomadic peoples on the Chinese for a few essential commodities. If the Chinese were willing to provide these goods peacefully to their neighbors, peace was possible. If not, only war could ensue.

I

TRADE OR RAID

The mountains and steppes along which the Great Wall was built divide continental Asia into two worlds, different from each other both physically and economically. The physical difference was described by Ch'iu Chu-chi (1148–1227), the famous thirteenth-century Taoist traveler, in his *Hsi-yu-chi:*[1] "Northward passing over the height of mount Yeh-hu Ling[2] gazing downward over the mountains of the T'ai-hang range,[3] I beheld scenery both beautiful and lovely; but looking toward the south, the only thing I could see was the cold desert and its arid grass. The atmosphere of the Middle-Land absolutely ceased from here!"[4]

The harshness of the physical environment in which nomadic people lived led them to depend on a pastoral economy to eke out an existence.[5] However, herding and hunting activities failed to provide nomads with some essential goods, and they became reliant on China for grain and cloth. This economic dependence, more than any other factor, was the chief cause for nomadic incursion into China.

Nomadic peoples possessed impressive fighting skills, and whenever they were unable to obtain the needed commodities through peaceful means, they resorted to aggressive military action to plunder agricultural areas. War could provide nomadic people with essential goods, enrich them, heighten the morale of their warriors, and strengthen the power of a "state on horseback."[6] In Chinese records, armed intrusions were called *lüeh-pien* (looting border areas), *t'ao-pien* (robbing in border areas), *k'uo-pien* (border encroachment), *ju-k'uo* (invasion), *ta-ju* (a great invasion), *shen-ju* (deep invasion), or *ta-chü ju-k'uo* (large-scale invasions), depending upon the size of the invaded area and the duration of the activity. Looting of border areas might occur during any season, but a "great invasion" or "large-scale invasion," penetrating the interior agricultural areas of China, usually occurred in the autumn when horses were stronger and the weather cool. Fall was an advantageous time to attack because agricultural products were most abundant and men, women and children were all busy and exposed in the fields instead of within the walled cities. Nomad invaders looted whole areas, took captives, and then retreated with their booty into remote regions before Chinese authorities could gather defense forces.

Despite their martial abilities, nomadic people were in a precarious position. Because they depended on the goods of their agriculturalist neighbors, who greatly outnumbered them, they constantly faced the danger of being assimilated. Their leaders knew that to survive as a people they must emphasize their cultural differences and distance themselves from the sedentarists who provided them with essential commodities. They could not safely settle the lands they conquered. Instead, they had to withdraw from the areas inhabited by the more numerous Chinese and commit themselves to their nomadic way of life. As a case in point, Ssu-ma Ch'ien recorded in his Shih chi the words of Chung-hang Yüeh warning Lao-shang, the Shan-yü of the Hsiung-nu (r. 174–161 B.C.), about this problem:

> The Hsiung-nu preferred food, cloth, and silk from the Han. Chung-hang Yüeh said, "The population of the Hsiung-nu is not as large as one of the Han's commandaries. But the reason that they are still powerful is only because their clothing and food are different, and nothing is needed from the Han. Now if you, the Shan-yü, change the custom, and love the goods from the Han, and if then the Han mobilized only two-tenths of their wealth, the whole of the Hsiung-nu would come under the Han's rule." Then he put on Han clothing and silk and he rushed on horseback among grass and thorns. He allowed his coat and trousers to be torn to pieces to show that these materials were not as good as woolen and fur garments. He rejected all the Han's food to demonstrate that it was not as good and as convenient as milk and curd.[7]

Most frequently nomadic intrusions were made to acquire sorely needed agricultural commodities rather than to secure territory or achieve some political objective. Bloodshed was not an aim in itself; rather it was required to obtain the desired goods. An accurate description of the motivation behind nomadic invasions is presented by Ssu-ma Ch'ien in his "Account of the Hsiung-nu" in the Shih chi; "On the attack, the [one who] kills the main enemy figure is rewarded with a cup of wine. The captured war booty is dispersed among [the warriors]; if they capture people, [they] make them slaves. Therefore, in their war each person struggles for his personal gain. [They] cleverly draw the enemy out, then attack [them]. When they see the enemy, they swarm like birds upon their profits. Upon defeat they scatter like the clouds. . . . "[8] Ssu-ma

Ch'ien suggests that the governing principle of Hsiung-nu tactics was that "if it is profitable [they] proceed; if it is unprofitable [they] withdraw. They are not ashamed of retreating."[9] Such nomadic pragmatism is apparent as early as the beginning of the Han era, as suggested by the willingness of the Hsiung-nu leader, Mao-tun, to abandon raiding Chinese frontiers if allowed to trade for essential goods.

In 209 B.C., three years before Liu Pang, the future Emperor Kao-ti (r. 206–195 B.C.), established the Han dynasty, an extremely capable and energetic Hsiung-nu *Shan-yü* emerged in the person of Mao-tun (r. 209–174 B.C.). Mao-tun was able to unify the Hsiung-nu tribesmen, and he quickly expanded Hsiung-nu power by launching successful military campaigns against the Yüeh-chih in the Kansu corridor, the Ting-ling and other nomadic peoples to the north, and the Chinese in the Ordos region. Because Mao-tun continuously raided Chinese territory and lured a number of Chinese generals and frontier leaders to defect to his cause, in the winter of 200 B.C., Han Kao-ti launched a massive military campaign against Mao-tun. However, Kao-ti fell into an ambush set by the Hsiung-nu leader which entrapped him, denying him supplies and reinforcements for seven days.[10] After his near disastrous attack against the Hsiung-nu, the Emperor Kao-ti adopted a policy of attempting to maintain peace through trade and intermarriage with the Hsiung-nu, to which his successors Wen-ti (r. 179–157 B.C.) and Ching-ti (r. 156–141 B.C.) adhered. This policy lasted for the next seventy years. Kao-ti dispatched a court official to escort a princess of the royal household to be the *Ou-shih* (wife) of the *Shan-yü* and to present to the Hsiung-nu silk, silk lining, wine, and grain each year in given amounts. It was proclaimed that the emperor and the *Shan-yü* were brothers. Ssu-ma Ch'ien suggests that these concessions led Mao-tun to reduce his invasions of China. This agreement between Mao-tun and Kao-ti became the basis for subsequent accords between the nomads and the Chinese.

In the "Account of the Hsiung-nu," in the *Han-shu*, there is a letter written by Mao-tun which he sent to Empress Lü, who as regent dominated the court for fifteen years after the death of her husband Kao-ti. This document shows that the nomadic ruler expressed his desire " . . . to exchange the things that I have for what I do not have."[11] However, prior to requesting trade, Mao-tun also proposed marriage to Empress Lü: "Your Majesty is lonely and I am lonesome. We, the two lords, all feel unhappy and have nothing with which to amuse ourselves."[12] Han officials regarded this as an insult towards the newly widowed empress, and some high court officials immediately advocated dispatching Chinese troops to punish this proud and ill-mannered leader. Incensed by the arrogance of the Hsiung-nu leader, few officials paid adequate attention to the request that goods be exchanged, even though this was what Mao-tun most eagerly desired. They failed to realize that Mao-tun may have proposed marriage simply to acquire, through the presentation of the dowry, the exchange of gifts, and the closer court ties that intermarriage would promote, additional Chinese commodities.[13] If the economic aspirations of Mao-tun were realized and peaceful trade was carried out, the frontiers between sedentarist and nomad remained peaceful, if not, war was substituted for peace.

Though neither Ssu-ma Ch'ien in the *Shih chi* or Pan Ku in the *Han shu* record the exact quantity of goods provided by the Chinese to the Hsiung-nu some lists of the gifts exchanged between Hsiung-nu *Shan-yü* and Han emperors do exist. During the reign of the Emperor Wen-ti there was an exchange of gifts between the Han ruler and Mao-tun to symbolize the restoration of peace after several border incidents:

> [Mao-tun] sent a *lang-chung* [department director] . . . to take a letter and to present one camel, two riding horses and two groups of pulling horses for carts. . . . [14] Formerly, in the sixth year of the Emperor Hsiao-wen [Wen-ti] [174 B.C.], the Han also sent to the Hsiung-nu . . . one embroidered coat, one embroidered long half coat, one brocade robe, one hair-dressing comb, one golden ornament belt, one golden belt and coat ornament, ten rolls of embroidery, thirty rolls of brocade, forty rolls of red satin and forty rolls of designed silk.[15]

The Hsiung-nu presented a camel and excellent horses suited for both riding and pulling chariots, and the Chinese offered fine manufactured goods. The quantity of items offered by the Han far exceeded those given by the Hsiung-nu.

These exchanges were often symbolic, designed to formalize friendship rather than supply the nomads with essential goods. In cases where a limited formal exchange of goods was all that occurred and no means was created to enable nomads to secure additional quantities of essential grain and cloth through the establishment of border markets or by the Chinese courts' bestowals or yearly payments, border raids might continue despite the apparent normalization of relations. The only way to diminish looting along the frontier of China was to establish a peaceful means of trade.

During the reign of the Emperor Ching-ti, the Han court attempted to stabilize trade with the Hsiung-nu in order to pacify them. The "Account of the Hsiung-nu" in the *Shih chi* states: "Throughout the reign of Hsiao Ching-ti, intermarriage with the Hsiung-nu was again carried out; the border markets were opened, and, as in the old agreements, gifts were given to the Hsiung-nu and princesses were sent [to the Hsiung-nu to marry]. [Therefore] until the end of the Hsiao Ching[-ti] period, although at times there were small encroachments along the border, there were no great invasions."[16]

Although Hsiung-nu nomads intruded into Yen (present-day Northern Hopei) in 148 B.C., Shang-chun (present-day northern Shensi) in 144 B.C., and Yen-men (present-day northern Shansi) in 142 B.C., it was determined that these encroachments were not serious enough to warrant a Chinese offensive. The peaceableness of the Hsiung-nu was fostered during Ching-ti's reign by the positive influence of border markets and the court-to-court exchange of goods.[17]

When Wu-ti (r. 140–87 B.C.) succeeded Ching-ti as emperor of the Han, he initially continued his predecessors policies for dealing with the Hsiung-nu: "After acceding to the throne, Emperor Wu-ti clearly made it his policy to continue to establish kinship through intermarriage, to tighten his control over frontier affairs, to treat outsiders nicely, to open the border market places, and to give more supplies to the outsiders. Therefore, the Hsiung-nu, from the *Shan-yü* down to [the commoners], all favored the Han and they came and went at will along the Great Wall."[18]

Although this policy stabilized the frontier, Emperor Wu-ti was distressed because the demands of the Hsiung-nu for grain, silk, and even cash payments had continually increased from the time when Emperor Kao-ti first established an accord with the nomads. The exchange of goods was decidedly one-sided. In essence, the Chinese court was "playing the role of a tributary state to the barbarians."[19] In 133 B.C., Wu-ti determined to free himself from making these payments by luring the Hsiung-nu into a trap near the city of Ma-i and destroying them. Wu-ti's plot is vividly described in Chinese sources:

> The Han [authorities] made an old man in the city of Ma-i, Neih I, their spy, assigning him to exchange goods with the Hsiung-nu. Tempting the *Shan-yü*, he pretended to betray the city of Ma-i. The *Shan-yü* believed him, and coveted the wealth and goods of Ma-i, and he violated the border of Wu-sai with a hundred thousand cavalry. The Han ambushed him with three hundred thousand soldiers . . . [They] tried to capture the *Shan-yü* and kill him. After that, the

Hsiung-nu discontinued the practice of intermarriage . . . and began to invade Han borders with increasing frequency. Even so, the Hsiung-nu desired the market places, and coveted Han goods. The Han often trapped them by the trick of opening the market place.[20]

Another description of the same important development reads:

[The court] secretly made Nieh I a spy [after which he feigned] escape to the Hsiung-nu, where he spoke to the *Shan-yü*: "I am able to kill the magistrate of Ma-i and surrender the city to you. [You] can take all the wealth." Nieh I [returned], chopped off the head of a condemned criminal and hung it on the wall of Ma-i as a signal. [Nieh I, reporting to the *Shan-yü*] said that the top official of Ma-i was already dead and [the Hsiung-nu,] should come quickly. The *Shan-yü* then passed the border and entered the fortress of Wu-chou with one hundred thousand horsemen. The Han were waiting in ambush with three hundred thousand soldiers, carts, horses, officers, and equipment in the valley of Ma-i. However, after crossing the border and before coming within one hundred *li* [Chinese miles] of Ma-i, the *Shan-yü* discovered [the ruse] and returned.[21]

There is little doubt that this tragic Hsiung-nu border raid was the personal creation of the Emperor Wu-ti. Because of avarice and desire to acquire the wealth of Ma-i, the Hsiung-nu *Shan-yü*, Chün-ch'en (r. 161–126 B.C.), nearly fell into Wu-ti's trap. The incident at Ma-i in 133 B.C. led to a formal break in the somewhat stable relations between the Han and the Hsiung-nu that had existed after the completion of Kao-ti's accord with Mao-tun in 198 B.C. With essential Chinese goods unavailable to them, Hsiung-nu raids along the frontier of China increased. These raids in turn prompted the ambitious Wu-ti to launch a great war against the Hsiung-nu which lasted throughout his reign. As suggested in the following two passages, the battles waged between Wu-ti and the Hsiung-nu were devastating economically, socially, and politically to both sides: "At the beginning [of the war], the Han . . . marched out in mass, encircled the *Shan-yü*, and killed or captured eighty to ninety thousand [enemies]; but many tens of thousands of Han soldiers died. Several hundred thousand Han horses also died. The Hsiung-nu suffered because of the remoteness of their retreat. Also, the Han could not return [to battle] because of the lack of horses."[22] "Before Wu-ti died, the Han troops entered deep [into Hsiung-nu territory] and chased [the enemy] for twenty years. The Hsiung-nu . . . suffered to the extreme. The *Shan-yü* and his followers continually sought [the reestablishment] of the intermarriage relationship."[23]

The Han-Hsiung-nu conflict led to a prodigious loss of life. For the

Hsiung-nu, the hardship of war was aggravated by the remoteness of their retreat. No longer were they near the borders of China, where they could obtain abundant supplies from the Chinese and conduct trade. They lost the rich grazing land on the south bend of the Yellow River and also their dominant control of the silk routes through Central Eurasia. There was a drastic decline in the Hsiung-nu standard of living as they were forced to squeeze essential goods from the nomadic peoples formerly subdued by them (the Wu-huan in the east, the Ting-ling in the north, and the Wu-sun in the west) rather than relying on the Chinese. This exploitation caused these once subdued peoples to rebel, while at the same time, because of the critical situation among the Hsiung-nu, there was growing internal dissension and unrest. It is not surprising that the Hsiung-nu recurrently attempted to establish peaceful trading relations with the Chinese. In 98 B.C., Hu-lu-ku *Shan-yü* dispatched an envoy to the Han with a document that read:

> On the south there is the Han and on the north is the powerful *Hu*. [We] the *Hu* are the proud Son of Heaven and do not worry ourselves over minor [problems of] ceremony. [I] now wish to open the great gate [to communicate] with the Han and to marry a daughter of the Han as [my] wife. [I also want the Han] to supply me with ten thousand *tan* [piculs] of grain, with wine, with five thousand *hu* [bushels, nominally ten piculs] of rice and millet, and with ten thousand rolls of new cloth. Other items should remain the same as in the old agreement. There will then be no border encroachments.[24]

The *Shan-yü* affirms that what the Hsiung-nu desired was trade. If it was possible to obtain sufficient quantities of Chinese grain and cloth through a negotiated peace, the Hsiung-nu would cease raiding the frontiers.

Relations between the Hsiung-nu and Han Chinese remained turbulent for over eighty years. About 54 B.C. the Hsiung-nu split into two rival camps, one in the north and one in the south. In 51 B.C., prior to the complete break between the southern and northern Hsiung-nu, Hu-han-yeh (r. 57–31 B.C.), the leader of the Southern Hsiung-nu, personally proceeded to the Han court to meet Emperor Hsüan-ti (r. 73–49 B.C.). He sought protection from his northern rivals, food, and manufactured goods. Hu-han-yeh offered homage to the Chinese emperor, presented tribute, and his left son in the Han capital of Ch'ang-an as a hostage. His submission to the Han court helped transform a relationship which, up to the time of Han Wu-ti, heavily favored the nomadic peoples into one which came to resemble the tributary relations conducted between the Chinese and nomadic peoples during subsequent periods.

After the audience, Hu-han-yeh was treated with special honors and his followers received enormous amounts of food, silk, silver, and gold. In fact, the Chinese lavished on the loyal Hsiung-nu a much higher level of gifts under this new tributary arrangement than they gave under the system of marital alliance.[25] The Southern Hsiung-nu were made Han mercenaries charged with guarding the Chinese border against the Northern Hsiung-nu. In 44 B.C., the Han and the Southern Hsiung-nu forced Chih-chih *Shan-yü* (r. 57–36 B.C.) of the Northern Hsiung-nu, who was Hu-han-yeh's rival, to abandon his homeland and migrate further from China into Central Eurasia. Hu-han-yeh then returned to the north and reestablished control over the traditional lands of the Hsiung-nu. He and his descendants remained obedient to the Han court, and, as a consequence, the quantity of rewards and bestowals presented by the Han continually increased.[26]

After Wang Mang (r. 9–23 A.D.) usurped the throne of the Former Han dynasty in 9 A.D., he achieved ephemeral success dealing with the Hsiung-nu by following earlier patterns of providing the nomads with the wealth of China: "In the second year of T'ien-fen (15 A.D.) . . . Wang Mang sent a great amount of gold and precious things to the *Shan-yü* and persuaded him to change his titles, such as *Hsiung-nu* [which has the meaning of furious slaves] into *kung-nu* [obedient slaves] and *Shan-yü* [khan] into *shan-yü* [a good man], and he bestowed upon him the seal and the sash. . . . The *Shan-yü* desired the gold and the precious things and outwardly agreed, but he violated the border as before."[27] It is interesting to note that this Hsiung-nu leader was willing to relinquish his title to secure essential commodities from the Han. However, he did not honor his agreement with Wang Mang. The Hsiung-nu raided China's borders, looted, and even penetrated into areas some distance south of the Great Wall. Unstable conditions persisted until internal conflict erupted amongst the Hsiung-nu in 48 A.D., at which time, in return for needed commodities and military support against their northern rivals, Pi, the leader of the Southern Hsiung-nu, surrendered to the Han.[28]

Emperor Kuang-wu-ti (r. 25–56 A.D.) allowed the Southern Hsiung-nu to migrate to the territory of Wu-yüan (the present-day Ordos area of Inner Mongolia), provided them with substantial economic aid, and transformed them into frontier guards who confronted the Northern Hsiung-nu and other northern nomads to protect the agricultural Chinese. The emperor dispatched an ambassador to confer the title of *Shan-yü* on Pi. During the ceremony, however, Pi was publicly humiliated by being required to bow in receipt of this imperial decree.[29] The Han court put great political pressure on the Southern Hsiung-nu to submit. Because this group of nomads was not as powerful as those who followed Hu-han-yeh a century earlier and because they depended on the Chinese for economic and military support against their northern rivals, the Han effectively exploited them. The Southern Hsiung-nu became separated from the remainder of the nomadic world and declined in power. However, the Southern Hsiung-nu presence immediately north of China denied the Northern Hsiung-nu direct access to the border, which limited their ability to secure adequate amounts of Chinese goods through either peaceful or violent means. As a consequence, Northern Hsiung-nu power also diminished, and massive defections of their followers occurred. Weakened by their dwindling numbers, the Northern Hsiung-nu were attacked from the south by the Southern Hsiung-nu, from the north by the Ting-ling, and from the east by the Wu-huan and Hsien-pei. In 91 A.D., following the pattern of the Hsiung-nu migration of 44 B.C., the Northern Hsiung-nu migrated into more remote parts of Central Eurasia.

At the height of Hsiung-nu power, it was said that a hundred barbarian tribes followed them,[30] but once the Hsiung-nu began their decline, it was impossible to retain the allegiance of their subordinates. Just as the Han had utilized the Southern Hsiung-nu to weaken the power of the more dangerous Northern Hsiung-nu, so too did they entice other nomadic groups, particularly the Wu-huan and the Hsien-pei, to challenge the Northern Hsiung-nu who had once dominated them.

From the late Chou period to the early Han dynasty, the Wu-huan and Hsien-pei people were collectively known as the Tung-hu (Eastern barbarians), because they were located east of the Hsiung-nu, somewhere in modern Inner Mongolia. Toward the end of the third century B.C., the Hsiung-nu *Shan-yü*, Mao-tun, conquered and subjugated the Tung-hu. The confederation split apart, with the Wu-huan remaining closer to China and their Hsiung-nu overlords. The Hsien-pei fled further east, possibly into eastern Inner Mongolia and even Manchuria. In 119 B.C., Han Wu-ti forced the Hsiung-nu to leave Inner Mongolia, and afterwards, the Chinese court attempted to drive a wedge between the Wu-huan and Hsiung-nu peoples. The Wu-huan were relocated near the Great Wall of China and enrolled in the Han tributary system.

Whereas active Wu-huan–Chinese interaction began during the reign of Han Wu-ti, the more distant Hsien-pei remained isolated from the Chinese court until the early years of the Later Han dynasty, about 49

A.D.[31] One particularly revealing passage from the Later Han period focuses on the effective use of rewards by the Governor of Liao-tung to persuade the Hsien-pei leader, P'ien-ho, to attack the Northern Hsiung-nu. In 58 A.D., P'ien-ho was also persuaded to attack the Wu-huan:

> In the twenty-first year of Chien-wu [45 A.D.], the Hsien-pei and the Hsiung-nu moved into Liao-tung [present-day Southern Manchuria]. The Governor of Liao-tung, Chi Yung,[32] defeated them. . . . Later the Southern Hsiung-nu surrendered to the Han and the Northern Barbarians were isolated and became weak. In the twenty-fifth year [49 A.D.], the Hsien-pei began to communicate and send envoys. Soon the Supervising Protector *[tu-hu]* [of the Hsien-pei], P'ien-ho, and others came to visit Chi Yung and petitioned to render service for the Han. Because of this, P'ien-ho was commanded to attack the Northern Hsiung-nu. . . . Henceforth, P'ien-ho sent troops to attack the Northern Barbarians every year. Upon the return of his forces, he usually brought the heads [of the Hsiung-nu] to Liao-tung to receive rewards. In the thirtieth year [54 A.D.], Hsin-chih-fen and other leaders of the Wu-huan tribe of the Ch'ih-shan area of Yü-yang [present-day Northern Hopei] had already invaded Shan-ku [the present-day southeastern part of Chahar]. In the first year of Yung-ping [58 A.D.], Chi Yung again bribed P'ien-ho to attack Hsin-chih-fen, the latter being defeated and killed. Consequently, all the Hsien-pei clan leaders came to surrender and to proceed to Liao-tung to receive rewards. The money was paid by [revenues collected in] both Ch'ing-chou and Hsü-chou [present-day Eastern Shantung and Northern Kiangsu] to the sum of two hundred and seventy million coins each year, as was usually the case. Consequently, at the time of the Emperors Ming[-ti] [r. 58–75 A.D.] and Chang[-ti] [r. 76–88 A.D.], the border was well protected, without any problems.[33]

P'ien-ho successfully fought both the Hsiung-nu and the Wu-huan for China, but the Chinese secured his services for a very high price. The regular annual payments to Hsien-pei chieftains of two hundred and seventy million coins was almost three times the amount given to the Southern Hsiung-nu during this same period.[34]

Relations between China and nomads north of its frontiers were often fluid and unsettled. Nomadic groups sometimes vied with one another to establish tributary relations with China in order to gain exchange opportunities and Chinese support against the threat posed by other nomadic groups. Of course, China frequently used this to its advantage. It is not surprising that, only a few years prior to encouraging the Hsien-pei attack on the Wu-huan, the Han court had enlisted the Wu-huan to spy on the Hsien-pei and assist the Chinese in their Han struggle to control their other nomadic neighbor. The *Hou Han shu* suggests that, as with the Hsien-pei, " . . . the Emperor [Kuang-wu-ti] bought over the Wu-huan with money and cloth":[35]

> In the twenty-fifth year [49 A.D.], Hao-tan, the headman of the Wu-huan on the west of the Liao River and nine hundred and twenty-two other persons led their people to turn to our culture, proceeded to the court to render tribute, and presented male and female slaves, cattle, horses, bows, arrows, and furs of tigers, leopards, and sables. At that time, the barbarians of the four directions, one after another, continually proceeded to the court to pay respects. The Son of Heaven ordered a great banquet to entertain them and bestowed upon them precious things. Some of the Wu-huan leaders desired to serve in the Imperial guards. Consequently, their leaders were granted ranks and titles, and eighty-one of them were made princes, marquises, and heads. They were all allowed to live inside the fortresses and were scattered in the commandaries along the border as spies for the Han in assisting the court to attack the Hsiung-nu and the Hsien-pei.[36]

In dealing with the Wu-huan, as with other nomads, the Han court achieved political gains, while the Wu-huan obtained economic and, to a lesser extent, political advantage. Bestowals of money, cloth, and other precious items encouraged nomadic tribes to surrender and pay tribute. However, the tribute presented by nomads was of greater symbolic than economic value. Among the items presented to Emperor Kuang-wu-ti by the Wu-huan, only the sable skins and horses were truly valuable.

A few decades after Emperor Kuang-wu-ti enrolled the support of both the Hsien-pei and the Wu-huan, the Hsiung-nu irretrievably lost their power. The Hsien-pei succeeded in filling the power void existing north of the Great Wall. The "Account of the Hsien-pei" in the *Hou Han shu* records their emergence: "During the Yung-yüan period of Emperor Ho-ti [r. 89–105 A.D.] . . . [the Han] defeated the Hsiung-nu, and the Northern *Shan-yü* escaped. The Hsien-pei thereupon occupied their land. Remnants of the Hsiung-nu numbered more than one hundred thousand and also called themselves Hsien-pei. Thenceforth, the Hsien-pei gradually grew prosperous."[37]

During the reigns of Ming-ti, Chang-ti, and Ho-ti, stable relations existed between the Han and the Hsien-pei, whose chieftains submitted to these Chinese rulers. All one hundred and twenty tribes of the Hsien-pei clans sent their sons to the Han court as hostages, where they were housed in specially built hostels. Hsien-pei leaders also accepted the authority of Han border officials. In return, they received large bestowals of gifts and cash as well as the opportunity to trade at frontier markets.[38]

Initially, the socio-political institutions of the Hsien-pei centered around Hsien-pei clan and tribal alliances, but the Hsien-pei ultimately sought to create a nomadic "state on horseback." As the Northern Hsiung-nu retreated, relations between the Hsien-pei and other nomadic groups became more volatile, with the Hsien-pei staging frequent raids to secure essential goods and expand their grazing areas and power. "[The Hsien-pei] looted along the [Han] border on the south, resisted the Tingling on the north, repulsed the Fu-yü on the east, attacked the Wu-sun on the west, and occupied all the old territories of the Hsiung-nu, all of which spanned [approximately] four thousand *li* east to west and seven thousand *li* south to north."³⁹

Hsien-pei power solidified under the leadership of Tan-shih-huai (d. 181 A.D.), and the Han dynasty viewed their growing strength as a threat. During the reign of Emperor Huan-ti (r. 147–167 A.D.), the court responded by ordering Lieutenant General Chang Huan, who was responsible for the supervision of the Southern Hsiung-nu, to attack the Hsien-pei, but he failed to subdue them. The court thereupon sent an envoy with a seal and sash to confer the title of prince on Tan-shih-huai and propose a marriage alliance with him. Tan-shih-huai rejected the offer, and the border intrusions and lootings worsened.⁴⁰

An interesting dynamic becomes evident as one studies the records of the interaction between the Han and the Hsien-pei. Before the Hsien-pei became a serious threat to the Chinese, they were nurtured by the court and allowed to obtain the agricultural commodities they needed through the traditional channels of intermarriage and frontier markets. The court hoped to utilize the less threatening Hsien-pei as a counter to Hsiung-nu and Wu-huan strength. However, even when markets existed, they were often used as ploys to enable the Chinese to capture or kill nomadic leaders judged to be a threat. Once Hsiung-nu power diminished and the Hsien-pei became a more serious threat, the demands of the Hsien-pei leaders for Chinese goods and titles rose dramatically. As a consequence, court policy vacillated, and the Hsien-pei decided to avoid the markets and obtain essential cloth and grain by plundering border areas. Weaker nomads who were unable by themselves to attack large cities or make significant incursions into the agrarian world were tempted to join forces with larger groups led by capable and charismatic leaders such as Tan-shih-huai. This expanded force could attack a large expanse of the Chinese frontier and penetrate more deeply into China, with the prospect of greater amounts of booty.

The key to Tan-shih-huai or any other nomadic leader's success lay with his ability to secure plunder from the Chinese and to equitably distribute it to those who supported him. A passage about another leader of the Hsien-pei, named K'o-pi-neng [d. 229 A.D.], suggests this: "[K'o-pi-neng] was supported as *ta-jen* [chieftain] because [he was] brave, powerful, fair in applying the law, and unselfish with what was gained. [He commanded] one hundred thousand horsemen. During an invasion, he ordinarily distributed captured wealth equitably and unselfishly before the eyes [of the public]. He was therefore able to win the masses over, [even] to the point that they would die for him. Chieftains of the other tribes all honored and were fearful of him."[41]

In order to sustain a "state on horseback" composed of several clans, the leader had either to provide each component an opportunity to enjoy the fruits of common victory or secure a treaty with the Chinese which allowed all his followers to trade and peacefully interact with the Chinese to obtain essential goods. It is likely that Tan-shih-huai refused to accept the title conferred by the Han and their proposal for intermarriage because there was an insufficient quantity of goods accompanying the royal title and imperial princess to enable him to strengthen his tribal alliance. In the nomad's cultural milieu, a Chinese seal and sash did little to glorify a leader. Without more useful and tangible goods accompanying the bestowal of titles, the establishment of ties with a Chinese court was a vain gesture.

This discussion of war and peace on the northern frontiers of China suggests that during the Han period, the Hsiung-nu, Hsien-pei, and Wuhuan peoples raided the borders of China whenever they were unable to secure essential foods and cloth from the sedentary Chinese through peaceful means. When farsighted Han emperors established markets and other mechanisms which enabled the nomads to secure needed commodities, peace was possible. However, relations between the nomads and the Chinese always remained volatile because the nomads frequently possessed superior fighting abilities, which tempted them to forcibly seize the goods they desired. At the same time, the Chinese were tempted to use the frontier markets and other exchange mechanisms to manipulate the nomads to the advantage of the court. The following brief overview of Chinese-nomadic relations from the end of the Han period through the Ming dynasty suggests that this pattern continued during subsequent periods of history.

As a powerful nomadic force north of China during the decline of the Han, the Hsien-pei became deeply involved in the struggle for power in China as that dynasty disintegrated. Hsien-pei's relations with Ts'ao Ts'ao, the founder of the Wei dynasty (220–264 A.D.) of the Three Kingdoms period (222–280 A.D.), suggests that the pattern of interaction between the nomad and agriculturalist courts changed little during the middle of the third century. The Hsien-pei leader, K'o-pi-neng, initially allied himself with Ts'ao Ts'ao and aided him in pacifying a rebellion led by T'ien Yin in present-day Hopei. He then joined with the Wu-huan when they revolted against Ts'ao. K'o-pi-neng's forces were defeated by Ts'ao's, and he was forced to retreat north of the Great Wall. However, he soon sent tribute to Ts'ao's Wei dynasty in northern China and sought to establish peace. The Hsien-pei leader's desire to normalize relations suggests that he was faced with the same economic difficulties that the Hsiung-nu had suffered. After he and his people withdrew from close proximity to arable territory toward more remote areas, it was difficult to acquire agricultural products, and during this time, the Hsien-pei were not strong enough to breech and loot the powerful Wei borders. Consequently, K'o-pi-neng was forced to negotiate peace with the Wei. The Wei court, eager to gain the Hsien-pei as allies, granted K'o-pi-neng the title Fu-i *Wang* ("Prince of Upright Subordination"), thereby suggesting his subordinate status to the dynasty. K'o-pi-neng accepted the title and took advantage of renewed ties with the Wei to lead three thousand horsemen in driving twenty thousand horses and oxen to the border markets for exchange.[42]

The Northern Wei dynasty (386–534 A.D.), which emerged more than a century after the Three-Kingdoms period, provides some insight into Chinese-nomadic relations towards the end of the almost four century period between the fall of the Han dynasty and the emergence of the T'ang dynasty. Although the T'o-pa founders of the Northern Wei dynasty were originally a nomadic people, they adopted in its entirety the traditional agrarian attitude toward the Jou-jan,[43] Khitan, and eventually the Turkic nomads along their frontiers. During intermittent periods of war and peace, T'o-pa rulers and Jou-jan nomadic leaders formed intermarriage ties, exchanged tribute, and developed trade relations. Again the stability of frontier relations between the agriculturalist and the nomad depended upon whether the Jou-jan acquired adequate amounts of grain and other indispensable products. This is evident from the following passage, drawn from the "Account of the Juan-juan" in the *Wei shu:*

> During the first year of Cheng-kuang [520] . . . the Emperor Su-tsung [r. 516–527] conferred on the King of the Jou-jan the title of Duke of Shuo-fang. . . . In the

first month of the second year [521], A-na-k'ui [r. 518–552] petitioned for permission to return [to the north]. . . . [The Emperor] decreed that two sets of fine armor, for both horse and rider, . . . and twenty-thousand *tan* of grain be given to A-na-k'ui and delivered at the border. . . . During the twelfth month of the third year [522], A-na-k'ui requested seeds for farming. By Imperial order ten thousand *tan* of [seed] grain were given to him. In the fourth year [523] a famine swept through the people of A-na-k'ui, so they violated the border and plundered. The Emperor Su-tsung ordered Yüan Fu . . . to be his royal emissary and stop them. Yüan Fu called on A-na-k'ui and was captured. After taking two thousand people, several hundred thousand official and private post horses, cattle, and sheep, A-na-k'ui retreated to the north. He apologized and returned Yüan Fu. The Emperor dispatched the . . . Great General, Prime Minister Li Ch'ung,[44] along with a hundred thousand troops to punish them. They advanced three thousand *li* from the border, reached the Gobi, but returned in vain without finding the enemy.[45]

The Jou-jan are described as a people who "moved south of the desert in the winter and retreated north of the desert in the summer."[46] A shortage of food and other essentials among the Jou-jan led A-na-k'ui to open relations with the Northern Wei court and to even request seed grain to plant in areas to the north of China.[47] Stable relations between the Northern Wei court and A-na-k'ui broke down when a severe famine forced the Jou-jan leader to raid the frontiers of China to obtain still more food for his people.

Khitan relations with the Northern Wei were more peaceful. The Khitan emerged from areas southeast of the great Gobi and grazed their herds just north of the Great Wall. Before they emerged as a great nomadic power, the Khitans did their utmost to maintain peaceful relations with the agrarian courts in order to obtain grain and other essential goods and for military purposes because the Jou-jan and later the Turks to their north were a serious threat to them. The "Account of the Khitan" in the *Pei shih* provides a summary of Khitan-Northern Wei relations:

During the third year of T'ai-ho [479], the Khitans . . . came to the east of the Pai-lang shui [river][48] to surrender with more than ten thousand people, three thousand carts, and animals. From this year on they continually presented tribute. Soon after famine broke out, the Emperor Hsiao-wen [r. 471–499] allowed them to come to the border to buy grain. Later, during the reigns of Emperors Hsüan-wu [500–515] and Hsiao-ming [515–527], they still sent missions to pay tribute.[49]

The Wei court was more generous in meeting the needs of the Khitan when they suffered food shortages, and allowed them to cross the border to purchase grain. As a consequence, it was unnecessary for the Khitan to loot the Chinese along the Northern Wei border.

Trade or Raid

When the Northern Wei dynasty split into eastern and western halves in 534, the Turks (T'u-chüeh) had already begun to displace the Jou-jan as the dominant nomadic force north of China. In little more than two decades, the rival states of Northern Ch'i and Northern Chou replaced the Eastern and Western Wei dynasties in China. Each state vied with the other to enroll Turkic military power as they sought to dominate China:

> The [Northern Chou] court entered into intermarriage [arrangements with the Turks] for peace and provided them with hundreds of thousands of rolls of satin and silk cloth each year. Turks in the capital were treated with high honors, clothed with embroideries, fed meat, and usually numbered in the thousands. Fearing raids and looting, the people of Ch'i also showered the wealth of their treasury upon [the Turks]. [The Turkic Khan] Tapar [r. 573–581] grew more proud and instructed his followers, "If my two sons to the south remain filial, why should [we] worry about the shortage of supplies."[50]

Under these circumstances, the Turkic khan found it unnecessary to cross the Chinese border to loot and raid. However, this situation did not last indefinitely. In 581, the Sui dynasty (581–618) was established with enough power to unify all of China. This powerful agrarian state no longer felt compelled to present silk, silver, and grain to the Turks to secure their support. It is said that, initially, the founder of the Sui dynasty, Emperor Wen-ti (r. 581–604) "treated the [Turks] as a problem of little importance."[51] This change in policy by the Sui court led to a renewal of border raids by the Turks led by Sha-po-lüeh (Ishbara, r. 581–587), the legitimate khan of the Turks. However, because there was continuous division and turmoil among the Turks, hostilities between Ishbara and the Sui dynasty were of short duration. Ishbara sought and obtained material and military support from the Chinese by forming a marriage tie with the Sui court. The nature of these efforts is suggested in the following passage drawn from "the Account of the Turks" in the *Sui shu*:

> On the tenth day of the ninth month of the year of the dragon [584], Ishbara . . . , the Son of Heaven, the Heavenly-born Khan of the Great Turk presents his letter to the Emperor of the Great Sui: "The envoy . . . arrived, and I have heard all the words that you have spoken to me. You the Emperor are the father of my wife, and therefore you are my father-in-law. Here I am the husband of your daughter, and so I am like your son. Although the two realms are different the disposition is the same. Now we have restored the old relationship of relatives and

this will never cease from the generations of our sons and grandsons to the tens of thousands of generations. Heaven will attest to this and it should never be taken ungratefully. All the sheep and horses here are the livestock of the Emperor, and all the silk and cloth over there belong to us here. Then what is the difference between us."[52]

By accepting a Chinese princess and making himself a son-in-law of the Sui emperor, Ishbara was able to satisfy the Sui court's desire for a hierarchical relationship while maintaining that "All the sheep and horses here are the livestock of the Emperor, and all the silk and cloth over there belong to us. . . . "[53] Eventually, Ishbara was challenged by Tarto Khan (r. 575–603) of the Western Turks and forced to move closer to the Chinese frontier to seek greater military support from the Sui. As his dependence on the Sui court grew, he was increasingly forced to admit Chinese preeminence, accept vassal status, and even send a son to the Sui court: "I recognize that the Emperor of the Great Sui possesses the realm of the four oceans and is in harmony with the will of Heaven above and is the only sage of the tens of thousands of generations. . . . Although the majestic court is far away to the south, I dare not overlook the ritual that a vassal should keep. Now I send my son to serve in the court. . . . "[54]

Despite adopting a humble demeanor towards the Sui to obtain continued Chinese support, Ishbara was not willing to abandon Turkic customs. He conceded that "the entire [Turkic] country wholeheartedly admires the culture of your country [the Sui],"[55] but recognized that the Turk "manner of dress, our hair style, our music, and our songs, these are old customs and are hard to change."[56] Fortunately Sui Wen-ti did not demand that the Turks abandon their culture.

Sui wealth and power continued to have a dramatic effect on Chinese-Turkic relations after Ishbara's death. A successor, Ch'i-min Khan (Tölis, r. 599–609) acceded to the throne after securing Sui help in the power struggle that occurred on Ishbara's death. He was much more submissive than his predecessor, having no reservations about declaring himself a vassal of the Chinese emperor. In 607, Ch'i-min Khan personally appeared at the court of the Emperor Yang-ti (r. 605–618) to present three thousand horses for which he was given a reward of twelve thousand rolls of satin. More surprising, he asked the Sui emperor to allow him and his people to adopt Chinese dress and customs. The emperor discouraged this arguing that: " . . . the superior man taught the people not to alter their customs; he allowed them to cut their hair, tattoo their bodies if it suited their natures, and wear different clothes of various styles according to everyone's convenience."⁵⁷ Before Ch'i-min Khan returned to his homeland the court entertained what is stated to have been thirty-five hundred persons at a banquet and bestowed two hundred thousand rolls of satin on the khan and his followers. The Sui court effectively used its wealth to pacify the Turks.⁵⁸

The *Sui shu* suggests that Ch'i-min Khan's successor, Shih-pi Khan (r. 609–618), also sought close ties with the Sui and in 615 journeyed to the eastern capital at Lo-yang to meet Emperor Yang-ti. However, without providing an explanation, the *Sui-shu* states that during that same year the Turks suddenly attacked the Sui and besieged the emperor at Yen-men.⁵⁹ This omission leads the reader to regard the Turks as unfaithful, but the biography of P'ei Chü, a T'ang authority on affairs of the Western Region, reveals that P'ei Chü counseled the Sui emperor to entrap and kill a nomad loyal to Shih-pi Khan, who, he felt, was a particular threat to the dynasty. This led to the Turks' attack:

> Chü again spoke to the Emperor saying, "The Turks are by nature quite simple and easily alienated from each other. Among them, however, are many other barbarians who are cunning and shrewd. It is they who guide [the Turks]. [I, your] vassal have heard that Shih-shu-hu-hsi is especially shrewd and much trusted by Shih-pi. [I] petition [your Majesty] to entice him into a trap and kill him." The Emperor gave his approval. Chü sent messengers to [Shih-shu]-hu-hsi to tell him "Now the Son of Heaven arranges for precious items to trade. Anyone who comes will receive fine things." Hearing this, [Shih-shu-hu-hsi] became greedy and believed the message. Without reporting to Shih-pi, he and his tribe rushed their herds into [the marketplace] in order to obtain the best opportunity for exchange. Troops under Chü waited in ambush near [the city of] Ma-i [present-day Shuo-hsien, Shansi], induced [Shih-shu-hu-hsi to enter], and executed him.⁶⁰

Sui Yang-ti then notified Shih-pi Khan that "Shih-shu-hu-hsi led his tribe here, said that [he] had rebelled against the khan, and requested that I receive him. I ought to have killed him because the Turkic khan is my vassal. He has been executed."⁶¹ Shih-pi Khan knew otherwise and broke relations with the Sui dynasty which left him free to form advantageous alliances with the future founder of the T'ang dynasty, Li Yüan, and other generals who were beginning to challenge Sui authority. The break with the Turks, coupled with the failure of Sui expeditions against Korea from 611–613, ultimately contributed to the fall of the Sui in 618.⁶²

When Li Yüan, the founder of the T'ang dynasty, emerged to challenge Sui authority, he sought Shih-pi Khan's support by declaring that "the population and the territory belongs to the Duke of T'ang; the treasures, cloth, goods, and precious things belong to the Turks."[63] Turkic nomads had little interest in interfering in China's internal politics or in occupying cultivated land, so Li Yüan appealed to their continuing desire for economic gain. An incident that occurred a short time later, dramatically portrays how Turkic involvement in early T'ang politics was primarily fostered by their continuing appetite for Chinese products. In 630, the Turk leader, Il Khan (Chieh-li, r. 620–630), threatened the T'ang by appearing with his cavalry under the city walls of the T'ang capital of Ch'ang-an. Emperor T'ai-tsung (r. 626–649) came out of the city and conversed on horseback with Il Khan and persuaded the Turks' leader to withdraw from Ch'ang-an without a fight. After the Turks' departure, the T'ang emperor noted that "although there were many [Turkic warriors], they were not well disciplined. The purpose of their ruler and [his] vassals [in entering China] was to gain profits."[64] He determined that the best T'ang strategy was " . . . to roll up our armor and put away our weapons and tempt them with jade and silk. The vain pride of those stubborn barbarians will begin from this point to cause their decline. This is to say, if we wish to take from them, we have to give to them."[65]

Another example of T'ang success in using economic means to pacify the Turks and even gain their support as a buffer against more hostile peoples is evident in the relations between the Emperor Hsüan-tsung (r. 713–755) and the Turkic leader Bilge Khan (r. 716–736), known to the Chinese as *Hsiao sha* (Small *Shad*). After becoming leader of the Eastern Turks in 716,[66] Bilge Khan had quietly allied himself with the Tibetan court.[67] Nonetheless, in 721, he sent an envoy to the T'ang court to request peace. No formal agreement was signed, but the T'ang ruler conceded the importance of trade to both countries in a letter to the Turks: "Our country buys Turkic sheep and horses, Turks receive our countries' silks. Both sides are abundantly supplied."[68]

In 727, Bilge Khan sent a minister to the T'ang court with a gift of thirty thoroughbred horses. The minister also presented to the court a letter which the Turkic ruler had received from the Tibetans, inviting him to join with them in a joint invasion against the T'ang. The Emperor Hsüan-tsung presented the Turkic khan immense rewards and opened a market for the Turks at Shou-hsiang ch'eng. Every year, at the market, the court presented the Turks with several hundred thousand rolls of silk and cloth. Bilge Khan sacrificed a military alliance with the Tibetans in exchange for the establishment of a border market with the T'ang. The T'ang, by richly rewarding the Turkic ruler, managed to avoid a dangerous alliance which would have threatened their southwestern, western, and northern frontiers.[69]

After the revolt of An Lu-shan and Shih Ssu-ming in 755-756, the T'ang court was forced to flee the capital. The Emperor Su-tsung (r. 756-762), having usurped power from his father, approached the Uighur people, who had displaced the Turks as the major force north of China, in a manner almost identical to that of his predecessor Li Yüan, the T'ang founder. He requested Uighur help in recovering the capital by stating his conditions for military cooperation: "the land and people belong to me; the jade and the silver, the boys and the girls will be given to the Uighurs."[70] The T'ang court was able to exchange wealth for military support. Significantly, this military assistance was not sought to pit barbarian against barbarian but rather to aid the T'ang in crushing internal dissent.[71]

At the end of the T'ang period, the Khitan emerged as a strong military force in the valleys of the Shira-Moren river. In 907, Yeh-lü A-pao-chi (r. 907-926) unified the Khitan tribes and concerned himself with expelling the Kirghiz from north of the Gobi and annexing the Kingdom of Po-hai (Parhei) in southern Manchuria. At this time, the Sinicized Sha-t'o Turks, who were establishing the Later T'ang dynasty in northern China, were warring with the Liang dynasty. Both states sought Khitan support in their struggle and offered lavish gifts to A-pao-chi and his followers. A-pao-chi accepted bestowals from both Emperor Wu (r. 907-922) of the Liang and Emperor Chuang-tsung (r. 923-926) of the Later T'ang, but in reality, he showed no inclination to become involved in the internal Liang-Later T'ang struggle. In fact, on occasion, the Khitan looted the Chinese frontier. This led one counselor of the Emperor Chuang-tsung to say: "[A-pao-chi] is tempted by the wealth of the Imperial Capital and is covetous of its wealth and commodities. He has no desire to establish a friendly relationship with a neighboring country."[72]

Although internal disruption in China invited nomadic intrusion, because the Khitan were busy consolidating their power north of China at the same time the Liang and Later T'ang were fighting for hegemony in northern China, there was less chance of full-scale war between the nomadic and agrarian worlds. The Khitans' incentive to wage war with her agrarian neighbors was also lessened because the crisis created by civil war in the south led many Chinese to flee their homeland and enter Khitan territories. Once settled, Chinese refugees produced crops and other goods for their nomadic rulers, thereby reducing the quantity of items the Khitans needed to obtain from the south. Chinese defectors also provided the Khitans with technical, bureaucratic, and administrative skills.

Military activity of a nonpolitical nature was abandoned by the Khitans when their khan, Yeh-lü Te-kuang, Emperor T'ai-tsung of the Liao dynasty (r. 927–947), agreed to provide military support to Shih Ching-t'ang in his attempt to usurp the throne of the Later T'ang. With the Khitans' support, Shih was able to establish the Chin dynasty (936–946). The Khitan were rewarded by the Chin court with enormous yearly tribute payments based on a "father-and-son" relationship and were also given sixteen counties including Yen (Peking) and Yün (Ta-t'ung). Gifts to the Khitans were so great that a heated debate occurred in the Chin court over whether this high level of offerings should be continued. The Khitans utilized the monies derived from the Chin court to incorporate the sixteen counties in Yen and Yün into their own territory. They made this the basis of the Liao dynasty.[73]

The Khitan Liao dynasty (907–1125) and its successor, the Jurchen Chin dynasty (1115–1234), dominated parts of northern China for more than three centuries. To the south, centered in the Yangtze River basin, the native Sung dynasty (960–1126) and the Southern Sung dynasty (1127–1279) controlled increasingly small areas of China. Although the Khitan and the Jurchen people occupied Chinese territory and therefore had direct access to the wealth of northern China, they maintained the nomadic tradition of forcing the Chinese dynasties south of them to frequently present to them their agricultural products and precious goods. Chinese presentations and yearly payments to the Khitan during the Sung dynasty are discussed in chapter five, but a brief summary of the evolution of Khitan-Sung market relations will be presented here.

In a document found in the "Monograph on Economy" in the *Sung shih*, it suggests that initially during the reign of the Sung Emperor T'ai-tsu (r. 960–976) "the Khitan were allowed to trade along the borders [of the Sung]. . . . "[74] Although Emperor T'ai-tsu wished to drive the Khitan out of the territories of Yen and Yün, which they occupied in 936, he had to consolidate his new regime. Providing the Khitan with desired goods at frontier markets promoted stability and enabled the founder of the Sung dynasty to unify his realm. The Khitan accepted the arrangement because their leader, Yeh-lü Te-kuang, had died in 947, and his successors were preoccupied with enhancing their power in northern China.

When the new emperor, T'ai-tsung (r. 976–997), ascended the throne, both Sung and Khitan power had grown. The situation along the frontier grew tense, and the Sung responded by establishing offices to regulate trade in specific commodities. In 979, Sung forces led by the emperor attempted to recover the territories of Yen and Yün but were defeated by the Khitan at Fan-yang. This led the Sung to close the borders to trade. However, despite decrees against commerce, smuggling activities mushroomed. In 986, the Sung again attacked the Khitan without success. This defeat led Emperor T'ai-tsung to decree an end to the conflict and once again the opening of markets: "It would be better, then, to allow trade along the border. From now on, garrison troops along the frontier should not disturb [traders]. . . . "[75] However, shortly thereafter, the court again forbade trade, and harsh measures, including the execution of illicit traders, were adopted to prevent illegal exchange. The Sung court prohibited trade to censure the Khitan for border disruptions, but also because they feared that Khitan spies were crossing the Sung frontier disguised as merchants.

In 991, the Sung again reversed its policy and opened its frontiers to trade, establishing markets and supervising offices at Hsiung-chou, Pa-chou, Ching-jung-chün, Tai-chou, and Yen-men-chai (present Hsiung-hsien, Pa-hsien, and Hsü-shui-hsien in Hopei province and Yen-men-chai and Tai-hsien in northern Shansi Province). In most cases, these were not the same places where trade was allowed earlier. Markets at Chen-chou and Ts'ang-chou in the central and southern parts of Hopei Province were closed, and markets at Tai-chou and Yen-men-chai were newly opened. Markets at Hsiung-chou and Pa-chou in present central Hopei remained open as before. The realignment of markets illustrates that trade activities were moving west.[76]

Khitan power reached its peak after the enthronement of the young Emperor Sheng-tsung (r. 983–1031, Yeh-lü lung-hsü) when his mother Empress Ch'eng-t'ien (r. 982–1009) administered the realm. The Sung feared that the Khitan would seek to avenge the Chinese invasions of 979 and 986 and prepared for war. However, before the first engagement, the treaty of Shan-yüan was negotiated in 1004, and peace was restored. The treaty required the Sung to present an immense "yearly payment" (sui-pi) to the Khitan. Later, in 1042, a second Sung-Khitan peace treaty was negotiated which increased still further the level of yearly payments exacted from the Sung.[77] As part of the accord of 1004, a new commercial center at Hsin-ch'eng (present-day Hsin-ch'eng, Hopei) was also opened along the banks of the Chü-ma River on the Sung-Khitan border. Shortly thereafter, three more border markets were opened to the Khitan. This trade was strictly regulated and northern merchants were forbidden to exchange goods with Sung merchants outside of the established frontier marketing system. The Sung sent officials from the capital to supervise marketing activities, set prices, and guarantee a profit to nomadic tradesmen. Careful regulation, coupled with set pricing, suggests that northern demand for southern goods far exceeded supply.[78]

Khitan traders desired to obtain the same goods coveted by earlier nomadic peoples: "fabrics, lacquers, and [both] glutinous and non-glutinous rice. . . . "[79] Tea is also on the list of traded commodities. They exported products of their pastoral economy (sheep, horses, and camels); luxury items such as spices, rhinoceros horn, and ivory; cotton cloth produced by Chinese living within the Khitan realm, as well as silver and money. The Sung court showed little interest in exporting its culture to nomadic peoples and prohibited the export of Chinese books other than Confucian documents and the nine scriptures. The use of bullion to purchase Chinese products suggests that there was less a demand for northern goods than vice versa.[80] The Khitans' ability to secure exotic products from distant regions is a testament to the extensiveness of international trade networks at this time. The inclusion of tea as an item of trade is unusual. Although it appears as an important item in Chinese-Tibetan commerce quite early, it does not make a regular appearance on trade lists between the Chinese and Mongols until after Altan Khan's conversion to Tibetan Buddhism in 1571. Whether the tenth-century Khitan people drank tea is still uncertain.

Trade between the Khitan and the Sung flourished after the accords of 1004 and 1042. As profits from the trade grew, Governor Chang Chaoyüan of Hsiung-chou petitioned Emperor Jen-tsung (r. 1023–1063) to divert monies made through the markets to increase the income of the state. The emperor reminded Chang that "the Former Emperor opened the markets in order to make it possible to exchange needed items, but did not plan for [any increase in income]."[81] The emperor remained committed to using trade as a means to preserve peace rather than enrich the dynasty. From 1004 on, Sung policy toward the markets was circumspect. Khitan rulers remained satisfied with Sung "yearly payments" or tribute, and the border markets provided the Khitan people with their essential needs. The trade markets were operative without disruption until the second decade of the twelfth century and relations between the Khitan and Sung courts remained stable.

As suggested in the following passages from the *San-ch'ao pei-meng hui-pien* and the *Sung shih*, about a decade prior to the capture in 1126 of the Sung capital of K'ai-feng by the Jurchen and the flight of the Sung court south of the Yangtze river, leading to the advent of the Southern Sung period, a debate occurred among Sung bureaucrats over whether to abandon peace with the Khitan and offer the more distant Jurchen concessions similar to those given to the Khitan in 1004. An alliance would thus be offered to the Jurchen to destroy the Khitan:

> Demanding the treaty be kept and the mission to the Jurchen be stopped, Cheng Chü-chung[82] rebuked Ts'ai Ching,[83] in the court saying " . . . In the reign of Ching-te (1004–1008), the Liao mobilized their whole country to invade us. Emperor Chen-tsung . . . went personally to punish them. Afterwards, . . . peace was reestablished. They kept the treaty for thirty-nine years and never invaded us. In the year Ch'ing-li (1042), the Khitan concentrated their forces along the border and requested the land south of the [Wa-ch'iao] Gate.[84] Emperor Jen-tsung sent Fu Pi[85] as envoy to visit them and agreed to increase the yearly payment. For the sake of people's lives, Emperor Jen-tsung did not use troops but kept the treaty. Thus, there was no disturbance anywhere and until now it has lasted one hundred and fourteen years. Today you tempt the Emperor Lord to break the treaty and to recover the land of Yen . . . " Ts'ai Ching answered, "The Emperor Lord hates to yearly pay five hundred thousand rolls of silk and taels of silver, so we advocated this." Chü-chung said: "Compare this five hundred thousand rolls of silk and taels of silver[86] with the one hundred million and nine hundred thousand that the Han paid to the *Shan-yü* of the Hsiung-nu, and seventy-four million and eight hundred thousand to the Western Region, then our payment to them is not a bad policy."[87]

The *Sung shih* passage provides more historical background and is more graphic:

> The Court intended to send envoys to the Chin to [plan] an attack by both parties against the Khitan to recover the territories of Yen and Yün. This was advocated by Ts'ai Ching and T'ung Kuan.[88] [Cheng] Chü-chung forcefully argued that this was no good and spoke to Ts'ai Ching: "Your Excellency, a minister and an elder of the state, cannot keep the treaty between two countries but rather makes trouble. It is not a good plan." Ching replied, "The Lord is tired of paying five hundred million in yearly payments. So it is." Chü-chung said, "Why does not Your Excellency compare the spending for peace with the barbarians with military expenditures of the Han dynasty? Your Excellency is actually doing the thing that will cause the livers and brains of millions to be splashed upon the ground." Consequently, the debate was temporarily suspended. Later, the Chin attacked several times and the

Khitan day-by-day weakened. Wang Fu[89] and T'ung Kuan once more advocated military measures. Chü-chung again said: "It is not good to delight in others' suffering and to take advantage of them. We should wait until they die by themselves. . . ."[90]

Southern Sung policy generally adhered to the principles earlier formulated by the Sung to deal with the Khitan Liao. However, unlike the Khitan, the Jurchen people were not pure nomads but rather relied upon a hunting, gathering, and agrarian economy. They also came to possess a larger segment of what is considered Chinese territory and more effectively utilized Chinese bureaucrats to extract the wealth of northern China to enrich their Chin state. Still, the Southern Sung adopted the Sung policy of lavishing goods on northern rulers, which was calculated to guarantee that the bounty of China fell into the hands of a nomadic ruler rather than that of his subjects, thereby creating a gulf between him and his people: "If the Liao establishes peace with the Sung, the khan will effortlessly receive the yearly payment and the benefit will go to the state [e.g., the khan and his court], and the vassals and underlings will not be involved; but if war breaks out the profit will go to the vassals and underlings, and the state will suffer the damage."[91] Yearly payments or bestowals became the gifts of the agricultural court to the rulers of a nomadic people. They were court-to-court exchanges which denied the generals and warriors of nomadic rulers the opportunity to divide the plunder derived through war and border raids. The danger of this policy to a Khitan or Jurchen ruler was that they might come to depend too much on Chinese offerings, thereby becoming rich and idle while the morale of their troops and officers, denied the opportunity to enrich themselves, collapsed.

The first nomadic people to completely dominate China were the Mongols, who established the Yüan dynasty, which lasted for almost a century (1271–1368). Although the Chinese Ming dynasty (1368–1644) drove the Mongols out of China, Mongol power north of China remained a serious threat. Mongol leaders who posed a dangerous challenge to Ming power included Esen (d. 1454), the leader of the Oirad Mongols[92] during the mid-fifteenth century; Dayan Khan (r. 1487–1524?), who reunified the Mongols at the beginning of the sixteenth century; Tümen Khan (r. 1558–1592), the great great grandson of Dayan Khan; and Altan Khan (d. 1583), the grandson of Dayan Khan and leader of the Right-Flank Mongols in the mid-sixteenth century.

All four of these powerful leaders contended with the Ming to secure quantities of grain and cloth for their people. Esen, Dayan Khan, and

Tümen Khan adopted titles suggestive of earlier Mongol power, indicating their eagerness to restore Yüan glories. In a document sent by Esen to the Ming court, he designated himself *Tai-Yüan t'ien-sheng tai-k'o-han* (the Heavenly empowered great khan of the great Yüan).[93] The reign title adopted by Batu-möngke was Dayan Khan, which many scholars suggest is a corrupted pronunciation of the title *Tai-Yüan Khan*, again referring to the Great Yüan. Tümen Khan showed his reluctance to deny past Mongol power when the leader of the Tümen *tümen*, Altan Khan, received the title Shun-i *Wang* (Prince of obedience and righteousness) from the Ming court. Although this secured for Altan Khan and his followers highly beneficial frontier markets and other exchange privileges with the Ming, Tümen Khan refused similar arrangements with the Ming court. Tümen Khan was a legitimate Chinggisid descendant and therefore the nominal leader of all the Mongols and the actual leader of the Left Flank Mongols. Tümen Khan's refusal meant that an institutionalized peace between Tümen's followers and the Chinese was never secured.[94]

At times, the Ming court was able to pit one Mongol leader effectively against another, thereby diminishing the nomadic threat to China. At other times, by establishing markets and presenting profuse offerings to nomadic leaders, the court simply purchased peace along the frontier.

Esen wanted to make war with the Ming and proposed that he and his brother-in-law, Toghto-bukha, the legitimate khan of the Mongols, join forces. Toghto-bukha and his people, who were called Ta-tan by the Chinese, ruled the east, while Esen, who was nominally vassal to Toghto-bukha, controlled the west or Oirad regions north of China. Toghto-bukha was reluctant to war with China and argued with Esen that "All of our food and clothing depend on the Great Ming. How can we do this and survive?"[95] At this time, Toghto-bukha " . . . paid tribute to the court every year. The Son of Heaven always rewarded him generously and treated him much more honorably than other barbarians. In letters he was entitled 'the Khan of the Mongols,' and [Ming] bestowals also reached his wives."[96]

When Toghto-bukha realized that with or without his support Esen was determined to war against the Ming, he reluctantly agreed to invade Liao-tung while Esen attacked China in the Ta-t'ung area. The *Ming-shih* tells us that "at first Esen underestimated the Middle Kingdom and desired to invade the capital. He was greatly disappointed to discover that the soldiers of the Middle Kingdom were powerful [and] that the cities and moats were fortified. On the other hand Toghto-bukha and Alagh Chih-yüan[97] sent their envoys to the court to establish peace and withdrew their forces. . . . "[98] As is well known, Emperor Ying-tsung (r. 1436–1450 and 1457–1465) personally directed the counterattack against Esen and was captured at T'u-mu.[99] Although Esen defeated the Ming Emperor in battle and took him hostage, Toghto-bukha had been handsomely rewarded for seeking peace and withdrawing from the alliance. Without Toghto-bukha, Esen's military advantage was lost, and Esen decided to return the emperor to China in return for economic rewards. Esen won victory on the battlefield, but suffered a setback because his ally felt he could profit more economically by normalizing relations with the Ming.

Dayan Khan was an important consolidator of Mongolian power north of China, who focused his efforts on reunifying his people rather than waging war against the Chinese. Some of his descendants, like Altan Khan, received generous rewards from the Ming and were willing to enroll themselves as tributaries to China, but others, like Tümen Khan, refused. Those who enrolled themselves as tributaries frequently grew complacent about military matters. According to the *Ming shih*, one grandson of Dayan Khan, the Small Prince Bodi-alagh Khan (r. 1524–1547) "was most rich and powerful. He had one hundred thousand archers, multitudes of animals, and wealth and money, and therefore he was a little tired of military activities."[100]

Another grandson of Dayan Khan whose relations with the Ming will be discussed later in this work is Altan Khan. Altan frequently warred with the Ming in order to force the Chinese to maintain frontier markets and continue a high level of gift presentation to his court. One document, presented by Altan to the court in 1571, reveals his dependence on the Chinese for essential goods and his willingness to maintain peace if he is provided with them:

> We, your vassals, have suffered an increase of population and a shortage of clothing . . . and on none of the borders were markets permitted to open. There was no way to satisfy our needs for clothing. Our felts and furs wear poorly in the summer heat, but it has been impossible to get even a piece of cloth. . . . We crossed the border and carried out improper activities. . . . Consequently, our people and horses were killed and wounded. . . . Since [I, your] vassal, received the Merciful Imperial Decree . . . and have been allowed to participate in the tributary markets . . . , please permit [us, your] vassals, to protect areas north of the desert and the bend area of the Yellow river and present tribute each year. We petition that the Imperial Decree should be sent to those border officials, ordering them to establish markets, and permit the Barbarians [Mongols] and the Chinese to carry out our trade once a year. . . . Thus, both Chinese and Barbarians [Mongols] may

enjoy a peaceful life. [I, your] vassal, with my brothers, nephews, sons, and grandsons will be grateful from generation to generation, and never rebel again. If there be any transgression, let Heaven punish us.[101]

This powerful nomadic leader fought and won numerous victories against Ming armies to secure essential Chinese goods for the Mongols. Eventually, a high level of gift presentation and market interaction was achieved between the Ming court and Altan, which was followed by a long period of peace. As Altan grew old, he and a number of his followers accepted Buddhism. Peace, the resultant prosperity achieved through interaction with the Chinese court, and the conversion to Buddhism led to the military decline of Altan Khan's Mongols. They seldom again posed a military challenge to the Ming.

This chapter has shown how, restricted by their physical environment and their life style, the northern nomadic tribes depended on the economic resources of their southern neighbors. Consequently, trade between the agriculturalists and nomads was requisite for peaceful co-existence. Whenever trade was cut off, the nomads waged war to secure grain, cloth, and other essential goods. In most instances, they abandoned violent means of securing goods if they could obtain the commodities peacefully. Sometimes, rulers such as Han Wu-ti chose to make war with the nomads rather than meet their demands, whereas at other times, Chinese courts successfully utilized the leverage provided them through their control of important goods to purchase peace with their hostile northern neighbors. In chapter two, the formulation of Chinese policies to deal with the nomadic peoples in order to achieve primarily political rather than economic objectives will be considered.

II

PEACE OR WAR

A major concern of all Chinese dynasties was conciliation of the non-Chinese peoples along their frontiers. Some dynasties adopted what was basically an activist or warlike approach to deal with potentially hostile nomadic neighbors. Others were more pacifistic and created markets and other exchange mechanisms to bring stability to China's borders. During some dynastic periods, both strategies or a combination of the two were adopted by different rulers. This chapter focuses on the ongoing debate within court circles over how best to deal with the threat posed by the continuous demand of nomadic peoples for essential agricultural goods. As suggested in chapter one, the interaction of a nomadic people with the Chinese was conditioned by economics (their dependence upon Chinese grain, cloth, and other goods). This chapter will show that Chinese interaction with the nomad, whether of a conciliatory or activist nature, was undertaken chiefly for political and military reasons.

Chinese bureaucrats, who felt that the establishment of various exchange mechanisms was the best method of promoting stability with the nomadic peoples, scrutinized the problems created by adopting an activist frontier policy. Yen Yu, a general of Wang Mang, who established the short-lived Hsin dynasty (9–23 A.D.), asserted that no aggressive policy for dealing with the nomads had ever worked. He criticized King Hsüan of the state of Chou (r. 827–782 B.C.), by suggesting that he adopted a "mediocre" policy and "pursued [the Yen-yün people] to the border and returned. He took the barbarian invasion just as the sting of an insect. It was enough to just knock them off."[1] Next, Yen Yu suggested that Han Wu-ti adopted the "worst" policy. He "selected generals, trained the troops, transported light provisions, and entered deep into barbarian lands."[2] Although the barbarians were seriously wounded, they periodically took revenge and, according to Yen Yu, war lasted for thirty years. China lay tired and wasted, which hastened the decline of the Former

Han dynasty. A third policy, which Yen Yu disparaged as "no policy", was adopted by Shih Huang-ti (r. 247–210 B.C.), of the Ch'in dynasty. He determined to complete the building of the Great Wall and garrison it, which exhausted Ch'in resources and contributed to the fall of the dynasty.

Yen Yu, as he focused on the logistical problems inherent in a long conflict on China's northern frontier, tried to persuade Wang Mang not to attack the Hsiung-nu, citing a number of concerns. First, it was difficult to get sufficient numbers of troops to the border at the same time. Second, provisioning troops was hard because frontier regions are barren and the inner commanderies of China are not linked together to effectively supply troops. Third, one soldier needs eighteen *hu* of grain to sustain him for 300 days of fighting. The most efficient way to transport this large quantity of grain to troops in the field was by oxen. Each ox needs twenty *hu* of grain for itself. However, because the lands in which the barbarians lived were sandy, salty, and lacked water and grass, past experience showed that oxen died within 100 days of the opening of a campaign. Fourth, there was a danger of epidemics. Fifth, the long and heavily laden supply trains made it impossible for the troops to effectively pursue the mobile and elusive nomad who can calmly withdraw and evade the Chinese armies.[3]

As did Yen Yu, those who cautioned their rulers against adopting aggressive policies toward the nomadic peoples sometimes added to their lists of logistical problems the observation that drawn-out confrontation sometimes led to the fall of dynasties. Chi Pu, a Han statesman who argued that punitive measures not be adopted by Empress Lü's court to punish the Hsiung-nu leader Mao-tun for his bold proposal of marriage to the widow of Emperor Kao-ti, defeated the pro-war advocates in argument by his assertion that "because the Ch'in [court] was entangled with the *Hu* [Hsiung-nu], Ch'en Sheng and others carried out their [internal] rebellions [which led to the Ch'in demise]"[4]

Those who advocated a nonantagonistic posture toward the nomadic people relied on frontier trade and markets, intermarriage, tribute exchange, and yearly payments and bestowals to provide the nomadic peoples with indispensable commodities in order to promote peace. The quantity of goods provided and mechanisms for presentation were determined by the ratio of real power existing between the two sides. When the power between a Chinese court and nomadic group was relatively equal, or when the nomadic state possessed superior strength, the Chinese court intermarried with the nomadic court, presented it yearly payments, and offered presents or tribute to it. Sometimes, when the Chinese possessed greater military power, they promoted peace with nomadic rulers through bestowals and border markets, but at other times, when a nomadic people were much less powerful than the Chinese, agrarian courts did not open markets or other trading mechanisms to them. A nomadic state generally had to possess enough strength to pose a threat to an agrarian court or become a viable ally against a still stronger nomadic group before a dynasty created the mechanism to promote the exchange of goods.

When the power of the nomadic rulers was equal to or greater than that of the agriculturalists, they often made enormous and onerous demands of the Chinese court. Still, as suggested in the following memorial by Sang Wei-han to Shih Ching-t'ang (the tenth century Chin dynastic founder, mentioned in chapter one, who relied heavily upon Khitan help to ascend the throne), continued payments were a better course of action than the provocation of war:

> War is a dangerous matter and if we reach a decision carelessly, how would we be sure of the outcome? . . . Those who deliberate [the issue of war or peace] might argue that Your Majesty's concession of supplies to the Khitan are really a waste and have brought about nothing but humiliation and disgrace. However, the view of your worthless vassal is completely different. Earlier emperors as heroic as Kao-tsu of Han still presented goods to Mao-tun, and, as martial, as Shen-yao [the Emperor Kao-tsu of T'ang] still considered himself as vassal to the Khan [of the Turks]. This means that they were flexible and talented in expedient measures, and that, whereas, the losses incurred were small, the gains were great. But if war breaks out on account of this matter, then military supplies will have to be shipped daily, and conscription and requisitions will have to be imposed year after year.[5]

Sang also observed that a war would exhaust the treasury and would enable generals to arbitrarily assume power. They might try to exceed their authority and endanger the positions of court bureaucrats. This would necessitate their stationing at the border to get them out of the capital, and strong military power on the frontiers of China could jeopardize the power of the central government.[6]

Advocates of military solutions for the threat that the nomadic states posed to China argued that relations between the nomads and the Chinese had become distorted and that only war could reaffirm the centrality of the Middle Kingdom and the emperor's pre-eminence as the "Son of

Heaven." For example, Chai I, a counselor to the Han Emperor Wen-ti, noted:

> The Son of Heaven is the head of the realm under Heaven. Why? Because [his position is so] high. The barbarians are the feet of the realm under Heaven. Why? Because [their position is so] low. Now the Hsiung-nu are boastfully and arrogantly invading and looting. They have reached the limit of insult and have become the utmost plague of the realm under Heaven. Yet [the] Han [court] annually presents [them] gold, silk, embroideries, and satin, which shows that the barbarians command and play the role of the lord above. The Son of Heaven [presents] tribute and fulfills the ritual of the vassal below. The feet are above, the head is below, and this hanging upside down is difficult to understand . . . [7]

Chai I's successor, Ch'ao Ts'o, gave similar advice to Emperor Wen-ti. He advocated the selection of competent generals, the improvement of military tactics, massive warfare against a less numerous opponent, the repair of the Great Wall and the construction of fortresses, and the forced migration of people to inhabit the border areas. He also proposed a more aggressive policy to reduce the power of the landed nobility and strengthen dynastic control. Ch'ao Ts'o's aggressive proposals led the threatened nobility to rebel, and Emperor Ching-ti, the son and successor of Emperor Wen-ti, decided to execute him.[8] As we will show, despite Ch'ao Ts'o's counsel, Emperor Wen-ti avoided conflict with the Hsiung-nu and relied on intermarriage, bestowals, and trade to secure peace.

Chinese courts adopted a wide range of policies to deal with nomads. As suggested in chapter one, the founder of the Han dynasty, Emperor Kao-ti, and his immediate successors concluded peace with the Hsiung-nu by promising their ruler the hand of a Chinese princess in marriage. They also pledged to provide the nomads with a fixed amount of annual gifts. In return, the Hsiung-nu vowed to maintain peace. Some rulers sought to pacify the nomads by opening border markets to guarantee them essential goods. Another mechanism to promote exchange and sooth the "barbarian" was a tributary relationship between nomadic rulers and sedentaristic courts. The Chinese hoped that tributary ties would awe the nomadic peoples with Chinese civilization and inculcate in them the desire to "come to submit" (lai-hsiang), and accept Chinese culture. However, the policies which promoted peace by offering nomadic people the material and cultural riches of China were often effective but frequently abandoned by the court. Chinese emperors often chose to use diplomacy and selective gift presentation to foment hostilities among the nomadic tribes. By "using barbarians to check barbarians" (*i-i-chih-i*) and "using barbarians to attack barbarians" (*i-i-fa-i*), they sought to prevent the formation of any major nomadic configuration that might seriously threaten the frontiers of China. Other rulers adopted even more extreme measures and encouraged their subordinates to assassinate hostile nomadic leaders or ensnare their followers. A more thorough analysis of the wide spectrum of Chinese policies towards the nomads will now be undertaken, by focusing on the Chinese court debates regarding the nomads during the almost two thousand year period encompassed by this study.

Sources on pre-Han interaction between nomads and the Chinese are almost totally lacking. Still, a few rare passages in the *Shih chi* provide useful information. It is evident that, occasionally during the Chou period, various states formed marriage alliances with the rulers of the Jung and Ti people and effectively utilized their military support in their struggle with other princely houses. For instance, the Marquis of Shen obtained Jung support to wage war against the Chou king, Yu. The Jung seized the king's wife, Pao-ssu, and the contents of the Chou treasury, and shortly thereafter, the Marquis of Shen was able to place a new ruler on the Chou throne.[9] By joining with the Jung nomads, the Marquis achieved his political objectives while the Jung satisfied their economic aspirations by looting the Chou treasury.

Another *Shih chi* passage suggests that Li Ssu,[10] although a Legalist, may have been one of the first Chinese statesmen to oppose aggressive warfare against nomads. This argument is not recorded in Li Ssu's biography but is cited in a memorial presented by the Han official Chu-fu Yen to support the pacifist position taken by Chu-fu at the court of Han Wu-ti. According to this Han statesman, Li Ssu argued that the Hsiung-nu nomads " . . . move like birds and are difficult to control."[11] They could not be captured because a lightly-equipped Chinese military force would quickly run out of supplies, and keeping supply lines open to a military force north of China was logistically impossible. Li Ssu also felt that "occupying the land [of the nomads] is not profitable [because if you] capture the people [you] cannot train and keep them."[12]

Chu-fu notes that Li Ssu's advice was rejected by Ch'in Shih Huang-ti, who dispatched the general Meng T'ien to combat the Hsiung-nu:

> The troops were in the wilderness without shelter more than ten years, and countless men died, yet they still were not able to cross the [Yellow] River and march into the north. It was not because the troops were too few and it was not because

the armaments were not sufficient . . . The transport of food supply was hastened from the country along the sea . . . northward to the [Yellow] river. It began with three thousand *chung*[13] and ended with one *tan*.[14] Men hastened to plant but could not fill the [army's] food demands; the women weaved but could not meet the [army's] tent needs. The people were tired and poor and unable to nourish the orphans, widows, the old, and the weak; their corpses dot the roadsides. Because of these things, the realm under Heaven began to rebel.[15]

Although adequate numbers of armed soldiers existed on the northern frontier, providing food and clothing to this massive army removed from the resources of agricultural China was an insuperable problem which impoverished the Chinese people. Chu-fu Yen and later Yen Yu, as suggested earlier in this chapter, both felt that Ch'in Shih Huang-ti's decision to wage war against the Hsiung-nu directly contributed to the demise of his dynasty.

The successful claimant to the throne of China after the fall of the Ch'in dynasty was Han Kao-ti, founder of the Han dynasty. Though counseled that fighting the nomad "is like attacking a shadow,"[16] in 200 B.C. Kao-ti made the same mistake as Ch'in Shih Huang-ti and attacked the Hsiung-nu leader Mao-tun, who gathered his forces in the valley of Tai (present-day northern Shansi). Mao-tun's forces successfully encircled Kao-ti at P'ing-ch'eng. Fortunately, Mao-tun was more interested in economicnomic than political or territorial gain. He therefore opened the encirclement and let Kao-ti escape hoping thereby to ingratiate himself with the Han ruler.

At this juncture, as suggested in chapter one, Han Kao-ti salvaged his situation by following the recommendations of his advisor Liu Ching, who proposed that Kao-ti offer a Chinese princess of the royal house in marriage to the Hsiung-nu leader. Liu Ching reminded Kao-ti that Han soldiers and the Chinese people were tired of war, yet they faced an army of three hundred thousand archers, led by Mao-tun, which could not be subdued. If Kao-ti offered Mao-tun a royal princess and sent with her a large dowry of splendid gifts, peace might be purchased. Liu Ching conjectured that "if she gives birth to a son, he will be the crown prince [in line] to become the *Shan-yü*. . . . Together with this [the princess and the dowry] you can send an eloquent man to cleverly influence them to know about ritual. While Mao-tun is alive he would be [your] son-in-law, when he dies [your] grandson would become the *Shan-yü*. It is unheard of for a grandson to compete against [his] grandfather. Then without war [they] can gradually be subdued."[17]

The marriage and bestowal policies of Kao-ti were pursued by his successors for more than a half century. Still, it was naive to believe that the son of a Chinese emperor's daughter would become a *Shan-yü*'s successor. The Han married many princesses to the Hsiung-nu court, but none of their sons actually became rulers in the nomadic world. However, inasmuch as intermarriage provided a mechanism for the peaceful exchange of goods, it contributed to the stabilization of the frontier. The sending of Chinese princesses to nomadic courts provided tangible evidence of the ongoing commitment by Chinese rulers to maintain peace.[18]

Correspondence sent to Lao-shang *Shan-yü* by Emperor Wen-ti suggests that he felt it was extremely important to maintain effective intermarriage ties and promote peace. Wen-ti's letter begins: "The Emperor politely greets the Great *Shan-yü* of the Hsiung-nu . . . on the north of the Great Wall in the kingdom of the archers the *Shan-yü* receives the mandate [of Heaven]; inside the Great Wall in the household of the robed-ones, We rule."[19] Wen-ti then affirms his concern that all under heaven have the food, clothes, and the other essentials needed to enable peoples to live in harmony. He admits that he had heard that evil and covetous men seeking personal gain had disrupted Chinese–Hsiung-nu relations. He then affirms his satisfaction that it is clear from the letter he recently received from the *Shan-yü* that "two countries [China and the Hsiung-nu] have already [again established] peace through intermarriage. The two lords are happy. The weapons are laid aside, the soldiers are resting and the horses are grazing."[20] Wen-ti follows with a significant statement affirming his commitment to provide the Hsiung-nu with the goods essential for their survival: "The Han and the Hsiung-nu are neighboring states facing each other. The Hsiung-nu are on the north where the land is cold and frost comes early. Therefore [We] order the officials to present to the *Shan-yü* grain, gold, silk and silk-products, and so on in a definite amount each year."[21]

Han Wen-ti clearly understood that the geographical limitations of the Hsiung-nu prevented them from producing agricultural products, making them dependent on the Chinese court for some essentials. When the machinations of unscrupulous Chinese, seeking personal profit at the expense of the nomads, denied them these goods, war broke out. The frontier could be pacified through the creation of new intermarriage agreements which would enable the Chinese court to provide definite amounts of goods to the Hsiung-nu.

Emperor Wen-ti's policy of promoting peace and stability with the nomads through intermarriage and bestowal policies was followed by his successor, the Emperor Ching-ti, but challenged by Ching-ti's son, Wu-ti. Han Wu-ti was a man of great talent and ambition who inherited the wealth and power accumulated during the previous six decades of prosperity and peace. As suggested in the following statement, Wu-ti grew irritated with the expense and the humiliation incurred by the Chinese through intermarriage politics: "We decorated the daughters to marry the *Shan-yü* and generously provided [the Hsiung-nu] with silk, embroideries, and other wealth. The *Shan-yü* . . . became more proud and their intrusions and robbings are endless. . . . "[22] In 133 B.C., when the Hsiung-nu again sent an envoy to request renewed intermarriage ties and additional gifts, Wu-ti encouraged a great debate at his court over the issue of whether to maintain peace by continuing to provide the Hsiung-nu with goods or promote war and seek to destroy the nomads once and for all.

One official named Wang Hui, a man from Yen who had been a border official and was experienced in nomadic affairs, argued that war was desirable because intermarriage arrangements usually last "for only several years" before they are transgressed. His position was challenged by the *Yü-shih tai-fu* (minister of censorship), Han An-kuo, who, adopting the language of Chu-fu Yen, stated that the Hsiung-nu " . . . move like the birds and it is impossible to control them."[23] A struggle with the Hsiung-nu is dangerous. Han argued that "it is not worthwhile to expand our territory by occupying their land, and it is impossible to increase our strength by subduing their people."[24] The majority of court officials favored Han An-kuo's position, so Wu-ti agreed to promote peaceful exchange.[25]

The issue did not die. In the following year, Wang Hui proposed that the court adopt the plan presented by Nieh I, described in chapter one, to ambush the Hsiung-nu at the Chinese city of Ma-i. He did not argue for a deep penetration into nomadic lands but rather for a quick surprise assault on a nomadic force deceived into entering China: "We will select the best horsemen and most powerful fighters to ambush [the enemy] from the shadows and to strategically utilize the landscape to prepare for the [struggle]. Our plan is settled; we may camp on their left and on their right or we may meet them from the front and cut them off from the rear. Then the *Shan-yü* will be captured and we will achieve total success."[26]

Wang agreed with Wu-ti that intermarriage policies had failed. In fact, they may have given the Hsiung-nu a false sense of power, which encouraged them to wantonly attack the frontier. Wang suggested that the court initiated the policies of conciliation, advocated earlier by Kao-ti, simply "to rest the hearts [of the people] under Heaven."[27] "Kao-ti [was a warrior accustomed to] wearing hard armor and holding sharp weapons."[28] Although Kao-ti's policies for the promotion of peace were suitable for his time, the deteriorating border situation under Wu-ti made an attack on the nomads a necessity. Wang attempted to show that there was precedent for an aggressive frontier policy toward the nomads, citing the attacks by Duke Miu of Ch'in[29] against the Western Jung, and Meng T'ien's consolidation, while serving Ch'in Shih Huang-ti, of China's frontier against the Hsiung-nu on the banks of the Yellow river. Wang insisted that "the Hsiung-nu can only be subdued with power and should not be treated with mercy. Now, the Middle Kingdom is in full splendor and the wealth has increased ten thousand times. To use one hundredth [of our power] to attack the Hsiung-nu is like shooting a strong arrow into a swelling to draw pus; there would not be hindrance."[30]

In the court debates of 134 B.C., Han An-kuo again represented the non-war faction. He suggested that although the Emperor Kao-ti was humiliated by Mao-tun in battle, he harbored no resentment against him and presented the Hsiung-nu gold and established intermarriage ties with the nomads. Han argued that the Emperor Wen-ti had also gathered Chinese troops to wage war against the Hsiung-nu, but he realized the futility of this and restored the marriage agreements. As a consequence, intermarriage and bestowal arrangements preserved peace and prosperity in China for generations and so "the footsteps of these two Sacred Ones are wise enough to follow."[31]

Han An-kuo asserted that during the Hsia, Shang, and Chou periods, the nomads were not subdued because they lived in remote areas "and could not be herded."[32] He cautioned against believing that things had changed:

> ... The Hsiung-nu are light, swift, and furious soldiers. They come like hurricanes and disappear like lightning. Travelling, bow-hunting, driving their animals for grazing and moving with no constant settlement is their way of life, which makes it difficult to control them. Now, [we] are planning the long disruption of the planting and weaving activities of the frontier commanderies [in order to mobilize for war] which is merely the normal way of life for the barbarians. [The costs] are not well balanced. Therefore, [I your] vassal, say it is better not to attack.[33]

Han believed that tactically and logistically the Hsiung-nu would be hard to defeat. Clearly, the time must be right before the initiation of any aggression against the nomad. The following passage suggests the dilemma which Han An-kuo believed Wu-ti's armies would face when attacking the nomad:

> Now [we] are [hurriedly] wrapping our armor to unthinkingly enter far into the enemy's land for an attack. It will be difficult to achieve any merit. If [we] march in a column [we] will be threatened from [both sides], yet if [we] march in a horizontal line the center will be cut off. If [we] go fast there will not be food, if we go slow there will be no gain. Before reaching one thousand *li* both man and horse will have nothing to eat. As the military principle says, this is sending booty to others . . . the benefit of reaching deep into [enemy land] cannot be seen.[34]

At the beginning of Emperor Wu-ti's reign, officials such as Han An-kuo emphasized the benefits of maintaining peaceful relations with the Hsiung-nu. However, Han power had grown to the point where it was difficult for Wu-ti to resist an attempt to destroy the Hsiung-nu once and for all. Wu-ti accepted the counsel of Wang Hui and tried to ensnare the Hsiung-nu at Ma-i. The Hsiung-nu evaded the trap and escaped. Because the plan failed, Wang Hui was beheaded. Nevertheless, a decades-long war resulted from the miscalculations of Wang Hui and of Wu-ti himself.

Once war broke out, although the conflict wrought havoc on the Chinese economy and administration, it was difficult to persuade Emperor Wu-ti to abandon his campaigns. As the costs of war grew to astronomical levels, the emperor established controls to regulate the marketing of such essential goods as salt, iron, and grain. This prevented private individuals from speculating in these commodities and diverted profits from their sale to state coffers. In 81 B.C., a heated debate over Wu-ti's policies occurred at the Han court which was recorded by the scholar Huan K'uan and preserved under the title of *Yen-t'ieh lun* (Discourses on Salt and Iron).[35]

The debate pitted Legalistically inclined administrators against Confucian bureaucrats. The Legalists argued that the Hsiung-nu had rebelled against Han authority and frequently raided and devastated frontier settlements. They deserved punishment for their unruliness and lawlessness, and, consequently, Emperor Wu-ti chose to war against them. As a result, governmental controls over the economy were necessary because the revenue needed for defense of the frontier had become inadequate.

Confucian scholars responded with the argument that "the ancients held in honor virtuous methods and discredited resort to arms."[36] They cited a more ancient source, possibly Lao-tzu, who stated that "the master conqueror does not fight; the expert warrior needs no soldiers; the truly great commander requires not to set his troops in battle array."[37] Confucian intellectuals insisted that military strength was unavailing unless rulers and ministers cultivated virtue and morality. If the Han state ordered its own house, the Hsiung-nu would clamor to submit, and there would be no need to war. Although the Confucian arguments offered in 81 B.C. failed to persuade Wu-ti to abandon war, the debates have provided subsequent scholars with a rich source of information on Confucian and Legalist attitudes toward frontier defense, governmental regulation of commerce, and the role of the scholar, peasant, artisan, and merchant classes in Chinese society.

The disdain of the Legalists for what they viewed as idealistic solutions to complicated problems is evident throughout the *Yen-t'ieh lun*, but it is also suggested in the following exchange, which occurred apart from the debates of 81 B.C., between Wu-ti and two of his advisors. A scholar named Ti Shan counseled Wu-ti that "since the time Your Majesty mobilized the army to attack the Hsiung-nu, the Middle Kingdom has suffered great emptiness and poverty. Observing from this point, it would be better to agree to intermarriage [with the Hsiung-nu]."[38] Wu-ti asked a Legalist advisor's view regarding Ti Shan's position. The Legalist replied that "this foolish scholar makes no sense."[39]

The historian Ssu-ma Ch'ien, who lived during the reign of Wu-ti, recorded the impact on China of Wu-ti's attacks against the Hsiung-nu in his "Monograph on the Economy." He suggests that the wars of Wu-ti were extremely bloody and affirms what is evident in the *Yen-t'ieh lun* about the enormous expense of the war. The Han court not only had to provision Chinese troops to prepare them for battle but also had to grant substantial rewards to those victorious in their fight against the nomads. For example, in 124 B.C, the great general Wei Ch'ing led six generals and more than one hundred thousand troops to attack the Hsiung-nu. They returned with the heads of fifteen thousand nomads. The following year, nineteen thousand heads were severed, and tens of thousands of captives were taken. The dynasty provided the victorious warriors with vast quantities of gold and other rewards. Another victim of the war was governmental administration. War bred corruption as "people manipulated the law for illicit gain. . . . Official posts were bought and crimes were forgiven of those who paid. . . . Shameless ones deceitfully posed as men of integrity. The men of martial ability were promoted."[40] Ssu-ma Ch'ien attributes both the decline of Han economy and the growth of administrative corruption to Wu-ti's military activities.

After Wu-ti's reign came to an end, the remaining emperors of the Former Han dynasty avoided launching large-scale campaigns against the Hsiung-nu for almost a century. However, Wang Mang, ruler of the short-lived Hsin dynasty from 9–23 A.D., adopted a more aggressive policy towards the nomads, and numerous border crises broke out.

When Han power was reestablished by the Emperor Kuang-wu-ti in 25 A.D., he sent envoys to the Hsiung-nu "to rehabilitate the old friendship and bring them gold and silk"[41] in an effort to reestablish intermarriage and exchange ties. The emperor was a conscientious and vigorous ruler determined to maintain peace even though various ministers advised him to adopt a more militant posture towards the nomads. The first test of Kuang-wu-ti's policies came in 30 A.D. when the *Shan-yü* of the Hsiung-nu began to regard himself as another Mao-tun. By invoking the memory of this powerful ancestor, he hoped to enhance his own prestige and secure more supplies from the Han. As Hsiung-nu demands increased, cries could be heard in the Emperor Kuang-wu-ti's court for war. The emperor ignored them and continued to provide the Hsiung-nu with essential goods.[42]

Again, in 48 A.D., when the Hsiung-nu split into two groups and the Southern Hsiung-nu surrendered to the Han and moved to the frontier adjacent to China, some court officials advocated taking advantage of Hsiung-nu weakness by allying with the Koguryo, the Wu-huan, and the Hsien-pei to attack the centuries old enemy. They observed that: " . . . the barbarians, both humans and animals, suffer disease and death. Drought and locusts have made their land turn red, and with their strength sapped by drought and disease they cannot even match a commandery. . . . How can we hang onto literary virtue and neglect military affairs?"[43] Emperor Kuang-wu-ti replied that he needed to concern himself with what was near and ignore that which was far. He felt that the advocates of war overestimated Han strength and underestimated the power of the Hsiung-nu. He cited the Taoist sage Huang-shih kung: "Tenderness is able to overcome hardness and weakness is able to overcome power, . . . [and] the one who manages broad lands, harvests nothing, [but] the one who manages broad virtue reaps [great] authority."[44] Emperor Kuang-wu-ti so forcefully declared his position against war that "from then on no general dared talk of a military campaign."[45]

The surrender of the Southern Hsiung-nu did not lead to a complete break between the Han and the Northern Hsiung-nu, who, as early as 52 A.D., petitioned the Han for peace, trade, and intermarriage.[46] It did, however, lead to a decline of Northern Hsiung-nu power. Trade was offered to the Northern Hsiung-nu to discourage border raids and provide the Han court with leverage in its dealings with the Southern Hsiung-nu and other nomadic groups. In 84 A.D, the Northern Hsiung-nu drove more than ten thousand cattle and horses to the frontier to trade with Han merchants. Princes and ranking officials coming to trade were accommodated in official residences and offered bestowals.[47] The Southern Hsiung-nu, disgruntled by Han support for their northern rivals, attacked the Northern Hsiung-nu in 85 A.D. and severely defeated them. Although the Northern Hsiung-nu leaders that were captured by the Southern Hsiung-nu were returned to the north by the Han, trade relations between the Han and the Northern Hsiung-nu never recovered.[48]

As suggested in chapter one, the split in Hsiung-nu ranks weakened both the northern and southern groups and left them vulnerable to Chinese manipulation and attacks by nomadic rivals, such as the Wu-huan and Hsien-pei. In 88 A.D. the young Emperor Ho-ti (r. 89–105) ascended the throne, only to be dominated by the Empress-Mother and her family, the Tou's. To increase their prestige and distract some officials from challenging their usurpation of power, the Tou family advocated an activist policy against the Northern Hsiung-nu. Among others, two officials emerged to challenge this adventurism. Lu Kung observed that the Hsiung-nu had been massacred by the Hsien-pei (he did not mention the Southern Hsiung-nu) and had retreated far to the west thousands of miles from the Chinese border. He argued that "now there are not problems along the border," and the court should consequently practice goodheartedness and uprightness. Taking advantage of the exhaustion and weakness of the Hsiung-nu to attack them would not be upright.[49] Sung I, another official, argued that "the benefits [of fighting the Hsiung-nu] have never compensated for the losses." Now that the barbarians are fighting the barbarians, it would be a mistake to intervene. Han policy should focus on getting the Hsien-pei to attack the Hsiung-nu and the Southern Hsiung-nu to struggle against the Northern Hsiung-nu.[50]

The counsel of Lu Kung and Sung I was not followed, and the court of Ho-ti sent the generals Tou Hsien and Keng Ping to attack the Northern Hsiung-nu. The Northern Hsiung-nu were in a weakened state and poorly prepared to challenge the Chinese armies. Their armies were exhausted because once the Southern Hsiung-nu settled on the borders of China, they had limited access to Chinese wealth. In addition, the expeditions of the Chinese general Pan Ch'ao,[51] commencing in 73 A.D., enabled the Han to secure the Tarim Basin and the silk routes and deny the Northern Hsiung-nu the vast wealth and supplies which they earlier derived from this source. As their economic situation deteriorated, they were forced to make excessive demands on the other nomadic groups that they originally dominated. These peoples rebelled and attacked their Hsiung-nu masters.

The Han armies sent by the Tou dominated court defeated the Northern Hsiung-nu who fled further into Central Eurasia. However, the Southern Hsiung-nu were prevented from occupying the territory left vacant by the Northern Hsiung-nu because the Hsien-pei filled the vacuum. Consequently, the Southern Hsiung-nu remained on the borders of China, dependent upon Chinese beneficence. Years later, following the great disturbances of the Han decline and the rule of Wei (220–264) and Chin (265–419), and following the great migrations of non-Chinese into China during the so-called Five Barbarian period (304–439), the Southern Hsiung-nu were assimilated into the densely populated Chinese sedentary society and disappeared as a distinct group.

In summation, it is evident that shortly after his near disastrous defeat to the Hsiung-nu in 200 B.C., Emperor Kao-ti adopted a policy which promoted intermarriage and the exchange of goods to insure peace between the Chinese and the Hsiung-nu. His successors generally followed his policies until the eruption of hostilities occasioned by Wu-ti's attempt to entrap the nomads at Ma-i. Once Wu-ti's reign ended, successors to the martial emperor adopted a less forceful approach toward frontier politics as they realized that to defeat the elusive Hsiung-nu in their homeland was a costly and nearly impossible venture, and that Han court objectives of securing peace on the frontiers could be better achieved through trade and diplomacy. The usurpation of the Han throne by Wang Mang led to another period of unrest between the Chinese and Hsiung-nu, as this ruler attempted to alter traditional relations with the nomads. From the founding of the Later Han dynasty by Emperor Kuang-wu-ti, relative stability was again achieved on the borders of China.

Throughout the Former Han dynasty, Chinese emperors did not treat the *Shan-yü* of the Hsiung-nu as a vassal but as the leader of an independent state. This is evident in the writing of the Chinese emperors to the *Shan-yü*, such as Emperor Wen-ti's recognition that north of the Great Wall the *Shan-yü* possessed the Mandate of Heaven. Again, the equality in relations is suggested by the manner in which the Hsiung-nu leader, Hu-han-yeh, was received by the Emperor Hsüan-ti when he appeared at the Kan-chüan Palace[52] seeking an alliance with the Han after the first split of the Hsiung-nu people in 55 B.C. Because there was little precedent for nomadic leaders to appear at a Chinese court, Chinese officials debated whether Hu-han-yeh should be received as a feudal prince or as the lord of another country? It was decided that "the *Shan-yü* is not covered by our correct calendar and, therefore, his country should be called the country of a rival *(ti-kuo)*.[53] For this reason, it would be better to receive him not as a vassal but to place him above the feudal kings."[54] The Han emperor and his ministers recognized the Hsiung-nu *Shan-yü* as the sovereign of an equal state, one who deserved to be treated as a guest and not as a subject.

Wang Mang began to alter the status of the Hsiung-nu by forcing them to use the title *kung-nu* (obedient slaves) rather than *Hsiung-nu* (furious slaves) and *shan-yü* (a good man) rather than *Shan-yü* (khan) when addressing the court.[55] He also changed the seals given by the court as symbols of authority to the Hsiung-nu leaders. The seals given to the Hsiung-nu by Emperor Hsüan-ti read, "The *hsi* [imperial seal] of the *Shan-yü* of the Hsiung-nu." Wang Mang changed it to read, "the *chang* [stamp] of the *Shan-yü* of the Hsiung-nu of the Hsin [dynasty] . . ."[56] In essence, he was relegating the Hsiung-nu ruler from the sovereign of an independent state to being a vassal of the Hsin dynasty. The Hsiung-nu, although deeply upset by this, did not immediately break with Wang Mang's court for fear of losing their access to essential goods from China. However, when Wang Mang attempted to divide the Hsiung-nu by sending presents and seals of authority to fifteen Hsiung-nu princes, the nomads attacked the frontier, and war broke out.

By 50 A.D., it is evident that the Southern Hsiung-nu accepted vassal status. As a response to a mission sent by the *Shan-yü* to the Han court, an envoy was dispatched to the Southern Hsiung-nu. "The *Shan-yü* welcomed the envoy and the envoy said, 'The *Shan-yü* must bow to receive the Decree.' The *Shan-yü* was startled for a moment, then bowed and entitled himself a vassal. After bowing he commanded the interpreter to tell the envoy, 'The *Shan-yü* has just been enthroned and feels shamed in front of his people. [I] ask the envoy not to insult me in front of the multitude.' All the Hsiung-nu nobles wept."[57] Comparing this incident with the treatment of the Hsiung-nu leader Hu-han-yeh during the

Former Han period, it is clear that the Former Han dealt, ostensibly at least, with the sovereign of a rival state whereas the Later Han dealt with the leader of a vassal state.

At the end of the Later Han dynasty, the Hsien-pei replaced the Hsiung-nu as the dominant northern tribe. However, the power of the Hsien-pei was not as great as that possessed by the Hsiung-nu. The Ts'ao court of the Wei dynasty (220–265 A.D.) considered itself superior to the nomads and refused to recognize earlier titles, such as *Shan-yü*, that had been granted to the nomadic leaders. They sought to assert Chinese authority by bestowing pure Chinese titles upon nomadic rulers. For example, in 220 A.D. they made K'o-pi-neng, a loyal prince of a small tribe of Hsien-pei, a Fu-i *Wang* (the Prince of upright subordination).[58] The court gave princely titles to other nomadic leaders as the Wei dynasty sought to win the allegiance of nomadic rulers to the sedentary court and weaken nomadic strength by creating rival centers of power. Nomads accepted the titles to gain prestige, win Chinese support against nomadic rivals, and secure trade privileges with the agricultural Chinese.

In the fourth century, the T'o-pa group of the Hsien-pei descended into and occupied northern China to establish the Northern Wei dynasty (386–534), the first dynasty of conquest in Chinese history. This period saw vast migrations of northern nomadic people into China proper.[59] Wave upon wave of nomads washed south into China only to disappear in the human sea of the agricultural populace. Although this laid the foundation for a stronger China with a more varigated culture, assimilation for the nomad minorities meant the outright erasure of their ethnic and cultural distinctiveness.

As suggested in chapter one, the T'o-pa court identified itself with Chinese culture and sought to establish relations with nomadic groups following earlier Chinese precedent. They were not beyond utilizing the nomadic peoples' desire for trade as a means to subordinate the herdsmen to an inferior status. This is evident in the way the T'o-pa Emperor, Su-tsung, treated the Jou-jan leader A-na-k'ui when he came to court in 520. The "Account of the Juan-juan" in the *Wei shu* states: "A-na-k'ui was placed in the middle of the court facing the north. The usher guided the princes, dukes, and others in ascending to the palace. A-na-k'ui was placed below the feudal princes. . . . Then A-na-k'ui was entitled 'Duke of the Shuo-fang Commandary, King of the Juan-juan' and bestowed with garments, crowns, carts, and canopies. His salary, followers, rituals, and guards equalled those of a feudal lord from the Imperial household. . . . "[60] A-na-k'ui's title of "King of the Juan-juan" was subject to legitimation by the Northern Wei court, an action which made him a ruler of a subordinate state. The title "Duke of a Commandary" (chün kung) was an even lower position than that of a feudal prince.

Evidence suggests that throughout the Ch'in and Han periods of Chinese history, sedentary courts seldom utilized nomadic forces to aid them in internal struggles. They might attempt to pit one nomadic group against another in the lands north of China, but they were reluctant to invite these formidable warriors to enter China to support them against internal rivals. However, from the sixth through the eighth centuries, nomadic people became intricately involved in internal Chinese politics. No longer were dynasties interacting with nomadic rulers simply to achieve the political objective of stabilizing the frontier; now, they cultivated nomadic support to aid them in securing and maintaining power within China.

An early example of this phenomenon is evident in the struggle between the states of Northern Ch'i and Northern Chou to gain an alliance with the Turks after the breakup of the Northern Wei dynasty into Eastern Wei and Western Wei halves and the subsequent fall of these states. Some evidence of the volume of bestowals from the Northern Ch'i and Northern Chou courts to win Turkic support has already been mentioned in chapter one. Ultimately, the Turkic leader, Mughan Khan (r. 533–572), allied himself with the Northern Chou dynasty and, with one to two hundred thousand Turkic cavalry[61], joined in attacking the Northern Ch'i capital of Chin-yang (present-day T'ai-yüan, Shansi) in 564. Northern Ch'i resistance was much greater than anticipated, the Turks retreated, and the leader of the Northern Chou forces reluctantly abandoned the campaign. "At this point, the Turkic Khan had [his] troops plunder on a grand scale. Within the seven hundred li from Chin-yang to Luan-ch'eng [present-day Luan-ch'eng, Hopei] the great majority of both humans and animals were captured and killed."[62]

It is clear that in this alliance the Turks and the Northern Chou were not working for the same objectives. The aim of the Northern Chou was to crush the Northern Ch'i, both politically and militarily, but Turkic efforts were directed toward plundering the region of its human population for labor and its agricultural stores for food. The Turks had no desire to fight a decisive war and destroy the Northern Ch'i, because they benefited economically and politically from the continuing struggle. One might even suggest that the Turks had adopted a Chinese strategy and reversed it as they sought to use Chinese to check the Chinese and to further their own advantage. In 577, the Northern Chou mobilized and attacked the Northern Ch'i. When it became apparent to the Turkic leader, Tapar Khan, that the Northern Ch'i might be crushed, he attempted to assist his former enemy, but Northern Chou forces crushed the Northern Ch'i before the Turks could intervene, putting an end to Turkic ability to profit from the Northern Chou-Northern Ch'i conflict.

The Sui unification of China in 589 gave rise to a period of north-south, sedentarist-nomadic confrontation. Within a quarter of a century, however, rebellious military leaders shattered China's unity and confronted the powerful Sui. These men organized several independent regimes and vied with each other for Turkic military assistance. It was again possible for the Turks to benefit from the internal disruption in China. Li Yüan, founder of the T'ang dynasty, approached the Turkic leader Shih-pi Khan for support. Li Yüan sent Liu Wen-ching to negotiate with Shih-pi Khan for assistance in attacking the Sui capital at Ch'ang-an. In return, Li Yüan promised that if "the people and the land should belong to the Duke of T'ang," "the wealth, silk, gold, and jewels will pass to the Turks."[63] Li Yüan, a successful bidder for the assistance of the Turks, paid a very high price for Turkic aid. Put simply, Shih-pi Khan extracted a promise from the T'ang founder that he would receive all movable wealth in China. The Khan's purpose in joining Li Yüan was not to occupy or administer the lands of China but to seize its riches.

Turkic assistance went not only to Li Yüan but also to his rivals. In 619, Shih-pi Khan's successor, Ch'o-lo Khan (r. 618–620), aided a dynastic claimant, Liu Wu-chou, but in 620 he abandoned Liu to aid the T'ang.[64] Liang Shih-tu was another dynastic aspirant who, during the chaotic period of Sui decline and T'ang emergence, proclaimed himself emperor of the Liang dynasty. He was aided first by Shih-pi Khan, then by Ch'o-lo Khan, and finally by Ch'o-lo Khan's successor, Il Khan. Once the T'ang consolidated its control, Liang Shih-tu fled China and lived at the court of Il-Khan, where he continually encouraged the Turks to invade China. However, Turkic support for Liang Shih-tu was undermined when he precipitously killed the chief of the Chi-hu, a non-Chinese people.[65]

An observation made by Liang Shih-tu suggests the Turks' rationale for supporting various Chinese regimes: "In the past, the Middle Kingdom was disturbed, divided into several countries, and because they were equally weak, [they] became subjugated to the Turks in the north."[66] Turkic policy was aimed at preventing the emergence of a powerful unified regime south of the Great Wall. The preservation of this division made it possible for the Turks to profit economically as each regime invited Turkic military intervention and rewarded it. Aside from this, there were numerous and convenient opportunities for the Turks to pillage during their campaigns.

Once the T'ang dynasty was established, continued alliance with the nomads on the terms mentioned above was impossible, as suggested by the following passage attributed to T'ang T'ai-tsung, the son of Li Yüan who ruled for a short time as T'ang Kao-tsu: "[Emperor] T'ai-tsung said to a minister in his service, 'Formerly, when the kingdom was about to be created, the Retired Emperor [Kao-tsu] entered into vassalage to the Turks for the sake of the people. How can We not hate this both in heart and mind? [We] wish to exterminate the Hsiung-nu [meaning the Turks] and cannot therefore rest and enjoy the taste of food.' "[67]

Emperor T'ai-tsung recognized that his father had granted immense concessions to the Turks to win their support, yet Turkic support for the T'ang state was tenuous and based solely upon the promise of further economic gain. In fact, even after the founding of the T'ang dynasty, the Turks secretly negotiated with a T'ang rival, Hsüeh Chü, who was occupying the southeastern part of Kansu, forcing Emperor Kao-tsu to send a minister "to bribe Il [Khan] with gold and silk." As a result, the Turkic Khan withheld his support from Hsüeh Chü and was induced to return to the Chinese a captured T'ang governor and the territory of Wu-yüan which the Turks had occupied.[68] Il Khan's decision to return the Wu-yüan area to the T'ang again suggests that, until the end of the T'ang period, although nomadic rulers might temporarily occupy and exploit agrarian areas, they had no intention of permanently governing the peasant populace. Consequently, when adequately rewarded, they were willing to return lands and even court officials to the Chinese. Still, once China was unified under the T'ang in 624, continuing Turkic demands, coupled with the threat posed by the Turks to T'ang armies, led T'ai-tsung to attack and crush Il Khan in 630.

Once the Eastern Turkic leader Il Khan was captured and defeated, Emperor T'ai-tsung attempted to "use barbarians to check barbarians" by seeking alliances with the Western Turkic and Sir-Tartush Turkic tribes against the Eastern Turks. The emperor also played lesser nomadic groups against each other within the major federations and implemented a different policy for entitling nomadic rulers. When T'ai-tsung honored a nomadic ruler, he granted him honorific titles which suggested subservience to the Middle Kingdom. He also organized the tribes on the basis of Chinese institutions. Among the Western Turks, two cousins competed for dominance, both of whom received gifts and titles from the T'ang court, thus encouraging the polarization between them. A-shih-na Mi-she was installed as Hsing-hsi-wang k'o-han (the Khan who restores that which was destroyed), Yu-chien-men ta-chiang-chün (the Great General of the Right Imperial Gate), and K'un-ling tu-hu (the Protector of K'un-ling) and was to rule five tribes. His rival Pu-chen was given the title of Chi-wang-chüeh k'o-han (the Khan who recontinues an extinguished line), Yu-wei ta-chiang-chün (the Great General of the Right Garrison), and Meng-ch'ih Tu-hu (the Protector of Meng-ch'ih). He was to rule five tribes.[69] Emperor T'ai-tsung continued the policies begun by Wang Mang and adopted by the Northern Wei of bestowing half-Chinese, half-Turkic titles on nomadic leaders to emphasize that they were servants of the Chinese court with power equivalent only to that of high ranking generals in T'ang government.

Emperor T'ai-tsung's relations with the Sir-Tartush Turks is also instructive. The Hsin T'ang shu indicates that I-nan, the leader of the Sir-Tartush Turks, allied himself with the T'ang against the Turkic leader Il-Khan. When Il-Khan was defeated in 630, the Sir-Tartush occupied the old lands of the Hsiung-nu with two hundred thousand select warriors. T'ai-tsung was able, through imperial decrees, to divide the Sir-Tartush between the two sons of I-nan into southern and northern tribes, thereby reducing the danger posed by the Sir-Tartush on China's northern frontier.[70] Effective T'ang diplomacy contributed to subsequent Turkic weakness and instability, which precluded any serious involvement of the Turks in struggles in China until Turkic power was destroyed by the Uighurs in 745.

The Uighur, another Turkic-speaking people, were, like the Sir-Tartush, a target for alliance as the T'ang tried to manipulate them to Chinese advantage. The dramatic rise of Uighur power is recorded in the Hsin T'ang shu: "The Turks were already exterminated, leaving only the Uighurs and the Sir-Tartush the most powerful. . . . The Uighurs attacked the Sir-Tartush, exterminated them and absorbed their land. . . . "[71] Uighur chieftains were appointed as feudal lords over the lands they controlled and were provided with Chinese official titles in order to absorb them into the Chinese orbit of administration. When

T'ang bestowals met the needs of their people, Uighur rulers willingly accepted these titles and the vassal status suggested by them. A clear example of an early Uighur khan accepting Chinese-style names in return for financial rewards is evident in the study of the Uighur leader Ku-li-pei-lo (r. 742–745). This eighth-century Uighur ruler, seemingly unconcerned about court reaction to his impressive title, presented credentials to the T'ang court in 744, entitling himself *Kutlug-Bilgä-Kül Khaghan* (the blessed wise Khan of all). The Emperor Hsüan-tsung bestowed upon Ku-li-pei-lo the title of Feng-i *Wang* (the righteous supporting Prince) and the Chinese-style honorary title, Huai-jen *Khaghan* (the remembrance of mercifulness Khan). Finally, in 745, when he killed the last Turkic Khan, he was made a general of the T'ang court with the title Tso hsiao-wei yüan-wai *ta-chiang-chün* (extra Great General of the left brave garrison).[72]

Ku-li-pei-lo was the last Uighur Khan who accepted the rank of *wang* (prince) or *chiang-chün* (general) from the T'ang. While Uighur power was on the increase, the T'ang court was threatened in 755 by the rebellion of An Lu-shan[73] and Shih Ssu-ming.[74] This forced Emperor Hsüan-tsung to abandon Ch'ang-an and escape to Szechuan. His son, Su-tsung, in present-day Ninghsia, proclaimed himself emperor in 756 and solicited Uighur military assistance in order to crush the rebel forces and restore the dynasty. From this time, the reliance of the T'ang court on the Uighurs led them to intermarry with the Uighur nobility, often in quite elaborate ceremonies with expensive exchanges of gifts[75] and grant the title of khan, rather than lesser titles, to Uighur leaders.

Su-tsung's request for aid from the Uighur leader Ko-le Khan (r. 745–759) did not go unanswered. In return for a promise that the Uighur would be rewarded with the "jade, silk, boys, and girls"[76] of China, the Uighur khan sent his heir-apparent, Yabkhu, with a force of cavalry to assist Su-tsung in the recapture of the capital Ch'ang-an. After capturing Ch'ang-an, the Uighurs were prevented from looting the city by Prince Kuang-p'ing.[77] However, after the eastern capital of Loyang was captured, T'ang officials could not prevent the Uighurs from ravaging the city for a three-day period. After the third day of looting, city elders gave the Uighurs ten thousand rolls of embroideries and fabrics as a reward for "liberating" them, and the pillage ceased. Yabkhu returned to Ch'ang-an, where he banqueted with Emperor Su-tsung. He was granted honorary titles and promised by the T'ang court annual payments of twenty thousand rolls of silk.[78] Aside from the opportunity to plunder, no other factor could have caused the Uighurs to shed their own blood to restore T'ang power.

The capture of Ch'ang-an and Loyang did not bring the T'ang civil war to an end. Soon after the enthronement of Emperor Su-tsung's successor, Emperor Tai-tsung (r. 763–779), the rebel, Shih Ch'ao-i,[79] son of Shih Ssu-ming, invited Teng-li-muo-yü (r. 759–780), the second son and successor of the pro-T'ang khan, Ko-le, to join him in destroying the T'ang and founding a new regime. Shih Ch'ao-i promised Teng-li-muo-yü "the wealth of the [T'ang] treasuries" for his assistance. The T'ang court countered Shih's offer by promising to continue the annual presentation of several tens of thousands of rolls of silk if Teng-li-muo-yü would help them.

It was not certain which side Teng-li-muo-yü would join. Although the now deceased heir-apparent, Yabkhu, had developed a good relationship with the future Emperor Tai-tsung while they captured Ch'ang-an and Loyang together, his younger brother, Teng-li-muo-yü, was less enamored of the T'ang. Two obstacles stood in the way of a T'ang-Uighur alliance against Shih Ch'ao-i. First, Teng-li-muo-yü harbored ill-feelings towards the T'ang, because they slighted him when T'eng's father, Ko-le Khan, requested a T'ang princess for him to marry. Beginning in 756, the Uighur leader and the T'ang court had begun an extensive exchange of imperial princesses for intermarriage. Ko-le Khan first adopted his wife's (khatun) younger sister as his daughter and offered her for marriage to a member of the T'ang imperial household. Later, Ko-le Khan himself accepted a daughter of Emperor Su-tsung as his wife.[80] However, Ko-le Khan's request for an imperial princess for Teng-li-muo-yü was denied, and a daughter of a T'ang vassal of Turkic blood was offered instead. The T'ang probably felt that, having formed intermarriage ties with the Uighur khan, there was little need for further intermarriage between the two courts.

The second obstacle hindering a T'ang-Uighur alliance revolved around the question of what route Teng-li-muo-yü's forces should take into China. Negotiations arose based not on military considerations but on the question of where the khan and his troops could best obtain adequate "supplies" as they marched to confront the forces of Shih Ch'ao-i. T'ang envoys strained to convince the khan to take the route farthest from the capital. They were less reluctant to allow the Uighurs to pass through more remote rebel-held areas. Once this problem was resolved and Teng-li-muo-yü had committed himself to the T'ang struggle, he mobilized not only his troops but also the "old, young, and women" and marched across the frontier. The Uighur khan's intention was not to wage a decisive battle but to gather the agricultural products and riches of China. His excursion into China was essentially a military visit to a Chinese bazaar.[81]

In the middle of the ninth century, the Uighur empire was destroyed by the Kirghiz. Remnants of the Uighur tribes migrated northward to the region south of the T'ien-shan Mountain range and to the corridor to the west of the Yellow River where they gathered at the city of Kan-chou (present-day Chang-i, Kansu). The T'ang dynasty fell shortly thereafter, in 907, when Chu Wen established the Liang dynasty (907–923) in northern China. In southern China a seventy year period emerged when the Ten Kingdoms struggled against each other to unify China, and during the next forty years in northern China, the Five Dynasties rose and fell in rapid succession. In 923, Li Ts'un-hsü of the Sha-t'o Turks ended the Liang dynasty and began the Later T'ang dynasty (923–934). The Later T'ang and the Uighurs in the Kan-chou area maintained trade relations. Although the Uighurs had moved westward from Mongolia, they were still interested in and received titles from the Later T'ang dynasty.[82]

The Kirghiz nomads who destroyed the Uighur empire were quickly challenged by the Khitan people when they emerged north of China, sandwiched between the Turks and the Chinese. Because the Turks were a serious threat to them, the Khitan sought protection from the T'ang and were frequently granted economic support and titles. The Emperors T'ai-tsung and Hsüan-tsung generally designated the leader of the eight Khitan tribes or clans with the Chinese-style official title of *ts'u-shih* (governor). Other leaders were provided with titles of prince, baron, or governor general. All titles forced the nomadic leaders to recognize that they were vassals of the T'ang "Son of Heaven".[83] These titles, although important to Sino-nomadic interaction, were less valued by the Khitan within their own realm, where nomadic leaders continued to rely on their own system of tribal alliance and openly used the title of khan.

Once the Khitan emerged as a dominant force north of China under the leadership of Yeh-lü A-pao-chi, both the Later Liang dynasty and the emerging Later T'ang dynasty in northern China sought Khitan support in their struggles against each other.[84] A-pao-chi accepted their bribes and inducements and sent horses to them in return, but, occupied with consolidating Khitan strength north of China, he refused to be personally drawn into a Chinese conflict, although he did lend some troops to the

Later T'ang.[85] However, the limited involvement of the Khitan in China's internal matters ended when Shih Ching-t'ang approached the Khitan leader Yeh-lü Te-kuang for help in the overthrow of the Later T'ang dynasty in order to establish the third kingdom of the Five-Dynasty period, the Later Chin dynasty of the Shih family (936–946). Shih Ching-t'ang[86] enticed the Khitan khan by offering him not only the traditional inducements of gold, silk, embroideries, and cloth earlier promised A-pao-chi but also a territorial prize, sixteen counties in what is now northern Hopei and Shansi provinces.

Shih Ching-t'ang's alliance with the Khitan enabled him to topple the Later T'ang and proclaim himself Emperor Kao-tsu, but it also enhanced Khitan power by enabling them to move their armies into and occupy the entire Peking area. At the Later Chin court, wrangling occurred over whether the new dynasty should war with the Khitan or acquiesce to their demands for wealth and goods. As noted in chapter one, Sang Wei-han, a court official, argued that war is a dangerous matter. He recognized that it is necessary to adopt a less active frontier diplomacy when the military strength of an agricultural court does not match that of the nomads. Shih Ching-t'ang accepted his advice. As will be shown in chapter four, subsequent Chin policies relegated the Chin court to a junior position in its relationship with the Khitan. This is suggested by the enormous payments annually presented to the nomads and by the Khitan insistence that they authorize the installation of any Chin emperor on the throne.

Emperor Kao-tsu's successor, who was called the young emperor, *shao-ti* (r. 943–946), attempted to free himself from the vassal relationship and warred against the Khitan. He failed in this struggle which resulted in the fall of his dynasty and enabled the Khitan to establish the Liao dynasty (947–1125), which, from its more northerly base, spread southward where it continued to occupy most of present-day Hopei province.

Khitan power was ultimately replaced by Jurchen hegemony as the latter established the Chin dynasty (1115–1234). The Jurchen Chin state penetrated into Sung territory and moved their frontier further south to the Huai river valley. As a result, traditional border markets disappeared, eliminating this valuable focus for nomadic-sedentarist interchange. The Jurchen were hunter-agriculturalists, not steppe nomads. They adopted a Chinese lifestyle and established a dynasty which was politically and economically more attuned to the traditional Chinese agrarian state. The Jurchen also followed traditional Chinese policies towards the Mongols. They heavily garrisoned the frontier[87] and relied more on force of arms and diplomacy than markets and exchange to deal with the nomads. The Jurchen granted titles to nomadic leaders and attempted to pit one nomadic group against the other. For example, *The Secret History of the Mongols* informs us that the Jurchen utilized Mongolian tribes to aid them in their struggle against the Tatar tribe. They established an alliance with the young Chinggis Khan and To'oril, the Khan of the Kereyid tribe, located in the central part of present Mongolia in the upper stretches of the Orkhon, the Tula, and the Selengge rivers. For their assistance in defeating the Tatar, the Prime Minister, Wang-jing (Wan-yen Hsiang) presented To'oril the rank of *ong* (Chinese, *wang*), which means prince, and Chinggis Khan the rank of *ja'ud khuri*.[88] From this point on, To'oril was known as Ong Khan. This suggests that before his power was fully developed, he preferred the rank or title given him by the agricultural court, which evidently increased his political prestige.

As Mongol power displaced Jurchen and then Southern-Sung power in China, Khubilai Khan (r. 1260–1294) created a dual system of government. He tried to preserve traditional Mongolian culture while adapting Yüan-dynasty (1271–1368) government to the Chinese pattern. He found it useful to give Chinese titles and ranks to Mongol princes and nobles in order to enhance the prestige of the Mongols in the eyes of his Chinese subjects. High Mongol military and civilian officials also received Chinese official names such as *t'ai-shih*, *ch'eng-hsiang*, *p'ing-chang*, *chih-yüan*, and *tsai-hsiang*. These titles were adapted into Mongolian forms such as *taishi*, *chingsang* and *tzaisang* and used until the middle of the sixteenth century. Ultimately, the meaning of the original Chinese words changed. For instance, *tsai-hsiang*, the term for prime minister, became the name of a minor local official.

In 1368, Chinese leaders of the Ming dynasty (1368–1644) drove the Mongols out of China. Ming policies toward the Mongols were, at times, warlike, but on other occasions, they focused on utilizing trade and the bestowal of titles to create conflict and division among the Mongols, thereby diminishing the threat of a unified Mongol attack on the northern frontier. From the beginning of the era, Ming policy was directed against the legitimist Mongol khans, the recognized successors of Khubilai Khan's Yüan dynasty. The Ming court, therefore, allied itself with lesser Mongolian tribes and particularly with Right Flank Mongols, such as Altan Khan.[89] As a rule, the legitimist khans refused to deal with the Ming court. From Ayur-shiridara (r. 1370–78) to Lighdan Khan (r. 1604–34), none accepted rank, title, or installation from the Ming dynasty.[90]

Soon after the retreat of the Mongolian khan from China, several Mongolian tribes, including the Uriyangkha in the southeast and the Chikin Mongols in the southwest, surrendered to the Ming.[91] Although the leaders of these tribes accepted Chinese titles and gifts, they were still at times subject to demands made of them by the Oirad and other more influential Mongolian tribes. Inasmuch as they were precariously balanced between powerful nomadic as well as agrarian forces, Uriyangkha and Chikin Mongol submission to the Ming was not total.

Because the prestige and power of the Uriyangkha and the Chikin Mongols was limited, the court also attempted to establish political contacts with Oirad Mongol leaders further to the west as a check on the power of the legitimist khans. The Oirad Mongols had had little contact with Mongol Yüan dynasty.[92] In 1403 the Ming Emperor Ch'eng-tsu (r. 1402–1424, commonly known by his reign title Yung-lo) dispatched envoys to Mahmud (d. 1425?), called Batula Chingsang (prime minister) in Mongolian materials,[93] to establish relations with the Oirad. Mahmud accepted the ranks and titles of the Ming and commenced to send tribute.[94] The *Ming shih* informs us that Mahmud then attacked and killed the legitimist khan. At this juncture, Oirad power itself seemed to threaten the Ming court, and Emperor Ch'eng-tsu turned his favor towards Arughtai, a supporter of the legitimist line and strong opponent of the Oirad. Arughtai was granted the title Ho-ning *Wang* (the Prince of harmony and peace) in order to enhance the policy of "using barbarian to check barbarians."[95]

The Emperor Ch'eng-tsu's policy of relying first on the Oirad to counterbalance the threat posed by the legitimist khans and then on Arughtai to weaken growing Oirad power failed. During his reign, Emperor Cheng-tsu carried out six invasions against the Mongols. The emperor personally led five of the six wars. Two were conducted against the legitimist khan, one against the Oirad, and three against Arughtai. Once on the return from another campaign, Ming forces were sent to loot the Uriyangkha because they showed some disloyalty to the court. It was clearly dangerous for the Mongols to form an alliance with Ch'eng-tsu.

He constantly waged war against the Mongols to achieve his political objective of subduing the nomads. In the next chapter, we will show that, more than a century later, Altan Khan, an influential Right-Flank Mongol, fought with the Ming to achieve his economic objective of insuring the opening of frontier markets and the regularized exchange of goods. In 1571 peace was established between Altan and the Ming court. Altan and almost all the male members of his household were given ranks and titles.[96] Subsequently, Altan's wife[97] and his later descendents[98] also received titles. The Ming court sought to use Altan and his descendents of the Right Flank Mongols to achieve the political objective of isolating the legitimist khans. Altan and his followers accepted the ranks and titles to achieve their economic objective of securing adequate stores of Chinese cloth, foods, and luxury items.

III

FRONTIER MARKETS

This work has suggested that a study of war and peace on China's northern frontiers cannot be divorced from a consideration of either the economic reliance of nomads on the agrarian society south of the Great Wall or the tendency of sedentary peoples to utilize this economic dependence to achieve their political objectives. Chinese courts sought to institutionalize interaction and thereby stabilize frontier relations between the Chinese and nomadic peoples through regulated frontier markets, intermarriage, yearly payments and bestowals, and offers of tribute. Beginning with a discussion of frontier markets, the next three chapters analyze these institutions. Unless one or more of these institutions was maintained to enable the exchange of goods, peace on China's northern frontier was virtually impossible.

The most revealing materials dealing with the impact of frontier markets on maintaining peace or contributing to war are found in documents of the Ming dynasty. Chapter three will focus solely on Mongol-Ming relations (1368–1644) and will show that on the northern frontiers of China peace was possible only when an effective marketing system was established: "Whenever tribute relations broke down, as was the case in the sixteenth century, when the Ming for decades consistently refused tribute from the Mongols, trade opportunities also disappeared (at least officially), and as a rule border raids ensued. Indeed, the Mongols . . . were determined to obtain the needed manufactures by raid and plunder if necessary."[1]

In 1368, Yüan dynastic dominance of China came to an end when the Mongols were forced from Daidu (Peking, also called Khan Baligh, the city of the khan). A series of expeditions were launched by Emperor T'ai-tsu (r. 1368–1398) against the Mongols to secure the new dynasty's political position. T'ai-tsu was followed as ruler of the Ming by a grandson, but, after a three-year civil war, a son of T'ai-tsu, Chu Ti, usurped the throne from his nephew and commenced the Yung-lo period (r. 1403–1424). Emperor Ch'eng-tsu was extremely active in his relations with the Mongols. At times he allied with them but more frequently made war against them. By the end of his long reign, this martial emperor controlled all of modern China proper and dominated most of the frontier regions from Hami, an oasis located to the far west of China proper in the southern foothills of the T'ien Shan in the Tarim river basin, eastward along the Great Wall into southern Manchuria.

Emperor Ch'eng-tsu tried to implement the traditional Chinese policy of "using barbarians to check barbarians" and "using barbarians to attack barbarians" to diminish the Mongolian threat posed to the newly emergent Ming dynasty. He also opened horse markets with less hostile northern peoples to obtain desperately needed horses for his armies struggling with recalcitrant Mongols and Jurchens. As a rule, the most consistent antagonists of the Ming court were the Chinggisid, or legitimate khans, the Great Khans, who were direct descendants of the dynastic rulers of the Mongol Yüan dynasty. Ming rulers also faced a serious challenge from the Oirad, or Western Mongols. As a partial balance to both of these groups, Emperor Ch'eng-tsu first secured support from the Uriyangkha Mongols, who professed loyalty to the Great Khan, but were persuaded to support the Ming court by the promise: "Those who choose to come to the Court will be given official [titles], will be allowed to remain on their own lands, and will be allowed to trade as they wish."[2]

Horse markets were crucial if Emperor Ch'eng-tsu was to succeed in forcibly consolidating China's northern frontier. Horses were the most important domestic animal in the nomad's world and the item of trade most coveted by the Chinese. In times of peace, Chinese peasants placed a higher value on the plow-pulling ox, but in times of turmoil, if the Chinese were to defend themselves successfully, it was absolutely essential that the court acquire the superior horses raised in the lush grazing areas north and west of China. With this in mind, shortly after the dynasty was founded, Emperor T'ai-tsu reestablished an active tea-horse trade, which had flourished as early as the Sung period, with Tibet. However, although the court sought to carefully regulate this trade by ordering the death penalty to convicted tea smugglers and by issuing separate halves of broken gold tablets to officially licensed Chinese merchants and their Tibetan counterparts and insisting that they match these tallies before trading, illicit trade was extensive and undermined the court's ability to secure good horses at inexpensive prices.[3] As a consequence, the Emperor

Yung-lo opened additional horse markets in Liao-tung, seeking mounts from the Uriyangkha Mongols and the Jurchen.

Three horse markets were established in Liao-tung: one at the southern gate of K'ai-yüan, created for the Hai-hsi Jurchen, one five li east of K'ai-yüan, and one at Kuang-ning both for the Uriyangkha Mongols.[4] Nomads preferred to trade their horses for cotton cloth, silk, and other desired items, but sometimes they were offered only coin and paper currency, which lessened the interest of the nomads in the markets and led to a decrease in the volume of trade.[5] In Liao-tung at this early date tea was not exchanged, as it was on the Tibetan frontier, because the Mongols acquired a taste for tea only after their conversion to Buddhism in the 1570's.

During his twenty-two-year reign, Emperor Ch'eng-tsu launched six invasions into Mongolia. When the invasion of 1422 ended in a stalemate, the emperor suddenly attacked the Uriyangkha who he distrusted because they remained vassal to the Mongolian khan. The Uriyangkha could not indefinitely balance themselves between rival nomadic and sedentary powers. Ch'eng-tsu's attack failed to bring stability to Uriyangkha relations with the Ming, and, in 1428, the Uriyangkha invaded Hui-chou (present Kharachin Right Banner, Inner Mongolia), forcing the Ming Emperor Hsüan-tsung (r. 1426–1435) to order Chinese forces into the area.[6] During the reign of Emperor Ying-tsung (r. 1436–49) continued Uriyangkha revolt caused the Ming to close the Liao-tung horse markets. Beginning in 1444 and again in 1445, the Uriyangkha presented horses as tribute to the Ming to seek pardon and the renewal of trade.[7]

Two major factors led the Ming court to ignore the supplications of the Uriyangkha. First, after the death of Emperor Ch'eng-tsu, the level of hostility between the Mongols and the Ming diminished, and, as a consequence, Chinese demand for war horses accordingly declined. Second, while Ch'eng-tsu was still the emperor, the Ming court made a conscious decision to ally itself with the Oirad Mongols, rivals of the Mongolian khan and his powerful vassal, Arughtai. As part of this new alliance, in 1438, the Ming court opened a horse market at Ta-t'ung for the Oirad Mongols.[8] The Ming court came to rely upon this trade and the extensive presentation of tribute horses by Oirad tribute missions to meet its needs for good mounts, horses which could now be turned against the Uriyangkha to quell their rebellion.

As suggested by the following passage, the Ming court's decision to utilize Oirad strength as a counterbalance to the continued threat posed by the Chinggisid khans and the challenge posed by the Uriyangkha ultimately backfired. "Formerly, Oirad emissaries had never exceeded fifty persons; [later] in order to obtain ranks and bestowals from the Court, [they] increased [the yearly mission] to more than two thousand people. The court issued several decrees ordering reductions, but each was ignored. Killing and looting occurred at the arrival and departure of each mission."[9] In the mid-fifteenth century, a Western Mongolian chief named Esen began to dictate tribute exchange patterns to the Ming by simply ignoring court quotas established on the number of Oirad envoys and merchants who could trade at the frontier and enter China to present tribute. After consolidating control over the Central Eurasian realm from Hami in the west to the Jurchen domain in the east, Esen posed a grave challenge to the Ming dynasty. After about a decade and a half of increasingly volatile exchange, Oirad-Ming relations completely collapsed.

A number of reasons are cited for the outbreak of hostilities. First, the "Monograph on Economy" in the *Ming shih* informs us: "By that time [1449], Esen brought tribute horses for exchange. The eunuch chief, Wang Chen,[10] cut down the price. [Consequently], Esen launched a large-scale invasion. . . . "[11] In other words, the eunuch Wang Chen, who is generally depicted in Chinese sources as the villain in the ensuing developments, changed the exchange rates at the horse markets and precipitated the crisis.

Second, "The Account of the Oirad" in the *Ming shih* states: "By that period, the court envoys to the Oirad seldom refused any of Esen's requests. Oirad emissaries increased to three thousand. Again, in their report they falsified their numbers in order to increase the size of their honorarium. But the Ministry of Rituals allotted payment corresponding to their true numbers, which amounted to only one-fifth of their request. Esen, humiliated and furious, incited all the barbarians to launch an invasion from various routes during the seventh month of the fourteenth year [Cheng-t'ung, 1449]."[12]

A third factor contributing to the outbreak of hostilities was false assurances given to Esen by Chinese interpreters that his son could marry a Chinese princess. When Esen sent the proper ritual objects to the Ming court to confirm the proposed betrothal, the court, unaware of the interpreters' promises, curtly refused him.[13]

Lastly, the situation at the market at Ta-t'ung had deteriorated. In the "Biography of Yang Shan" in the *Ming shih* it is hinted that the silk and other fabrics offered for exchange to the Oirad were of poor quality, badly cut, and otherwise damaged.[14] Mongols were approaching the court in greater numbers, behaving in unruly fashion, and offering poorer horses as tribute to the court. They were demanding higher levels of bestowals and rewards, yet receiving goods of poor quality. In addition, they complained of being mistreated and deceived by Chinese bureaucrats and merchants. Esen's answer to this dilemma was war.

Esen's invasion of China in 1449 and his capture of Emperor Ying-tsung has been vividly described.[15] Fortunately for the Ming, after seizing the emperor, Esen did not press his advantage but hesitated before advancing toward Peking. The Ming court rallied, shored up the defenses around the capital, and after a short siege, Esen withdrew with the emperor still captive. The Ming court responded to Ying-tsung's capture by placing his younger brother on the throne as Emperor Ching-ti (r. 1450–1457). With the ascendance of a new emperor, Esen lost the leverage he retained when Ying-tsung was still regarded as the "Son of Heaven." In addition, as mentioned in chapter two, Esen also faced the defection of his ally, the Mongolian Khan Toghto-bukha, who now made peace with the Chinese.

Esen now sought to rebuild his relationship with the Ming. He released his captive, but the new emperor, enthroned during Ying-tsung's absence, turned Oirad envoys away, fearing they might assist those at court seeking to place his older brother back on the throne. While hostilities continued, it was impossible to maintain any border marketing system that could peacefully supply the Oirad with needed goods. As a consequence, in 1450 and again in 1451 the Western Mongols invaded and looted the frontier. Fortunately for the Chinese, civil war now broke out among the Mongols. In 1453, Esen clashed with and killed Toghto-bukha and took for himself the title Khan of Mongolia. Esen soon came in conflict with Alagh, another powerful leader of the Oirad, and was killed in 1454. The power structure established by Esen immediately collapsed enabling the leaders of the Eastern Mongols to recover the symbolically important throne of the khan. In 1457, the Ming emperor, Ying-tsung, also successfully staged a coup d'etat and regained the throne taken from him while he was a captive of Esen. He changed the chronicle title of his reign to T'ien-shun and entered the second half of his reign (1457–1464).

Relations between the Mongols and Emperor Ying-tsung remained chaotic. No institutionalized marketing system was created, which led to frequent border unrest. In 1458, Bolai of the Kharachin tribe moved from Kan-chou in the west to invade Liang-chou and Chen-fan (present-day midwestern Kansu) and then moved eastward along the border areas of present-day Shensi to Ta-t'ung and Hsüan-fu (present-day Shansi and Hopei). In 1462, Bolai's aggression ceased when his demand to present "tribute" was accepted by the Ming court.[16]

Chinese-nomadic relations remained turbulent during the reign of Ying-tsung's successor, Emperor Hsien-tsung (r. 1464–1487). Shortly after the new emperor ascended the throne, the nomadic leader Morikhai[17] challenged Bolai for dominance in Mongolia, and in 1465 war between the Chinese and the Mongols broke out again. The "Annals of Hsien-tsung" inform us that during his more than twenty year reign, invasions occurred one after the other from Liao-tung (in southern Manchuria) to Lung-hsi (in western Kansu). Only during a short period from 1475 to 1479 were some leaders of the northern nomadic world allowed to send their envoys to present tribute horses to the court.[18] A short period of trade then ensued as the Liao-tung horse markets were reopened in 1478.

The horse markets were reopened for two strategic reasons. First, it is apparent that the Ming Chinese again desperately needed horses. A passage in the "Monograph on Military Affairs" in the *Ming shih* states that "at the beginning of the Ch'eng-hua [period, 1456], horses became more and more rare, and the people became poorer, but horses were truly scarce."[19] Second, although the Uriyangkha Mongols had recurrently rebelled against the Ming through the period of Esen's insurrection, which led the dynasty to close the markets in Liao-tung, a Chinggisid khan named Mandughuli had arisen whom the Uriyangkha were unwilling to follow. Consequently, they migrated towards the Great Wall and asked the Ming to open markets for them. The emperor determined that rather than drive the Uriyangkha back into the arms of the khan it would be better to provide them with essential goods and seek to deepen the division between them.[20]

Ming efforts to stabilize frontier relations by normalizing trade with nomads were short-lived. By 1480, Chu Yung, a man of little courage and limited capabilities as a fighter, was made "General of barbarian pacification" (P'ing-lu *chiang-chün*) and led a force of Ming troops to attack a nominal vassal of Mandughuli Khan, Ismail of the Yungshiyebu tribe. The exact impact of this shift in Ming policy is generally unclear, but it transformed a period of somewhat stable relations into a period of violent border looting.

The situation on the frontier remained chaotic for about a decade until the youthful Batu-möngke, better known in Mongolian sources as Dayan

Khan and in Chinese sources as Little Prince (*hsiao-wang-tzu*), was established as khan. He directed his efforts at ending internal disunity, reestablishing the power of the khan, destroying rivals, and expelling the Oirad. Absorbed in consolidating his power north of China, Batu-möngke had little interest in raiding the Chinese frontiers and provoking conflict with the Ming. In 1488, "the Little Prince presented a document requesting that he be entitled Great Khan of the Great Yüan (Tai-Yüan tai-*k'o-han*). At that time the court was trying to treat [him] deferentially, and [the request] was accepted".[21] In both 1488 and 1490, the Little Prince was allowed to present tribute and conduct trade. In 1488, when he sent one thousand five hundred persons to the customs station, the governor of Ta-t'ung, Hsü Chin, was instructed to allow five hundred persons to proceed to the capital. The *Ming shih* informs us that in 1490 the " . . . military forces at Ta-t'ung were strong, and border defenses were fully prepared. When the tributary missions [of the Little Prince] came to the customs station, they dismounted from [their] horses and removed [their] bows and arrows. They were careful to obey orders, and no one dared quarrel."[22] It is important to note that, although this was a period of intermittent war, the Ming court's decision to open trade to Batu-möngke led this Mongol to restrain his troops and proved a positive preventative measure against the outbreak of conflict. A period of five years of relative peace followed.[23]

Dayan Khan divided Mongolia into right and left flanks and in each flank organized the tribes into three *tümen*. He placed the Left Flank under his personal command and made the Right Flank subservient to him. In 1510, the Right Flank rebelled against the khan. He quickly suppressed the insurrection and appointed one of his own sons, Bars-bolod, to rule over it, giving him the honorific title, *jinong* (deputy khan). Because he had another name, Sayin-alagh, Bars-bolod was known in Chinese sources as Sai-na-la or A-chu.[24] Bars-bolod was the father of Altan Khan. Dayan Khan also forced the Uriyangkha tribe to accept his control and made them a *tümen* of the Left Flank. As his power grew, relations between the Ming and Dayan Khan deteriorated.[25]

During the reign of the Ming emperors Wu-tsung (r. 1506–1521) and Shih-tsung (r. 1521–1567), war was the dominant form of interaction between the Mongols and the Ming, and avenues for peaceful trade were cut off. Until 1571, the engagements were violent and fought south of the Great Wall. In 1514, Dayan Khan's armies converged upon all of northern and central Shansi, where there was a prodigious loss of life.[26] In

1517, the Little Prince led fifty thousand cavalry into northern Shensi and after a massive two day battle, withdrew, with the Chinese claiming victory.[27] From this point until Altan Khan emerged in the 1540's to war with the Ming, there were no great nomadic invasions, but border intrusions never ceased.[28] From 1533 on these intrusions became more and more serious.[29]

After the death of Bars-bolod, his eldest son Gün-bilig inherited the *mergen jinong* (deputy khan of wisdom) title and the ownership of the Ordos *tümen* north of the Shensi border, and the younger brother of Gunbilig, Altan, received twelve clans of *Tümed* north of the Shensi border.[30] At this time, conflict was most frequently initiated by the relatively independent Right Flank descended from Bars-bolod, whereas the Left Flank Mongols grew complacent because of their wealth and power.

Altan Khan continued the Right Flank tradition and penetrated the frontiers of China in search of essential commodities. His brother and the Mongols of the Ordos *tumen* sometimes joined him. He had few political objectives other than to force the Ming court to recognize his requests that tributary relations and frontier markets be established. The Ming court's negative response provoked long periods of violent war, followed by short periods of negotiation with the Mongols and court debate about barbarian affairs. The remaining pages of this chapter are devoted to studying the debate, negotiation, and accords (or lack of accords) reached during the crisis years of 1541–2, 1550, and 1570. A thorough study of Altan's relations with the Ming dynasty reveals many things. First, Altan's objectives were primarily economic and not political. Second, nomadic incursion was the catalyst for Ming debate and the Chinese response. Third, the soundest course of action for the Ming court proved to be the establishment of frontier markets rather than a continued denial of trade to the Mongols. Finally, the benefits derived from market concessions outweighed the costs incurred in maintaining tribute and market relations. In other words, once the markets were established, they worked.

The crisis of 1541–2 was created when, in 1541, Altan sent an envoy, a Chinese named Shih T'ien-chüeh, to visit Governor Shih Tao at the Ming fortress of Ta-t'ung to request the opportunity to present tribute. The governor forwarded Altan's petition to the court where the emperor "ordered that it be rejected," directed that troops be sent to reinforce Hsüan-fu and Ta-t'ung, and "announced an award for the heads of Altan and [his ally] Abughai."[31] Despite the hostile response by the court in

1541, the next year Altan again sent his envoy to Ta-t'ung. However, "Governor Lung Ta-yu arrested Shih T'ien-chüeh and chopped him into pieces at the bazaar. Lung Ta-yu was [subsequently] elevated to the next higher official rank, and those officials involved in the execution were all promoted and rewarded."[32]

Altan responded to this treachery by ravaging most of present-day Shansi Province. "The bandits were indignant and carried out a great invasion and massacred villages and fortresses."[33] In 1544, Mongol forces entered present-day western and west-central Hopei, forcing the Ming court to place Peking on alert.[34] However, Altan's military activities involved only a portion of the Right Flank Mongols. Their penetrations were different in kind and degree from the twelfth-century Mongol invasion of the Jurchen Chin dynasty. Altan's desire was to seize booty and convince the Ming to reopen peaceful trade; he had no other political objectives.

After releasing a captured Ming centurion of the Yü-lin Garrison[35] who promised to persuade the court to open tribute relations, Altan Khan again sent envoys to Ta-t'ung in 1546 and 1547.[36] The commanders at the fortress, aware of the elevation of Lung Ta-yu after his execution of Altan's earlier envoy, killed them and presented their heads to the court to obtain merit. The court official, Weng Wan-ta, critical of the activist foreign policy of the dynasty, condemned "the mischief of the border officials" and advocated that the court execute them for killing Altan's envoys. He suggested that tribute relations in the early Hung-chih period (1488–1505) had brought comparative peace to the border areas and urged the court to negotiate with Altan. In his memorial he observed that "If there is an outbreak of invasions, the tribes will profit, but if [they are] allowed to pay tribute, the leaders will profit."[37] Weng clearly realized that Altan recognized the advantage of court-to-court exchange, which would enrich the Mongolian leader without obligating him to divide the goods he acquired with his subordinates. Weng's efforts proved futile. The emperor remained committed to war and reproved Weng for writing an improper memorial.[38]

Although markets were not opened to Altan in 1546 and 1547, in 1548, two markets were operating at Ning-hsia and Yen-sui to service the Ordos Mongols, particularly the nephew of Altan, Lang *Taiji* (Baisangghur *Taiji* in Mongolian sources). A passage in the *Ming shih* suggests that after looting parts of present-day Kansu, " . . . several tens of thousands of bandits again stationed themselves outside the fortress of Ning-hsia and prepared to launch a great invasion. Government forces repulsed them. . . . [By that time] horse markets had been opened in the two cities of Yen-sui and Ning-hsia, and five thousand horses were exchanged. The chieftain, Lang *Taiji*, restrained his tribesmen, and there were no further incidents until the markets were closed."[39] Although these markets diminished the aggressive activity of the Ordos Mongols, the Ming court did not expand the marketing mechanism across the entire border region.

The Ming failure to open markets to Altan led him to again invade China during the autumn of 1550. His forces ravaged T'ung-chou and devastated more than thirty prefectures in the vicinity of the Ming capital.[40] When his horsemen appeared near the gates of Peking, Altan released a captive official of the imperial stable and ordered him to deliver a document to the court demanding the opportunity to pay "tribute."[41] The appearance of Altan's armies at the gates of the capital forced the court to reconsider Ming frontier policies:

> Minister Hsü Chieh[42] said that "at present, the barbarian troops are stationed in the suburb, but we have no preparations for either attack or defense. It would be convenient to allow the barbarians to render homage, but there is the prospect that in the future we will be unable to satisfy their demands." The emperor replied, "If it will be beneficial for the kingdom, [We] will not withhold furs, cloth, pearls, and jade." [Hsü] Chieh said "If [their demands] are limited to furs, cloth, pearls, and jade, that will be satisfactory; but what should we do if [they request] something to which [we] should not agree."[43]

It is safe to assume that some kind of understanding was reached between the court and Altan because he and his forces withdrew from China. During the following spring, Altan again petitioned the Ming authorities at Hsüan-fu and Ta-t'ung to allow him to present "tribute" and open frontier markets. He even sent his son, Toghto, to Ning-yüan pu (a castle east of Kalgan, near Hsüan-fu) to urge the frontier authorities to carry his petitions to the Ming court. Toghto gave horses to the border officials and left hostages with them. A short time later, as another sign of his sincerity, Altan Khan turned over two Ming soldiers who had defected to his camp.[44]

Altan's successful invasion of China coupled with his reaffirmation of a desire to open trade relations with the Ming led to a heated debate among Ming officials over issues of peace, war, and trade with the Mongols. The chief proponent of establishing tribute and market relations with the Mongols was the Count of Hsien-ning, a man named Ch'ou Luan,[45] who was ultimately appointed generalissimo to deal with the enemy.[46] The spokesman for those committed to a continuation of the activist frontier policies of the past decades was Yang Chi-sheng, a counselor of the Ministry of Military Affairs. In a rather long memorial translated as a footnote in this monograph,[47] Yang presented ten objections to allowing Altan to offer tribute and trade at frontier markets and criticized Ch'ou Luan and his colleagues for developing five erroneous theories leading them to promote five falsehoods to the court. Study of this memorial clarifies the basic arguments used by both factions in this debate.

Yang's arguments supporting continued hostility toward Altan and his followers can be broken into several categories. First, he simply argued that war was a better course of action than peace. He asserted that "The Lord Emperor is brilliant and heroic. The kingdom flourishes, and there are countless brave and strong men . . . so why is it impossible to capture the barbarian chieftain and exterminate the people and their seed. . . . "[48] Besides, the Chinese anticipate that the Ming will fight the barbarians. If the court determines to promote peace after being humbled by the Mongolian armies at the gates of Peking, both the emperor's subjects and the invaders will question the military capabilities of the Ming. This would not only invite further barbarian incursions but equally dangerous "the masses will rise up as bandits."[49] Yang suggested that the court not delay fighting Altan because currently Ming soldiers were indignant towards him. If markets are opened and peace is promoted, it will be difficult to maintain morale in the army and prepare for a future struggle.

A second concern voiced by Yang in his memorial to Emperor Shih-tsung was that the barbarians had insulted the court and opening markets meant capitulating to them. He argued that "a dignified Celestial Court's disgracing itself by trading with dogs and sheep bears no difference from switching the positions of a hat and shoes."[50] Yang's opinion reflected the view that a Chinese court was able to accept tribute from barbarians and bestow rewards upon them for their obedience, but it could not engage in trade with them on an equal basis. The recognition of equality suggested by the opening of markets would be disgraceful and analogous to switching "hat and shoes." Yang inquired as to whether "the so-called tribute today [is] the same as that from subordinates who came to pay respects to the king in ancient days?"[51] He then suggested that the present tribute was "nothing but a large bribe [to the enemy] to maintain an improper peace for a short time."[52]

Yang's third objection was that frontier markets promote corruption, are costly, and provide the Chinese with little to benefit the state. Yang realized that frontier officials and merchants at Hsüan-fu, Ta-t'ung, and elsewhere were generally in collusion with the barbarians. As long as the Ming court restrains interaction between Chinese on the frontier and the nomads, "they are afraid of the law and dare not run wild."[53] However, once the markets are opened, the court will be unable to monitor the activities of all those who flock to them to trade, resulting in further concert between unscrupulous Chinese and nomads and "immeasureable disasters."[54] Yang also observed that the court would be forced to send hundreds of thousands of taels of silver to the markets to purchase horses from the Mongols, but "the horses are purchased only for expeditions against the barbarians. If the markets lead to peace, then where are the horses to be used? Moreover, why should the barbarians give us good horses?"[55]

Yang's fourth concern was expressed in his ninth objection:

> These dogs and sheep are untrustworthy and constantly changing. Now, when we send an important minister to carry gold and silk to the border, they may not abide by the agreement and may refuse to come. Or, because of the markets they may attack the customs area and invade. Or, they may come to the market to trade today but invade tomorrow. Or, they may send their masses to invade and say that it was done by other tribes. Or, they may bring weak horses but ask for a high price. Or, because they sell horses, they may ask for excessive rewards. Or, they may demand something beyond what we can bear. As it is, we are unable to hobble them, but they are able to fool us. We will thus be trapped in a shrewd plot by the northern barbarian.[56]

The response by those advocating the opening of markets was stated by Ch'ou Luan and his colleagues. They first suggested to the emperor that there was historic precedent during the Ming period for opening markets. During both the Yung-lo (1403–1424) and Ch'eng-hua (1465–1478) periods, horse markets were established in Liao-tung for the Hai-hsi Jurchen and the Uriyangkha Mongols. Now, it seemed propitious to open markets to trade with Altan Khan and his followers. Next, Ch'ou Luan suggested that when Altan recently petitioned for the opportunity to present tribute and trade, he showed proper submissiveness, presented hostages, and even returned Chinese rebels to the court.[57] Third, advocates affirmed that the markets would not suggest Mongol-Chinese equality but rather trading outlets intricately linked to the tributary system, allowing only those enrolled as tributaries who showed proper deference to the court the opportunity to trade.

To these initial arguments, supporters of market and tributary relations added still others. Fourth, they suggested that by opening the markets you could hobble the barbarians. Mongols depended on and coveted Chinese goods and also derived substantial profit from trading for them at Chinese markets. It was argued that if markets were created that provided the nomadic people with adequate quantities of these goods to feed and clothe themselves and, in addition, make a profit by selling surplus commodities to others, the once confrontational Mongols could be reigned in for fear that the markets would be closed if there was a disturbance.[58]

Advocates also suggested that the Ming court desperately needed horses and would therefore personally benefit from the normalization of trade. Recurrently throughout the Ming period, the Chinese court lacked sufficient numbers of good mounts. After the Cheng-t'ung period (1449) and again at the beginning of the Ch'eng-hua period (1465), there was a scarcity of horses.[59] The *Ming shih* shows that "In the twenty-ninth year [of Chia-ching, 1550], Altan invaded while the *T'ai-pu* [Ssu, the Imperial Service Bureau] was short of horses. . . . This situation continued until the forty-first year [1562], when it was arranged to confer official posts on those who donated horses to the army."[60] It was argued that opening frontier markets and developing tribute relations with Altan Khan would stop this chronic shortage of horses.[61]

A sixth justification for establishing markets was that trade would enable the Chinese to win the hearts of the nomads so that they would ultimately desire to pay tribute. Once enrolled as loyal tributaries, they would recognize the superiority of Chinese culture and *lai-hsiang* "come to submit."[62]

Lastly, supporters of opening markets argued that "military action is unpropitious and should not be carried out carelessly."[63] Although Altan represented only a segment of the Mongolian tribes north of China's frontier, he had proven his military prowess by reaching the gates of the capital. Ming armies were in disarray. At this juncture, it would be futile to attack Altan and pursue him into the Gobi. Peace was the better policy. Besides, some officials felt that, when advantageous, it might be possible to use the markets to trick or trap Altan.[64] The *Ming shih* suggests that "the border officials were afraid of [war] and bought off [the enemy] through interchange markets."[65] Many who voiced proposals in support of developing a market-exchange system fall into this category. Through his successful invasions of the Chinese frontier and capital regions, Altan set the tone for these discussions. He, in fact, forced a Chinese response.

As was often the case in Chinese history, especially during the last decades of Ming rule in the seventeenth century, architects of frontier policy, whether pacifist or activist, were highly vulnerable to court censure. Yang Chi-sheng presented his arguments to the emperor fairly late in the deliberation process. Although his activist posture was reminiscent of that practiced by Emperor Shih-tsung throughout the previous decade, in 1550, the Ming emperor was preparing to abandon war and seek peace through the opening of markets. His response to Yang's memorial was scathing: "The emperor said, 'This matter was memorialized by border vassals long ago. Why did Yang Chi-sheng not speak before? After the envoy has already been sent, submission of this blasphemous memorial carelessly hinders border affairs and disturbs the hearts of the people.' "[66] The emperor ordered the imperial guards to arrest Yang and turn him over to the *Chen-fu ssu* (Office of Suppression and Pacification) to be examined and flogged. Afterwards, Yang was demoted and sent to be a scribe of the Ti-tao Prefecture of Shensi (presently in Kansu). In 1553, when he again became involved in court intrigue, Yang Chi-sheng was executed.[67]

Ch'ou Luan's position at court was also precarious. High officials initiating peace proposals frequently were suspected of treason. Many government officials felt they desired to open markets only so they could privately deal with the Mongols in order to enrich themselves. Other officials supported Ch'ou Luan's proposals to open markets but only reluctantly, because faced with military reality, they felt there was no alternative. As a consequence:

> The court discussions were usually harsh and condemnatory of the horse market as an erroneous policy. They tried to find one person on whom to fix the blame. Fearing the opprobrium, the Count of Hsien-ning, Chou Luan, memorialized [the Throne] and said, "The reason that [I, Your] vassal advocate the opening of the horse market is to facilitate secret preparations for war. Now all along the frontier and within [the court] there are those plotting to kill [me, Your] vassal. [They] purposefully neglect defense efforts in order to draw the barbarians [into war] and have them destroy the market agreement as early as possible so that Your Majesty will entertain doubt concerning [me, Your] vassal. [I, Your] vassal am worthy of nothing, but what of the affairs of the kingdom? Please, issue a clear decree to the vassals ordering them to strengthen their preparation for war.[68]

As suggested in the above discussion, the debate over frontier matters polarized the court, but Emperor Shih-tsung ultimately recognized the continuing threat posed to the borders as well as the capital by Altan Khan and decided to open markets for trade.

The initial proposals of Ch'ou Luan and his supporters suggest the terms of the arrangement offered to the Mongols. First, the markets were to be opened in recognition of the willingness of Altan and his followers to "restrain their tribes and refrain from violating the border."[69] Second, one hundred thousand taels of silver were to be allocated to the Minister of Military Affairs for the purchase of a set quota of horses from the Mongols which would enable the Mongols to buy satin, silk, and other goods to satisfy their needs. Third, a civilian official expert in border affairs and well known to the nomads was to proceed to Ta-t'ung with a military officer, the governor, and the governor-general to declare the opening of markets. Fourth, a minister especially deputed by the court was to monitor market activities, act as judge and arbiter in handling disputes, and return annually to the capital to memorialize the throne. Fifth, it was suggested that the markets be opened four times each year.[70]

The emperor referred these proposals to the Ministry of Military Affairs for discussion. The ministry agreed that the markets should be opened, but urged that this be only a temporary arrangement. It also asserted that opening the markets four times each year was too frequent, and that offering one hundred thousand taels of silver to the barbarians for horses was excessive. Ministry officials cautioned that the nomadic peoples "animal-like desire is like a deep gorge, so that it might be difficult to restrict it in the future."[71]

The emperor accepted the counsel of the ministry on one point and decreed that the markets be opened only twice annually, but on the other, he held firm to the suggestion that the Mongols be offered one hundred thousand taels annually for their horses. In his decree to open markets, he insisted that civilian and military vassals and garrison commanders provide the court with thorough reports of their activities. He also revealed a major concern of the dynasty with the markets when he cautioned all officials to "arrest the spies, and prohibit private contacts and struggles for gain which may lead to a dispute or the disclosure of border intelligence."[72] Lastly, he called the retired Vice Minister of Military Affairs, Shih Tao, to come to the capital and appointed him to oversee the implementation of these new policies from Ta-t'ung.[73]

The emperor's proposals were acted upon almost immediately and led to the opening of markets in 1551 and 1552 at Hsüan-fu and Ta-t'ung.[74] The *Ming Shih-lu* states that the horse market at Ta-t'ung was opened at the fortress of Chen-ch'iang pu. Altan and his son Toghto and their followers exchanged more than two thousand seven hundred horses there.[75] However, the *Ming shih* states that "while the Ta-t'ung market was open, he [Altan] would strike at Hsüan-fu, and while the market at Hsüan-fu was open, he would invade Ta-t'ung. . . . Nevertheless, the tribes benefited from the horse markets and were reluctant to launch a greater attack."[76] Altan's raids provided critics of the frontier markets the leverage needed to persuade the emperor to close the markets and led the Ming to again adopt a hostile attitude toward the Mongols. Ch'ou Luan, who had successfully persuaded the court to implement the market system, became the scapegoat for its failure and like Yang Chi-sheng was executed.[77] There followed almost two decades of uninterrupted warfare between the Mongols and the Ming.[78]

Why, after struggling for more than a decade to persuade the Ming court to open markets to exchange goods, did Altan and other tribes jeopardize these newly created institutions by raiding Hsüan-fu and Ta-t'ung? Moreover, why did the court so quickly abandon a marketing mechanism that led these Mongols to be "reluctant to launch a greater attack"? The "Annals of Shih-tsung" in the *Ming shih* fails to provide an explanation, but the "Account of the Ta-tan" suggests that several Chinese who had embraced the rebellious traditions of the White-Lotus (Pai-lien) Sect of Buddhism fled across the frontier to evade authorities. Knowing that during times of peace Altan might extradite them to Chinese authorities, they fomented unrest and encouraged the Mongols to raid the frontier.[79]

The *Ming Shih-lu* suggests that bureaucratic mismanagement was a second reason for frontier unrest:

> At Ta-t'ung, since the return of Minister Shih Tao to the capital, those barbarians who sought to exchange cattle and sheep for grain and beans, after a lengthy wait, received no answer, so they dispersed into [small groups] and engaged in daily robbery. During the eleventh month [of the twenty-ninth year of Chia-ching, 1550], they crossed the border in great force and looted and captured a great many people and animals. The governing official dispatched an interpreter both to rebuke and conduct an inquiry. Altan answered evasively, saying "these poor barbarians have no where from which to obtain food. It is impossible to stop [them] by prohibition only. Although the law of the Middle Kingdom is strict, is there no theft among

the people? It is possible for me to restrain myself [but] it is impossible for me to forbid [my] subjects."[80]

In this instance, bureaucratic delay may have been the result of court debate on the prudence of providing the nomads with grain and beans that might be used to feed Chinese defectors,[81] but most certainly it was always difficult for the nomads to deal with the bureaucracy at the frontier markets.

A last factor that undermined the stability of the newly created marketing system was the hostility of many nomads and Chinese towards the markets. Chinese hostility towards the markets has already been shown by the study of the debate over whether to open them or not, but nomadic resentment to the markets deserves further attention. Nomadic raids may have occurred for any of the following reasons. First, as suggested above, Altan could not guarantee the behavior of his subjects let alone Mongolian groups not loyal to him who were critical of the arrangement. Second, many Mongols in Altan's camp may have felt that the one hundred thousand taels of silver annually allocated to purchase horses simply were not adequate to provide the Mongols with the resources needed to obtain coveted goods. This would explain their raids on Hsüan-fu when the Ta-T'ung market was opened and their raids on Ta-t'ung when it was closed and trade was being conducted at Hsüan-fu. The critic of frontier markets, Yang Chi-sheng, suggested this danger before the markets were created when he asked, "is the profit from the horse trade sufficient to meet the needs of their multitude? If not, why should they observe words spoken in vain and harness themselves?"[82] Emperor Shih-tsung's rejection of the Ministry of War's proposal, that the monies allocated to purchase horses be diminished, suggests that he realized the validity of Yang's observation. Yet, was the allocation of one hundred thousand taels of silver to purchase horses sufficient? Third, the benefits accruing directly from "tribute" and the markets were monopolized by tribal leaders and nobles, whereas only booty seized in raids was distributed evenly among all those involved in military activities. It is therefore understandable that there were those in Altan's camp who felt that the successful opening of markets would decrease their income.

The ease with which markets were abolished and border hostilities again erupted must have been disconcerting to Altan and the Ming court officials interested in maintaining trade and tribute relations. However, once the markets were closed, it was virtually impossible to stop the spiral of warfare and promote the exchange of goods. In fact, Emperor Shih-tsung decreed that Chinese officials who opened markets would be executed.[83] When a new Ming ruler, Emperor Mu-tsung (r. 1567–1572), ascended the throne, it initially looked as if warfare would continue. In 1567, Tümen Khan and Altan jointly crossed the frontier and destroyed huge sections of present-day central Shansi as well as the Peking area and other parts of Hopei. The *Ming shih* states that "several tens of thousands of men and women were killed, . . . and the capital was alarmed."[84] However, because of the fortuitous surrender of one of Altan's grandsons and the actions of a courageous Chinese official, Wang Ch'ung-ku, the court shifted its policies and again opened the frontiers of China to trade.

In October of 1570,[85] Bagha-achi, the grandson of Altan Khan through his third son Tebeg *Taiji*, surrendered to Wang Ch'ung-ku, the Viceroy of the Hsüan-fu and Ta-t'ung areas. After his father's death, for some reason, the boy's mother had been put to death by Altan, and subsequently, he had been reared in the household of Altan by the Great Qatun herself. Although deeply loved by both Altan and his wife, when Bagha-achi was about eighteen, he and his grandfather violently quarreled. The cause of the rift revolved around Bagha-achi's decision to take as a second wife the daughter of a certain T'u-ch'e-chin of the clan Uushin. However, before the marriage was completed, Altan took this girl and sent her to marry another nomadic ruler who threatened war against Altan because Altan had fallen in love with a girl promised to him in marriage and had taken her for himself. Through the offer of the girl promised to Bagha-achi, Altan avoided war. Disillusioned, Bagha-achi and a small group of followers surrendered to the Chinese.[86]

Wang Ch'ung-ku determined to use this surrender to the court's advantage. He realized that Bagha-achi's defection provided the Ming with three options. First, Altan's grandson might be exchanged in return for the extradition of a number of Chinese fugitives. Second, if Altan refused to bargain for the return of Bagha-achi and began to raid the frontiers, the Chinese could threaten to kill Bagha-achi in order to constrain the Mongolian leader. Third, should Altan abandon Bagha-achi, the Ming could use Bagha-achi to encourage Mongolian defections. Moreover, when the aging Altan died, Bagha-achi could be allowed to return to Mongolia to set up a tribe loyal to the Ming to challenge one which would be controlled by Altan's eldest son.[87]

Wang Ch'ung-ku persuaded the court to allow him to treat Altan's grandson graciously and to offer him the title of *Chih-hui shih* (military director). At the time of Bagha-achi's surrender, Altan was fighting the Tibetans. Because Bagha-achi's departure was sudden, Altan thought he might be dead and immediately returned to the frontier of China to search for his grandson. When he discovered that Bagha-achi had surrendered and Wang had treated him well and was willing to negotiate terms for his release, Altan responded immediately. Wang proposed that Altan turn over to the Ming authorities Chao Ch'üan and other Chinese defectors and promised that if they were presented the next morning Bagha-achi would be returned that same evening.[88]

As suggested by the following passage, Altan's response was partially determined by his wife, the Great Qatun: "The old chieftain loved his grandson very much, but his wife loved him still more. The old chieftain was afraid of her. As [Bagha-achi had surrendered because of the old chieftain's behavior], she hit him [i.e., Altan] with a firebrand saying: 'even if the Chinese should demand your head, I am going to give it! I only want my grandson!' "[89] However, as evidenced by a passage from the *Ming shih*, it is clear that another factor weighed heavily in Altan's determination to negotiate with Wang: "My grandson has now surrendered to China; this is an opportunity created by Heaven. If, by good fortune, the Son of Heaven confers upon me [the rank of] prince, making me head of all the northern tribes, then who will dare turn on us to [make] disaster?"[90] Altan and the Ordos Mongols had invaded Tibet in 1566 and again in 1571 and were committed to challenging the Oirad Mongols in the northwest. An understanding with the Ming court would free Altan's forces in the east for his campaigns against his other enemies. Tribute and market exchanges would also provide Altan with essential commodities and the opportunity for extensive profits. Consequently, Altan complied with the demands of Wang Ch'ung-ku and turned over the defectors. He also requested titles for himself and his relatives and the reopening of frontier markets.[91]

Once Bagha-achi was returned, Altan sent envoys to Wang to express his gratitude and pledge to him that he would defend Ta-t'ung. Wang then asked Altan to help persuade Tümen Khan, Köndüleng, and the *Jinong* to render tribute. Köndüleng headed the Kharachin tribe of Mongols, and the Ordos Mongols were led by Noyandara *Jinong*. Both of these tribes belonged to the Right Flank and were descendants of Bars-bolod.[92] Altan was the oldest of the Bars-bolod lineage, which enabled him to convince them to accept Wang's offer to present tribute. However, although at this time Altan was more powerful than Tümen, he had little leverage with him. Tümen was the Great Khan of Mongolia, descended from Chinggis. It was difficult for the khan to present tribute to the leader of the enemy, and Tümen refused Wang's offer. The legitimist khans, for the most part, remained hostile to the Ming. Wang determined that with Tümen isolated his best course of action was not to provoke him. He ordered Ming troops not to set fire to Tümen's pastures[93] or to attack him north of the frontier. This aroused critics at court, bringing about another contentious debate regarding war, peace, and trade on the frontiers of China.

Wang entered this debate in a favorable position. Using only diplomacy to achieve his objectives, he had persuaded Altan to turn over Chinese defectors within his camp to Ming authorities and also to urge two other important nomadic leaders to present tribute. Altan had also shown a willingness to accept Ming titles and a hierarchical relationship with the court. Wang Ch'ung-ku added to these achievements several persuasive arguments in support of creating markets. First, Wang reminded the court that during the past autumn when Altan pushed east, "the capital was in a serious state. It was even arranged to gather brick and lime to block the gates and protect the city."[94] Wang admitted that "the enemy's strength is not as great as it was, and our troops are not as weak as before . . . ,"[95] but this admission was in reality a disclosure of the true state of Ming forces, which, though not as weak as before, were still incapable of resisting Mongol invasions. He observed that if peace was not established by opening the markets, then there would be "no way to put a stop to [military] alarms. Financial resources will be exhausted, and even wise people will be unable to remedy the aftermath." On the other hand, "if the Court allows Altan to receive rank and pay tribute, there will be peace along the border regions for several years. [We] can utilize this period for [defense] preparations. If the enemy forsakes the agreement we can either attack or defend with the financial strength we will have accumulated over several years."[96]

Wang moved cautiously in formulating his second argument, for it was essential for him to show that although Emperor Shih-tsung forbid border officials to open markets, he "did not forbid the northern enemy to offer presents for peace."[97] Wang argued that he sought to enroll Altan as a loyal tributary to the dynasty and the opening of markets was part of the tribute exchange process. Wang suggested that there are ample examples of previous times during the Ming when rank was conferred and tribute accepted from nomadic princes and insisted that the current *rapprochement* with the Mongols was not merely a response to military threat. Altan was not demanding trade on the basis of equality, but rather seeking to be enrolled as a loyal tributary, and the tributary markets opened to him would not differ from those created earlier at K'ai-yüan and Kuang-ning in Liao-tung. Wang suggested that Altan's change in attitude towards the Middle Kingdom was evident in his willingness to accept the Ming rank of Shun-i *Wang* (Prince of righteous obedience), thereby recognizing his subservience to the court. It was also apparent because of the submissive tone in his petitions to the throne, because of his willingness to turn over Chinese dissidents in his camp, and in his role of persuading other nomadic princes to offer tribute. Wang ended his plea by stating, "in later times, Altan may be unable to maintain his health, and it may be impossible to control the tribes after his death."[98] Now, was clearly the best time to show "that the magnificent Celestial Court countenances faraway subordinates who come to express their submission to the King. . . ."[99]

Critics of Wang were numerous. Minister Kuo Ch'ien argued that "the horse markets were forbidden by the former emperor, and they should not be permitted."[100] The Supervising Censor, Chang Tuan-fu, worried about Wang's unwillingness to provoke the nomads while negotiating a settlement. He cautioned him against neglecting to prepare for possible long-range wars as he sought to achieve immediate merit. A group of six individuals centered around Minister Chu Heng felt that conferring ranks on and accepting tribute from the Mongols was acceptable but markets should not be established. They held the view that the Celestial Court would disgrace itself by trading with "dogs and sheep."[101]

During the debate the court was polarized. Twenty-five officials believed that Wang's proposals should be adopted and markets opened. Twenty officials were against abandoning the existing policy. As cited earlier, six supported the position that conferring ranks and accepting tribute was suitable but that the establishment of markets was inappropriate. Based on these discussions the emperor determined to implement an eight point program formulated by Wang Ch'ung-ku. The text of Wang's proposals, minus items seven and eight which are missing, are recorded in the "Account of Ta-tan" in the *Ming-shih*.

In item one of his proposal, Wang suggests that Altan Khan be conferred with the rank of *wang* (prince); his major relatives such as Old

Ba'atur,[102] Sengge Khong-*Taiji*, and Noyandara *Jinong* be given the title *tu-tu* (governor-general); his younger brothers, nephews, sons and grandsons up to forty-six branches of the family be granted the title of *chih-hui* (directors); and his sons-in-law through more than ten branches be designated *ch'ien-hu* (heads of one thousand households of soldiers). The granting of ranks or titles was evidence that the Ming court accepted them as vassals and welcomed them as tributaries.[103]

Before the implementation of this first proposal, the court official Wang Chih-hao suggested that the offer of rank to Noyandara *Jinong* be delayed until he stopped his aggression against the frontier for one or two years. Wang Ch'ung-ku, in response, memorialized the throne: "Altan and the *Jinong* are uncle and nephew by blood and respond to each other as head and tail. We are now retaining the uncle but releasing the nephew, locking up the head but setting the arms free. Altan would certainly call the followers of the *Jinong* to come east of the Yellow river to trade at Hsüan-fu and Ta-t'ung. If the traders cannot supply his needs, the *Jinong* will join with Altan to disturb Shensi. Then problems will increase for the four garrisons along the border."[104] The emperor agreed with Wang Ch'ung-ku, and Noyandara *Jinong* was given a title.[105]

The second item in Wang's proposal dealt with presenting tribute. Once the Ming court conferred titles upon an individual, he was expected to offer tribute. However, because the presentation of tribute provided an individual with the opportunity to travel to the capital, secure gifts and bestowals from the court, and enrich himself through trade, the Mongols clamored to join tribute embassies. More than 100 years earlier, during the Cheng-tung period (1436–1449), the Ming dynasty had lost control of the tribute presenting process. Toghto-bukha Khan and the Oirad leader Esen had recurrently sent tributary missions composed of two to three thousand members. The Ming court had been overwhelmed by the costs involved in receiving and hosting these missions. Although it had made frequent attempts to persuade the Mongols to send tributary missions less frequently and to reduce the number of envoys in these missions, its efforts had been utterly ignored by their "tributary obligors," the Mongols. Wang Ch'ung-ku therefore proposed to regulate tribute presentation carefully. He suggested that "differences [in the amount of tribute presented] between the chiefs of the tribes should be decided according to the size of the tribe. . . . "[106] However, "each year, in all, tributary horses should not exceed five hundred head, and envoys should not exceed five hundred persons . . . , [and] only sixty envoys should be allowed to proceed to the capital, and the others should wait at the border."[107] Tribute horses were to be divided into three categories, and under no circumstances should old and skinny horses be accepted. The envoys were to be given appropriate bestowals and awards and to be allowed to purchase cloth, fabrics, and other essential items.

The third point in Wang's eight-point program established procedures for the tribute-presentation process. Envoys were required to present their documents and have their tribute inspected at Ta-t'ung in the spring and then follow set routes, accompanied by Chinese guards, to the capital. This would minimize the disruption created by the emissaries as they travelled through China; enable the court to prepare accommodations, food, and transportation for the mission; and discourage them from being disorderly or using the journey to Peking to gather information that might jeopardize China's security.

In the fourth point of his program, Wang established the guidelines for creating markets. He stipulated the items to be exchanged: "oxen, horses, hides, furs, horse tails and so forth, . . . for satin, silk, cloth, pots and so forth."[108] Markets were to be established at Ta-t'ung north of the Left Garrison on the outer side of the border at Wei-yüan pu; at Hsüan-fu at the Right Garrison of Wan-chüan on the outer side of the border at Chang-chia k'ou (Kalgan); and on the other side of the border at Shui-chüan ying in Shansi. They were to be opened for only one month intervals and no more than three hundred persons were to be allowed during a market day in any one market.[109] Five hundred Ming soldiers were to be stationed at each market to maintain control.[110]

In item five, Wang proposed that two rolls of cotton cloth be rewarded to each Ming soldier stationed to guard a market. This would promote integrity by supplementing his income and discourage him from becoming involved in illicit exchanges with Mongols. Each Mongolian chieftain was also to be awarded two rolls of satin and two rolls of silk to encourage his good behavior. The sixth and last item recorded in "the Account of the Ta-tan" dealt with the disposition of political prisoners. Neither China nor the Mongols were to harbor political refugees from the other. Items seven and eight of Wang's proposals are included in the Ming shih-lu and deal with special considerations on border policies and warn military leaders against falsifying battle reports and troop strength in order to obtain rewards.[111]

At the start of the implementation of Wang Ch'ung-ku's program, the Ming emperor Mu-tsung issued an imperial decree summarizing the unfolding of relations between Altan Khan and the Chinese and conferring upon him the title of Shun-i *Wang*:

> Our T'ai-tsu, the Lofty Emperor, received the Mandate of Heaven and became ruler of all directions, and Ch'eng-tsu, the Literate Emperor, abiding by [the will of] Heaven, succeeding to the throne, pacified the nine frontiers, and all people within and without the state submitted without exception. After Our succession, respectful of Heaven, following the example of ancestors, merciful toward all living beings, [We] tolerate and nourish the *Hu* [foreigners of the north] and the *Yüeh* [foreigners of the south] without discrimination. Recently, your grandson came to surrender, and [We] issued special orders to border officials to provide him with protection, food and clothing, rich entertainment, and a safe return. You were moved by Our mercy and were willing to subjugate [yourself] as a vassal, to pay tribute year after year, to be a vassal from afar forever, and return all rebellious traitors as an expression of [your] faithfulness. Border officials have written many memorials and petitioned repeatedly. We believe tribute from the northern foreigners was paid in many dynasties, and it is a customary ceremony in our country. You admire China and surrender as a vassal and petition with obedience and sincerity. This is recognized as coming from one who understands deeply the way of Heaven. We are extremely pleased, accept your petition, and make you Prince Shun-i, with *tu-tu* or other official titles to be bestowed upon your younger brothers, sons, and the tribal chieftains[112] so you might live in your homeland from generation to generation to graze and hunt. . . . [113]

Altan's reply, given in "The Memorial for Tribute from Altan Shun-i *Wang* of the Northern Barbarians," is found in the *Hsüan-lan-tang tsung-shu*. The document was probably written by a Chinese official and "polished" to satisfy the expectations of the court.[114] The self-effacing style of this memorial makes it difficult to believe that it was submitted unedited by a nomadic leader whose power and prestige compared with that of the Great Khan and who had successfully invaded China for almost fifty years. Nevertheless, Altan's presentation of this memorial to the court effectively testifies to his firm commitment to restore peace with the Ming for the sake of economic exchange. After showing proper deference to the court (". . . the most honorable of all realms under Heaven is the Celestial Court of the Imperial Ming . . . ", *et cetera*),[115] Altan summarized factors which contributed to earlier Ming-Mongol confrontation and the reasons why he now sought peace:

> In earlier years, the Little Prince [the khan] presented tribute and received bestowals from the Celestial Court. In recent years, the tribes have been drawn in by treasonous people and have forfeited the bestowals. [We, your] vassals [have suffered] an increase of population and a shortage of clothing . . . and on none of the

borders were markets permitted to open. There was no way to satisfy our needs for clothing. Our felts and furs wear poorly in the summer heat, [but] it has been impossible to get even a piece of cloth. Incited and guided by Chao Ch'üan, we crossed the border and carried out improper activities. Although [we] plundered the cities and met our needs, our people and horses were killed and wounded. In recent years, the border generals sent troops continually to destroy, kill, and kidnap our families and people, to loot our horses and set fire to our pastures outside the border. [Life] became difficult for both people and animals, [especially] during winter and spring. This of course was caused by the evil that we committed, which was caused also by Chao Ch'üan.[116]

It is easy to see why Wang Ch'ung-ku insisted that Chao Ch'üan and other Chinese defectors be turned over to the court as a precondition for the establishment of tribute relations and markets. Still, Altan boldly stated that his border incursions were necessitated because frontier markets were closed, and there had been an increase in population among his people and a shortage of cloth garments, since fur and felt clothing were totally unsuitable to wear in the hot summer months. Altan continued his memorial with a summary of the events leading to this point in negotiations. He then petitioned that his nephew, the *Jinong*, be given official titles, that he be allowed to present tribute each year, and that markets be established to permit him to annually trade with China. The Mongolian leader made no demands for territory. He remained consistent in seeking economic and not political objectives. He simply sought the opportunity to present tribute and conduct trade.[117]

As suggested, Altan accepted several humiliating preconditions to secure peace and gain the opportunity to trade for Chinese goods. He turned over his Chinese advisors to the Ming for punishment, recognized the hierarchical relationship between the Middle Kingdom and his tribe, and accepted the humiliating title of Shun-i *Wang*. However, as the following passage recorded by a relative of Altan, Saghang Sechen *Taiji* suggests, Altan's submissiveness to the Ming, although criticized by Tumen Khan and others, was not perceived by all Mongols to be total surrender: "[Altan] carried out invasion and destruction against China. The people of the Ming felt greatly threatened and sent envoys to Altan to present him with the title of *Sun Ong*[118] and a golden seal and to petition for peace. In the year of the White Sheep [1571], at sixty-six years of age, Altan ruled the great nation together with [Emperor] Lung-ch'ing of the Great Ming."[119] This is an interesting example of how different the perceptions of Mongols towards a major event in Chinese-nomadic relations could be from those of the sedentarist.

However, many Mongols doubted the veracity of those who claimed that the Ming submitted to Altan to seek peace. Tümen Khan, who had warred with Altan against the Ming just a few years before the settlement, was particularly critical of it. He noted that "Altan was made Shun-i *Wang*. . . . Altan is my slave and was made a prince. My will cannot be satisfied."[120] Altan was ostensibly subordinate to the Great Khan, and his separate arrangement with the Ming created a fissure between Altan and the Great Khan of the Mongols. The khan was left with the choice of accepting a politically demeaning arrangement with the Ming in order to satisfy his economic needs or reaffirming his personal commitment to struggle against the Chinese and seize the goods essential to him. Tümen Khan rallied the Uriyangkha Mongols and the Hai-hsi and Chien-chou Jurchen tribes of present-day Manchuria, who still accepted the Khan's authority,[121] in "attacking the old enemy Kitad *ulus* [China],"[122] and vied with Altan for the loyalty of other tribes north of China.

Although the opening of markets to Altan did not bring peace to the entire northern frontier of China, border markets were advantageous to both Altan and the Ming court. Altan secured the goods he desired and the Ming court stabilized relations on at least one section of its frontier. The "Biography of Wang Ch'ung-ku," the architect of the marketing system, records:

> [Wang] Ch'ung-ku then broadly summoned [Chinese] merchants and traders to trade cotton, cloth, and cereal for fur and hide. [They came] from far away—from the Chiang-huai and Hu-kuang [areas]—and gathered under the fortresses along the border. [The officials] collected tax from them to meet the need for bestowals and rewards. The government provided gold and cloth to the greater and lesser tribal heads who yearly traded horses of a definite quota. [Wang] Ch'ung-ku usually appeared at Hung-ssu pu each year to publicize the magnificence and mercy [of the Court]. All the tribal [people] bowed before [him] and no one dared to quarrel. From then on the frontier areas were released. East from Yen-yung west to Chia-yü, all soldiers and civilians of the seven garrison [districts] along several thousand *li* [of] the border enjoyed a happy situation. No military weapon was used and seventy percent of the expenditure was reduced.[123]

The trade settlement reached between Altan and the Ming was of national rather than local scope. Merchants from present Kiangsu, Hupei, Hunan, and even Kwangtung gathered at these markets. To keep the markets open, Altan's followers were expected to abide by the rules established at the markets and refrain from any hostile border raids. Order prevailed in the market areas on a line from Hsüan-fu and Ta-t'ung in the east to Ning-hsia and Kansu to the west. As a consequence, Chinese military expenditures fell by seventy percent.

In the regions Altan controlled, he actively policed the frontier to prevent aggressive actions against the Chinese that might lead the Ming to close the markets. Shortly after the markets were opened, Altan discovered that Köndüleng, his younger brother and the powerful leader of the Kharachin tribe of the Right Flank Mongols, and Sengge, Altan's eldest son, chose to support Tümen Khan when he decided to wage war on the Chinese. These two chieftains could not thwart the market policy of Altan, but they had no intention of disobeying the Great Khan. Altan dealt with the threat with the warning that: "Hsüan[-fu] and Ta[-t'ung] are my markets. Do not trouble them."[124]

Once, when Altan journeyed to Kökönor to visit the Third Dalai Lama, Ching-ba'atur, the second son of Köndüleng, who became a leader of the Kharachin tribe after his father's death, followed the advice of Tumen Khan and invaded the frontier. Altan returned eastward, and persuaded Ching-ba'atur to abandon his struggle. After joining again with Altan, Ching-ba'atur even punished his own followers who refused to abandon their loyalty to Tümen Khan's policy.[125]

The "Account of the Ta-tan" in the *Ming-shih* states that "since Altan agreed on the matter of the markets, he has served the court prudently. If his subjects plundered the frontier people, [he] punished them . . . and required their apology. . . . "[126] Another example of Altan's role in promoting peace occurred when two of his sons, Bingtu, who was stationed at Sung-shan north of Lanchou, and Bintu, located near Kökönor west of Ho-chou (present-day Lin-hsia, Kansu),[127] grew unruly and threatened the frontier.[128] Bingtu was becoming involved in Tibetan affairs and desired to open a way through present Szechwan province to take the third Dalai Lama to Mongolia. The garrison officials in Szechwan suggested that this would provoke war and asked Altan to intervene. Altan replied that the fundamental problem between the Ming court and Bingtu was economic: "[officials in] Kansu refused to open a market place for him, and Ning-hsia is too far away and too difficult to reach. So, even if I forbade him, I do not think the problem would dissipate entirely."[129]

Altan's concerns were confirmed by the successor of Wang Ch'ung-ku, Fang Feng-shih, who suggested to the Ming emperor that markets be opened in Kansu. Fang was aware that if access to markets remained difficult, and new markets were not opened Altan was powerless to restrain even his sons from encroaching upon China's frontier. The emperor ordered the Governor of Shensi to deal with the matter, and, in 1574, two markets were opened in Kansu.[130] Having derived this benefit, Altan monitored the activities of his followers to ensure that these markets were not closed. For example, "During the eighth month of the eighth year [of Wan-li, 1580] Bintu invaded Tibet, capturing people and animals under [Ming] jurisdiction. His market place was therefore closed by imperial order. Hearing of this, Altan sent him a reproof and compelled him to return what he had plundered. . . . His father's [Altan's] obedience pleased the Emperor, . . . who allowed the market to reopen."[131]

The "Biography of Tung I-yüan" in the *Ming shih* states that "after Altan presented tribute along the border, military alarms at Hsüan[-fu], Ta [-tung], and the three garrison areas of Shansi [Ning-wu, Yen-men, and Shansi] all ceased."[132] However, despite the success of the markets established by Wang Ch'ung-ku in promoting peace, his successor, Fang Feng-shih still had to argue persuasively against detractors at court to ensure that Wang's policies were not abandoned. In 1577, another debate occurred over whether to continue the peaceful policies encouraged by the establishment of trade relations or abandon the markets and adopt a more strident position toward Altan and his followers. This debate provides us with a final opportunity to consider the advantages and disadvantages of market arrangements between Ming China and the Mongols.

In defense of the markets, Fang Feng-shih first reflected on frontier conditions before the market settlement was reached in 1570: " . . . corpses of the soldiers were exposed in the fields, people wandered homelessly, cities and towns were ruined, food supplies were exhausted, border officials were unable to protect even themselves and the court was so occupied [with these problems] that there was no time to eat."[133] He then noted the dramatic change that occurred after the settlement:

> Relying on Your Majesty's Celestial sense of strategy during the past eight years, the population has increased daily along the nine borders,[134] defenses strengthen daily, cultivated land increases, trade and commerce are flourishing, and people along the border are beginning to realize the joy of living. The northern tribes present tribute sincerely and dare not violate the agreement. Sometimes during the year they make certain requests, which are granted as it is convenient. When they receive even one cake or pastry they usually bow and smile. If anyone, like Dalad-Mingghantu, who plundered the people and demanded rewards, requires punishment, and it is reported to Altan, he lowers his head and obeys the order without dispute.[135]

In this memorial, Fang expresses concern about the advancing age of Altan. He admits that Altan is a crucial factor in maintaining stability on the frontier and conjectures that once he is dead, "the tribes will not be unified, and the shrewd ones among them will struggle for power and seize any pretext to launch an invasion."[136] Fang then reveals that for the Ming court the chief objective of the market arrangements is political, for if the frontier becomes chaotic, he argues that:

> ... the only measure we can undertake is to reject their tribute, close the market, close the gates and watch diligently, yet still prevent the border generals from doing something thoughtlessly in order to fix blame on the enemy and maintain our uprightness. Exactly how to dispose of the matter will depend on the strategy employed by later peoples. In border matters there is no rigid form or definite measure that is proper. The only solution is for the court to appoint a suitable person to implement a proper decision, so why should we be biased in favor of keeping the markets open and accepting tribute while not making any plans for war and defense? Again, I, your vassal have heard that there is no good policy for resisting the barbarians. War is disastrous, intermarriage is disgraceful, and bribery is shameful. Today, tribute is not intermarriage, and markets are not bribery. When there are markets and tribute there is no war. . . . [137]

Fang's proposals sound Machiavellian. He takes exception with those who suggest that there are no good frontier policies, "[that] war is disastrous, intermarriage is disgraceful, and bribery is shameful." For Fang, the key to successfully dealing with the Mongols is flexibility. He recognizes that frontier markets must be backed by strong military force and challenges those who assert that the marketing system established in 1570 is dependent on intermarriage and bribery and thus not consistent with maintaining the hierarchical relationship that must exist between China and other countries. He also affirms that *"WHEN THERE ARE MARKETS AND TRIBUTE THERE IS NO WAR. . . . "*[138]

Critics of frontier markets were numerous. Meng I-mai, the Imperial Censor of Nanking, is representative of those who felt that maintaining the markets was both unduly expensive and also humiliating:

> The border officials daily neglect border defenses and are committed against both superiors and subordinates. . . . Fishermen catch fish by leaving the bait, but it has never been heard that they fed the fish with the bait. Now fine silk and embroideries of the Middle Kingdom become the ordinary barbarian dress. Although it is said to be [gifts in return for] tribute, it is really nothing but flattery of them. Border officials have taken the tributary markets as an excuse to buy off barbarians, and the barbarians loot and plunder freely. . . . [139]

As suggested by the following excerpt from the "Monograph on Economy" in the *Ming shih*, the conception that the markets were unduly expensive is evident even in Chinese dynastic histories:

> In the fourth year of Lung-ch'ing (1570), a grandson of Altan, Bagha-achi, surrendered. This precipitated a discussion about conferring rank, assessing tribute, and establishing an interchange market. Subsequently, the interchange markets were reopened at Hsüan-fu and Ta-t'ung. The borders remained quiet for some time, but the cost of pacification was very great. To meet the need for maintaining [the market], the court reduced the salaries of the troops and the sentinels. The bestowals increased year after year but so did the [Mongols'] demands. Again the officials took all possible advantage in the management, so the cost of border affairs unduly increased.[140]

Fang dealt with officials who felt the costs of markets were prohibitive by directly addressing the issue. To the critic who suggested that "there is no way to satisfy their desires, and wasteful expenditures increase daily,"[141] Fang replied with explicit figures comparing former expenses of entertaining nomads, purchasing horses, and maintaining an army to fight them with current costs. He insisted that there had been a reduction of seventy percent in costs under the frontier-market system established in 1570.

Other officials claimed that "there are too many enemy emissaries. It is a disaster."[142] Fang replied that the mechanisms created by Wang when the markets were established to strictly limit the number of envoys allowed to enter the markets and also those entitled to cross the frontier were still functioning. The restricted time frame for the presentation of tribute and for trading in frontier markets also still existed.[143]

It is almost certain that, as in previous periods, despite Fang's efforts to prevent it, cheating and corruption of all sorts existed in the markets created for Altan Khan. Throughout the entire Ming period, strict regulations were established at the frontier markets. Everyone who came to the markets had to be registered and could trade only during a set time period. They could not carry bows and arrows, and, except for the day of exchange, they were forbidden to come near the walls of the fortresses.[144] The Ming regulated the types of goods that could be exchanged in order to prevent the sale of weapons, bronze, and iron to non-Chinese.[145] Despite this, it is evident that Chinese officials frequently cheated Mongols,[146] sold them inferior products, and involved themselves in smuggling and other activities. The Mongols responded by selling the

Chinese inferior horses[147] and by involving themselves in smuggling activities.[148] Nomads exchanged seals with other nomads and delivered tribute using the names of other frontier leaders. They also used the marketing system to spy against the Chinese.[149]

Peace was maintained between the Ming and regions where Altan Khan held sway, but elsewhere, particularly in the east, where the Ming failed to establish and maintain effective tributary markets, recurrent conflict occurred. Tümen Khan and his followers along the northeastern borders of China never stopped their invasions of China. The "Account of the Ta-tan" states that " . . . Tümen of the east ordered his masses to invade across the border of Liao[-tung] several times. . . . After Emperor Shen-tsung (r. 1573–1620) ascended the throne [1573, they] invaded every year. . . . During the winter of the seventh year [of Wan-li, 1579], Tümen entered the camp at Chin-chou with forty thousand horsemen."[150] It appears that war continued between the Left Flank Mongols and the Ming throughout the remainder of the sixteenth century. This is suggested by the fact that in 1598 the well-known general, Li Ju-sung was killed in a light cavalry attack on Tümen's base.[151]

The situation in the northeast changed somewhat after Li Ch'eng-liang was again appointed commander of Liao-tung in 1601:

> By that time Tümen, Jongnon,[152] and Ba'atur[153] had already died, so invasions and looting had gradually decreased. Two markets for horses and lumber were again opened in the frontier areas of K'ai-yüan and Kuang-ning. All the tribes were attracted by the benefits available at the markets and strove to pay tribute. As a consequence, during the eighth year of [Li] Ch'eng-liang's second term as commander, trouble rarely occurred east of the Liao [River]."[154]

Tümen Khan died in 1592, and his son, Buyan *Taiji*, ruled from 1593 to 1603. He was less able to control the Mongol tribes traditionally loyal to the khan. In particular, the Uriyangkha, were becoming increasingly independent. The opening of frontier markets induced the Uriyangkha and other tribes to rely on trade and abandon plunder to obtain needed goods. However, the markets for the Mongols remained open in Liao-tung only until 1607.

Buyan Khan's short reign was followed by that of his son Lighdan, also known as Khutughtu Khan, who ascended the throne in 1604, at the age of thirteen.[155] During Lighdan's reign, the khan's power of direct rule over other tribes collapsed, and Mongol tribes formed alliances with many different groups. The last selection in the *Ming shih* under the heading

"Account of Ta-tan" records that during his reign the Naiman and seven other Mongolian tribes offered tribute to the Ming court. Some tribes allied themselves with Manchu power, while others identified themselves with Mongols of the Right Flank which had separated themselves from the khan's direct authority during Altan's lifetime. Some tribes sought to avoid entanglements in the inevitable struggles by migrating northward, where they joined with the Khalkha Mongols, who generally remained independent of and neutral in these conflicts. Nevertheless, until sometime after 1614, Great Khan Lighdan never altered his position in dealing with the Ming and continued to launch raids against them.[156]

Just as Tümen Khan's policy of hostility towards the Chinese began to be abandoned by his allies after his death so also were the trade markets implemented through the efforts of Altan abandoned by his followers after his demise. Altan died in 1583 and was succeeded by his grandson, Chürüge. In 1587, Chürüge accepted the title of Prince Shun-i, but afterward migrated westward with his followers away from the Ta-t'ung, Hsüan-fu, and Shansi border areas. This was disconcerting to the Ming, who, in 1591, cancelled Chürüge's market rewards (shih-shang). Had Chürüge been more powerful, this cancellation of his marketing privileges would probably have led to war, but it did not.

Chürüge's departure left the border areas unoccupied and other tribes now rejected the unequal marketing arrangements and the humiliating terms of Altan's peace and engaged in raiding the borders. First to challenge the Ming marketing system were the Kökönor Mongols under Kholochi *Noyan*, who breeched the frontier in 1588. They were joined in their struggle against China by the Ordos Mongols, led by Boshightu[157] and Jongdolai.[158]

The decision to keep markets open to the descendants of Altan was contingent on Chürüge's cooperation with the Ming. After heated debate, officials appointed by the pro-market grand secretary, Shen Shih-hsing,[159] persuaded the court that, despite the unrest created on the frontier by Chürüge's departure, it would be unfair to punish all the tribes because of the error on the part of Chürüge. When, in 1592, the Ming garrison commander at Ning-hsia, Po-pai, rebelled, the Ming court asked Chürüge to assist in crushing the uprising. At the time Chürüge was returning to the east. The test of Chürüge's loyalty would be his willingness to extradite Po-pai. He captured the rebel and delivered him to the Ming, which is reminiscent of Altan's surrendering of Chao Ch'üan a few decades earlier. For this, Chürüge's market privileges were restored.[160] Because he again desired to obtain Chinese goods at border markets, Chürüge was enticed back to the frontiers of China, where he acted as a buffer against more hostile nomads and a challenge to Chinese defectors.

During the first quarter of the seventeenth century, relations between various nomadic groups and between the nomads and the sedentarists of China were highly fluid and volatile. This can be attributed primarily to the decline of Chinese power, the fragmentation of Mongolian power, and, at the same time, the dramatic rise of Manchu power northeast of China. When the leader of the Manchus, Nurhachi, declared himself Khan of the Manchu in 1616, the entire structure of frontier politics changed. Indeed, the threat posed by the Manchus to the Ming dynasty was so great that after the reign of Emperor Shen-tsung (r. 1573–1620), the annals section of the *Ming shih* records only two short entries of conflict between the Ming and the Mongols as more and more time was devoted to the Manchus. Fortunately, the "Account of the Ta-tan" in the same work presents a somewhat fuller account.

The frontier situation in the northwest remained dynamic and tense. In 1616, the Ming commander Tu Wen-huan defeated a leader of the Ordos Mongols, Mongkeshiri,[161] several times on the Yen-sui border (present-day northern Shensi). This led a number of influential Mongol leaders, including the *Jinong*,[162] Sechen *Taiji*,[163] Daiching,[164] Shaji,[165] Kholochi, and Bayantai,[166] to petition for markets.[167] By this period, Mongol power was so diffused that the leaders of numerous tribes sought the security offered by trade and tribute relations with the Ming. Still, we are informed by the "Account of the Ta-tan" that in 1621 and again in 1622 the *Jinong* abandoned market relations to launch massive raids in the Yen-sui, Yen-an, and Huang-hua-yü areas. In 1623, Daiching abandoned trade and began to raid the Kansu area.[168]

In the northeast, the rise of the Manchus led to a dramatic change in frontier relations. Lighdan Khan, fearful that Mongolian tribes ostensibly under his control might form alliances with the Manchus, responded to Ming overtures and formed an alliance with the Chinese to counter the growing Manchu threat:

> Then Wen Ch'iu, the Governor-General of Chi(-men) and Liao[-tung], ... and others bribed [Lighdan Khan] with rewards in order to have him ally with Chokhor and other tribes to defend against the Great Ch'ing [the Manchus]; he was paid four thousand [taels] of silver. In the next year (1620) ... the bestowal was increased to forty thousand [taels]. Khu[tughtu] [Lighdan Khan] then declared that he would assist the Middle Kingdom and requested [continuous bestowals]. ...[169]

Lighdan Khan's alliance failed to prevent tribes of the Left Flank from joining with the Manchus, and, in fact, drove many Mongols of the Right Flank, which had distanced themselves from the khan's authority, into the arms of the Manchus, because they feared the growth in Lighdan Khan's power now that he was allied with the Chinese. After Lighdan allied himself with the Ming, the Manchus attacked and defeated the Mongols under Chokhor, allies of Lighdan who also had ties with the Ming. Lighdan, in turn, attacked the Kharachin and other Mongols to the west. In 1629, Lighdan attacked the Yen-sui and Hung-shui-tan border areas of China and demanded from the Chinese an increase in his rewards. When the Ming court failed to provide them, Lighdan Khan abandoned his pro-Ming policies, which were repugnant to many of his followers, and finally joined the Manchu camp.[170]

The Manchus were now the prevailing power north of the Great Wall. They were not a typical nomadic "state on horseback," desirous only of sharing the economic wealth of an agricultural society. Instead, the Manchus were a non-Chinese people with territorial ambitions and the ability to rule the Chinese population through the Chinese elite. In appearance, the Manchus resembled those who earlier had established dynasties of conquest in China, especially the Jurchens of the Chin period. Like their Jurchen predecessors, the wealth derived from pastoral herding and hunting activities was heavily supplemental by agricultural production undertaken in the Liao and Sungari river basins. Before their conquest of China, there was significant contact between the Manchus and Chinese living in the Liao-tung area which led them to adopt some Chinese institutions as they consolidated their strength. A degree of Sinicization of the Manchus occurred before the conquest of China, which made them more successful rulers of China once they marched inside the Great Wall.

In summary, this chapter has shown that Altan Khan's continuous wars against China to secure goods that were essential to him and his followers provoked a heated debate among the Chinese, leading to the creation of a highly effective marketing system. Although there clearly was unrest on all borders north of China during the last few decades of the Ming dynasty, supporters of the markets suggest that " . . . along the border of Hsüan[-fu] and Ta[-t'ung], the condition of subjugation continued unchanged until the end of the Ming dynasty."[171] Others, less willing to be generous, assert that "From the Hsüan[-fu] and Ta[-t'ung area] to Kansu there was no military mobilization for twenty years,"[172] or that

"... since the agreement was made, there has been no change within these thirty years."[173]

Ming historians suggest that, prior to the creation of these markets, peace with the Mongols had never endured for a twenty-year period. Furthermore, this peace was achieved after Altan, his sons, and his brothers had engaged in war with China for decades.[174] The creation of a stable marketing system for Altan and his descendants, based at Ta-t'ung, Hsüan-fu, and Shansi enabled the Mongols to satisfy their economic needs by acquiring essential cloth and grains without raiding the frontiers of China. At the same time, it provided the Chinese with a mechanism to accomplish their political objectives of stabilizing the frontier and forcing the nomads, however fictional it was in reality, to recognize Chinese centrality in the universe. The noted Ming-Mongol scholar, Henry Serruys, boils the need for this arrangement down to a simple formula: "tribute and trade or raids."[175]

IV

TRIBUTE AND BESTOWALS

In chapter three it becomes evident that for more than a quarter of a century the aggressive actions of a nomadic leader, Altan Khan, set the agenda for the court debates of the mid-sixteenth century on frontier affairs. Incursions by Altan and other Mongolian rulers were often followed by demands for tribute and trading opportunities. Frequently, Chinese dynasties were forced to abandon hostile policies towards the nomadic peoples and establish for them costly tributary and marketing relations. However, one should not suppose that all nomadic people had a deep-seated desire to be transformed and accept Chinese culture. Many were reluctant to accept tributary arrangements which suggested they were inferior to the Chinese. Nomadic rulers interacted with China because, through frontier markets and the mechanisms of bestowals, yearly payments, and intermarriage, they could enhance their own power by acquiring essential Chinese goods and the leverage provided by an alliance with the Middle Kingdom. At times, but certainly not always, nomadic leaders humbly addressed the Chinese court, following the dictated patterns of the tributary system in order to acquire these benefits. However, they were merely adhering to a set formula which, in turn, forced the Chinese to "present", or "bestow," on them gifts and yearly payments frequently worth far more than the value of the tribute nomadic rulers offered to the court. Gifts and payments from the Chinese were often forcefully exacted, which suggests nomadic superiority to the Chinese, at least in terms of military prowess.

Chapter four continues the discussion of the institutions created by the Chinese to stabilize frontier relations, focusing on tributary exchange. It will show that the relationship between China and her nomadic neighbors was generally determined by the relative power of each. Chinese historical records suggest that the nature of Chinese-nomadic interaction was generally determined by China. They imply that China's impressive culture and more importantly her immense wealth, coupled with the desperate need of nomadic people for Chinese goods, led the nomadic rulers, of their own volition, to come to the borders of China to seek recognition as a tributary state in a hierarchically arranged "Chinese world order." Chinese records might lead one to believe that once enrolled as a tributary state, nomadic people consciously or unconsciously accepted Chinese culture and dutifully acted as an inner shield against more aggressive "outer barbarians." However, through this discussion of the presentation of nomadic tribute and the concomitant Chinese offers of bestowals and yearly payments, it will become clear that, throughout much of the history of Chinese-nomadic interaction, the amount of and frequency with which goods were exchanged was often dictated by nomadic leaders, which was highly advantageous to them and might better be regarded as Chinese tribute to the nomadic rulers. Henry Serruys in his masterful study of the Ming tribute system supports this assertion:

> "We are used to speaking of barbarians offering the tribute to the emperor and at least theoretically acknowledging his suzerainty, . . . yet, in fact, it was the Ming empire which paid the Mongols . . . for calling themselves subjects and for relative security on the northern frontiers. If foreign missions traveling to the Ming capital constituted a form of flattery and were proof of China's prestige abroad, China had to pay a steep price for the prestige. Under the circumstances, it is not surprising that the Mongols thought of the tribute system as a tribute paid to them, not the other way about. Mongols and Chinese understood the tribute system quite differently. . . . "[1]

A thorough discussion of the institutional framework for the presentation of tribute, bestowals, and yearly payments need not be presented here because, as was the case with frontier markets, analysis of marketing and tribute-exchange procedures have already been published.[2] For our purposes, it is noted that all items exported to China by officially recognized people from "beyond the pale of civilization," as well as gifts from nomadic rulers to their Chinese counterparts, were regarded by the Chinese as tribute and given the title of either *hsien*, *ju-kung*, or *t'ung-kung*, each meaning tribute. All items provided by the agricultural court to nomadic peoples and the presents from the emperors of China to the khans were referred to either as bestowals, *tseng-lai* or *shang-tz'u*, or yearly payments, *sui-pi*. The rationale used by the Chinese court to give nomadic rulers bestowals was to suggest that bestowals were a recognition of merit of those who came to submit to China. Consequently, a carefully chosen terminology was used to suggest the superiority of the Chinese ruler who, because of his munificence, bequeathed these bestowals on his subjects. At times, when nomadic power was equal or superior to that of the agriculturalists, nomadic leaders demanded a less elevated terminology, and, as a consequence, bestowals were designated as gifts from the agrarian court to the nomadic ruler. Goods conveyed might be of greater worth than traditional bestowals yet only be designated as gifts.

Bestowals were presented to nomads on a number of different occasions. For instance, the Chinese court presented bestowals directly to members of tributary missions which supposedly came specifically to accept them. The court also sent "bestowal missions" to the frontiers of China to offer gifts to nomadic leaders. In addition, at times, there were *ad hoc* bestowals, rather hurriedly presented to rebellious nomadic leaders to defuse a tense situation. Ming sources reveal that by the end of the sixteenth century the presentation of bestowals was routinized. Sometime after the accord was reached between the Ming dynasty and Altan Khan in 1570, both "monthly bestowals", *yüeh-shang*,[3] and "market bestowals", *shih-shang*,[4] were created, enabling the court to frequently present gifts to key nomadic leaders.[5]

Yearly payments were presented by the Chinese court to nomadic powers as early as the Han period. The amount of gold, silver, silk, grain, and other goods the Chinese offered a northern neighbor depended on the relative strength of each party. Clearly, during certain eras of Chinese history, these payments were huge and made only under duress. Although payments to the nomadic states are hidden behind the mask of carefully selected terms and couched in the rhetoric of tributary formulas, in reality many Chinese dynasties were presenting tribute to nomadic powers stronger than they in order to avoid conflict. Because the value of bestowals and yearly payments frequently exceeded the value of tribute offered China, bestowals and yearly payments were another means by which nomadic people secured essential Chinese goods. As suggested by Serruys, tribute and trade enabled China to avoid raids. Although extremely expensive to the sedentarist, trade and the presentation of gifts was infinitely less costly than military alternatives.

A good place to begin an analysis of the Chinese implementation of bestowal and yearly-payment mechanisms is with the interaction between Han Kao-ti and the Hsiung-nu *Shan-yü*, Mao-tun, already discussed in chapter one. When Kao-ti determined that he must avoid further conflict with the Hsiung-nu, he sent a princess of the royal household to be a wife to Mao-tun, but equally significant, he committed the Han court "to annually present a specific quantity of silk, cloth, wine, rice, and food to the Hsiung-nu."[6] In addition to these yearly payments, an abundant exchange of gifts occurred,[7] heavily weighted to provide nomadic rulers with goods of much greater value than those received by the Han court. When discussing yearly payments and the exchange of goods at this time, the historian Ssu-ma Ch'ien used the word *hsien,* which means to present, to offer, or to give tribute to describe the action of the nomadic ruler, and the words *i,* meaning to send or give, or *feng,* to present, when discussing the Han response.[8] Ssu-ma Ch'ien recognized the basic equality in the Han-Hsiung-nu relationship and did not use the word *tz'u,* to bestow, suggestive of Chinese superiority, which was generally used during subsequent periods.

As suggested in chapters one and two, Emperor Kao-ti's policies of maintaining peace through market and exchange mechanisms were followed by his successors for the next half century, but they were increasingly attacked by chauvanistic Chinese officials who were critical of the courts' submissiveness to nomadic rulers. For example, Chia I, an official in Emperor Wen-ti's court asserted that "now the Hsiung-nu are boastfully and arrogantly invading the looting. They have reached the limitation of insult. . . . Yet the Han annually presents gold, silk, embroideries, and satin, which shows that the barbarians command and play the role of the lord above. The Son of Heaven pays tribute and fulfills the ritual of the vassal below."[9]

When Emperor Wu-ti came to power, he desired to end the immense outflow of Chinese goods given as bestowals and yearly payments to the Hsiung-nu and conspired to entrap the Hsiung-nu at the frontier market of Ma-i. When his conspiracy failed, war broke out. After several bloody encounters, Wu-ti sent his minister Yang Hsin to meet with the Hsiung-nu *Shan-yü* to discuss the possibility of reestablishing intermarriage ties to promote peace, but one of the Han ruler's terms was unacceptable to the nomadic leader. Wu-ti asked the *Shan-yü* to send the Crown Prince as a hostage to the Han court, to which the *Shan-yü* replied: "This is not the old agreement. According to the old agreement, the Han usually sends princesses and a definite quota of satin, silk, and food stuff to fulfill the purpose of intermarriage, and we, the Hsiung-nu, stop disturbing your border lands. Now you want to change the old tradition and ask to have my son be a hostage. Of this there will be no possibility."[10] The Hsiung-nu would not accept Han alteration of the intermarriage and bestowal arrangements, and the war continued.

A dramatic change in Hsiung-nu-Han relations did not occur until 51 B.C., when internal conflict among the Hsiung-nu caused Hu-han-yeh to lead the Southern Hsiung-nu to the borders of China to surrender. The rupture in Hsiung-nu solidarity weakened the nomads and denied the Southern Hsiung-nu leverage in negotiations. As a result, diplomatic interaction between the Chinese and the Hsiung-nu, which from Kao-ti's time had been conducted on the premise of basic equality, was altered to infer a lord-vassal relationship. Goods from the Han were no longer presented (*feng*) but rather bestowed (*tz'u*), and the *Shan-yü* was forced to leave his son as hostage in the Han capital. However, although the basic arrangement between the court and the Hsiung-nu was changed to suggest Chinese superiority and nomadic deference, the Han court was unable to free itself from providing for the needs of their new ally. When Hu-han-yeh appeared before the Han emperor he was lavishly bestowed with gifts:

> The Han Court treated him with special honor and placed him above all the princes and barons.... The Emperor bestowed on him hats, belts, clothing, a golden seal, a purple sash, jade vessels, daggers, swords, one bow, four arrows, ten ceremonial spears, one ceremonial cart, one saddle, fifteen horses, twenty catties of gold, two hundred thousand coins, seventy-seven coats, eight thousand rolls of embroidered and designed silk, and six thousand catties of lining silk.... In addition the Emperor ordered the border officials to transfer 340,000 bushels of grain to his supply of food.... [11]

The Southern Hsiung-nu depended on the Han court for essential commodities and effectively extracted them from the Chinese dynasty. As suggested by the following figures, Han bestowals to Hu-han-yeh steadily grew. In 49 B.C., two years after his initial surrender, Hu-han-yeh again appeared at the Han court. The Han court increased the number of coats given him to 110, the embroidered and designed silk bestowed on him to nine thousand rolls, and they offered him 8,000 catties of lining silk.[12] In 33 B.C., the *Shan-yü* of the Southern Hsiung-nu was given double the bestowals of 49 B.C. in clothing, brocades, and lining silk.[13] In 25 B.C., the court increased the bestowals to twenty thousand pieces of brocade, silk and cloth, and twenty thousand catties of lining silk.[14] And by 1 B.C., when the *Shan-yü* came to court, the bestowals were increased to 370 coats, 30,000 rolls of embroidered and other silks, and 30,000 catties of lining silk.[15]

Following Hu-han-yeh's surrender to the Han court, the Emperor Hsüan-ti and his immediate successors utilized the Southern Hsiung-nu desire for economic aid and military assistance to transform a once hostile nomadic group into an ally of China. By 44 B.C., the Han-Southern Hsiung-nu alliance led the Northern Hsiung-nu to flee their homeland and allowed the Southern Hsiung-nu to occupy it. Next, Han policy makers effectively stopped the flow of goods from the western regions of Central Eurasia, particularly the silk route areas of the Tarim Basin, to the Southern Hsiung-nu making them completely dependent on the Han for economic support. This left the Southern Hsiung-nu with little choice but to express continued obedience to the Han, but it also forced the Chinese court to increase its economic assistance to the Southern Hsiung-nu to guarantee peace. As suggested by the Chinese historian Pan Ku, although costly, the policy worked: "Since the time of Emperor Hsüan-ti, for several generations, there was no war alarm along the northern border. The people were prosperous and the herds of cattle and horses fully covered the wilderness."[16]

As might be expected, a growth in Hsiung-nu power coupled with the chaotic conditions in China at the time of Wang Mang's usurpation led the Hsiung-nu to challenge Chinese assumptions of Chinese-nomadic inequality. Soon after the turmoil caused by Wang Mang ceased, the *Shan-yü* Hu-tu-erh-shih-tao-kao-jo-ti stated to the Later Han court:

> The Hsiung-nu and the Han originally were brothers. When disturbance broke out among the Hsiung-nu, Emperor Hsüan-ti assisted Hu-han-yeh in becoming the *Shan-yü*. Therefore, we entitled ourselves as vassals in order to honor the Han. Afterwards, the Han was also disturbed, and the throne was usurped by Wang Mang. We, the Hsiung-nu, also dispatched our forces to attack him and emptied his border. The whole realm under Heaven was stirred up, and the people returned to the Han. That Wang Mang was defeated and the Han was restored is to our merit. Therefore, the Han should honor us and we should confront each other as equals.[17]

Hsiung-nu aspirations to reestablish relations with China based on assumptions of equality were dashed when civil war again broke out among the Hsiung-nu in the middle of the first century A.D. Once again, the Southern Hsiung-nu surrendered to the court to seek military and economic assistance from the Chinese. When the *Shan-yü* Pi sent his envoys to the Han, they recognized the hierarchical relationship between the two courts by presenting themselves "as representatives of a satellite state in vassalage, bearing with them the precious things of [their] country...."[18] Pi also sent his son to serve the Chinese emperor[19] and later publicly showed his submissiveness when he bowed to receive the Han emperor's decree that he be entitled *Shan-yü*, which was conveyed to him by an ambassador of the Han court.[20]

The submissiveness of the Southern Hsiung-nu was rewarded by lavish bestowals and yearly payments, following the precedent established a century earlier. However, if one compares the level of payments with those given to Hu-han-yeh, they are smaller,[21] which confirms our belief that the second group of Southern Hsiung-nu to submit to China were not as powerful as the first. Bestowals were presented to the Southern Hsiung-nu *Shan-yü* at the end of each year. The nomadic leader would send an envoy to the court to present memorials and offer his son to the throne. In return, the Han sent envoys to the *Shan-yü* with a wide range of bestowals and yearly payments, which often included substantial amounts of grain as well as thousands of head of cattle and sheep.[22] By this time, as suggested by documents relating to the death of Pi in 55 A.D., the policy of presenting bestowals as a means of condolence and comfort was also practiced.[23] Bestowals were also given to princes, nobles, family members of the *Shan-yü*, and other important nomadic leaders to win their favor.

Hsiung-nu submissiveness continued throughout the remainder of the Han, as suggested by the discussion in chapters one and two of the effective Han manipulation of the Wu-huan and Hsien-pei after the Hsiung-nu declined. However, once the Han dynasty fell, the relative strength of nomads vis-à-vis the agrarian dynasties in a now fragmented China changed significantly. Nomadic rulers could now seek alliances with one court against another and demand larger bestowals and yearly payments. They, of course, were less willing to adopt an obsequious attitude toward these weakened agrarian states.

Jou-jan interaction with the Northern Wei dynasty during the early sixth century provides evidence of this change in nomadic-sedentarist relations. The Jou-jan frequently struggled with the Northern Wei dynasty established in northern China. This led them to attempt to establish diplomatic ties and obtain aid from the states of Sung, Southern Ch'i, and Liang to the south of Wei by sending to them tribute missions. However, actual relations between the Jou-jan and these dynasties were unfettered by notions of lordship or vassalage.[24]

Jou-jan leaders also sought to stabilize relations with the Northern Wei dynasty. Before the Northern Wei ruler Shih-tsung (r. 500–515) ascended the throne, the Northern Wei court granted bestowals to and intermarried with the Jou-jan.[25] However, as early as 506, Shih-tsung rejected further proposals for intermarriage and insisted: "Peaceful relations cannot now be assured, unless [you] are sincerely willing to perform the proper rituals as a subordinate state and to show that you will not neglect your fealty."[26] His decrees exaggerated the stature and greatness of his "Heavenly Reign" and led to continued conflict between his dynasty and the Jou-jan. In 518, a new emperor, Su-tsung, again rebuked envoys sent by the Jou-jan for "negligence in performing proper rituals of respect and obedience."[27] As suggested in chapters one and two, relations between the Jou-jan and the Northern Wei remained volatile, even though in 520 the Jou-jan leader A-na-k'ui appeared at the Northern Wei court and showed proper submissiveness in order to obtain needed grain and livestock. Notwithstanding the continued overtures to the court, it is obvious that, for the most part, the Jou-jan were little interested in accepting subordinate status to the Northern Wei or Chinese culture.

When the Northern Wei split in 534 giving rise to the Eastern Wei and Western Wei and ultimately to the rival states of Northern Ch'i and Northern Chou, a new nomadic power, the Turks, rose to contest with them. Because Turkic power was formidable and an alliance with nomadic rulers might give an advantage to one agrarian court in its struggles against the other, both the Northern Ch'i and Northern Chou sought the support of the Turks:

> Since the intermarriage agreement was carried out, the Court of Chou annually gave [chi] them a hundred thousand rolls of satin and silk. . . . Fearing their invasion and looting, the Ch'i people also poured out the wealth of their treasury to them. T'a-po [Tapar Khan] became very proud, saying to his followers: "As long as my two filially pious sons on the south exist, why should we worry about a shortage of goods?" In the second year of Chien-te [573], T'a-po sent emissaries to present horses as tribute [hsien].[28]

It is interesting to note that in the above passage Chinese historians failed to admit the actual relationship between the Turks and the states of Northern Ch'i and Northern Chou. The author describes the Chou offering to the Turks using the term *chi* (to give) even though it is clear that in this case the term *hsien* (to offer tribute) is more appropriate. Even more striking is the effort to describe the gift of horses sent by the Turkic khan as a tributary offering which clearly it was not.

Once the Sui dynasty was established in 581, Turkic relations with this Chinese state were explosive. When the Emperor Wen-ti "showed [the Turks] little deference,"[29] the Turkic khan Ishbara led what Chinese sources say was a force of four hundred thousand mounted archers to invade China.[30] However, because rivals of the Western Turks challenged Ishbara, he quickly abandoned hostility toward the Sui and sought an alliance with them. Ishbara was forced to move closer to the Chinese frontier to avoid his enemies and became dependent on Sui aid. As his power relationship with the sedentarist court changed, the credentials presented by Ishbara to the court also changed. He no longer addressed himself as "the Heaven-born . . . Khan of the Great Turk, Wise Saint under Heaven . . . ,"[31] but now he more humbly approached the court as "the Khan of the Great Turk, [I, your] vassal. . . . "[32] Ishbara and his successors established close ties with the Sui and early T'ang courts, and a regular exchange of tribute for bestowals followed. The Turks petitioned for the opening of border markets, which Sui Wen-ti quickly allowed. As early as 589, Turkic envoys appeared at the frontier of China with ten thousand horses, twenty thousand sheep, and five hundred head each of camels and oxen to present as tribute.[33]

As Li Yüan, the future T'ang Kao-tsu, struggled to establish a dynasty, he vied with the Sui and with other aspiring dynasts to gain Turkic military support. More than a decade after successfully establishing the T'ang, his son, Emperor T'ai-tsung, admitted: "Formerly, when the state had just been settled, the Father Emperor Kao-tsu, for the sake of the people, presented tribute to the T'u-chüeh [Turk] and falsely served them as a vassal. . . . "[34] However, this admission of Chinese submission to the Turks to secure needed military assistance is again hidden by the terminology chosen by Chinese dynastic historians reporting at a later date. For instance, they suggest that Shih-pi Khan "sent his envoy . . . to pay as tribute *(hsien)* two thousand horses and to command five hundred soldiers to join us."[35] They also state that "the words in the letters of the Turks were usually impolite and always demanding something. Emperor Kao-tsu, because the realm under Heaven had just been settled, usually treated them courteously and gave *(tseng-lai)* them more gifts of great value. However, their desires had no end, and their demands were without limitations."[36]

Shih-pi Khan had no reason to pay tribute to the emerging T'ang emperor; rather, it is the T'ang ruler who was forced to induce the Turkic khan to assist him. Consequently, when describing Emperor Kao-tsu's presentation of goods to the Turks, the historians use of the term *tseng-lai* is inaccurate. The strict meaning of *tseng* is to give, but *lai* means to bestow or to give from a superior to an inferior. Inasmuch as Kao-tsu "served them as a vassal" it is incorrect to suggest that he bestowed anything on his lord. It is clear that the use by Chinese historians of terms connoting tribute presentation or the offering of bestowals does not always reflect the true situation.

Sui and early T'ang leaders did not take Ishbara and his successors for granted. When Ishbara died in 587, the Sui court sent a *fu* (funeral gift) or *tseng* (gift of condolence) of five thousand rolls of silk to his successor.[37] A little over three decades later, in 619, the Turk ruler Shih-pi Khan died. Although Shih-pi Khan had not always been a faithful ally of the T'ang, the T'ang court offered his successor Ch'o-lo Khan (r. 619–620) a funerary gift of thirty thousand rolls of silk.[38] This impressive gift, six times larger than that bequeathed earlier, led Ch'o-lo Khan to draw closer to the T'ang and helped stabilize Turkic-Chinese relations. As the quantity of goods presented by the court increased, the ritualistic significance of the offering became less important than the political and economic significance.

Turkic dominance of the lands north of China ended in the mid-eighth century. The Uighur people became the next important nomadic group to interact with China. Scholars trace the Uighurs to the earlier T'ieh-le, or Tölös, mentioned as tributaries of China in the *Sui shu*.[39] The Tölös are, in turn, believed to have descended from the Kao-ch'e, who allied themselves with the Northern Wei. At the end of the fifth century, the Kao-ch'e were a minor tribe threatened by the powerful Jou-jan. As a consequence, in 490, A-fu-chih-lo, the headman of the Kao-ch'e, sent envoys to the Northern Wei. He presented two arrows as tribute and said, "the Jou-jan are thieves against the Son of Heaven. [I, Your] vassal, admonished them but was rejected. Therefore [I] rebelled against them and came here to independently establish myself. [I] would like to punish and exterminate the Jou-jan for the Son of Heaven."[40]

The Northern Wei emperor, desirous of finding allies who he might pit against the Jou-jan, dispatched an envoy to investigate the Kao-ch'e and instruct them in the proper presentation of local products to the court. This was followed by the formation of an alliance in which the Northern Wei encouraged the Kao-ch'e to attack the Jou-jan and in return allowed them to pay tribute. The exchange of goods between the two courts was stabilized but not extensive, suggesting that the Kao-ch'e were only a minor force in frontier politics. Still, the Kao-ch'e acquired agricultural goods, manufactured goods, and, most intriguing, a wide array of court ceremonial items, which included musical instruments along with eighty musicians, sedan chairs, and ceremonial umbrellas and fans.[41]

The Uighurs, descendants of the Kao-ch'e, were a major factor in T'ang history. As suggested in chapter two, initially Uighur rulers accepted a subordinate position to China, were given honorary titles, and exchanged their goods for essential items from the agrarian court. However, after the An Lu-shan rebellion in 755, the T'ang emperor Su-tsung sought Uighur assistance in overthrowing the rebels and the court became highly dependent on Uighur aid. As a consequence, formal relations between the T'ang and the Uighurs changed dramatically. Intermarriage arrangements increased and "annually the Court gave them (the Uighurs) twenty thousand rolls of silk, causing them to come to Shuo-fang chün (present Ling-wu area of Ning-hsia) to receive the bestowals."[42] This "bestowal" again is misrepresented by Chinese chroniclers who should more appropriately suggest that the Uighurs came "to receive a gift." The annual presentation of twenty thousand rolls of silk was offered as a reward to the Uighurs and is similar to the *sui-pi* (yearly payments) subsequently given by the Sung dynasty to the Khitan Liao, the Jurchen Chin, and the Tangut Hsia from the eleventh to the thirteenth century.

Uighur power was displaced by the Kirghiz in the fourth decade of the ninth century. One element of the Uighur migrated to the area near the T'ien-shan range, and another settled in the Chi-lien mountain range in the Kan-chou area of present-day Kansu Province and continued their contact with China. After the T'ang dynasty fell in 907, the Uighurs interacted with the individual dynasties of the Five-Dynasties period, the Liang, Later T'ang (Sha-to), Chin, Han, and Chou, following the pattern established during the early T'ang between Tibetan rulers and the Chinese court: "For generations [they] called the Middle Kingdom *chiu* [father-in-law or uncle on the mother's side], and when the court bestowed documents [to the Uighurs] it usually called them *sheng* [sister's son]."[43] From the Uighurs' point of view, since earlier khans married T'ang princesses, the uncle-nephew relationship should remain even though there had been dynastic change.[44] Uighur contact with the dynasties in northern China continually increased. The Uighurs were clever in commercial activities and concentrated their attention on economic gain. They primarily traded horses and jade to the Chinese to obtain Chinese silk and other products,[45] and it is probable that they secured high quality jade, as well as sable skins and yak tails, which they also exported to

China, from the other group of Uighurs located in the T'ien-shan, where these items were more readily available.

It is evident in the *Wu-tai shih-chi* that during the Five-Dynasties period the tribute and trade policies of the Later T'ang were highly favorable to the Uighurs and other nomads. Emperor Ming-tsung (r. 926–933), of the Later T'ang dynasty, established markets open to all the barbarians along his frontiers. He "bought all the horses without any differentiation and usually paid a much higher price than they were worth. [In addition], transportation and accommodation were also supplied [by the Court]. Those who approached the capital would be received by [Emperor] Ming-tsung in the palace and entertained with food and drink. After getting drunk they would sing one after the other in turn and talk about their customs in great enjoyment. When they left, they would again be richly rewarded. . . . "[46] In time, the emperor was persuaded by his ministers to limit his lavish entertainment of foreign tributaries which, they asserted, was annually costing the court one million in cash. Ming-tsung reconsidered his policies and instructed border officials to purchase horses and other goods at the frontier and stop Uighur envoys from coming to his court.[47]

Uighur relations with sedentary courts continued after the Sung dynasty came to power in 960. Sung emperors desired to adopt the traditional policy of allying with a distant nomadic people in order to attack one nearby, and, therefore, encouraged the Uighurs to attack the Hsia (Tangut), which would alleviate Tangut pressure in the northwest. The Uighurs were interested in maintaining tributary relations in order to trade but were unwilling to engage the Tangut in battle. During the Sung period, the court became quite concerned about extensive Uighur trading activities, noting that Uighur merchants were scattering and settling in Shensi province. They feared that frequent contact between Uighur and Chinese merchants might threaten the security of border areas.[48] This concern was justified, for it is clear that when viewing the "Table of the Subordinate Countries" in the *Liao shih*, the Uighur were also maintaining tribute and trade relations with the Sung's hostile neighbor, the Khitan Liao.

Khitan relations with agrarian courts can be chronicled from the latter half of the fifth century, when they established trade relations with the T'o-pa Northern Wei to secure needed foodstuffs. A study of Khitan-Chinese tributary and trade interaction provides a particularly rich supply of information on T'ang, Five Dynasties, and Sung relations with the nomad and sustains the thesis that the relative power of the sedentarist and nomad courts dictated the nature of tribute and market exchanges. It also suggests that relations between the Khitan and the Chinese seldom adhered to the guidelines set by the tributary system.

Throughout the early history of this people, the Khitan found themselves sandwiched between large agrarian states: the To-pa Wei, Sui, and T'ang, and between equally threatening nomadic powers: the Jou-jan, Turks, and, later, the Uighur. Located on the southeast of the Gobi, the Khitan moved close to the Chinese frontier and sought protective relationships with the Chinese. They quickly established a reputation as "the most impolite, stubborn, and arrogant [people] of all the barbarians. . . ."[49] While their strength was growing, the Khitan regularly offered tribute to the Sui and T'ang, thereby securing essential commodities without needing to attack the frontier. However, the T'ang, sensitive to possibly alienating the more powerful Uighur, did not confer official ranks on Khitan leaders.[50]

In 907, the T'ang dynasty fell, and the Khitan, now the pre-eminent power north of the Great Wall, were courted by a number of rival states seeking to dominate northern China. Li K'o-yung, the Sinicized leader of the Sha-to Turks in Shansi, attempted to form a league with the Khitan ruler Yeh-lü A-pao-chi and use the military capability of the Khitan to help him expand the power of his Later T'ang dynasty in China. A-pao-chi chose to focus his efforts on consolidating power north of China and refused to personally involve himself in the struggle, although he did lend some Khitan troops to the Later T'ang.[51]

Chinese historians suggest that Yeh-lü A-pao-chi led either seventy thousand or three hundred thousand warriors to Yün-chou (Ta-t'ung) to meet Li K'o-yung and presented him with one thousand horses and "tens of thousands" of sheep and oxen. Of course, the presentation of these gifts required offerings from the Later T'ang court in return. The *Chiu Wu-tai shih* informs us that "[they] shook hands, conversed happily, and entered into a sworn brotherhood,"[52] and the *Liao shih* states that "[they] exchanged their robes and horses and became sworn brothers."[53] Neither source suggests that A-pao-chi's gifts in any way suggested a tribute offering. In fact, the sworn brotherhood suggests just the opposite. Later, A-pao-chi publicly proclaimed to a Later T'ang emissary: "I and the former lord east of the [Yellow] river [Li K'o-yung] entered into a brotherhood, and now the Son of Heaven south of the river [Emperor Chuang-tsung] is my son."[54] Despite this evidence, later entries in the "Annals of Chuang-tsung" and the "Annals of Ming-tsung" in the *Chiu Wu-tai shih* incorrectly describe all items delivered by Khitan envoys to the Later T'ang court as tribute.⁵⁵

Because conditions in northern China were chaotic, many Chinese crossed the Great Wall to settle as refugees on Khitan lands. Once there they began to farm and provided the Khitan with increasing food supplies,⁵⁶ which made the Khitan less dependent on trade with China. The Khitan diminished tribute and trade relations with dynasties established in north China and, when exchange was conducted, sought fewer agricultural products and more manufactured goods.

Khitan non-interference in northern China ended in 936 when the Khitan khan, Yeh-lü Te-kuang, committed his troops to Shih Ching-t'ang to fight against the Later T'ang dynasty. When Yeh-lü Te-kuang's forces joined those of Shih Ching-t'ang, the Khitan ruler stated: "I came from three thousand *li* away for this righteous deed. . . . This matter must be accomplished. . . . Now I install you as the Son of Heaven. . . . You should ascend the Imperial throne . . . and use Chin as the title of the kingdom. We will forever be the states of father and son. . . . "⁵⁷ Once the Later T'ang were defeated, Yeh-lü Te-kuang turned over the surrendered troops and five thousand horses to Shih Ching-t'ang, the new Chin emperor Kao-tsu, and once again affirmed that the Khitan would maintain the role of father in a new father-son relationship.⁵⁸

The Khitan exacted from this newly created state important concessions in return for their military assistance. Although this had seldom happened before in the East Asian realm, Yeh-lü Te-kuang demanded territory from the court of an agricultural sedentary society as a reward for support: "The Chin conceded the land under the jurisdiction of Yu-chou and the land of Hsin-chou, Wu-chou, Yün-chou, Ying-chou, and Shuo-chou as a bribe to him."⁵⁹ This is a dramatic departure from earlier T'ang agreements with the Turks and the Uighurs, when both sides agreed that "people and land belong to the Duke of T'ang; treasures, silk, gold, and precious things belong to the Turks."⁶⁰

The Khitan also demanded that the Chin accept the status of vassal and present substantial yearly payments to them: "The Emperor Kao-tsu of Chin [Shin Ching-t'ang] usually sent envoys to visit the Khitan Khan to present memorials and to call himself a vassal. Besides the yearly presentation of three hundred thousand rolls of silk, he also presented each year precious jade, special precious things, and even the foodstuffs of the Middle Kingdom. The messengers traveled along the road every day."⁶¹

Sui-pi, or yearly payments, were institutionalized at this time. Besides yearly payments, the Khitan pressed the Chin court for gifts during various festivals and at the New Year to celebrate special events, or to mourn the death of members of the Khitan imperial household. "At times, when [Yeh-lü] Te-kuang requested something and the answer was a little unsatisfactory, the Khitan envoys would come to reprove. Kao-tsu of Chin usually condescended to serve him."[62]

When Emperor Kao-tsu died in 942, his son Shih Ch'ung-kuei ascended the throne, determined to change the humiliating relationship between the Chin and the Khitan. He announced that, although his father had been installed by the Khitan, he was enthroned by the Middle Kingdom. Consequently, in dealing with the Khitan, he was willing to call himself "grandson but not vassal."[63] This Chin declaration generated a debate in Khitan circles between those who desired to again humble the Chinese by launching a war against them and those who were willing to maintain peace if the Chin would increase the yearly payments and allow the Khitan to occupy additional areas of Chen and Ting (present Chengting and Ting-hsien in Hopei Province). During this debate, Empress Shu-lü, the wife of Yeh-lü A-pao-chi and mother of Yeh-lü Te-kuang, recognized that historically nomads were the catalysts for nomadic-Chinese interaction. Although an advocate for peace, she observed that trade concessions were generally secured from the Chinese only after war was waged and the sedentarists were forced to seek peace.[64]

The hopes of Empress Shu-lü and other Khitan officials to secure additional economic concessions in return for a softening of the hierarchical relationship between the Khitan and the Chin were not realized, and war broke out. In 946, Yeh-lü Te-kuang occupied Pien-ching (K'ai-feng), the capital of Chin. Shih Chung-kuei, the Chin emperor, was captured, and the Khitan leader personally occupied the dragon throne and declared the creation of the Liao dynasty. However, the Khitan had little experience in ruling a sedentary agricultural society and failed to utilize Chinese-style institutions to rule the Chinese majority. Khitan efforts to expand their holdings in China failed and forced them to withdraw their forces back to the sixteen prefectures of Yen and Yün which the Chin had earlier conceded to them.

In 960 most of China was again unified by the Sung dynasty. As the relationship of power between the Chinese and the Khitan changed, it was likely that the Chinese would seek a more favorable arrangement with the Khitan. Initially, war between the Khitan and the Chinese was averted because both the Sung and the Khitan were preoccupied with the consolidation of their internal bases of power. However, in 976, Emperor T'ai-tsung ascended the throne, determined to recover Chinese land earlier ceded to the Khitan by the Chin. T'ai-tsung conducted two expeditions against the Khitan, one in 976 and the other in 986, both of which failed.

The defeat of their armies twice within a little more than a decade forced Sung diplomats to reassess their foreign policy towards the Khitan. In 988, the Sung official, Chang Ch'i, suggested that the best strategy to adopt against strong enemies was active forward defense: "If they [the enemies] come, be fully prepared to resist them; if they depart, resist the temptation to pursue them."[65] However, Chang Ch'i realized that the Sung was ill-prepared to adopt such a policy and reached the conclusion that the only diplomacy available to the dynasty was "to put away one's armor and bows, use humble words, send generous gifts, send a princess to obtain friendship, and transport goods in order to establish firm bonds; although this would diminish the emperor's dignity, it could *for a while* end fighting along the three borders."[66]

The Sung court was slow to implement Chang Ch'i's proposals to strengthen relationships with the Khitan, and, in 1004, the Mother Empress, Ch'eng-t'ien (r. 982–1009) of the Khitan Liao dynasty, prepared to invade the Sung. The new Sung emperor, Chen-tsung, desired to avoid war and sent an envoy with instructions to a former Sung vassal who then lived among the Khitan, Wang Chi-chung,[67] to secretly negotiate peace. During these exploratory discussions "The Emperor of Sung called the Mother Empress 'aunt' "[68] and promised to annually provide the Khitan with one hundred thousand taels of silver and two hundred thousand rolls of silk.[69] Although the Sung prime minister, K'ou Chun, cautioned against making too many concessions to the Khitan to obtain peace, he desired "to force the [Khitan] envoys to recognize the Khitan as a vassal to the Sung and to return the lands of Yen and Yün."[70] The Sung emperor was not so intransigent.

Regarding the question of yearly payments, Emperor Chen-tsung sent his envoy to the Khitan with the instructions that "if it [the sum demanded by the Khitan] is under one million, it will be agreeable."[71] Perhaps he realized that it was more economical to make annual payments than to wage war, for one Sung official suggested that such payments constituted less than one or two percent of military expenditures during wartime.[72] However, before the envoy commenced negotiations with the

Khitan, K'ou Chun summoned him to his tent and said: "Although the Imperial instruction is otherwise, you should not agree to more than three hundred thousand. If it surpasses three hundred thousand, I will execute you!"[73] The envoy succeeded in preserving his life and also negotiating the Treaty of Shan-yüan, which promised yearly payments to the Khitan within the guidelines of K'ou Chun as well as the opening of frontier trading markets.

The peace signed in 1005 lasted until 1042, when the Khitan again amassed their forces along the border of the Sung and demanded further concessions. Demands made by the Khitan included more Chinese territory, intermarriage ties between the two courts, continued recognition of Sung submission to the Khitan as evidenced in the language used in the presentation of yearly payments, and an increase in the level of yearly payments. Although the "Annals of Jen-tsung" in the *Sung shih* gives no account of the Khitan-Sung peace negotiations, the "Biography of Fu Pi," the Sung emissary in the peace process gives a full account. Because these negotiations are highly revealing, a rather lengthy excerpt is quoted here:

> The Khitan stationed their troops along the border and sent the vassals Hsiao Ying and Liu Liu-fu[74] to demand the land on the south of the Wa-chiao gate. . . . The [Sung] emperor Jen-tsung . . . had Fu Pi accompany them. . . . Hsiao Ying secretly told Fu Pi of the desire of his lord and said: "If it is agreeable, please agree. If not, then fulfill one of his desires. That will be enough." Fu Pi reported all of them, but the Emperor agreed only to the increase of yearly payment and to allow the Khitan ruler's son to marry a daughter of a member of the imperial household. Then Fu Pi was appointed the emissary as a response. After his arrival . . . Pi called on the Khitan lord . . . and said that " . . . if the country of the north maintains friendship with the Middle Kingdom, the lord himself will monopolize all the benefits and the vassals will have nothing to gain. If war breaks out, then all the profits will go to the vassals and the lord himself will be responsible for the disasters. Therefore, those who advocate war are all planning for their personal gains". . . . Liu Liu-fu said: "My lord feels ashamed to receive gold and silk, but insists on obtaining ten prefectures. How about that?" Pi answered: "The emperor of my court said: 'We must keep the country of Our ancestors. How dare We unjustly give away the country of Our ancestors. How dare We unjustly give away the territory to someone else? The thing that the court in the north demands is nothing more than tax and rent. We cannot endure more killing of the people of our two countries, and, therefore, we yield Ourselves and agree to increase the yearly payment instead. But if you insist on obtaining the land, then it is desirable to break the agreement. . . . If the country on the north begins the battle, then the fault will not be Ours!' " Later Liu-fu said: "My Lord, after hearing the words of glory and shame from your excellency, began to feel agreeable. Now the only thing that we need to discuss is the marriage." Pi said, "Marriage easily creates ill will. When

the elder princess of our court goes to marry, her dowry does not exceed one hundred thousand strings of money. How can it compare with the endless benefit of the yearly payment?" The Khitan lord commanded Pi to return and said: "We will wait until you come back again, and then decide the selection. You come with the credential and oath." . . . Later, after Pi arrived, the Khitan did not again ask for marriage but only desired to increase the yearly payment, saying: "The gifts that were sent us from the court on the south should be called *hsien* [presents] or *na* [offerings]. Pi resisted it. . . . The Khitan Lord said: "You should not resist. It also happened in early times." Pi said, "In the early days it was only the case when Emperor Kao-tsu of T'ang borrowed troops from the Turks and entitled the gifts of that time as *hsien-na* [presents or offerings]. Afterward, Il Khan was captured by Emperor T'ai-tsung, and when occurred such a ritual again?" . . . The Khitan Lord . . . then said: "We will send someone to discuss this with your court." Again the Khitan sent Liu Liu-fu to come as an envoy . . . and finally, the court gave them the yearly payment as *na* [an offering].[75]

This document reveals that the primary objective of the Khitan in their negotiations with the Sung was economic. They sought to ensure that the amounts of goods received as gifts and yearly payments from the Chinese were increased. Consequently, while threatening war, they requested intermarriage, realizing that the Sung court would then offer them additional gifts and dowries. They also demanded more Chinese territory, which, if ceded to them, would enable them to squeeze more revenue from the hapless Chinese. By demanding territory, they also obtained a bargaining chip which could be abandoned during negotiations in return for additional economic concessions.

Khitan demands for territory and intermarriage were effectively deflected by the Sung envoy Fu Pi. In response to the serious threat posed by Khitan mobilization, Fu Pi adeptly reminded the Khitan ruler that war was not advantageous to him. He noted that from the time of the Hsiung-nu, nomadic custom dictated that "in their campaigns, they distribute their booty and make slaves of their prisoners. Therefore, in war, everybody strives for his own gain."[76] On the other hand, bestowals and yearly payments would go directly to the Khitan court and need not be shared with a ruler's subjects.

Fu Pi persuaded the Khitan court to relinquish their demand for more Chinese land by ensuring them that they would be compensated by an increase in yearly payments. He also induced the Khitan to abandon their requests for imperial intermarriage by suggesting that dowries and gifts offered at the time of marriage were not as great as imagined. If the primary interest of the Khitan khan was to secure valuable gifts, the Sung would commit themselves to raise the annual yearly payments. The *Liao shih* informs us that the Sung committed itself to increase the annual presentation of silver by one hundred thousand taels and the amount of silk by one hundred thousand rolls.[77]

A major hurdle in the negotiation process was the language which would be adopted by the Sung when presenting annual payments. Fu Pi's biography in the *Sung shih* states that the Khitan demanded that precedent be followed and these payments be called *hsien* (presents) or *na* (offerings). The Sung resisted, arguing that such terms were used only on rare occasions as when T'ang Kao-tsu depended on the Turks for troops. It is clear that an understanding was reached which basically satisfied the demands of the Khitan, but it is not certain what terms were used because of the contradictory statements in various sources. "The Biography of Fu Pi" states that the Sung agreed to use the quite flexible term *na*, or offering,[78] but the "Annals of Hsing-tsung," in the *Liao shih*, suggests that the yearly payment was called tribute or *kung*.[79] In the *Liao shih*, the "Biography of Liu Liu-fu," the envoy of the Khitan in the negotiations, records that "the term settled on was tribute *chin-kung* and the Sung agreed to entitle the yearly payment as *kung* (tribute)."[80]

As suggested above, stable relations between the Sung and the Khitan were maintained only because the Sung were willing to annually present vast amounts of Chinese wealth to their powerful northern neighbor. Sung policy towards the other great nomadic threat to the dynasty, the Tangut Hsia realm, located along the silk routes of the Kansu corridor, including territories to the east and south of the Ho-lan Mountains and in the agricultural zone along the east and west banks of the westernmost extension of the Yellow river loop, also relied on yearly payments to promote peace. Because of the continuing threat posed to the Sung by the Khitan, it was imperative that the Chinese court maintain stable relations with the Tangut.

Sung gifts to the Hsia were so large that the Tangut Crown Prince, Li Yüan-hao (r. 1032–1048), cautioned his father against becoming too dependent on the Sung and too willingly accepting the status of vassal. The success of Sung policy is evident in his reply: "The father warned him, saying, 'I employed the army for a long time, and [now I am] tired. Our people have been wearing embroidered silk for thirty years. This is a favor of the Sung. We should not be ungrateful.' "[81] The Crown Prince answered: "Wearing hide and wool to herd animals is convenient for the nature of the Tanguts. The birth of a hero would make him a king or a hegemon. Where is the need for embroidery and silk?"[82] Li Yüan-hao recognized the danger of a nomadic people becoming economically dependent on the supplies of an agricultural society. His words reflect the same fear felt by Chung-hang Yüeh, who warned the *Shan-yü* of the Hsiung-nu not to depend on Han goods,[83] and Tonyukhukh, who exhorted the Turkic Khan not to change the Turks' nomadic way of life by imitating the pattern of the Chinese T'ang.[84]

After Li Yüan-hao became the ruler of the Tangut Hsia, he unsuccessfully made war on the Sung for seven years. When his resources were exhausted, and he could no longer sustain the conflict, the Tangut ruler signed a peace accord with the Sung in which the Sung committed themselves to offer the Tangut bestowals and yearly payments "as in the old agreement," which set the level of yearly payments at "two hundred fifty-five thousand units of silver, embroidery, silk, and tea."[85] The Tangut ruler agreed to "entitle himself as a vassal, to accept the proper calendar of the Sung and all the imperial documents that were bestowed on him as decrees."[86] However, he retained the right to appoint his own officials and entitle himself emperor within his own country. Sung diplomats thus avoided the humiliation of presenting yearly payments to the Tangut as tribute, as was the case with the Khitan. Although the Hsia court accepted a vassal relationship with the Sung, their leader still remained independent within his own realm.

The emergence of the Jurchen northeast of the Khitan Liao and Tangut Hsia states in the early twelfth century had a dramatic effect on frontier relations. The peace established between the Khitan and the Sung by the Treaty of Shan-yüan in 1005 brought stability to China's borders for more than a century. However, with the rise of the Jurchen, many Sung officials argued that the Khitan treaties should be abandoned and an alliance made with these outer "barbarians". Negotiations between the Jurchen and the Sung led to a treaty arrangement in 1123, which committed the Jurchen to aid the Sung in destroying the Khitan. The Jurchen Chin also promised to restore to the Sung territories in present Northern Hopei and Northern Shansi occupied by the Khitan for almost two centuries. In return, the Sung agreed to regard the Jurchen as the legal successors of the Khitan Liao which obligated the Chinese court to continue yearly payments to the Jurchen at the levels stipulated in the Shan-yüan treaty of 1005. In addition, the Sung agreed to compensate the Jurchen for land-tax revenues they would lose by allowing the Sung to occupy the Northern Hopei and Northern Shansi areas after the Khitan defeat.[87]

As predicted by some Sung officials, after the defeat of the Khitan, it was not long before the accord of 1123 broke down that the Jurchen continued to move south into Sung territory. In 1126, before the Sung capital at K'ai-feng was occupied, a feverish exchange of correspondence occurred between the desperate Sung and the Jurchen. During these negotiations, the Sung emperor was forced to style himself as nephew, using his personal name, and address the Chin emperor as elder uncle. In return for withdrawing their armies, the Jurchen demanded cession of the three prefectures of T'ai-yüan, Chung-shan, and Ho-chien, payment of a huge indemnity in addition to continued annual payments, and the sending of an imperial prince to serve as hostage in the Jurchen camp. Although an agreement was signed, it lasted only months, and in January 1127, K'ai-feng was taken by the Jurchen. The Sung imperial household fled south of the Yangtze river to Hang-chou, giving rise to the Southern Sung dynasty.[88]

Fourteen years of war followed before the Southern Sung and the Jurchen finally agreed to peace in 1141, based on the following terms: "It was decided to divide the territory from the middle stream of the River Huai. The two regions of T'ang and Teng[89] were conceded to the Chin, and two hundred fifty thousand taels of silver and two hundred fifty thousand rolls of silk were to be presented annually.[90] The Southern Sung were also to declare themselves vassals of the Chin.[91]

The first payments to the Jurchen approximated those which earlier were given to the Tangut Hsia. As noted previously, initial payments to the Khitan had also been at a comparable level, ranging below the three-hundred-thousand-unit mark.[92] However, it is clear that as Khitan power increased, they exacted higher levels of yearly payments from the Sung until they reached the five-hundred-thousand-unit range in the mid-eleventh century.[93]

The pattern of Sung "bestowals" and the nature of the relationship between the Chinese and the Jurchen continued to depend on the relative strength of each party. When, in 1161 the Jurchen leader Hai-ling-ti was assassinated in an army camp during an expedition against the Southern Sung, there was a period of internal disruption in the Jurchen Chin state before his successor, Emperor Shih-tsung (r. 1161–1189), reestablished order. In 1164, the Southern Sung used this opportunity to negotiate a reduction of the yearly payments offered the Jurchen by one hundred thousand taels of silver and one hundred thousand rolls of silk. However, the Southern Sung did not challenge the existing boundaries between the two countries. The Southern Sung emperor also continued to recognize the Jurchen ruler as "Uncle Emperor of the Great Chin" and accept for himself the humble position of "Nephew Emperor of the Sung."[94]

A little more than forty years later, in 1206, the Southern Sung minister Han T'o-chou attacked the Jurchen and suffered a serious defeat. Once again the relationship between the two countries and the amount exacted as yearly payments changed. At this time, the Chin court demanded the head of Han T'o-chou, which it received, as a precondition for establishing peace.[95] From this juncture, Jurchen exactions were short-lived because in 1206 the Mongolian leader Chinggis Khan became the Great Khan of Mongolia. By 1214, Mongol pressure on the Jurchen capital of Chung-tu (Peking) forced the Jurchen to flee to Pien-liang (K'ai-feng). Even while the Mongols besieged Chung-tu, the Jurchen emperor continued to send envoys to the Southern Sung, demanding yearly payments.[96]

The last effort to stabilize a critical situation on the borders of China through the mechanism of yearly payments was initiated without imperial authorization by Prime Minister Chia Ssu-tao of the Southern Sung dynasty. In 1259, the Mongolian khan, Mongke (r. 1251–1259), invaded Szechwan and sent his younger brother Khubilai (r. 1260–1294) to attack O-chou (present Wu-ch'ang). Chai Ssu-tao "secretly dispatched Sung Ching [and others to the Mongolian military camp], petitioning to present themselves as vassals and to make yearly payments."[97] Shortly after this event, Mongke Khan died, and, after further discussions with Sung Ching, Khubilai, satisfied with the pledges made to him by this envoy, withdrew. However, Chia Ssu-tao did not report the secret peace talks to the emperor. Rather, he falsely announced a great military victory over the Mongols. After ascending the throne in 1260, Khubilai dispatched envoys to Hao Ching[98] and others to demand fulfillment of the pledges. The envoys were all either secretly imprisoned or killed by Chia Ssu-tao, providing the pretext for the Mongolian invasion of the Southern Sung, which ended Sung rule in 1279.[99]

The final remarks in this chapter will focus on Ming-Oirad Mongol relations until 1454, when Oirad power collapsed after the death of Esen. As suggested in chapter three, early Ming rulers sought to develop close relations with the Oirad to counter the threat posed to the Ming by the legitimist khans, descendents of the Yüan emperors, of the Eastern Mongols. They sought to check and balance the barbarians against other barbarians by adopting "the equal practice of the hard and the soft," by persistently putting pressure on the more powerful Mongol force and providing aid to the weaker. However, it will become evident that in their dealings with the Oirad, the Ming had a "tiger by the tail," for the Oirad proved impossible to control and ultimately came to dictate to the Ming court the level of tributary exchange.

The Ming emperor Ch'eng-tsu was especially active in "using barbarians to check barbarians." When Kuei-li-chih, apparently Ugechi-khashakha of the Oirad,[100] illegally usurped power from the legitimate descendant of the imperial household of the former Yüan dynasty, the Ming court encouraged his action by bestowing silver and silk on one of his military commanders and also on his prime minister, thereby hoping to form an alliance.[101] However, Kuei-li-chih's rule was short-lived, and Emperor Ch'eng-tsu found himself struggling against the next leaders of the Eastern Mongols, Bunyashiri Khan[102] and Arughtai. In 1410, both Bunyashiri Khan and Arughtai were badly defeated in separate battles with Ch'eng-tsu. A short time later Arughtai opened tribute relations with the Ming court. Because of his submission, Ch'eng-tsu returned to Arughtai his older brother and younger sister, who had been captured earlier, and bestowed on Arughtai the title Ho-ning *Wang* (the Prince of peace and tranquility).[103]

Emperor Ch'eng-tsu still had to deal with Bunyashiri Khan. As early as 1403, the Ming had begun to develop tributary relations with the Oirad leader Mahmud,[104] and these relations were of great value and led the Ming in 1409 to grant the title of Shun-ning *Wang* (Prince of obedience and peace) on Mahmud. In 1412, Mahmud attacked and killed Bunyashiri Khan. After this success, he sent envoys to the Ming emperor demanding weapons and other bestowals. Ch'eng-tsu granted these gifts to Mahmud saying to his ministers: "The Oirad are proud, but it is still not worthwhile to find fault with them."[105]

By 1414, Ch'eng-tsu determined that the Oirad threat was greater than that posed by the Eastern Mongols, and he allied himself with his former enemy Arughtai to wage war against Mahmud. At Ula'an-Khoshi'un he fought a severe but indecisive battle against the Oirad and returned to Yen-ching (Peking). Shortly thereafter, the Oirad, faced with the continuing threat posed by the Eastern Mongols led by Arughtai, presented tribute to the Ming, released an imperial envoy they had taken hostage, and sought to reestablish ties with the Chinese court. Ch'eng-tsu told his ministers that "it is not worthwhile to compete with the Oirad. Receive their presents and accommodate their envoys."[106]

It is evident that Emperor Ch'eng-tsu practiced duplicity in his relations with the Eastern and Western Mongols, but as noted in the following passages, Mongol potentates were also unscrupulous in their actions towards the Chinese. The first passage is the observation of a rival of the Oirad leader Mahmud which questions the seriousness of Mahmud's intentions: "After the assassination [of Bunyashiri] and establishment of himself [as khan], Mahmud of the Oirad became proud and without restraint, desirous of assuming status equal to that of the Middle Kingdom. While [he] sends envoys to the court, the object of his will is not [obedience] but gold, silk and other goods."[107] However, the Eastern Mongols exhibited the same tendencies and were equally difficult to deal with: "Arughtai's submission to the Ming resulted from his fear of Oirad oppression. He was forced to move south to seek a haven close to the Great Wall. Within several years, both human and animal populations had increased. As a result, he treated our envoys with impudence and imprisoned many. Often, his tributary missions plundered [the people] as they returned."[108]

After Emperor Ch'eng-tsu's death in 1424, the Oirad Mongols gained control over the lands north of China. By 1434, they defeated the Eastern Mongols and arranged a marriage between the elder sister of Esen, the future leader of the Oirad, and the young khan of the Eastern Mongols, Toghto-bukha.[109] From this juncture on, because their strength had greatly increased and Ming efforts to "use barbarians to attack barbarians" were less effective, both the Eastern and the Western Mongols began to increase the frequency and the size of their "tributary missions" to the Ming, thereby making greater demands on the Chinese court.

The Chinese rationalization for the maintenance of the tributary system was that it allowed the "barbarians" to "revere the Celestial way and honor the court."[110] The Chinese also suggested that the presentation of tribute evoked a natural response by Chinese courts to offer bestowals to the envoys and, in turn, send emissaries to grant bestowals to nomadic rulers in order to demonstrate a Chinese emperor's kindness and graciousness to those who come from afar. Participants in tributary missions, even those who joined the missions exclusively to trade, received special treatment and were supplied all their provisions once they entered China. Yet it is important to note that after Emperor Ch'eng-tsu's death, for two full decades until the fall of Esen in 1454, the Mongols set the level of bestowals, and the Ming were forced to respond. As suggested by Henry Serruys, the Ming were really paying tribute to the Mongols to achieve their political objectives. An effort will now be made to chronicle the dramatic escalation in demands made by the Mongols on the Ming court.

> A passage in the *Ming Shih-lu* suggests the court dilemma: Formerly in the beginning of Cheng-t'ung [1436], the Oirads sent envoys to come to the capital to offer tribute. The court also sent envoys to the Oirads who stayed there until the next year and came back together with the barbarian envoys. Every year it was the same. But the barbarian envoys were very covetous. It was impossible to satisfy their desires and they always caused trouble. The chief of the barbarians requested the goods of the Middle Kingdom, and increased their demands each year. Sometimes they asked for many expensive and luxurious things which we did not have. Even so, the court always tried to give those things to them if they were ready in hand. Our envoys often flattered the barbarian chief, and promised to give whatever he asked. But if he got half, or less than what he asked, the barbarian chief always got very angry . . . [and] even held our envoys and refused to send them back.[111]

When the tributary system operated as the Chinese desired, a quota was established which set the number of envoys allowed to travel to the court and frontier markets as well as the level of tribute presentations offered in return for court bestowals. During the Ming period, there is ample evidence that this system broke down. An interesting passage in the *Ming Shih-lu* relates how one emissary of the Ming went to the court of Toghto-bukha to offer him bestowals of silk lining and colored facing. However, after receiving these gifts, Toghto-bukha asked for additional bestowals for his chieftains, which was not anticipated by the Ming court. Rather than deny him unscheduled payments, the envoys borrowed 668 rolls of satin, three sets of facing and lining silk, and 5870 rolls of cloth from members of the Chinese retinue and soldiers to give to the Mongols.[112]

Another more serious problem faced by the Ming were the inflated numbers of nomads traveling to the court to present tribute in order to receive rich bestowals and trading opportunities in return: "In the early days, Oirad missions to the court usually consisted of less than five persons. Now, envoys sent by Toghto-bukha or Esen number approximately one thousand, plus traders."[113] The Ming informed the Mongols that this huge increase of nomads coming to the capital to present tribute placed a terrible strain on the Chinese soldiers and people who needed to provide food and lodging for them and insisted that the numbers decrease.[114] The emperor also upbraided the nomads for their unruly behavior: " . . . last year envoys and traders were too numerous; some among them were intoxicated, violated public order, [and] beat and injured soldiers and workers along the road. With envoys so numerous, such transgressions are inevitable. Be aware of Our desire for continued hospitality and warn your retinue to respect ritual and law and avoid misconduct. . . . "[115]

Under Esen and Toghto-bukha, tributary missions came to resemble trade caravans and yet the Chinese refused to recognize them as such. They continued to invest them with tributary status to maintain the Chinese claim that their nation was the center of the universe.[116] One might think that the Chinese willingness to meet the increased demands of the Western and Eastern Mongols would guarantee continued stability on China's frontiers, but in 1449 an Oirad-Ming war broke out. After the Ming Emperor was captured at T'u-mu, the Chinese envoy Yang Shan met with Esen in 1450 and suggested Chinese bewilderment in the following manner: "During the reign of the Retired Emperor [Ying-tsung], [you], the *Tai-shih*, usually sent tributary missions of three thousand people. Each year [you] were offered numerous gifts; the roads flowed continually with gold and silk. Why then did you violate our friendship and attack [the Middle Kingdom]?"[117] Esen responded that the prices he received for horses had been reduced, the silk he received was cut and disfigured, some of his envoys failed to return, and the level of bestowals had been reduced. Esen's perception that the Ming court had failed to sustain support for him and his people at the levels he had come to expect led Esen to war with China in hope of obtaining even greater riches from the Chinese.[118]

This chapter has shown that nomadic states presented tribute primarily for economic reasons. The presentation of tribute assured nomadic rulers that they would receive not only frontier trading privileges but also valued bestowals and yearly payments in return. Yearly payments were received by the Hsiung-nu *Shan-yü*, Mao-tun, as early as the Han period, which set a precedent for the huge demands made on the Sung and Southern Sung dynasties by the Khitan Liao, Tangut Hsia, and Jurchen Chin states. Bestowals were also presented throughout these dynastic periods, with the level of presentation determined by the relative power of the sedentary and nomadic states. During the Ming period, bestowals made in the context of tributary exchange to Oirad Mongols increased dramatically until the mid-fifteenth century decline of Mongol power after the death of Esen. Although bestowals and yearly payments were in reality exacted frequently from Chinese courts and extremely costly to maintain, they did provide Chinese courts with an alternative to expensive and dangerous warfare with their nomadic neighbors.

V

INTERMARRIAGE

This chapter will examine the effect of intermarriage on Chinese-nomadic relations. Although we have divided our discussion regarding the mechanisms through which the nomadic people exchanged what they produced for the essential commodities they desired from China into three chapters, they are all intricately interwoven. In fact, it is tempting to suggest that princesses of imperial households were regarded by sedentarists simply as another form of bestowal offered to nomadic rulers in return for frontier products and security along the borders. In this same light, nomadic leaders sought intermarriage for the same reasons they sought access to frontier markets or yearly payments. Intermarriage meant dowries and wedding gifts and equally important closer relations with agrarian courts. This enabled nomadic states to obtain more easily the prized commodities of China. Intermarriage proposals were sometimes the first thing requested by nomadic rulers seeking to normalize relations with China. A study of intermarriage relations provides yet another means to show that in approaching China, nomadic leaders were primarily interested in obtaining necessary commodities. On the other hand, it becomes quite apparent that Chinese courts utilized intermarriage primarily for political reasons, as they sought to quiet unrest along the frontier, drive a wedge between one nomadic group and another, or form alliances enabling them to "use barbarians to attack barbarians."

This chapter will briefly survey representative examples of intermarriage between sedentarist and nomad, commencing in the Han period. It will focus on the Han, Sui, and T'ang dynasties, which were especially committed to utilizing intermarriage as an important element of their foreign policy. It will also examine various conquest dynasties, especially the T'o-pa Wei, who adopted these traditional intermarriage policies. On the other hand, Sung and Ming emperors did not promote intermarriage, and the nature of Mongolian Yüan and Manchu Ch'ing intermarriage relations are different enough from the traditional policies of the Han, Sui, and T'ang that they will not be studied here.[1]

In earlier chapters, the interaction of the Hsiung-nu leader, Mao-tun, with Han Kao-ti has already been discussed. However, one factor in the formulation of Kao-ti's intermarriage policy, which sought to make Mao-tun a son-in-law, so his son might become the grandson of the Han emperor and not compete against his Han grandfather, warrants fuller discussion. When Kao-ti determined to provide Mao-tun with an imperial princess, he was instructed by his counselor Liu Ching: "If Your Majesty cannot send the eldest princess but rather [sends another daughter] of the Imperial Household or [a daughter of Your Majesty's] royal concubines as a princess, they will know that and will not honor her. Then that [intermarriage covenant] will be of no use."[2] Kao-ti accepted this counsel and determined to send his only daughter by Empress Lü to marry Mao-tun. However, he failed to gauge the crisis that this would create within his own household: "Empress Lü wept day and night and said, 'I only [gave birth to] the crown prince and one daughter. How can [we] throw her away to the Hsiung-nu?'"[3] The emperor relented, selected another girl from a member of the imperial family, entitled her the eldest princess, and sent her to marry Mao-tun. The Hsiung-nu leader knew that the girl presented to him for marriage was a surrogate for Kao-ti's daughter, but as was to be the frequent case later, Mao-tun accepted the girl in order to solidify his relations with the Han court and obtain the dowry, gifts, and opportunity to trade that came through intermarriage.

There is evidence to suggest that the intermarriage policies with the Hsiung-nu initiated by the Han founder were followed by many of his successors. For example, a passage in the *Han shu* states that "[Emperor] Hsiao Ching-ti again carried out an intermarriage [policy] with the Hsiung-nu; the border markets were opened, gifts were given to the Hsiung-nu and princesses were sent [to the Hsiung-nu to marry] as in the old agreement. [Therefore] until the end of the Hsiao Ching[-ti] period, although at times there were small encroachments along the border, there were no great invasions.[4]

However, Emperor Wu-ti adopted a hard-line, aggressive policy toward the Hsiung-nu and stopped further intermarriage between the two courts. Once war broke out, Wu-ti attempted to isolate the Hsiung-nu and sought allies to fight against them. He contacted the Yüeh-chih (Kushan), the Ta-hsia (Bactria), and married the Princess Hsi-chün, the daughter of the Prince of Chiang-tu, to the King of Wu-sun. Wu-ti hoped that through intermarriage he could gain the Wu-sun as an ally some distance from China in order to attack the Hsiung-nu flank.[5]

A few passages in the *Han shu* illuminate the situation faced by this young princess sent to the Wu-sun. First of all, it is clear that the Wu-sun were also being courted by the Hsiung-nu, because the king of the Wu-sun, K'un-mo, accepted a Hsiung-nu bride, whom he designated the "Lady on the Left" at the same time he received the Han princess, whom he designated the "Lady on the Right." Second, it is evident that the princess was as much a diplomat as a wife. Princess Hsi-chün went to the Wu-sun accompanied by several subordinate officials, eunuchs, and several hundred servants, carrying with her the insignia of the court, imperial objects, and many splendid gifts. Once she arrived, she built her own palace to live in and "met with K'un-mo again and again, entertained [him] with wine and food, and bestowed rolls of silk on the followers of the king."[6] Third, there is no doubt that this young girl suffered greatly. She could not directly communicate with her husband because of the language barrier, and in addition, we know that K'un-mo was old and therefore could not be much of a companion to her. In fact, he proposed that she be wed to his grandson Ts'en-tsou.[7] Princess Hsi-chün was against this union and informed the Han that she did not want to marry him. She received a reply from Wu-ti: "Follow the custom of the country and join together with the Wu-sun to oppress the *Hu* [Hsiung-nu]."[8] She assented to Wu-ti's command and married Ts'en-tsou. When K'un-mo died, Ts'en-tsou became the next ruler of the Wu-sun. A song composed and sung by Princess Hsi-chün suggests her despair:

> My family married me
> To the other side of the Heaven;
> And trusted me in a foreign country
> To be married to the King of Wu-sun.
> The yurt is my house,
> And the felt is my wall.
> The meat is my food,
> And the sour milk is my drink.
> Living here [in a foreign country],
> I am always longing for my native soil,
> Wishing to turn into a yellow crane
> And fly back to my homeland.[9]

The *Han shu* informs us that when the Emperor Wu-ti heard the words of this song, he pitied Hsi-chün and sent envoys to her every other year with tents, satins, embroideries, and clothing in order to make her life more bearable. When Princess Hsi-chün died, the Han court selected another girl, Princess Chieh-yu, the granddaughter of the Prince of Chu, and continued the intermarriage tie with Ts'en-tsou.[10]

Later in the Han period, after the bloody wars of Wu-ti and after the Hsiung-nu themselves broke into two factions, Han rulers never used intermarriage as a means to strengthen their relationship with either the Northern or Southern Hsiung-nu. Towards the end of the reign of Emperor Kuang-wu-ti in the middle of the first century A.D., Han policy generally relied on maintaining firm ties with the Southern Hsiung-nu and utilizing them as a buffer on the frontiers of China against the more hostile Northern Hsiung-nu or other nomadic groups. However, this did not prevent the Northern Hsiung-nu from continuing to importune the Han court for intermarriage arrangements and better trading ties.

Generally, the Han viewed the frequent overtures of the Northern Hsiung-nu as a sign of weakness, and although these nomads assured the Han that if relations were stabilized they would lead traders from the western regions to the frontiers of China to trade, the Han frequently rejected their pleas. They feared that intermarriage with the Northern Hsiung-nu would increase their prestige and therefore their strength while at the same time it would reduce the confidence of their Southern Hsiung-nu allies. Occasionally, a counter view surfaced, as suggested by the counsel given to Emperor Kuang-wu-ti by an official in the interior ministry, Pan Piao[11]: "[I, your] vassal, think that the more they pay tribute, the more it indicates their poverty and the more [they] show friendliness, the more it indicates that they are afraid [of us]. At the present time, . . . [we] should not reject the North. According to the principle of the haltering policy [toward the barbarians], there is no reason not to respond. It would be good to reward [them] with bestowals a little more valuable than those they have brought as tribute."[12]

Our understanding of relations between agrarian and nomadic courts during the more than three and one half centuries from the fall of the Han to the rise of the Sui and T'ang has focused on the Northern Wei dynasty. As early as 432, the T'o-pa Wei court formed intermarriage ties with the Jou-jan north of their frontiers. The initial intermarriage arrangement was reciprocal. In 432 a Northern Wei princess was sent north to the Jou-jan, and in 433 the younger sister of Wu-t'i, the Chih-lien Khan of the Jou-jan, was sent south for marriage. During the Northern Wei and subsequent Western Wei and Eastern Wei as well as the Northern Chou and Northern Ch'i dynasties, there are many citations of nomadic princesses being sent to agrarian courts for intermarriage. The following passage from the *Wei shu* suggests the reasons why the Northern Wei court agreed to intermarry with the Jou-jan:

> In the beginning when We ascended the throne, the evil ones were not yet under control, [the countries of] the four directions were not yet subdued, and there were rebellions everywhere. The Juan-juan were making trouble on the north of the desert. . . . Therefore, in order to pacify them, [We] struggled with great effort and even forgot to eat at noon or sleep in the night, . . . and, therefore, there have been [military] expeditions to the northwest all these years. The transportation obligation caused the people to labor, and they suffered from their agricultural losses. In addition, there were floods and droughts which made the people's wealth unequal. Some of them could not support their families and others, who were even poorer, could not satisfy their own needs. We had great pity on them. Now the four directions are following the right course and military actions are gradually decreasing. It is time to reduce taxes and let the people enjoy a rest.[13]

The Northern Wei elected to intermarry with the Jou-jan to halt their long and bitter struggle, which had left the Northern Wei state exhausted. However, initial intermarriage ties with the Jou-jan only partially succeeded in bringing peace along the frontier.[14] Throughout the last half of the fifth century and first two decades of the sixth century, there was intermittent conflict between the Jou-jan and the Northern Wei and little intermarriage. Generally, T'o-pa leaders of the Northern Wei resisted forming intermarriage ties with other nomadic states or with the Chinese. Their intermarriage efforts were generally directed towards defectors from the nomadic or other independent states to hasten the integration of these people into Northern Wei society.[15]

Northern Wei unwillingness to utilize trade and tribute exchange as a means to stabilize relations changed when Emperor Ching-tsung (r. 528–530) ascended the throne. He realized that the Jou-jan leader, A-na-k'ui, was a serious threat to his dynasty and recognized general parity between the two states by allowing A-na-k'ui "to not mention his name at the time of Imperial reception and not to title himself as vassal when presenting a document."[16]

A short time later, the Northern Wei dynasty broke into two halves, the Western Wei and Eastern Wei dynasties, which in turn gave rise to the short-lived Northern Chou and Northern Ch'i dynasties. Throughout this period of disruption, the Jou-jan and the newly emerging Turks found these competing states receptive to their demands for intermarriage and tribute exchange proposals. A-na-k'ui proposed to the founder of the Northern Ch'i dynasty, Kao Huan,[17] that Kao Huan marry his daughter and make her his chief wife to draw the two courts more closely together. Kao Huan reluctantly accepted. He asked his first wife "to retire from the main hall and had [the Jou-jan Princess] live [there]."[18]

As A-na-k'ui consolidated his ties with the courts of northern China, he was approached by the Turkic khan, Tümen, who sought intermarriage relations with the Jou-jan: "A-na-k'ui, Lord of the Ju-ju [Jou-jan], was angry and sent a messenger to [the Turks] to scold [Tümen] saying, 'You are my blacksmith slave. How dare you suggest this!' Tümen became angry. [He] killed the messenger, and severed relations [with the Jou-jan]. . . . "[19] This incident led Tümen Khan to form intermarriage relations with the Northern Chou, and to attack the Jou-jan. In 552, the Turks defeated the Jou-jan in battle and became the major nomadic power north of China.

The states of north China then competed to form intermarriage ties with the Turkic leaders. During the reign of Ssu-chin (Mughan Khan, r. 553–572), the rival courts of Northern Chou and Northern Ch'i both bid for the right to marry his daughter. The Turkic khan first promised her to the state of Northern Chou, but when Northern Ch'i promised a larger dowry and related gifts, Ssu-chin vacillated. In 565, the Northern Chou sent several experienced diplomats, together with a traveling palace, one hundred and twenty attendants, and official gifts to persuade the Turkic khan to send his daughter with them to the Northern Chou court. When they arrived at the Turks' camp, they found representatives of the Northern Ch'i already there. A three year struggle between the two courts to win the hand of the Turkic princess followed. Envoys of the Northern Chou continually reproved Ssu-chin for faltering on his initial agreement to them but made little progress until a fortuitous thunderstorm arose, which blew for more than ten days, destroying much of Ssu-chin's camp. The Turkic ruler took this as a punishment from heaven for not adhering to his initial pledge to the Northern Chou and subsequently agreed to send his daughter to the Northern Chou court. When she arrived in 568, Emperor Kao-tsu personally went out to receive her. We are told that she was beautiful and polite, and that she deeply impressed the emperor. When her husband, Kao-tsu, died, and Emperor Hsüan-ti (r. 578–579) ascended the throne, she was made an Empress Dowager. When she died in 582 at the age of thirty-two, she was buried by the new Sui emperor with full honors at the tomb of her husband, Emperor Kao-tsu of the Northern Chou.[20]

Intermarriage

In 577 the Northern Chou dynasty destroyed the Northern Ch'i state, its chief rival for domination of northern China. When the Northern Ch'i dynasty fell, Kao Shao-i, the Ch'i Prince of Fan-yang and the Governor of Ting-chou (west central Hopei), fled to the Turks and sought the protection of the Turkic ruler Tapar Khan. The khan established Kao Shao-i as the emperor of Ch'i, vowed vengeance on his behalf, and raided the area of Yu-chou (northern Hopei). At the same time, he petitioned the Northern Chou state for intermarriage, suggesting he wished to stabilize relations.[21]

The Yü-wen family of the Northern Chou dynasty desired to bring peace to the frontier and form an alliance with the Turks, enabling them to focus their efforts on consolidating their power in China. They were even more concerned with diminishing the threat posed to them by Prince Kao Shao-i of the recently vanquished Northern Ch'i state. Therefore, when Tapar Khan proposed the creation of intermarriage ties, the Northern Chou quickly responded by offering him the hand of the Princess Ch'ien-chin, the daughter of the Prince of Chao, a member of the imperial household. However, they made this marriage contingent on the willingness of the Turks to extradite Prince Kao.[22]

Tapar Khan initially refused to send back the Northern Ch'i prince and, in 579, again raided the frontier, this time in the area of Ping-chou (central Shansi). Finally, the Northern Chou court sent the envoy Ho Jo-i[23] to the court of Tapar Khan, and Prince Kao's fate was sealed. Kao Shao-i's biography in the *Pei-Ch'i shu* says that "the Chou people [desired] to purchase him from Tapar and sent Ho Jo-i to persuade [the Turks to extradite him]. Tapar was still indisposed to comply. Finally, [Tapar] pretended to hunt with Shao-i in the southern territory and had [Ho] Jo-i capture him."[24]

Kao Shao-i's story is tragic but so also is the story of Princess Ch'ien-chin, who was offered as the purchase price for the Northern Ch'i prince and, as a consequence, was forced to leave the sumptuous court of the Northern Chou state and move north of the Great Wall into the camps of the "barbarians." Actually, Ch'ien-chin's departure from northern China at that time was fortuitous because a short time later, in 581, the general Yang Chien, better known in Chinese history as Emperor Sui Wen-ti, usurped the Northern Chou throne and massacred the father and a brother of Ch'ien-chin. By 589, Wen-ti destroyed the dynasties to his south and unified China under the Sui dynasty.

While Sui Wen-ti consolidated his power in the south, he also faced a changing situation to the north. Princess Ch'ien-chin's husband, Tabar

Khan, died in 581, forcing the Sui court to deal with the new Turkic khan, Ishbara. Because of Wen-ti's usurpation of power and slaughter of her family, Ch'ien-chin, now widowed, had little reason to return to China, but the emergence of a new ruling house in China also jeopardized her position in the Turkic camp. Consequently, when the new khan, Ishbara, approached the Sui court requesting that he be given a Chinese princess as a wife, "Princess Ch'ien-chin voluntarily petitioned to alter her family name [from Yü-wen to Yang], to be a daughter of the Emperor [Wen-ti]."[25] This action would make her a member of the new imperial household, and she could then be offered to Ishbara in marriage. One can imagine what must have passed through the mind of this young lady as she sought to become the daughter of the man who had butchered her father and brother so recently.

Sui Wen-ti accepted the idea, gave the princess the family name of Yang, and changed her title to Princess Ta-i.[26] Ch'ien-chin, now Ta-i, was accompanied by the court official Chang-sun Sheng to the court of Ishbara to be presented to her new nomadic master. One might think that Ishbara would have questioned the presentation of an adopted Northern Chou princess to him as a legitimate member of the Yang family, but the Turkic khan did not differentiate between the two families inasmuch as they were both members of the Chinese ruling class.

The formal presentation of Ta-i at the court of Ishbara provides insight regarding the Turkic ruler's perception of himself and about his views considering intermarriage. Initially, when Chang-sun Sheng presented the imperial decree from Sui Wen-ti to Ishbara, he refused to stand up and bow, because he regarded himself as of equal or even superior stature to the Chinese court. The Sui envoy, tactfully dealt with this problem by saying: "Both the [lords] of the Turks and the Sui are the Sons of Heaven of the Great Kingdoms. The Khan refused to stand up; how can I disagree? But the *Khatun* [Queen] is the daughter of the Emperor; therefore, the Khan is the son-in-law of the Great Sui. How can [the Khan] refuse to honor the father-in-law?"[27] Ishbara accepted this rationale and told his ranking officials, "I have to bow to the father-in-law. I shall obey."[28] Despite the awkwardness of submitting to his father-in-law, Ishbara was willing to do so because this new familial relationship enabled him to claim the silk, cloth, and other riches of China.[29]

Once Princess Ta-i was accepted as a wife by Ishbara her influence in the Turk camp depended on continued close ties with the Sui dynasty. Yet, despite this, she must have hated Sui Wen-ti, the man who now professed to be her father, for his destruction of the Northern Chou state and her family. There is evidence to suggest that Princess Ta-i used her influence in Turkic ruling circles to plot against the Sui dynasty. In 593, a defector from the Turk's camp claimed that she was seeking to ally with Liu Ch'ang, the duke of the state of P'eng, to overthrow the Sui.[30] A passage in the *Sui shu* also informs us that after her husband Ishbara died in 587, she was accepted as the wife of Tu-lan Khan (r. 588–600) and "caused several border disasters."[31]

Princess Ta-i was a threat to the Sui, and when the Sui envoy Chang-sun Sheng informed the emperor that as she conversed with him "her manner and words were not polite," the emperor ordered Chang-sun to kill her.[32] Ever the adept politician, Chang-sun manipulated the Turks to secure her demise. At this time, two rival Turks were both petitioning the Sui court for intermarriage. The court determined that Jan-kan (also known as Tölis Khan), a son of Ishbara, had few troops, little power, and would be easy to pacify and train. Chang-sun Sheng suggested that the other Turk, Yung-lü "vacillates and is unfaithful," and "if he becomes more powerful, it will be difficult to deal with him later."[33] Consequently, the Sui did not offer a princess to Yung-lü to marry, but sent an emissary to Jan-kan with the following message: "Unless he first killed Princess Ta-i, the marriage could not be promised." As a result, Jan-kan slandered the princess in front of her husband Tu-lan Khan. Tu-lan grew angry and killed the princess in her camp.[34] A second explanation for Ta-i's death suggests that Tu-lan Khan simply responded to a request made by an envoy specifically sent by Sui Wen-ti that she be executed.[35]

Princess Ch'ien-chin, later to become Princess Ta-i, was wife to three nomadic rulers. She became a pawn in Northern Chou politics, but rose in stature among the Turks to challenge the Sui emperor who had destroyed the Northern Chou state and her family. Ultimately, the Sui ruler ordered that Ch'ien-chin be killed. As suggested by the following poem written by her in 589, she lived a life full of tragedy and despair:

> Rise and fall like the dawn and night,
> The way of the world is rootless as the duckweed,
> Glory and splendor are difficult to preserve,
> Ponds and chambers will be leveled.
> At present, where is wealth and honor?
> Aimlessly exhausting [myself] in painting.
> Wine and drink never provide happiness,
> How can music and song produce the melody?

> Originally I was a child of the Royal Household,
> [Now] darting around the camp of barbarians.
> Seeing both success and failure,
> The emotion in [my] heart is unrestrained.
> It's the same from the ancient times.
> I am not alone in my complaint.
> The feeling of a far-married woman was
> Described by the song of Ming-chün.[36]

As a postscript to the tragic story of Princess Ch'ien-chen, it is worth noting that the Sui court's promise of an imperial princess for Jan-kan proved efficacious. Jan-kan, the Turk who slandered the princess and caused her death, ultimately became Ch'i-min Khan or I-chen-tou Khan, also known as Tölis Khan, and reigned over the Turks from 599 to 609. As suggested in chapter one, he was extremely loyal to the Sui. Ch'i-min Khan was first given a princess of the imperial household named An-i as a wife. The Sui emperor ordered that he also be presented with lavish gifts to promote dissension among the Turks.[37] The favor shown to Ch'i-min Khan led his rival, Yung-lü, to rebel and plunder the frontier, but Ch'i-min Khan agreed to move his people south to live at the old Chinese garrison of Tu-chin. From that vantage point, he watched the movements of Yung-lü and other Turks and reported them to the Sui who could then take effective countermeasures against them.[38]

Princess An-i died before the reign of Ch'i-min Khan was completed, and, as a consequence, the court offered I-Ch'eng, another princess of the imperial household, to him in marriage. Princess I-Ch'eng suffered a fate similar to that of Princess Ch'ien-chin. When Ch'i-min Khan died, his son Ch'o-chi-shih became Shih-pi Khan and petitioned to marry Princess I-Ch'eng. It was the custom, because of the exogamous clan-to-clan marriage traditions among the nomads, for a son to marry his father's wife, yet, judged by Confucian moral values, this was regarded as "bestial." However, to further the objectives of the Sui court, I-Ch'eng was forced to adhere to nomadic customs and become the wife of Shih-pi Khan. I-Ch'eng outlived Shih-pi Khan and also became the wife of Ch'o-lo Khan and finally of Il Khan. While among the Turks, she witnessed the fall of her beloved Sui dynasty and the rise of the T'ang. Like Princess Ch'ien-chin she was drawn into the internal struggles in China. I-Ch'eng tried to persuade the Turks to support her blood relative, Yang Cheng-tao,[39] as he sought to restore the Sui dynasty. When, in 630, the T'ang defeated and captured Il Khan, Princess I-Ch'eng was killed by T'ang soldiers.[40]

An analysis of the interaction between nomadic and agrarian courts from the Northern Wei through the Sui dynastic periods suggests that although nomadic rulers frequently sought to initiate intermarriage ties with agrarian courts, their requests were generally accepted only when nomadic states posed a serious threat to an agrarian state or were viewed as a possible ally that might help one sedentary court as it struggled against another. Royal marriage with the Jou-jan or the Turks was encouraged for military or diplomatic advantage. The money and gifts offered the nomads reflected the price an agricultural state was willing to pay to achieve its political aims. As suggested by the carefully considered response of the Turkic khan Ssu-chin to the requests of both Northern Ch'i and Northern Chou to marry his daughter, nomadic rulers also carefully ascertained what advantages might accrue from forming marital ties with agrarian courts.

Unlike the Sui, the T'ang dynasty was slow to intermarry with the Turks. In the "Table of Princesses" in the *Hsin T'ang shu*, there is only one entry that records the marriage of a Chinese princess to a Turk during the early T'ang. This marriage was between the daughter of Emperor Kao-tsu and a member of the Turkic Khan's household, A-shih-na Tu-erh. However, A-shih-na Tu-erh left his people and identified himself with the T'ang court before the intermarriage occurred, so it is likely that the marriage was more a personal one or one undertaken to assure his loyalty to the T'ang court rather than one orchestrated to improve T'ang-Turkic relations.[41]

Eventually, two officials, Feng Lun and P'ei Chü, emerged to formulate T'ang intermarriage policy: "The evil hearts of Feng Lun and P'ei Chü were bad enough to destroy the Sui, but they were knowledgeable enough to support the T'ang."[42] Feng Lun and P'ei Chü tired of the meddling of the Eastern Turks in early T'ang politics. As suggested in chapters one and two, as the T'ang dynasty struggled for power, the Eastern Turkic rulers Shih-pi Khan, Ch'o-lo Khan, and Il-Khan promoted unrest in China by supporting dissenting generals and others opposed to the founding of a T'ang state. Feng Lun attempted to persuade Emperor Kao-tsu to reject intermarriage ties with the meddling Eastern Turks and intermarry with the Western Turks instead: "At present, the important matter is to establish distant allies and to attack the [enemy] in our vicinity."[43] As suggested by the following statement, P'ei Chü also supported this policy: "After the [Eastern] Turks had encroached over the border several times, Emperor Kao-tsu joined in an alliance with the Western Turks. Consequently, the [Western] Turks petitioned for marriage. The emperor said: 'Their location is too distant from us. They may be of no use in a time of need. What shall we do?' [P'ei] Chü said, 'The northern barbarians [Eastern Turks], having enhanced their power, are disturbing the border every year. If we temporarily promise them [intermarriage], [we] can show [to the Eastern Turks] that we have aid from the outside. . . . ' "[44]

Following the advice of P'ei Chü and Feng Lun, T'ang Kao-tsu promised intermarriage to the Western Turkic leader T'ung-yeh-hu (r. 618–630), but "just then Il Khan [of the Eastern Turks] invaded and the route to the western barbarians was cut off. Consequently, the marriage agreement was not carried out. . . . "[45] Subsequently, the Eastern Turk leader, Il Khan, was defeated by the T'ang in 630, and taken to the T'ang court. The Sui princess I-Ch'eng was immediately killed. After the death of Il Khan, when the Western Turk Khan, Sha-po-lo Tieh-li-shih, requested intermarriage in 635, he was "warmly and politely soothed" but not granted a marriage agreement.[46] One might conjecture that having defeated Il-Khan of the Eastern Turks, the T'ang no longer felt it imperative to link themselves to the distant Western Turks through intermarriage.

The power of the Eastern Turks under Mo-ch'o (r. 691–716) quickly revived, posing a threat to the T'ang. In 698, Mo-ch'o demanded that the T'ang return to him the *Shan-yü* Protectory, located in the old Turkic territory of the great loop of the Yellow river, and hundreds of Turkic households which had surrendered to the T'ang during the middle of the Hsien-heng period (670–673) and had been allowed to settle in the six regions along the Chinese frontier. He also petitioned to be made a son of Empress Wu (Tse-t'ien, r. 684–704) by being allowed to marry his daughter to a member of the imperial family.

At first, the T'ang court rejected his demands. "Mo-ch'o, greatly indignant, used impolite and proud words, arrested our [the T'ang] envoy, . . . and threatened to kill him."[47] The T'ang relented and drove the surrendered Turk households away from the frontier, gave Mo-ch'o the forty thousand *shuo*[48] of seeds and the three thousand farm tools which he had requested, and sent Wu Yen-hsiu,[49] the Prince of Huai-yang, the son of the Prince of Wei, to go to the Turks to accept the daughter of the Turkic khan. Prince Wu was accompanied by a large entourage carrying "gold and silk in great quantity to the barbarian headquarters."[50]

Through the use of force, the khan coerced the T'ang court to capitulate. But, when Prince Wu arrived, Mo-ch'o rejected him as a candidate to marry his daughter with the following speech: "I wished to marry my daughter to the son of the Son of Heaven of the Li family, and now you bring the son of the Wu family. Is this the son of the Son of Heaven? We, the Turks, have been subjugated for several generations. Now I heard the seeds of the Son of Heaven of the Li family have not yet been entirely exterminated. Now I am going to move my troops to help them!"[51]

Mo-ch'o raised the banner of revolt against Empress Wu who, as a concubine of both T'ang T'ai-tsung and his son Kao-tsung, elevated herself to the position of widowed mother-empress and ultimately adopted the title of emperor, thereby threatening to end the T'ang dynasty established in the name of the Li family. In 660, as Kao-tsung's health began to fail, Empress Wu secured informal regental power, and, in 690, after Kao-tsung's death, she deposed her son from the throne and assumed the title of emperor, the only woman in Chinese history who formally bore the title. She then established the Chou dynasty and ruled until 705.[52] Despite the offer by Empress Wu to intermarry with the Turks, Mo-ch'o held Prince Wu captive and used his supposed loyalty to the deposed Li family to justify attacking Empress Wu's regime and win sympathy from the Chinese who remained loyal to the original imperial household. This kind of political maneuver by a nomadic ruler toward a Chinese court is rare.

Mo-ch'o first requested intermarriage with the court of Empress Wu in 698. After rejecting Prince Wu Yen-hsiu, he made a second request in 703. Despite Empress Wu's willingness to discuss intermarriage and bestow on the Turks numerous gifts, Mo-ch'o again invaded the frontiers of China. The *Chiu T'ang shu* informs us that: "the Government troops were defeated and six thousand soldiers were killed. Then the bandits proceeded to invade Hui-chou and other countries. [They] looted more than ten thousand horses from the herds on the right side of Kansu and departed. . . . "[53]

Contradictory materials in T'ang sources make it difficult to determine how successful subsequent T'ang rulers were in creating effective intermarriage policies with the Turks. A passage in the *Hsin T'ang shu*, in which Mo-chi-lien, the Turk ruler Bilge Khan, and the envoy of the T'ang Emperor, Yüan Chen, discuss intermarriage suggests that these efforts frequently failed. Bilge Khan had earlier invaded the T'ang border, after which he asked for peace and proclaimed his willingness to honor the Son of Heaven as father. Bilge Khan was allowed to present tribute, after which he asked the T'ang court to form an intermarriage arrangement with him. As will be shown in the following passage, Yüan Chen used Bilge Khan's recognition of the T'ang emperor as his father to justify T'ang unwillingness to form intermarriage ties with the Turks:

> [The Khan] spoke to [Yüan] Chen and said, "The Tibetans are the seeds of dogs and they intermarried with the T'ang. The Hsi and the Khitans are my slaves and princesses were also given to them to marry. But why have the Turks, after asking so many times, always been rejected?" [Yüan] Chen replied, "[You] the Khan are the son of the Son of Heaven. Is it possible [to give his own daughter] to marry his own son?" Mo-chi-lien said, "No, these two barbarians were also given the (Imperial) family name, but even so they still received princesses to marry. Then why [in my case] is this impossible? Moreover, the princess is not the daughter of the Emperor. Of course, I dare not select [the true one], however, we have asked for marriage so many times but all were rejected. We are ridiculed by other countries." [Yüan] Chen agreed to petition for him.[54]

Bilge Khan criticized T'ang intermarriage policies because they favored Tibet, the Khitan, and the Hsi and because they hid behind the fiction that the princesses sent to marry Turkic rulers were truly daughters of the T'ang emperor himself. Because they were not, there would be no problem of incestuous relationships.

A letter presented to Bilge Khan by the T'ang emperor in 721 presents a contradictory appraisal of the success of previous T'ang-Turk intermarriage arrangements. "Formerly [our] country and the Turks were engaged in peace and intermarriage, [therefore] both the Chinese and the barbarians enjoyed peace and the armies had their rest. [Our] country bought sheep and horses from the Turks, and the Turks accepted silk and cloth from our country. Both sides were richly and fully supplied."[55]

Bilge Khan lived during the reign of the Emperor Hsüan-tsung which was a relatively peaceful period in T'ang-Eastern Turk interaction. However, this did not prevent the T'ang from developing intermarriage ties with the Khitan, Hsi, and other nomadic groups as a counterbalance to Turkic power north of China. The Khitan and the Hsi were precariously positioned between the more dominant T'ang and Turkic powers, which forced them to adopt a fluid policy for dealing with their neighbors. To the T'ang, neither the Khitan or the Hsi posed the same threat as the Turks, and, consequently, when intermarriage ties were formed, the T'ang sent daughters of imperial relatives and less important court families to marry with these nomadic leaders. Dowries and bestowals provided the Khitan and the Hsi were also smaller.[56]

Because the Tibetans were mentioned by Bilge Khan in his criticism of T'ang intermarriage policies, a brief digression away from our discussion of the Turkic and Mongolian peoples who are the chief focus of this study seems appropriate. The partly nomadic, partly agricultural Tibetans on the western frontiers of China were a serious threat to the T'ang. Consequently, the T'ang court established marriage ties with the kings of Tibet. The Hsin T'ang shu informs us that as early as 632 the "first great Tibetan emperor"[57] Songtsan-gambo (d. 650), began sending envoys to T'ang China. He had heard that leaders of the Turks as well as his rivals, to dominate the Kökönor area, the T'u-yü-hun,[58] were being given T'ang princesses to marry. As a result, he sent an envoy with presents to the T'ang court to propose an intermarriage arrangement with China. When his request was refused, Songtsan-gambo attacked the T'u-yü-hun and invaded Sung-chou (present-day Sung-p'an, Szechwan). After his attacks, he again sent an envoy to present gifts to the T'ang and announce that he was willing to receive a T'ang princess. He told his followers that: "If the princess does not come, I will launch a further invasion."[59] The T'ang relented and, in 641, sent Princess Wen-ch'eng, a daughter of the imperial household, to Songtsan-gambo together with five thousand taels of gold and other precious gifts.

Clearly this first Tibetan-T'ang marriage agreement was imposed on the Chinese by the Tibetan king. Interestingly, the Tibetan king allowed himself to be greatly influenced by this Chinese bride sent to his court. He built a city for the princess; he forsook all woolen materials and began to use silk garments, imitating the style of the Middle Kingdom; and he sent the sons and younger brothers of Tibetan dignitaries to China to study poetry and the classics. He also invited T'ang scholars to Tibet. The peace secured by the marriage of Princess Wen-ch'eng to Songtsan-gambo lasted until the deaths of T'ang T'ai-tsung in 649 and the Tibetan king the following year.[60]

A second effort to develop intermarriage ties with the T'ang was initiated shortly after Tibet successfully defeated T'ang forces in 696 on the borders of T'ao-chou. At the time, T'ang forces faced military threats not only from Tibet but also from the Eastern Turks and Khitan. The T'ang made an intermarriage agreement with Tibet contingent on the Tibetan return of the Kökönor region and the T'u-yü-hun to China. T'ang peace proposals sowed seeds of discord among the Tibetans because the proposals appealed to one faction at court but were rejected by another. Ultimately, the T'ang court abandoned the Tibetan initiative and agreed to a political marriage with the Eastern Turks rather than with Tibet.[61]

The decade following this failed initiative was a chaotic one for Tibet, culminating in a power struggle at court after the death of the Tibetan king in 704 and the emergence of the ruler Khridesungtsan (r. 704–755).

In China, the year 705 witnessed the restoration of the Li family to the T'ang throne on the death of Empress Wu. These internal developments proved propitious to the creation of a new intermarriage arrangement. As early as 707, the Chinese had decided to conclude a marriage agreement with Tibet, and in 710 a young princess was sent to the Tibetan court.[62]

The princess was Chin-ch'eng, the daughter of Prince Yung (Li Shou-li) of the imperial household. This princess left for Tibet with a huge entourage, including an important general, a band of musicians who could play the music of Kuei-tzu (present Ku-ch'e, Sinkiang), and numerous craftsmen. Before she departed, the T'ang emperor bestowed on her "several tens of thousands of rolls of silk," pardoned the criminals and convicted murderers in Shih-p'ing district, exempted the people of the district from paying rent or taxes for a full year, and renamed the district Chin-ch'eng in her honor.[63]

This new intermarriage alliance did not stop hostilities along Tibetan-Chinese frontiers. A few months after Chin-ch'eng arrived in Tibet, Chinese armies invaded and plundered northern Tibet. The Tibetans were indignant that T'ang forces had committed such a faithless act. They demanded and received compensation from the T'ang court for these deeds. However, after the marriage, Tibetan armies were also guilty of raiding areas in present-day Kansu. In response, the T'ang emperor sent an envoy to the Tibetan court asking Chin-ch'eng to intercede and bring hostilities to an end. Her intercession led the Tibetan king to apologize to the T'ang court. He claimed that he had been led astray by his border generals and pledged in the future not to forget the special relationship between China and Tibet created by the marriages of Princess Wen-ch'eng and Princess Chin-ch'eng to Tibetan kings.[64]

Intermarriages between T'ang and Tibetan courts did not bring a complete end to the conflicts between the two. Tibet continued to pose a serious threat to China where Tibet's eastern and China's western frontiers collided or to T'ang China's more distant interests along the silk routes in Central Eurasia. Moreover, the mid-eighth century rebellion of An Lu-shan and Shih Ssu-ming also seriously challenged T'ang power. Internal unrest coupled with Tibetan and other external challenges to the T'ang dynasty led the Chinese court, as early as 756, to form intermarriage ties with the Uighurs who had replaced the Turks as the major nomadic power outside China. The T'ang hoped to utilize Uighur troops as mercenaries to confront rebels inside China and help to check Tibetan aggression in the west.

The first proposal for intermarriage between the T'ang and Uighur courts was initiated in 756–757 by the Uighur khan Ko-le. Ko-le Khan informed the T'ang that he wished to marry his daughter to a member of the T'ang imperial household. The T'ang agreed and prepared the son of Prince Pin, Li Ch'eng-ts'ai, who had earlier been sent by the Emperor Su-tsung as ambassador to the Uighurs, for the ceremony. Reminiscent of the Chinese practice of elevating a royal relative or lesser member of the imperial household to the status of princess and then marrying her to a nomadic chieftain, Ko-le Khan "appointed the younger sister of the *Khatun* as his [nominal] daughter so she could marry Ch'eng-ts'ai. . . . "[65]

The successful intermarriage of this T'ang prince and Uighur princess led Ko-le Khan to commit more than four thousand cavalry troops to help the T'ang suppress internal rebellion.[66] It also led to one of the most important events in the Sino-nomadic history of intermarriage. In 758, Ko-le Khan personally asked to marry a daughter of the T'ang emperor Su-tsung. It is clear that the T'ang emperor was reluctant to send his own daughter to the Uighur Khan. However, Su-tsung knew that sending someone other than his own daughter to marry Ko-le Khan would antagonize the Uighur ruler and invite a Uighur attack. In addition, the T'ang would lose Uighur support against internal rebellion and the threat posed by Tibet. Faced with few other options, the emperor conferred on his youngest daughter the title of Princess Ning-kuo and prepared her to travel north to marry Ko-le Khan.[67]

The marriage of Princess Ning-kuo to Ko-le Khan provides an excellent means to explore the Chinese-nomadic institution of intermarriage. One is first impressed by the seriousness with which both courts prepared for the marriage ceremony. Emperor Su-tsung designated a number of key court officials to participate. Li Yü, the Prince of Han-chung,[68] was appointed the ambassador to confer the title of *Ying-wu wei-yüan Bilge Khan* on Ko-le Khan. The imperial nephew, Li Hsün, was appointed the vice-ambassador and the director of the marriage ceremony. The emperor personally accompanied Princess Ning-kuo to the Tz'u-men station of Hsien-yang, and charged his prime minister, P'ei Mein,[69] to journey to the border with the princess. The carefully orchestrated acceptance of the T'ang marriage entourage by the Uighurs also suggests elaborate preparations and attention to ceremonial details.

It is clear that this was an intermarriage arrangement in which both the Uighur and the T'ang recognized the basic equality of the two powers. This is particularly evident in a passage in the *Chiu T'ang shu*, recording the initial interaction between Li Yü and Ko-le Khan. When Li Yü arrived at the royal tent of the Uighur leader to confer on him by imperial decree the title of *Ying-wu wei-yüan Bilge Khan,* the Khan asked him what relation he was to the T'ang Emperor. He replied: "The cousin of the Son of Heaven of T'ang."[70] "[The Khan] again asked, 'Who is the one standing in front of you?' Yü replied, 'The eunuch Lei Lu-chün.' The Khan then said, 'The eunuch is a slave. How dare [he] stand before you!' Lei Lu-chün, very frightened, jumped backward and stood there."[71] Having made apparent how important it is that one recognize his proper station in life, Ko-le Khan confronted Li Yü with a question suggesting that the Uighur state was superior to that of the T'ang by asking: "There is the ritual between the lords and vassals of the two countries. Why do [you] not bow?"[72] Li Yü presented the same argument offered to the Turk Khan Ishbara when the Princess Ta-i was given to him as a wife. He admitted that formerly the Middle Kingdom presented daughters of members of the royal family who were given the titles of princess and adopted as daughters of a Chinese emperor to marry nomadic rulers. However, Princess Ning-kuo was actually a true daughter of the Emperor Su-tsung. "[She] is talented and beautiful and comes here from ten thousand *li* [away] to marry the Khan."[73] Li Yü reaffirmed that Ko-le Khan was a son-in-law of the Son of Heaven. It is Ko-le Khan who, rather than sitting to receive the imperial decree from the T'ang emperor, should stand and show his respect to his father-in-law. As was the case with Ishbara, Ko-le Khan relented and stood to receive his new title.

Throughout the T'ang period, intermarriage gave the Chinese court additional leverage when interacting with nomadic groups. Emperor Hsien-tsung (r. 806–820) pointed out that princesses were given in marriage to the Uighurs because "the northern barbarians [Uighurs] were meritorious to the Court, whereas the western barbarians [Tibetans] disturbed the border."[74] Princess Ning-kuo courageously consented to marry Ko-le Khan, even though she was still a young girl and he was an old man. As she left her father at Tz'u-men station to journey to the Uighur camp, the *Chiu T'ang shu* suggests that while she wept she told her father: "State affairs are important. Even though [I] die, [I] shall not regret [this]!"[75] Princess Ning-kuo's resolve was clearly tested for during the second year of their marriage, in 759, Ko-le Khan died. Princess Ning-kuo was then asked to follow Uighur custom and commit suicide.[76] Ning-kuo responded by saying:

According to the ritual of our Middle Kingdom, after the death of the husband [the wife] should remain in bereavement, to weep both morning and evening at the place [where his name tablet is arranged] for three years. Now the Uighur took a wife [from the Middle Kingdom] and therefore [you] should follow the way of the Middle Kingdom with admiration. If [you] insist on following your own way, why should [we] engage in marriage [with a country] ten thousand li away?[77]

Though Princess Ning-kuo avoided committing suicide, she did follow the Uighur tradition of cutting and disfiguring her face. However, because she had not given birth to a son and was the daughter of the T'ang emperor, she was ultimately allowed to return to China.

The fate of another T'ang princess married to Ko-le Khan was not so fortuitous. At the time Princess Ning-kuo was sent to marry the Uighur Khan, the Emperor Su-tsung also sent the daughter of Prince Jung as a concubine for Ko-le Khan.[78] She was given the title Little Princess Ning-kuo and was presented as an extra gift by the T'ang in recognition of the importance of the occasion. When Ko-le Khan died, she was not allowed to return to China, but following Uighur custom, she was taken as a minor *khatun* by the old khan's successor, Teng-li-muo-yü Khan. She gave birth to two sons, but both were killed in a Uighur court power struggle. Finally, in 791, she died while still among the Uighur.[79]

The marriage of the Princess Ning-kuo and the Little Princess Ning-kuo led to a period of active intermarriage between the Uighur and T'ang courts. Through the study of subsequent marriages between these two dynasties, it is possible to clarify the nature of the marriage ceremony and the level of gift exchange which occurred. While Ko-le Khan was still alive, he requested that a T'ang princess be provided for his second son, the future Teng-li-muo-yü Khan. However, the T'ang court relied on the close relationship that had developed between the Uighur Crown Prince Yabkhu and the Chinese heir-apparent, Prince Kuang-p'ing, as the cornerstone of their foreign policy.[80] As a consequence, they slighted the second son by not offering him a princess of the imperial household but rather the daughter of Pu-ku Huai-en, a vassal of Turkic origin as a wife.[81] T'ang plans to promote close Sino-Uighur relations through Prince Yabkhu were dashed when Ko-le Khan accused him of a criminal offense and killed him.

In 759, the slighted second son succeeded Ko-le Khan as Teng-li-muo-yü Khan. T'ang policies now had to adjust to this dramatic change in Uighur politics. When it became apparent that Teng-li-muo-yü Khan might support the rebellion of 762–763 of Shih Ch'ao-i against the T'ang, the T'ang sent Teng's father-in-law, Pu-ku Huai-en to admonish him not to break with the court. A short time later, in 768, when his first wife died, the T'ang offered a younger daughter of Pu-ku Huai-en to the Uighur khan and bestowed on him twenty thousand rolls of designed silk. The account of this event in the *Hsin T'ang shu* suggests that at this time the finances of the state were exhausted and the mission to present the future bride to Teng-li-muo-yü Khan traveled to the Uighur camp only by conscripting the horses and camels of ministers and officials.[82]

Gift exchange at the time of intermarriage was tantamount to trade. The Uighur court received valued goods that it could, in turn, bestow on those loyal to it. After receiving substantial gifts in the form of a dowry and bestowals from the T'ang court, Ko-le Khan presented "embroideries, silk, cloth, gold, silver, and instruments to his officials and chieftains." In the exchange, the Uighur presented to the Chinese court "five hundred horses and one hundred sable fur coats. . ." as gifts and as a "bride price" or presents for engagement.[83] Both the horses and the sable coats were highly sought after by the Chinese.

The level of Uighur-T'ang gift exchange offered during intermarriage increased from this period. In 787, the Uighur Alp Küchlüg Bilge Khan dispatched an envoy to present tribute and petition for intermarriage. Emperor Te-tsung (r. 780–804) promised the Chinese Princess Hsien-an to the khan. The envoy was summoned to an audience and presented a portrait of the princess to show the Uighur leader. In addition, the T'ang allowed that border markets be established and gave fifty thousand rolls of silk to the Uighurs in recognition for the horses presented.[84] In 788, Alp Küchlüg Bilge Khan sent a princess to the capital of the T'ang accompanied by more than one thousand persons. He presented two thousand horses to the T'ang and he and his envoys were granted rich bestowals in return.[85]

In 821–822 the number of envoys and amount of goods involved in court-to-court exchanges were even higher. When the Uighurs came for Princess T'ai-ho, Bilge Ch'ung-te Khan sent two thousand troops to escort her. The T'ang allowed five hundred persons to cross the frontier and proceed to Ch'ang-an while the rest remained at T'ai-yüan. The Uighur Khan's mission presented the T'ang twenty thousand horses and one thousand camels.[86] Although there is no record of the Chinese gifts presented in return, each envoy that arrived at the capital undoubtedly received a rich bestowal and those who remained at the frontier were regarded as emissaries of the Uighur khan and allowed to enrich themselves through trade. Tradition dictated that the value of Chinese goods presented to the nomads should exceed the value of the offerings made by the nomads to the court.

The best record of the marriage ceremony itself concerns the marriage in 822 of the Uighur ruler Bilge Ch'ung-te Khan to the Chinese princess T'ai-ho. Princess T'ai-ho was the daughter of the deceased Emperor Hsien-tsung. Before she departed, as was the custom, the T'ang emperor Mu-tsung (r. 821–824) conferred on the princess important titles. On the day she left, he and other high officials accompanied Princess T'ai-ho to the T'ung-hua gate where " . . . all the officials were formally lined up . . . the ceremonial guards were splendid and the whole population of the Capital came to watch [the procession]."[87] The minister of the interior, who was also designated the great general of the left imperial guard, Hu Cheng,[88] was to represent her and be the T'ang ambassador at the Uighur camp.

When the court procession was about one hundred *li* or two nights' journey from the Uighur camp, the khan demanded a private visit with the princess before the formal marriage ceremony was conducted. Hu Cheng would not allow this. After the arrival of the princess, an auspicious day was selected for the khan to confer on the princess the title of *Khatun* of the Uighur, symbolizing the completion of the marriage.[89] There follows an account of the event:

> [On that day] the Khan ascended the chamber first and sat facing the east. A woolen yurt was set up under the chamber to accommodate the Princess where the barbarian princesses taught her barbarian etiquette. Then the Princess took off T'ang clothing and wore the barbarian costume. One elderly woman who served her [had her] come to the front of the chamber to bow towards the west. The Khan was sitting and looked on the Princess. [She] bowed again, then entered the woolen yurt to take off the costume she had worn and put on the dress of *Khatun*. It was a long skirt and a large robe light red in color with a golden decorated hat like a horn pointing forward. Coming out again from the chamber [she] bowed to the Khan as in the earlier ceremony. The barbarians prepared a large sedan chariot with curved windows and a small seat in the front. The usher guided the Princess to ascend the sedan chair. The ministers of the nine clans of the Uighurs carried the sedan chair in turn and following the direction of the sun turned towards the right [clockwise] nine times in the courtyard. The Princess then descended from the chariot and ascended the chamber to sit together with the Khan, both facing the east. The ministers and officials then began to pay their respects to the court audience and at the same time bowed to the *Khatun*. The *Khatun* also had her own court with two ministers to serve [her] there. When [Hu] Cheng was prepared to

return, the *Khatun* gave [him] a banquet in the court camp. She felt lonesome and wept for a whole day. . . . [90]

The Sung and Southern Sung courts did not rely on intermarriage as had the T'ang and Sui dynasties. In lieu of providing coveted Chinese goods to hostile neighbors through the vehicle of dowries and marriage gifts, the Sung offered huge yearly payments, *sui-pi,* to the Tangut, Khitan, and Jurchen people along their frontiers. However, in 1126, when the Jurchen Chin occupied the Sung capital of Pien-liang, present K'ai-feng, and captured the Sung emperors Hui-tsung (r. 1101–1125) and Ch'in-tsung (r. 1126–1127), bringing an end to the Northern Sung dynasty, many young women of the imperial household were forced to marry Jurchen notables. The "Biography of the Princesses" in the *Sung shih* records that "Hui-tsung had thirty-four daughters. . . . Fourteen of them died young and the rest were all brought to the north."[91] A graphic account of the fate of the Sung imperial household is presented in the *Chin shih:*

> The two commoners [of the Sung, former Emperor Hui-tsung and his son Emperor Ch'in-tsung] . . . were presented [to the Court]. [The Chin emperor] bestowed [the title of] Hun-te *Kung* [Duke of Stupid Virtue] to the father and [the title of] Ch'ung-hun *Hou* [the Marquis of Double Stupidity] to his son. . . . On the *kui-yu* day . . . of the sixth month . . . of the eighth year [1134] . . . the Imperial Decree ordered the six daughters of the *Hun-te Kung* to be the wives of members of the Imperial Household.[92]

After achieving victory, the Jurchen forced the daughters of vanquished Sung leaders to marry them. However, these captive daughters had no official relations with the court of the Southern Sung, which continued to rely on yearly payments rather than intermarriage as a means to promote stability along its frontiers.

The Tangut Hsia and Jurchen Chin dynasties who dominated northern China after the fall of the Sung soon found themselves facing a serious threat posed by growing Mongolian strength. Royal marriages between the Hsia and Chin courts and the Mongols led by Chinggis Khan occurred, but only when the Mongols were about to subdue or had already defeated the Hsia or Chin enemy. The status granted to these princesses by the Mongolian court was much less than that given Chinese princesses during earlier periods. There was no notion of in-law relations between the Mongols and these courts. Intermarriage with the Mongols was imposed on the Chinese as a condition for peace and the relationship between the

Mongols and the Chin or Hsia was simply that between conqueror and conquered. Although the offering of a bride to the Mongolian khan often led to the withdrawal of Mongolian armies, the most plausible argument for the retiring of these troops is that they had secured all the booty they could carry back to Mongolia rather than a sought after princess.[93] This is suggested by several documents referred to in the previous footnote, but especially evident in one found in *The Secret History of the Mongols*:

> [The Jurchen] Prime Minister Ong-jing[94] persuaded the Khan of Chin saying, "the Mandate of Heaven and Earth designate that it is the time to transfer the Great Throne. The Mongols come with tremendous power. . . . If [you] the Khan of Chin agree, we will negotiate surrender to the Mongolian Khan. . . . " [They] surrendered, presented a daughter with the title of Princess to Chinggis Khan, and brought gold, silver, and silk cloth from Jungdu [Chung-tu] to [our] soldiers to have them take as much as their strength could carry. Since [they] surrendered, Chinggis Khan therefore accepted their proposal, withdrew the forces that had conquered the cities one by one and returned. . . . Our soldiers took as much silk cloth as they could carry.[95]

There is little doubt that the booty secured through the peace treaty was as important an inducement for the Mongolian withdrawal as receipt of a daughter of the imperial family with the title of princess.

Intermarriage was an effective and relatively inexpensive tool utilized by some agrarian courts in their relations with nomadic leaders, but officials still debated the relative strengths and weaknesses of these policies throughout Chinese history. Those critical of intermarriage were unwilling to ignore the terrible human cost exacted through this institution. The author of the *Hsin T'ang shu* angrily addresses this question when he states:

> The virtuous young girls of the Imperial Family became the minor wives in the yurts. The nice people were sent to [marry in] the desert. . . . The ones who bore the titles of the daughter of the Emperor were not distinguished from the barbarian women, to be taken as wives by their sons and to follow their bad customs. The reason that the Middle Kingdom is different than the barbarian people is only that [we] recognize the distinction between father and son and man and woman. Such beautiful, charming ladies were destroyed by the foreigners. This was extremely disgraceful; however, the rulers and the vassals of the Han were not ashamed![96]

Li Chiang, the Minister of Rituals in the court of Emperor Te-tsung during the T'ang period, presented the following argument in support of intermarriage. He suggested that those who criticize intermarriage fail to recognize that although the costs of intermarriage seem high, perhaps as great as the entire annual income from one prefecture, they are minimal when compared to the expenses encountered through warfare:

> "If we use the tax of one prefecture as the expenditure for [inter]marriage, is [it] not that [we] spend less but achieve more? But if [we] are stingy in the marriage expenditure and refuse to give [a princess in marriage] and mobilize the Imperial forces to carry out a northern campaign with at least thirty thousand troops and five thousand cavalries, [we] cannot defend or attack. If [we] try to win a complete victory, then in only one year [we] will be exhausted because of the military and food supplies. Can that be matched by the tax of one prefecture?"[97]

Li Chiang, as had numerous officials before him, recognized that war was an extremely costly and ineffective way to bring stability to China's northern frontiers. Intermarriage, bestowals, yearly payments, and frontier markets, though costly, provided a better means of obtaining peace with the nomadic peoples by delivering to them the textiles, foods, and other goods they needed.

VI

CONFLICT OR CALM

For a period of two thousand years, trade was the chief determinant of peace and war between the nomadic and Chinese peoples along China's northern borders. The nomadic peoples were dependent on a few key products produced by the agriculturalist Chinese, particularly grain and cloth. When they were able to peacefully obtain these goods through the mechanisms of trade, bestowals, or court-to-court intermarriage arrangements, stability along China's frontiers was possible, but when they were denied ready access to these essential commodities, war was almost a certainty.

About 200 B.C., the Hsiung-nu and Han Chinese successfully developed marketing, bestowal, and intermarriage institutions which insured the flow of necessary goods from sedentarist to nomad and negated the need for conflict, yet the Han and subsequent Chinese dynastic rulers and nomadic leaders north of China often abandoned these mechanisms, and war ensued. Why were these institutions that promoted peace so frequently cast aside?

This concluding chapter will first examine the importance of trade to the nomads by chronicling the wide range of goods that they traded to secure immense quantities of silk, grain, and other essential commodities from China. Inasmuch as trade was necessary to maintain peace between the Chinese and the steppe nomads, the last part of this chapter will explore three factors which undermined marketing, bestowal, and intermarriage institutions, and, as a consequence, increased the chances of war. They are: (1) the prejudice and mistrust felt by nomad and also sedentarist toward the other; (2) the ineffectiveness of Chinese dynasties in implementing frontier trading policies and regulating unscrupulous frontier officials; and (3) the chaotic nature of the frontier, rife with unsavory characters and illicit trading activities.

The Chinese historian Ssu-ma Ch'ien described the nomadic lifestyle of the Hsiung-nu: "They follow [their] herds and move. Their domestic animals are mainly horses, cattle, and sheep. Their rare livestock includes camels, donkeys, and mules. . . . They are forever moving about, following the waters and grazing fields. They have no cities, houses or farming lands. . . . As is their custom while there is peace, they herd their flocks and hunt game for a livelihood."[1]

The goods exchanged by nomadic peoples with China were derived from this herding and hunting livelihood and sometimes through trade with more distant people. In the "Monograph on Economy" in the *Shih chi*, Ssu-ma Ch'ien notes that "in the north there are multitudes of horses, cattle, sheep, wool and fur, tendons and horns, and copper and iron."[2] As evidenced by the following passage, it is clear that prior to the Han period, at least in some regions along the frontier, trade was extensive and the nomadic peoples offered the animals they herded for treasured Chinese goods:

> Lo of the Wu-shih, when his livestock increased, sold them in exchange for excellent silk cloth; and, from time to time, he presented [this silk] to the king of the Jung [the barbarians]. The barbarian king multiplied the price to ten times and paid him in animals. Consequently, [Lo] measured his cattle and horses with the [number] of the mountain valleys [where he placed his herds]. The First Emperor of the Ch'in [Shih Huang-ti] made Lo's [position] almost equal to a feudal lord, and commanded him to visit the Court together with the Court officials.[3]

Lo was a man living along the borders of China who became extremely wealthy trading valued silk cloth to nomadic people at ten times its worth for "valleys" of livestock. Although this trade may have been conducted outside a government-regulated market system,[4] Lo was honored and treated almost as a feudal lord by the Ch'in Emperor.

In addition to cattle, horses, sheep, and other animals, nomadic people also offered the Chinese furs and hides in exchange for Chinese commodities. The "Monograph on Economy" in the *Shih chi* records that each of the big cities of China annually consumed "one thousand pieces of fox and sable skins and one thousand *tan* of lamb skins."[5] A notation in the *Han shu* suggests that, "because the fox and sable furs were expensive, the number was given, and, because the lamb skins were cheap, they were measured by their weight."[6] Fox and sable furs were exported to China by nomadic hunters and trappers working in the Great Hsingan Mountains and the wooded areas north of the Gobi.

From the earliest records of the Ch'in and Han periods until the seventeenth century, it is clear that nomadic peoples bartered primarily their furs and animals, particularly horses, to the Chinese for desired goods. A few representative passages will affirm this. A passage in the *Hou Han shu* states that "in the twenty-eighth year of Chien-wu [52 A.D.], the Northern Hsiung-nu again sent envoys to the court, tributed horses and fur coats, and again asked for an intermarriage agreement. . . . "[7]

The Wu-huan and the Hsien-pei people, who created the most powerful nomadic states after the Hsiung-nu decline, also traded their livestock and furs: "In the twenty-fifth year [of Chien-wu, 4A.D.], Hao-tan, the leader of the Wu-huan on the west of the Liao [River] and others . . . admired [our] culture. They led their people to the court and presented their tribute, male and female slaves, cattle and horses, bows and the furs of tigers, leopards and sables."[8] And again, "The Hsien-pei are a branch of the Eastern Barbarians [Tung-hu]. . . . Their animals, which are different than those of the Middle Kingdom, are wild horses, great horned goats, and *chiao-tuan* cattle. The bow made from horns is commonly known as the *chiao-tuan* bow. Besides, there are sables, *na*, and ermines. Their skin and hair are tender and soft and they are known as the best furs under heaven."[9]

Other passages suggest that after the decline of the Wu-huan and Hsien-pei, the Jou-jan " . . . tributed horses, animals, and sable and *na* furs [to the court] yearly."[10] [In 629, the Uighurs] "presented sable skins as tribute,"[11] and "between the era of K'ai-yüan [713–741] and T'ien-pao [713–755] they [the Hei-shui Mo-he] came to the court eight times and presented the eyeballs of whales, sable, and white rabbit skins."[12]

Trade in animals and furs did not diminish with the emergence of the Uighur people, although a greater diversity of other goods derived through trade along the silk routes or with more northerly nomadic groups was sometimes presented to sedentary courts. Once they were forced by the Kirgiz to migrate in the middle of the ninth century from Mongolia into Kan-chou, the Uighurs expanded the range of products they offered as tribute and trade to the T'ang court and, after the fall of T'ang, to the courts of the Five-Dynasties period. The land of the Kan-chou Uighurs was said to produce:

> jade-yaks,[13] green wild horses,[14] one-humped camels,[15] white minks,[16] antelope horns,[17] sal ammoniac,[18] seal testicles,[19] diamonds,[20] red salt,[21] and the skins of wild horses. Their land was good for the production of white wheat, Tibetan wheat, yellow hemp, green onions, leeks, and carrots. They used camels to farm.[22] In the fourth year of Ch'ang-hsing [933], the Uighurs came and presented a pair of white falcons, and Ming-tsung [of the Later T'ang] commanded that they be

released.²³ From the time of Ming-tsung, [the Uighurs] usually came to the Middle Kingdom to sell horses. All the precious jade that they brought with them would go to the county magistrates, and the people who transgressed the regulation and bought [the jade] would usually be punished. . . . ²⁴

Following the decline of the Uighur people, the Khitan came to dominate the Yen and Yün regions of northern China south of the Great Wall. The *Chiu Wu-tai shih* informs us that "[in] the second year of T'ien-fu [937] . . . Yi-li-bi, the envoy of the Khitans arrived and presented two hundred horses, ginseng, sable skin, ambling horses, and wooden bowls."²⁵ Another passage from the *Sung shih* records: "Along the border the markets were established. . . . All the goods sold by the offices remained as the old, with the addition of silk, cloth, lacquer wares and rice. The imported items were silver money, cotton cloth, sheep, horses, and camels."²⁶ Although the Khitan occupied parts of northern China and established the Liao dynasty, they still depended, as did other nomads, on the Chinese for silk, cloth, and rice. They continued to rely on pastoral products to trade for these goods, and although they conducted extensive trade with other peoples, they were forced to use silver to purchase needed grain and cloth from the Sung Chinese.

A passage in the "Monograph on Economy" in the *Liao shih* suggests how extensive the Khitan trading network with other nomadic peoples was: "The market places were established at Hsiung-chou,²⁷ Kao-ch'ang,²⁸ and Po-hai²⁹ to transfer the goods of the Southern Sung, the Northwestern tribes, and the Koguryo. Therefore, the Jurchens took [their] gold, silk, cloth, honey-wax, and other medical products, and the Tieh-le, Mo-ho, Yü-chüch and other tribes took [their] clam-pearl, gray ermine, sable and fish skin, cattle, sheep, horses, camels, woolen-cloth, and other items to come and exchange with the Liao."³⁰

Khitan and later Jurchen power was ultimately displaced by that of the Mongols, who dominated China during the thirteenth and much of the fourteenth century. Once the Mongols were forced north of China by the native Ming dynasty, the goods exchanged by the nomads for sought-after Chinese items were still primarily derived from their herds and from hunting activities:

In the tenth year of Cheng-t'ung [1445], Pir Mahamed and others, the envoys of the Oirad, came and paid a tribute of eight hundred horses, one hundred thirty thousand pieces of gray ermine skins, sixteen thousand pieces of white ermine skins, and two hundred pieces of sable skins. The Emperor thought this was too many and commanded the officials to take the best ones among the horses and ten thousand pieces of the grey and ten thousand pieces of the white ermine skins but to accept all the sable skins, and he commanded the envoys to sell the rest by themselves.[31]

Throughout the two-thousand-year period of this study, nomadic leaders bartering their furs and animals with China sought primarily to acquire fine silk and other cloths as well as grain from their agrarian neighbors. They sought Chinese textiles because of the comfort they provided when worn and their value as mediums for exchange with other more distant peoples, and grain was essential as a supplement to the nomadic peoples' meat and milk based diets.

In this study, it has been suggested that perhaps the first definitive exchange arrangement between powerful nomadic and sedentarist rulers along the borders of China was achieved by Han Kao-ti and Mao-tun. In addition to an intermarriage provision, this agreement committed the Han court "to yearly present a definite quantity of silk, cloth, wine, rice, and foodstuffs to the Hsiung-nu."[32]

As suggested in chapter one, Chung-hang Yüeh, an advisor to Lao-shang, a later *Shan-yü* of the Hsiung-nu, feared that the luxurious Chinese goods sent to the nomadic court might lead it to abandon its nomadic way of life. Indeed, among the relics excavated from the tomb of a Hsiung-nu nobleman at Noyan-uul (Peoples Republic of Mongolia), there are about equal amounts of Chinese embroidery and finely woven Hsiung-nu woolen textiles.[33] This suggests the degree to which the Hsiung-nu nobility had come to accept Chinese manufactured products.

In 51 B.C., Hu-han-yeh proceeded to the Han court of Emperor Hsüan-ti, who received him with special honors. The catalogue of gifts presented to this Hsiung-nu leader suggests that textiles and food grains were the chief items coveted by the Hsiung-nu: "There were swords adorned with jade, ceremonial swords, one bow with four arrows, ten ceremonial lances, one cart, saddle and bridle, fifteen horses, twenty catties of gold, two hundred thousand pieces of money, seventy-seven sets of clothing and quilts, eight thousand pieces of embroidery, satins, and all kinds of silk, and six thousand catties of crude silk. . . . Also, [Hsüan-ti] commanded the border officials to gather the grain and foodstuffs, altogether [there were] thirty-four thousand *hu* to supply them with food."[34]

About a century later, in 48 A.D., the Southern Hsiung-nu again appeared at the Han court to surrender. The bestowals made to the Southern Hsiung-nu at this time were almost identical to those presented a century earlier to Hu-Han-yeh, with the exception that an additional 36,000 head of cattle and sheep were presented to the Southern Hsiung-nu.[35] It was unusual for the Chinese to present livestock to a nomadic people, but war with the Northern Hsiung-nu had forced the Southern Hsiung-nu to flee their homeland and seek safe haven along the borders of China. Because their flight was a hasty one, they were unable to wait for their slower animals to move southward; only their herds of horses could move fast enough to follow them as they evaded the pursuing Northern Hsiung-nu. Consequently, in 48 A.D. and again five years later,[36] the Han found it expedient to provide the Southern Hsiung-nu with sheep and cattle when they allowed them to settle south of the great bend of the Yellow River to act as a buffer against more hostile northern nomadic peoples.

The descriptions in Chinese sources of the Wu-huan and Hsien-pei differ little from those given earlier of the Hsiung-nu:

> They are experts in riding and shooting and following the waters and grass to pasture their animals, and they have no definite place to live. They use yurts as their homes, and all the yurts point towards the east. They hunt birds and animals every day. They eat meat, drink milk, and wear wool and skins. . . . The land is good for the planting of green millet and *tung-ch'iang*. *Tung-ch'iang* looks like rush bush, but in reality it is the seed of mallow, ripening in the tenth month [November]. They prepare white wine from this, but they do not know how to make yeast. They depend on the Middle Kingdom for their supply of seed and grain. The *ta-jen* leaders are able to make bows, arrows, saddles and bridles, and to forge metals to make arms. They are able to dress hides, embroider, and weave woolen clothes.[37]

It is apparent that the Wu-huan and Hsien-pei, like earlier nomads, depended primarily on a pasturing and hunting economy. Although they engaged in some agricultural activity, their techniques were underdeveloped, their production inadequate, and they were forced to rely on imports of Chinese seed and grain to augment their supplies.

Study of the relationship between the nomadic Jou-jan and the more sedentarist T'o-pa Wei dynasty established in North China during the fifth and sixth century also suggests the dependence of the nomadic peoples on their southern neighbors for cloth and food. The "Account of the Juan-juan [Jou-jan]" in the *Wei shu* provides a list of the gifts from the Wei Court to the Jou-jan leader A-na-k'ui in 520 A.D.:

> The Emperor ordered bestowed on A-na-k'ui two sets of fine, shiny man and horse armor, six sets of *Wu* iron man and horse armor, two long lances adorned with

silver threads and white tassels, ten red-lacquered long lances with white tassels, ten black-lacquered long lances with pennants, two silk-adorned bows with arrows, six red-lacquered bows with arrows, ten black-lacquered bows with arrows, six red-lacquered shields with swords, black-lacquered shields with swords, twenty red-lacquered drums and horns, two five-colored embroidered quilts, thirty yellow silk quilts, one embroidered robe for private use, hats, one dark-red lined jacket, twenty dark-red robes and hats, one thousand silk robes of different colors, one pair of dark-red, narrow opening trousers, a lined coat and the attached items, one pair of purple narrow opening trousers, a lined coat and the attached items, eighteen small tents, six yellow cloth tents, one thousand bushels of newly cooked rice, eighty bushels of fried wheat, fifty bushels of fried nuts, four bronze pots . . . two fine iron pots . . . two black-lacquered bamboo wire containers, two girl slaves, five hundred . . . horses, one hundred twenty camels, one hundred cattle, five thousand sheep, ten red-colored painted plates, and two hundred thousand bushels of grain to be provided at the garrison place on the border.[38]

The principle articles the Wei court presented to the Jou-jan leader were finely manufactured ceremonial weapons, silk apparel, animals, and food. The cooked rice, fried wheat, and fried nuts were provisions for A-na-k'ui's trip back north, but the two hundred thousand bushels of grain were clearly intended to supplement the Jou-jan people's diets. As suggested in chapter one, despite massive shipments of Chinese grain northward to feed the Jou-jan people, famine broke out in 523 among the Jou-jan, and A-na-k'ui was forced to lead his people south to raid the frontiers of China.[39]

The Turkic people north of China during the Sui and T'ang periods conducted large-scale exchanges of their livestock for Chinese silk and other cloth. For example, in 607 the Turkic ruler Ch'i-min Khan "came to have an audience with [Emperor Sui Yang-ti] at his royal pavilion and presented three thousand horses. The emperor was greatly pleased and bestowed two thousand rolls of satin on the Khan. . . . The Emperor entertained Ch'i-min, and the tribal chieftains, three thousand five hundred persons, at his great pavilion with a banquet and bestowed two hundred thousand rolls of satin in accordance with their ranks."[40] The importance of this exchange was recognized by Sui and T'ang rulers, as suggested by this statement attributed to Emperor Hsüan-tsung of the T'ang: "Formerly, our country carried out intermarriage agreements with the Turks; and both the Chinese and the barbarians enjoyed peace, and the troops rested. Our country bought sheep and horses from the Turks, and the Turks received satin and silk from our country. Consequently, both they and we were rich and bountiful."[41]

Khitan and Jurchen relations with the Sung and Southern Sung dynasties have already been discussed in earlier chapters. It was suggested that stability along the Khitan and Jurchen frontiers with their southern neighbors was only secured when the Chinese provided them with massive yearly presentations of silk, silver, and grain. In the thirteenth century, the Mongols invaded China and established the Yüan dynasty. Mongolian leaders sought to improve the lives of their people by seizing the wealth of China and shipping it northward. As was the case with earlier nomadic peoples, the goods acquired from the sedentary Chinese were chiefly satin and silk products, although gold and silver were important secondary items.

Once the Mongols fled China and the Ming dynasty was established, the basic items included in nomadic-sedentarist exchange remained nomadic livestock and Chinese textiles and grain. This is suggested by the fact that the Ming court, recognizing that the basic exchange between the Mongols and the Chinese was that of horses for silk, set the amount of silk to be offered the Mongols for a certain grade of horse: "Toghtobukha *Wang* [Khan] and Esen *Tai-shih* of the Oirad both sent envoys to the Court to present horses as tribute. In order not to disappoint the people from afar, it was decided to pay four rolls of embroidered satin with lining silk and eight rolls of silk for each first-class horse; two rolls of embroidered satin with lining silk and two rolls of . . . silk for each middle-class horse; one roll of silk sackcloth and eight rolls of silk for each third class horse; and the reward for a bad horse would be given according to the regulation."[42]

Evidence of continuing Mongolian interest in securing grain from the Chinese also exists. In one instance, the desire for grain was the consequence of famine: "Famine broke out in Uriyangkha and other areas. The Mongols wished to exchange horses for grain. . . . This was decided . . . for each good horse fifteen *tan* of grain and three rolls of silk . . . for each colt five *tan* of grain and one roll of cloth."[43] However, it is clear that during the sixteenth century, when Altan Khan struggled to normalize relations with the Ming, he requested trade in grain as well as silk and other commodities at a time when his people were not subject to famine: "In the thirtieth year of Chia-ching [1551], Altan again petitioned to exchange cattle and horses for grain and beans, also asking for workers and Imperial decrees [authorizing the Mongols to come to the borders for trade]."[44] Once markets were effectively established between the Mongols and Ming merchants in 1571, the "Account of the Ta-tan" in the *Ming shih* suggests that "the barbarians came with gold, silver, furs, hides, horse-tail hair, and other items, and the traders and salesmen came with satin, silk, cloth, pots, and other items for exchange."[45] The "Biography of Wang Ch'ung-ku", the Ming statesman most instrumental in successfully creating the markets, states that: "Wang Ch'ung-ku then broadly summoned merchants and traders to trade cotton, cloth, and cereal for fur and hides. . . . "[46]

Henry Serruys believes that during the sixteenth century thousands of Chinese settled in Mongolian territory, established villages, and began to farm. Mongolian rulers came to depend on the grain produced by these immigrants, yet periodically the Mongols found it necessary to acquire grain through trade with China to guarantee that the mushrooming Chinese populace was fed. The presence of Chinese peasants cultivating Mongolian lands created a dilemma for Ming officials. Some officials insisted that grain exports from China were going only to feed Chinese allies of the Mongols, who could not be induced to return as long as grain continued to flow across the frontier. Others argued that too firm a policy of restricting grain exports in order to force Chinese renegades in Mongolia to accept repatriation would deny the Mongols the agricultural products produced by China, leaving the nomadic people without adequate provisions, which would force them to again raid the frontier to acquire grain and other supplies.

Nevertheless, the Chinese living in Mongolia did not produce sufficient grain to meet the demand of the Mongols, which left them dependent on grain shipped from the south to supplement their diets. Esen, Altan, and other Mongolian leaders continued to importune the Ming court for additional supplies of grain, cloth, and other products for the native people as well as the new arrivals.[47] Because of the need of nomadic peoples to obtain Chinese grain and cloth, the maintenance of peace along the Great Wall depended on trade, tribute, and intermarriage arrangements between the nomadic and Chinese states. However, prejudice and mistrust, the ineffectiveness of Chinese governments to implement frontier trading policies, and the chaotic nature of the border areas led to the recurrent breakdown of exchange mechanisms. As a result, calm on the borders was replaced by conflict.

Chinese disdain for their northern neighbors has been suggested in earlier chapters. Nomadic peoples north of China were seldom deferentiated one from another, but simply grouped together and given pajorative titles such as *i* (eastern barbarians), *man* (southern barbarians), *ch'iang* (western barbarians) or *hu* or *ti* (northern barbarians). These terms denigrate the nomads because they suggest that southern barbarians were worm-like *(man)*, western barbarians were goat-like *(ch'iang)*, and northern barbarians were animal-like *(ti)*. The terms *i* and *hu* are general and cannot be linked to animal qualities.

Stereotypical qualities were assigned to all barbarians regardless of where they came from or what their motives were in approaching the Chinese court: "The barbarians *(i ti)* are covetous for gain, they have long hair, they button their [clothes] on the left side, and are human faced [but] bestial hearted."[48] Such simplistic and critical views of nomadic peoples too frequently led Chinese rulers to view contact with nomadic states only as deleterious to the Chinese state. They assumed that the northern barbarians knew nothing of affection or friendship but only of greed, and, as a consequence, the Chinese adopted aggressive measures against them.[49]

Nomadic rulers found it difficult to accept the Chinese assertion of cultural superiority. They reasoned that cultural superiority should create an infrastructure conducive to military might, yet clearly the preponderance of military power most frequently was held by the nomadic peoples. Leaders of the nomadic states were unwilling to accept subordinate status to a country whose frontiers and cities they could destroy. As suggested in chapter one, for more than a century and a half Hsiung-nu hegemony north of China was recognized by the Han court, who offered trade, intermarriage, and bestowals to the Hsiung-nu to secure peace along China's frontiers. Then, in 51 B.C., because of civil war among the nomadic peoples, the *Shan-yü* Hu-han-yeh was forced to accept vassal status to the Han court. About a half century later, leadership of China was usurped by Wang Mang, after which a weakened Han court was able to reestablish itself. At this juncture, the Hsiung-nu approached the Chinese and suggested that the Han court recognize that once again military parity existed between the nomadic and Chinese peoples. The Hsiung-nu insisted that the Chinese no longer treat them as vassals. From this point on, nomadic rulers frequently challenged the Chinese assumption of superiority by refusing to kowtow to envoys sent by Chinese emperors, by insisting that they were sovereign over the lands north of China, and by demanding trade on terms advantageous to them. Even when a ruler such as Altan Khan condescended during the sixteenth century to accept a title suggesting his deference to the Chinese court, his subjects and other nomads realized that in reality it was Altan who benefited most from the exchange relationship which he had dictated to the Chinese emperor.[50]

The Chinese regarded all those who had not embraced Chinese culture as barbarians. However, nomadic peoples did not rush to accept Chinese culture, and, as a consequence, peoples with antipathetical life styles confronted one another. Unlike the Chinese, nomadic peoples did not use a great number of pajorative terms for the Chinese. For instance, the most critical term used by the Mongols to refer to the Chinese was to call them the *khara Kitad* (black Chinese).[51] Nomadic people viewed the Chinese as impolite and improperly raised, but they did not manifest the deep seated prejudice so evident in the Chinese view of nomadic peoples. As suggested by the frequent requests for Chinese musical instruments, some nomadic rulers were interested in Chinese music. Sometimes nomadic leaders requested Chinese books, which, aside from important philosophical texts, were generally denied them. However, after Altan Khan's conversion to Tibetan Buddhism in the sixteenth century, the Mongols became more interested in Tibetan religious paintings and Buddhist literature and had the *Tripitaka* translated from Tibetan. Generally, styles of nomadic dress were retained, even when Chinese silk was utilized in the making of the apparel.

As suggested in chapter one by Chung-hang Yüeh's warning to the Hsiung-nu *Shan-yü* during the second century B.C., nomadic rulers were aware that it was dangerous to adopt Chinese customs. A Turkish Orkhon inscription of the eighth century provides additional insight:

> The Chinese people, giving us limitless amounts of gold, silver, alcohol [grain], and silk always had sweet speech and luxurious treasures, and seducing us with this sweet speech and luxurious treasure, they strongly attracted faraway peoples to themselves, who settled close by, and then absorbed their evil practices. . . . Having given yourselves over to seduction by their sweet words and precious gifts, you, O Turks, have perished in large numbers. . . . Evil people instructed a part of the Turks, saying, "To him who lives far away, the Chinese give poor gifts, but to him who lives close by, they give fine gifts." By these words they instructed you, and now you, people, not possessing true wisdom, have heeded their words, and having approached right up [to China] have perished there in great numbers. Thus, O Turks, when you go into that country you come to the edge of death, but when, on the other hand, you stay in your Otukan fastnesses, and only send caravans [for trade or tribute] you have no woes at all.[52]

Just as the Chinese disliked nomadic people, so also did the nomad despise and mistrust the Chinese. The nomadic peoples took great pride in their mobility and freedom. They were not tied to one spot as were the sedentarists, and their land was not denuded by the plow as was that to their south but still possessed skin *(körösü)*. They disdained those who worked on their knees in mud and dirt in the skin-less (körösü-ügei) south. Few nomadic peoples abandoned their herds to plant seeds, although some allowed captured or fleeing Chinese to cultivate areas north of China's frontiers.

Fostered by the inherent conflict that often emerges between peasant and herdsmen, cultural differences, and deep-seated prejudice, enmity and mistrust often existed between the Chinese and nomadic peoples. Such mutual antagonism was a deterrent to stable relations between the two.

A second factor which contributed to nomadic-Chinese discord was the failure of the Chinese dynasties to implement effective frontier trading policies or regulate military and civilian officials. Stable nomadic-Chinese relations depended on the maintenance of viable exchange mechanisms. All too often, Chinese dynasties failed to adequately regulate frontier trade, which left nomads vulnerable to unscrupulous Chinese officials and merchants, who often bilked them of their possessions.

In Mongolian there is no true word for merchant, so that eventually the word most commonly used to refer to merchants was *naimai*, which was derived from the Chinese word for buying and selling *maimai*. Sometimes the Mongols referred to merchants by using the much more revealing word *khudaldaa* (the verbal form) or *khudaldugha* (the written form), which is derived from the root *khudal*, meaning "to lie", combined with the suffix *dugha*, which suggests "action". The Chinese often regarded nomadic peoples as foolish, and the nomadic peoples felt the Chinese were shrewd and could not be trusted. Far too often, the nomad was cheated at the marketplace, which created ill-will, mistrust, and instability along the frontier.

Merchants were not the only Chinese who deceived and mistreated the nomads. Far too often, ambitious or simply ill-advised officials failed to implement frontier trading policies, or worse still, sought to use the market places to entrap and destroy nomadic forces. Frontier officials sometimes sought to gain court recognition and rewards by initiating hostile and aggressive actions toward the nomads. Both frontier and court officials generally found it safer to advocate an activist military approach toward the nomadic peoples than to encourage reliance on markets and exchange mechanisms to promote stability.

The nature of Chinese autocratic government contributed to the ineffective dynastic control of frontier trading activities. Throughout the two-thousand-year period of this study, Chinese dynasts, for the most part, derived their wealth by controlling the agrarian sector of society.

With the exception of the implementation by some dynasties of monopolistic control of the production and sale of salt and a few less essential commodities, Chinese emperors drew little income from the regulation, taxation, or direct involvement in mercantile activities. They came to regard agriculture as the primary occupation of the people and welcomed the constructive contributions of scholars or artisans to the stability of the state. However, the merchant was held in low esteem, for he contributed nothing materially or intellectually to society but made his profit merely by exchanging goods already produced. In fact, Confucian philosophers warned dynasts that when the government involved itself in marketing activities it "entered into financial competition with the people, dissipating primordial candor and simplicity and sanctioning propensities to selfishness and greed. As a result, few among our people take up the fundamental pursuits of life, while many flock to the nonessential. . . . "[53]

Anti-marketing prejudice led many Chinese rulers to ignore or even evade their responsibilities to regulate frontier markets. Rulers such as Han Wen-ti, who affirmed that the Han and the Hsiung-nu were neighbors and, as a consequence, that the Chinese would provide those from the land of cold and frost with grain and silk products,[54] and Emperor Ming-tsung of the Later T'ang, who established markets open to all nomadic people,[55] were the exception to the rule. Most emperors regarded the incessant nomadic demands for trade as an annoyance and viewed exchange with nomadic peoples as economically disadvantageous to China. As a consequence, they established markets or other exchange mechanisms only when forced by military threat to do so. Because war or the threat of attack was often the only vehicle open to nomadic peoples to force Chinese rulers to open markets, once the exchange mechanisms were established, the climate of hostility often remained and far too frequently exchange agreements were abandoned by the Chinese as the markets were used to ensnare and destroy the nomadic peoples.

The nature of Chinese bureaucracy also mitigated against preserving stability along the frontier. Chinese dynastic government funneled absolute power into the hands of the emperor, who made decisions about nomadic-Chinese affairs after considering the counsel of a few close scholar, eunuch, or imperial advisors. Although officials could send memorials to the throne expressing their views about frontier policy, active debate was limited to members of key ministries or a few individuals having direct access to the emperor.

What is striking about these debates is how dangerous they were to those who participated. In 1421, after Fang Pin incurred the wrath of Emperor Ch'eng-tsu for questioning the wisdom of a third attack against the Mongolian leader Arughtai, he committed suicide rather than face censure.[56] When a bureaucrat chose to defend a general who had become a scapegoat for a failed policy, as the Han court historian Ssu-ma Ch'ien did, the emperor could order him castrated,[57] or as suggested in chapter three, an official might fail to realize there was a subtle change in court thinking, as did Yang Chi-sheng during the Ming period, and advocate an activist policy towards the Mongols when the emperor was moving towards placating them with markets and exchange agreements. For this, he was censured, judicially investigated, and ultimately executed. However, supporting a position momentarily favored by the throne was also tenuous, as suggested by the fact that Ch'ou Luan, Yang Chi-sheng's rival in the debates of 1550, was also executed once the market arrangements implemented by him were abandoned. Those, such as Ch'ou Luan, who supported the creation of markets and other exchange mechanisms to promote stability along China's frontiers, were generally more vulnerable to censure than those who argued for an aggressive military approach toward the nomadic peoples. This is evident in the constant reiteration by the pacifists that they sought only to create exchange mechanisms to gain time to prepare China militarily to confront the "barbarians."

As might be expected, military leaders faced an even graver danger of being censured than their civilian counterparts. When they failed in battle with nomadic forces, they sometimes were demoted, banished, had their goods and property confiscated, and were beaten or even executed. But, if they achieved success, they were handsomely rewarded. Courts often monitored a general's success in battle by counting the collected number of heads of enemy soldiers. This led generals to order the slaying of non-belligerents to meet established quotas and receive a given level of rewards. It was important to military officers to persuade the court that they were aggressive in combating their nomadic rivals. Even when there was relative peace or when nomadic leaders sought to open negotiations with the Chinese by sending ambassadors to frontier garrisons, Chinese leaders often dealt harshly with them, as suggested in chapter three when several envoys sent by Altan Khan to explore the possibility of negotiating peace were summarily executed by garrison commanders, one of which was rewarded with promotion by the Ming court for his brash action.

Fighting along the frontiers of China was sometimes initiated by Chinese officers seeking to build a reputation for themselves and secure the rewards granted to the victors. The following passage records the activities of the powerful court eunuch Wang Chih, the general Chu Yung, and another member of Wang Chih's clique, Ch'en Yüeh:

> [Wang] Chih was young and preferred military activities. Ch'en Yüeh persuaded [Wang] Chih indirectly that [he] should carry out a campaign against Fu-tang-chia to establish a reputation in border affairs and reinforce his own position. [Wang] accepted this. [He had the Court] appoint the Count of Fu-ning, Chu Yung, and he himself as supervisors of the troops. After the troops returned, [Chu] Yung was entitled Duke Pao-kuo [the Duke who protects the state], [Ch'en] Yüeh was promoted to Yu tu-wei *chien-shih* [supervisor of the Right Flank of military officers] and [Wang] Chih received an increase in his rice stipend. [Wang] Chih again accepted Wang Yüeh's suggestion that he issue a false report informing [the court] that Ismail had crossed the border. The [Emperor] instructed [Chu] Yung and [Ch'en] Yüeh to launch a campaign into the west, and made [Wang] Chih the military supervisor. [Ch'en] Yüeh was made Count of Wei-ning and [Wang] Chih's rice stipend was again increased. Soon afterwards, Fu-tang-chia invaded Liao-tung, and Ismail invaded Ta-t'ung. The killing and looting went on everywhere.[58]

The Chinese attacks against Fu-tang-chia and later Ismail were unprovoked. They were launched simply to build the reputations and secure rewards for those leading the Chinese forces. Seven to eight years of war followed, and although Ming forces ultimately suffered heavy casualties, the architects of the fighting were all handsomely rewarded for their initial successes against nomadic forces.

Court disinterest in frontier markets, coupled with the remoteness of frontier regions from the hub of administrative activity, guaranteed frequent delays before the court answered the requests of the nomadic peoples. As suggested in chapter three, in 1550, some Mongols asked to exchange cattle and sheep for grain and beans. When frontier officials failed to respond, the Mongols raided the borders to obtain the goods they needed. Tenuous central control over China's border regions forced frontier military and civilian authorities to take the initiative in discharging their responsibilities. Unfortunately, some Chinese officials used their office only to enrich themselves, regardless of the consequences to border stability. In chapter four, it was suggested that the Mongolian leader Esen warred with China because he felt mistreated by frontier and central-government officials. In 1449, after stable relations were established between Esen and the Ming court, the Ming eunuch Wang Chen ordered a reduction in the price offered the nomadic peoples for their horses. Esen, angered by this breech of contract, invaded China. When peace was restored, Esen was asked why he launched a war when the Ming had been offering him such high levels of bestowals. Esen replied: "Why was the price of horses reduced? The silken rolls sent to me were mostly cut and disfigured. Our emissaries usually failed to return. In addition, yearly bestowals were also reduced."[59] Esen felt that he was being mistreated by high and low officials alike. The eunuch Wang Chen arbitrarily modified the exchange agreements while corrupt minor officials were cutting and disfiguring the rolls of silk presented to Esen by the court.

Duplicity on the frontier is also evident in the actions of Ming officers toward the nominal vassal of the Ming, the Uriyangkha Mongols. One passage states that "[the Uriyangkha] still came to render tribute because [they] desired the benefits derived from bestowals from the Middle Kingdom. Nevertheless, they detested the killings carried out by border generals, and as a result plotted revenge."[60] The random killing of Mongols by Chinese along the frontier sometimes gave way to a systematic slaying of the Mongols: "[Li] Ping said, 'Areas outside the Great Wall were originally the pasture lands of the tribes, and [this] does not constitute invasion of [our] borders. An indiscriminate massacre carried out merely on the chance that it would enhance someone's prestige is not a matter of which [I, your] vassal would like to hear.' "[61] And as suggested in chapter one by the story of Han Wu-ti's attempt to ensnare the Hsiung-nu at Mai, nomads were sometimes massacred at frontier markets. This was true of the Uriyangkha as well:

> At the beginning of the Hung-chih period [1488–1505], [the Uriyangkha] usually looted border areas near Ku-pei [a gate of the Great Wall north of Peking] and K'ai-yüan [present-day Liao-ning Province]. The governing official, Chang Yü, the Commander, Li Kao, and other [officials], by subterfuge, trapped three hundred [Uriyangkha] when they came to the market area and executed them. Consequently, [the Uriyangkha] to the north allied with Toroghan, asked him to avenge [the deaths] and carried out several invasions in the areas of Kuang-ning [present-day Pei-chen, Liao-ning] and Ning-yüan [present-day Hsing-ch'eng, Liao-ning.][62]

Other passages in the *Ming shih* suggest that in 1465 conflict broke out between the Uriyangkha and the Ming because a border official named Wu Kuang "betrayed the goodwill of the Three Garrisons [Uriyangkha] by his covetous desire for bribes . . . ,"[63] and in 1478, "The official interpreters, Liu Hai and Yao An, carried out intrigues for illegal gain. The tribes of To-yen [Doying] complained, disturbed Kuang-ning, and refused to come to the markets. The minister of military affairs, Wang Yüeh, petitioned [the Court] to order a deputy general and an administrator to supervise an investigation to determine whether there had been any corrupt activities. As a consequence, [Liu] Hai and [Yao] An were punished according to the crimes [that they had committed]. . . . "[64]

Border officials were sometimes ruthless in the means they used to destroy the enemy.[65] In 1641, the Governor of Kansu, Lü Ta-ch'i had just repulsed an attack by a Mongolian force incited by a recently censured Chinese commander. When the Mongolian leader, Erdeni *Khong Taiji*, approached the Great Wall to request rewards, "[Lü] Ta-ch'i then pretended to provide gifts and rewards [to tempt them to come] but poisoned the fountain where [they] watered their horses, which killed countless of their masses."[66]

Because a number of scholars have already elaborated on the excesses of the nomads at the frontier markets or on the road to various courts to offer tribute,[67] this work has not dwelt upon this subject. Still, it is important to note that nomadic merchants and envoys frequently took advantage of the laxity of Chinese administration to spy, rape, pillage, illicitly trade, and carry out other misdeeds while in frontier areas or travelling to and from a Chinese capital. Like the Chinese, nomadic leaders and their followers committed perverse acts toward their neighbors, which contributed to instability between nomadic and sedentarist states.

Still, some nomadic and Chinese leaders realized that if peace was to be maintained, the cycle of recrimination must be broken. Each party must look inward and seek to better order its own house rather than justify his own criminal acts by pointing to the other's. As suggested in chapter three, Altan Khan and Wang Ch'ung-ku were two such individuals. Wang Ch'ung-ku was the frontier official who negotiated with Altan Khan the agreements leading to the peace of 1570–71. While Altan Khan was attempting to police the frontiers north of China and persuade his supporters to adhere to the new settlement, Wang Ch'ung-ku, made the following criticism of the incompetence and fraud practiced by Ming border officials:

> In the three decades from the *hsin-ch'ou* [year] of Chia-ching [1541], the border was violated constantly, and many border officials were punished because of misconduct. Border generals and lieutenants even bribed bandits [Mongols] to obtain peace, but some of the funds were utilized by [the bandits] in a contrary manner. Those who were captured and who arranged some manner of returning [to the

Middle Kingdom] were usually killed, which was falsely reported as military victory. Although there was no way to learn the enemy's situation, the enemy was usually aware of [our] troop movements.[68]

Clearly, at times, the court failed to regulate frontier officials effectively. However, because of bureaucratic malaise, even scrupulous border officials could not be certain that the central government would expeditiously respond to their requests. They also faced the constant danger that court intrigue might reach down to them and cause their censure. It was dangerous for officials along the northern frontiers of China to show bold initiative. Many chose the safer course of action and bribed or coerced critics of their local administration into silence. Many also illicitly offered nomadic leaders additional remunerative incentives to ensure quiet on the frontiers. These officials chose a safer option based on the assumption that by doing little that was constructive there was less chance of upsetting the status quo. They hoped only to maintain peace within their jurisdiction until their short tenure in office was completed and they could gain appointments in a safer realm.

Governmental ineffectiveness in implementing frontier policies and regulating border officials is a second major reason why exchange agreements were abandoned and war broke out. It is now possible to explore a third and related factor contributing to the frequent hostility between the nomadic and Chinese peoples. The chaotic nature of frontier regions allowed the development of wide-ranging smuggling activities and havens along the border for unsavory characters. Illicit trade activities weakened the established exchange mechanisms created to promote peace. As suggested by Owen Lattimore, "war is likely to break out first at the margins of a society and to begin with those classes that are least 'typical' or 'normal.' "[69]

Throughout history, the Chinese legal system banished the dregs of Chinese society to frontier regions, where they joined disillusioned, poorly trained, and poorly cared for military personnel. Criminals of all sorts were sent north along with censured political figures who were also exiled to the borders. Along China's northern frontiers were others who were fleeing Chinese justice and some who had rebelled against the dynasty. The frontier, on both the nomadic and the Chinese side of boundaries, was riddled with impoverished Chinese peasants intermingling with unsettled nomadic herdsmen in a fluid and volatile mix. Along the frontiers, subtle changes in the environment occurred, contributing to the diversity of farming and nomadic activities undertaken on these lands.

Thieves abounded in great numbers, governmental control was minimal, and quick profits could be made through illicit trading activities. The chaotic nature of China's northern borders made it difficult for the Chinese dynasties to establish stable exchange mechanisms with nomadic peoples in order to promote peace.[70]

The dynasties attempted to limit illicit trade because it deprived the court of profits, contributed to disruption, and enabled nomadic peoples to acquire weapons or other contraband goods, particularly strategic materials such as iron, which could subsequently be crafted into lethal weapons.

There is little information in Chinese sources regarding the nature or extent of contraband trading during the periods investigated in this study. However, at times, it must have been extensive. In chapter one, it was shown that Emperor Wu-ti was able to lure the Hsiung-nu to the market town of Ma-i by promising them contraband. By 121 B.C., the sale of illegal goods to nomadic peoples was such a problem that Han Wu-ti arrested and executed five hundred merchants at Ch'ang-an for selling contraband goods, probably iron vessels, to members of the entourage of a Hsiung-nu *Shan-yü* in the Han capital.[71] Archaeological excavations of a Hsiung-nu or Wu-huan burial site also reveal sizeable cashes of iron weapons and implements produced in Han China. These could only have reached nomadic leaders as contraband, because the Han court did not present weapons to nomadic rulers as gifts or allow them to be exchanged at regulated frontier markets.[72]

Further evidence that contraband trade during the Han dynasty was extensive is revealed by a passage in "The Account of the Hsien-pei" in the *Hou Han shu*. Here the court official Ts'ai Yung warns the emperor about campaigning against the increasingly powerful Hsien-pei, who have armed themselves with sharp weapons produced with Han iron:

> After the Hsiung-nu escaped, the Hsien-pei became powerful and occupied the land. They have one hundred thousand powerful and well-trained troops. Primarily [because] the supervision and control of the frontier areas has not been tightened enough, many good metals are being smuggled [out], so that the best iron is totally possessed by the Hsien-pei bandits. Moreover, there are Chinese escapees helping them to plan further activities. Now their weapons are sharper and their horses are faster than those of the Hsiung-nu.[73]

During the era of division between the Han and Sui dynasties, sedentary courts continued to attempt to regulate trade between the Chinese and nomadic peoples. In 553, the founder of the Northern Chou dynasty, Yü-wen T'ai,[74] was campaigning against the nomadic T'u-yü-hun, who controlled the silk routes along the corridor to the west of the Yellow river, when he "captured 240 barbarian merchants, six hundred camels and mules, and tens of thousands of rolls of all kinds of silk."[75] He confiscated the goods of these merchants on the pretext that they had been obtained outside the government-regulated marketing system.

Little information exists regarding smuggling during the T'ang period, but there is one passage in the *Hsin T'ang shu* which suggests that some illegal trading centered around Manichaen priests. "The *Mo-ni* came to the Capital and each year dealt in the western market. Many merchants traded with them illegally."[76] The word *Mo-ni* is the Chinese transliteration for the priesthood of Manichaeism. Manichaen priests enjoyed a favorable position in China because, in the mid-eighth century, they converted the Uighur khan T'eng-li-mou-yü to Manichaeism. By this time, the T'ang depended on Uighur military support to sustain their dynasty, so when the Uighur khan insisted that the T'ang treat Manichaens well, the Chinese court was careful not to antagonize them.

The Sung dynasty issued numerous decrees in their attempt to control frontier trade. In 988, when regulated frontier markets were closed because of unrest with the Khitan, there was an outbreak of smuggling. The Sung responded by warning that "anyone who transgressed the laws [against illicit trading] would receive the death sentence. Any northern merchant illegally entering the interior land and trading would be beheaded on the spot where he is arrested."[77] The subsequent issue of similar decrees suggest that the Sung effort was not completely successful. In 1067, "the people of the border areas were strictly forbidden to deal in unauthorized trade with the Hsia."[78] In 1076, a "law of punishment and rewards" was issued to deter unauthorized trade with foreigners.[79]

As suggested by the following passage, Ming problems with smuggling were extensive: "This year, in the luggage of the envoys of the Oirad, there were many helmets, much armor, many swords, arrows, and other forbidden iron goods. There were all the things of the greedy people and traders of the Ta-t'ung and Hsüan-fu areas. It proves that the order had not been tightly carried out! Henceforth, you must clearly proclaim the prohibition. Anyone who repeats the former wrongdoings will cause all of you to be punished!"[80]

High profits tempted merchants and craftsmen to smuggle strategic materials to the Mongols. The Ming court was aware that "there were people who possessed iron tools who sold them to the envoys of the Oirad for great gains."[81] The trade became so blatant and serious that the emperor ordered his own secret police, the Embroidery Uniform Guards (*Chin-i wei*) to investigate smuggling activities and arrest and imprison violators.[82]

In reality, during the Ming period, influential eunuchs and some important governmental officials participated in smuggling activities, undermining the court's efforts to curtail illegal trade. For instance, an entry in "The Biography of Eunuch Wang Chen" in the *Ming shih*, states: "Formerly, Kuo Ching, the Governor of Ta-t'ung, made many dozens of large jars of arrowheads every year, and by the order of Wang Chen, he presented them to the Oirad. The Oirad usually rewarded him with excellent horses."[83] Other passages in the *Ming shih* reveal that near the end of the fifteenth century, Shen Ying, who was the commander of the garrisons at Ta-t'ung and Ning-hsia, ordered his servants to trade with the nomads clandestinely. "Consequently, the barbarians crossed the border and exchanged [their goods] for iron tools."[84]

Another form of exchange that occurred along the frontier was the presentation of ransom in return for kidnapped or captured Chinese. This type of exchange often assumed widespread proportions. For example, the *Hsin T'ang shu* states that "during the disturbance of the Sui dynasty, many Chinese people were captured and taken to the barbarian land. The Court sent envoys to bring gold and silk as ransom to redeem eighty thousand men and women who were to be reinstated as citizens."[85] Later, once the T'ang dynasty was more firmly established, the court tried to resist extortion by denying nomadic leaders trading opportunities until captive Chinese were released.[86] During the mid-fifteenth century, the Oirad leader Esen captured Emperor Ying-tsung, but failed to extort money or goods from the Ming dynasty. However, on occasion, the Ming court paid ransom to the Mongols for captive Chinese.[87] There can be little doubt that these activities helped destabilize the frontier.

Although this study has focused on relations between the Turkic and Mongolian nomads and China during the two-thousand-year-period from the second century B.C. to the seventeenth century A.D., the basic tenets of our thesis are affirmed when one studies nineteenth century relations between the Middle Kingdom and the "barbarians" from the Great Western Ocean (*ta hsi yang*), particularly the British.

From the seventeenth century on, the British began to trade with China and became increasingly dependent on Chinese silks and teas (a different fare than the grain eaten by nomads, but still considered by the Chinese as essential to the well-being of the "barbarians" who sought it). Although the British commanded formidable military forces and boasted that the sun never set on their empire, Lord MacCartney and his successors failed to persuade the Ch'ing court to grant them political and economic concessions. As suggested by the continuing correspondence between the courts of Britain and China,[88] the British discovered that the Chinese, and their Manchu overlords, were chauvinistic, arrogant, self-centered, and condescending towards them. The British were allowed to trade only under highly circumscribed conditions at the frontier trading depot open to Westerners at Canton, but they were forbidden to interact with any merchants not licensed to participate in this regulated trade or correspond directly with the court, except as vassals paying homage to the "Son of Heaven." As was the case with the Turks and Mongols, the British also found it difficult to find goods to trade which the Chinese desired. Consequently, during the first two centuries of British-Chinese exchange, the British were forced to purchase the silks and teas of China with silver and gold bullion.

By the beginning of the nineteenth century, the British began to challenge the restrictive Chinese system. First, they illegally exported opium to China, enabling them to purchase the coveted Chinese teas and silks without parting with their bullion. When, in 1840, the Chinese official Lin Tse-hsü seized the British stores of opium readied for the market, the British went to war. There were numerous factors which led the British to war with China, but many were identical to those leading nomadic peoples during earlier eras into conflict. Like earlier barbarian peoples, the British were chauvinistic and had grown tired of Chinese prejudice and mistrust and the Chinese insistence that they accept subordinate status. They were frustrated with the marketing system and the officials who ran it and weary of the chaotic conditions in the trading area created by illicit smugglers, pirates, and other rabble which the Chinese were unable to control. However, as was the case with nomadic peoples throughout Chinese history, war with China was undertaken to better secure goods the British felt were essential to the well-being of their country.

Throughout history, trade was the chief determinant of frontier stability between China and the nomads who were dependent on some goods she produced. Peace was possible when either frontier markets, the exchange of nomadic tribute for Chinese bestowals and yearly payments, or court-to-court intermarriage relations enabled the nomads to obtain grain, cloth, and other essential commodities. Although other explanations have been posited to explain nomadic-sedentarist conflict, war was most often precipitated by the breakdown of exchange mechanisms occasioned by mutual enmity and prejudice, the inability of dynastic governments to regulate self-serving Chinese merchants and officials, and the instability of nomadic-sedentarist frontiers.

NOTES

INTRODUCTION

1. Several excellent studies have been completed on the horse trade between nomadic peoples and the Chinese. For example, see S. Jagchid and C. R. Bawden, "Some Notes on the Horse-Policy of the Yüan Dynasty," *Central Asiatic Journal* 10:246–268 (December 1965); Denis Sinor, "Horse and Pasture in Inner Asian History," *Oriens Extremus* 19.1–2:171–183 (December 1972); Morris Rossabi, "The Tea and Horse Trade with Inner Asia during the Ming," *Journal of Asian History* 42:136–168 (1970); Tani Mitsutaka, "A Study on Horse Administration in the Ming Period," *Acta Asiatica* 21:73–97 (1971); H. G. Creel, "The Role of the Horse in Chinese History," *American Historical Review* 70.3:647–672 (April 1965). An excellent description of the use of horses by pastoral nomads and the prestige acquired by those who owned them can be found in Sevyan Vainshtein, *Nomads of South Siberia: The Pastoral Economies of Tuva*, ed. and intro. Caroline Humphrey, tr. Michael Colenso (Cambridge, 1980), 65–72.
2. Walter Goldschmidt, "A General Model for Pastoral Social Systems," in L'Equipe écologie et anthropologie des sociétés pastorales, ed., *Pastoral Production and Society* (Cambridge, 1979), 15–16.
3. Caroline Humphrey, "Introduction," to Vainshtein, 13–18. Vainshtein's chapter on Tuvinian agriculture is excellent, 145–165.
4. Humphrey, 17.
5. Ibid. See Vainshtein's chapter on Tuvinian crafts, 198–232.
6. The impact of cultural incompatibility as an agent of friction between the nomad and the sedentarist is discussed by Wolfgang Weissleder, "The Promotion of Suzerainty Between Sedentary and Nomadic Populations in Eastern Ethiopia," in Wolfgang Weissleder, ed., *The Nomadic Alternative* (The Hague, 1978), 275–288. Goldschmidt's article, cited above, considers the characteristics of pastoral in contrast to agricultural life. He believes that the chief determinant of the social order is the relationship between man and the resources he depends on and suggests that the differing demands made on herdsmen and farmers accounts for the conflict between them. See Goldschmidt, 15–27.
7. Hsiao Ch'i-ch'ing, "Pei-ya yu-mu-min-tsu nan-ch'in ko-chung yüan-yin ti chien-t'ao," *Shih-huo yüeh-k'an* 1.12:610 (March 1972).
8. Ibid.
9. *Chang Wen-chung kung ch'üan-chi*, Wan-yu wen-k'u ed., "Shu-tu," 8:362–363, cited by Yang Lien-sheng, "Historical Notes on the Chinese World Order," in John K. Fairbank, ed., *The Chinese World Order* (Cambridge, Mass., 1968), p. 31.
10. Yü Ying-shih, "Han Foreign Relations," chapter 6 in Denis Twitchett and Michael Loewe, ed., *The Cambridge History of China* (Cambridge, 1986), I, 433.
11. Paul A. Cohen suggests that the great preponderance of scholarly work done by Westerners during the 1950s and 1960s focused on the Western challenge to traditional China and how this challenge had been met or on the impact of modernization on China. Until recently, Westerners seldom studied Chinese-nomadic interaction even though relations with the nomad remained the paramount focus of Chinese concern well into the nineteenth century. See Paul A. Cohen, *Discovering History in China* (New York, 1984).
12. Arnold J. Toynbee, *A Study of History* (London, 1934), III, 396.
13. Ellsworth Huntington, *The Pulse of Asia* (Boston, 1907).

14. This work will utilize the somewhat less well known term Central Eurasia to refer to the central part of the Eurasian land mass generally occupied by nomads. For an explanation of the suitability of this term to describe this area, see Denis Sinor, *Inner Asia: A Syllabus*, (Bloomington, Ind., 2nd ed. 1971), 1–5.

15. Toynbee, 395–454.

16. G. F. Hudson, "Note by Mr. G. F. Hudson," in Ibid., 453–454; Owen Lattimore, "The Geographical Factor in Mongol History," in Owen Lattimore, ed., *Studies in Frontier History: Collected Papers 1928–1958* (New York, 1962), 241–244.

17. Gareth Jenkins, "A Note on Climatic Cycles and the Rise of Chinggis Khan," *Central Asiatic Journal* 18.4:217–226 (1974).

18. Joseph Fletcher, "The Mongols: Ecological and Social Perspectives," *Harvard Journal of Asiatic Studies* 46:11–50 (1986).

19. Frederick J. Teggart, *Rome and China: A Study of Correlations in Historical Events* (Berkeley, 1939), vii.

20. Ibid., v–xi.

21. Ibid., 225.

22. Ibid., 230.

23. Ibid., 231.

24. Ibid., 232.

25. Ibid., 148–223.

26. Christopher I. Beckwith, *The Tibetan Empire in Central Asia* (Princeton, 1987), 173–196.

27. Ibid., 193.

28. Two theoretical articles support Barfield's premise that nomadic states emerged as a response to the growth of sedentarist power on their borders. William Irons formulates the hypothesis that "among pastoral nomadic societies, hierarchical political institutions are generated only by external political relations with state societies, and never develop purely as a result of the internal dynamics of such societies." See William Irons, "Political Stratification Among Pastoral Nomads," in L'Equipe . . . , ed., 362. Philip Burnham, another anthropologist, independently reached the same conclusion. See Philip Burnham, "Spatial Mobility and Political Centralization in Pastoral Societies," in Ibid., 349–360.

29. Thomas J. Barfield, "The Hsiung-nu Imperial Confederacy: Organization and Foreign Policy," *Journal of Asian Studies* 41.1:54 (1981).

30. Ibid., 47.

31. Marceau Gast has written about the importance of loot in maintaining stability in the nomadic society of the Kel Aghaggar in the Sahara. Kel Aghaggar society was dominated by a warrior group that exploited a class of tributary nomadic pastoralists. Although exploited, the pastoralists were presented booty acquired by the warriors from raids on neighboring peoples. The exchange of tribute from the nomadic pastoralists for booty helped ensure the perpetuation of the Kel Aghaggar. See Marceau Gast, "Pastoralisme Nomade et Pouvoir: La Societé Traditionnelle des Kel Aghaggar," in L'Equipe . . . , ed., 201–220.

32. Barfield, 52.

33. Ibid., 52–54.

34. Chusei Suzuki, "China's Relations with Inner Asia: The Hsiung-nu, Tibet," in Fairbank, ed., 180–197; Joseph F. Fletcher, "China and Central Asia, 1368–1884," in Ibid., 206–224; and David M. Farquhar, "The Origins of the Manchus' Mongolian Policy," in Ibid., 198–205.

35. Morris Rossabi, "Introduction," in Morris Rossabi, ed., *China Among Equals* (Berkeley, 1983), 1–12.

36. Tao Jing-shen, "Barbarians or Northerners: Northern Sung Images of the Khitans," in Rossabi, ed., 66–86; and Wang Gungwu, "The Rhetoric of a Lesser Empire: Early Sung Relations with Its Neighbors," in Rossabi, ed., 47–65.

37. Walter Goldschmidt, 16, agrees. He states that "no pastoral nomadic society is entirely free of involvement, either directly or indirectly, with agricultural products." *Peace, War, and Trade* . . . also recognizes the interdependence of the nomad and sedentarist. Owen Lattimore admits that the exchange of goods was important to all nomadic peoples, but insists that "the steppe nomad can withdraw into the steppe, if he needs to, and remain completely out of contact with other societies." (See Lattimore, "The Geographical . . . ," 253). Still, Lattimore spends much less time studying the completely self-sufficient nomad, isolated in the remote vastness of the Central Eurasian steppe than he does nomads living along the frontier between herdsmen and peasants. He believes that scholars must understand the dynamics of frontier exchange and politics to clearly assess Chinese-nomadic relations. See especially, Owen Lattimore, *Inner Asian Frontiers of China* (New York, 1951).

38. A. M. Khazanov, *Nomads and the Outside World*, tr. Julia Crookenden (Cambridge, 1984), 82, quoting V. V. Barthold, "Tadzhiki. Istoricheskii ocherk," *Sochineniia* (Moscow, 1963), vol. II, pt. I, 460.

39. Khazanov, Nomads . . . 5.

40. Ibid., 212.

41. Ibid., 203.

42. Ibid

43. Ibid., 205.

44. Ibid., 206. See also, A. M. Khazanov, "Characteristic Features of Nomadic Communities in the Eurasian Steppes," in Weissleder, ed., 124.

45. Khazanov, *Nomads* . . . , 234.

46. Ibid., 235–236.

47. Khazanov, "Characteristic . . . ," 119–125.

48. Vainshtein, 80.

49. Khazanov, "Characteristic . . . ," 123.

50. In seeking peace with the Khitan Liao dynasty, the Sung statesman Fu Pi argued: "If Liao establishes peace with the Sung, then Liao will easily receive the yearly payment and benefits will pass to the state Khan. If Liao engages in war with the Sung, all benefits will pass to the subjects, and damage will be done to the state Khan." See Toghto et al., *Liao shih* (completed 1344, reprinted Taipei, 1967), 19, chi 19, "Annals of Hsing-tsung" III, 3a. Fu Pi's words swayed the Liao emperor Hsing-tsung and a long-lasting peace was established. Later, in the 1540's, the Ming official Weng Wan-ta used the same argument in seeking to secure peace with the Mongol leader Altan Khan. He stated that "if there is an outbreak of invasions the tribes will profit, but if allowed to pay tribute, the leaders will profit." See Chang T'ing-yü and others, *Ming shih* (completed 1736, reprinted Taipei, 1967), 198, chüan 86, "Biography of Weng Wan-ta," 24a–25b.

51. An especially good analysis of Sung relations with the Liao and Chin states is found in Herbert Franke's "Sung Embassies: Some General Observations," in Rossabi, ed., 116–148.

52. Yü Ying-shih, "Han . . . ," 390–391.

53. Liu Hsü and others, comp., *Chiu T'ang shu* (reprinted Taipei, 1967), 57, chüan 7, "Biography of Liu Wen-ching," 5a.

54. For elaboration on these points, see Benjamin I. Schwartz, "The Chinese Perception of World Order, Past and Present," in Fairbank, ed., 276–288, and John K. Fairbank, "A Preliminary Framework," in Ibid., 1–19.

55. For a fine study of Ming frustrations in trying to restrain unruly Mongols through the tribute system see, Henry Serruys, "Sino-Mongolian Relations during the Ming II: The Tribute System and Diplomatic Missions (1400–1600)," *Mélanges Chinois et Bouddhiques* 14:1–650 (1967).

56. Integrating Tibetan-Chinese relations into this study is difficult because Tibetan power was built on a sedentary as well as a nomadic base. As such, the Tibetan style of warfare, Tibetan objectives in fighting, and the manner in which Tibetan courts interacted with China differed from that of steppe nomads. During the T'ang dynastic period, Tibet contended with China not only to dominate the Tarim Basin and other strategic parts of Central Eurasia, but it also coveted what was considered by Chinese to be their territory in parts of present-day western and northwestern China. This forced the T'ang to seek alliances against Tibet with Uighur and other nomads who were judged to pose a lesser threat to the Middle Kingdom because they seldom occupied Chinese territory. The Tibetan-Chinese rivalry sometimes erupted into war, but occasionally, as will be shown in chapter five, intermarriage and tributary mechanisms were adopted to stabilize relations. During the T'ang era, tributary relations and treaty arrangements between China and Tibet were based on terms of equality. Unlike relations between steppe nomads and the Chinese, which were initiated by nomads primarily for economic reasons, intermarriage and tributary ties between Tibet and China were maintained more for political purposes. An assessment of Tibetan-Chinese rivalry from the seventh to the ninth century, when the Tibetan threat to China was perhaps the greatest, is available in Christopher I. Beckwith's *The Tibetan Empire in Central Asia*.

57. For the purposes of this study, the term Jurchen is used primarily to refer to the conquerors of northern China who founded the Chin dynasty in 1115. The term Manchu refers to the Jurchen who adopted this title in 1635. They occupied Yen-ching (the future Peking) in 1644 and extended Ch'ing dynastic rule over all of China during the following half century. A good starting point for studying the Jurchen during the Chin period is provided by Tao Jing-shen, *The Jurchen in Twelfth-Century China* (Seattle, 1976). For assessments on the consolidation of Ch'ing power in China, see Lynn A. Struve, *The Southern Ming 1644–1662* (New Haven, 1984), and Frederic Wakeman, Jr, *The Great Enterprise* (Berkeley, 1985).

58. See chapter five.

59. Sechin Jagchid, "The Uighur Horse Trade during the T'ang Period," in Walther Heissig and Klaus Sagaster, ed., *Gedanke und Wirkung (Thought and Practice)* (Wiesbaden, forthcoming).

60. Toyama Gunji, *Kinchōshi kenkyu* (Kyoto, 1964). The two studies related to early Chin-Mongol conflict are found on 421–443 and 472–564.

61. Sung Lien et al., *Yüan shih* (completed 1369, reprinted Taipei, 1967), "Annals of T'ai-tsu," chi 1, 15b.

62. Ibid., 146, "Biography of Yeh-lü Ch'u-ts'ai," 7b.

63. For assessments on Chinese merchant exploitation of the Mongols, see Robert H. G. Lee, *The Manchurian Frontier in Ch'ing History* (Cambridge, Mass., 1970), and Lattimore, *Inner*. . . .

64. Ibid., and Sechin Jagchid, "Shintai Moko no chiho seiji seido," *Moko* 83 (April 1939).

65. Sechin Jagchid, "The Manchu-Ch'ing Policy towards Mongolian Religion," in Walter Heissig, ed., *Tractata Altaica, Denis Sinor, Sexagenario Optime de Rebus Altaicis, Merito Dedicuta* (Wiesbaden, 1976), and Sechin Jagchid, "The Rise and Fall of Buddhism in Inner Mongolia," in A. K. Narain, ed., *Studies in the History of Buddhism* (New Delhi, 1980).

I. TRADE OR RAID

1. The *Hsi-yu chi*, written by Li Chih-ch'ang, also known as *Ch'ang-ch'un chen-jen hsi-yu chi*, is the famous travelogue of Ch'iu Chu-chi about his visit to Chinggis Khan, who was then in Afghanistan. For information on Ch'iu Chu-chi, see a brief record in Sung Lien et al., *Yüan shih* (completed 1369, reprinted Taipei, 1967) 202, chüan 89, "Biography of Monks and Taoists," 9a–10b. See also Yao Ts'ung-wu, "Ch'iu Ch'u-chi nien-pu," *Tung-pei-shih lung-tsung* (Taipei, 1959), II, 214–276.
2. Yeh-hu Ling is located about ten to fifteen miles east of present-day Kalgan.
3. T'ai-hang is the chief mountain range between present-day Hopei and Shansi.
4. *Ch'ang-ch'un chen-jen hsi-yu chi*, 258.
5. A passage from the *Discourses on Salt and Iron*, cited in Yü Ying-shih's, *Trade and Expansion in Han China* (Berkeley, 1967), 40, describes the conditions under which the Hsiung-nu nomads, contemporaries of the people in Han dynastic China lived:

> The Hsiung-nu live in the desert and grow up in a land which produces no food. [They are the people who] are abandoned by Heaven for being good-for-nothing. They have no houses to shelter themselves, and make no distinction between men and women. They take the entire wilderness as their villages and the *ch'iung lu* tents as their homes. They wear animal's skins, eat meat raw and drink blood. They wander to meet [others] in order to exchange goods, and stay [temporarily on some pastures] in order to herd cattle.

The term *ch'iung lu* refers to round hut and suggests the traditional nomadic yurt.
6. The Chinese referred to important nomadic states as *ma-shang hsing-kuo*, or "states on horseback," thereby recognizing their great mobility and the different relationship nomadic people had with their land. For a fuller discussion of the nature of nomadic states, see Sechin Jagchid and Paul Hyer, *Mongolia's Culture and Society* (Boulder, Colorado, 1979), 245–296.
7. Ssu-ma Ch'ien, *Shih chi* (reprinted Taipei, 1967) 110, chüan 50, "Account of the Hsiung-nu," 16a. Another excellent example of this concern with assimilation is evident in Tonyukhukh's counsel to Bilge Khan (r. 716–734) found in Liu Hsü et al., comp., *Chiu T'ang shu* (reprinted Taipei, 1967) 194 I, chüan 144 I, "Account of the Turks," I, 14b:

> Because Bilge Khan received many Chinese refugees who surrendered to him, he conceived of a plan to build new cities and temples. Tonyukhukh said, "this will be a serious mistake. The Turkic population is very small and does not even reach one percent of that of the T'ang. The only reason that we are able to resist them is because we are able to migrate on the steppes. We search for pastures and water, but have no definite place to stay. Besides, we have a vigorous life of shooting and hunting, and everyone learns the art of war. When we are weak we can retreat and hide ourselves in the mountains and forests. Although the T'ang has many soldiers, it still cannot affect us. If we began to establish cities to live in and to change our customs, then when we are defeated we will be swallowed up by the T'ang. Moreover, the custom of the temples is to teach people to be benevolent and weak. This is not good for the development of martial arts and the struggle for power. Therefore, these should not be established." The Khan strongly agreed with his advise.

See also the entry in O-yang Hsiu, Sung Ch'i and others, *Hsin T'ang shu* (reprinted Taipei, 1967) 215 II, chüan 140 II, "Account of the Turks," II.
8. *Shih chi* 110, chüan 50, "Account of the Hsiung-nu," 11a.

9. Ibid., 2a.
10. Yü Ying-shih, "Han Foreign Relations," in Denis Twitchett and Michael Lowe, ed., *The Cambridge History of China* (Cambridge, 1986), I, 384–386. For a complete discussion of the Han foreign policy debate undertaken at this time, see chapter two.
11. Pan Ku and Pan Chao, *Han shu* (reprinted Taipei, 1967) 94 I, chüan 64 I, "Account of the Hsiung-nu," I, 10a–b.
12. Ibid.
13. Additional discussion of this development occurs in chapter five.
14. Each group contained four pulling horses.
15. *Shih chi* 110, chüan 50, "Account of the Hsiung-nu," 14a, 15a–b.
16. Ibid., 20b.
17. Ibid., 11, chi 11, "Annals of Ching-ti," 6a–b.
18. Ibid., 110, chüan 50, "Account of the Hsiung-nu," 20b–21a.
19. Yü Ying-shih, *Trade* . . . , p. 43. For the court debate on whether to maintain earlier policies or abandon them for war, see chapter two.
20. *Shin chi* 110, chüan 50, "Account of the Hsiung-nu," 21a–b.
21. *Han shu* 52, chüan 22, "Biography of Han An-kuo," 19a–b.
22. *Shih chi* 110, chüan 50, "Account of the Hsiung-nu," 21a–b.
23. Ibid., 26b.
24. *Han shu* 94 I, chüan 64 I, "Account of the Hsiung-nu," I, 29b.
25. Yü Ying-shih, *Trade* . . . , 43–45. For a more complete discussion of the transformation of Han-Hsiung-nu relations at this time from one based on marital alliances which favored the nomads to one that came to resemble the traditional tributary system, see Yü Ying-shih, "Han . . . ", 394–398.
26. For further discussion, see chapter four.
27. *Han shu* 94 II, chüan 64 II, "Account of the Hsiung-nu," 2b.
28. See chapter four, for a discussion of the Chinese response to this situation.
29. Fan Yeh, *Hou Han shu* (reprinted Taipei, 1967) 89, chüan 79, "Account of the Southern Hsiung-nu," 5a–6a.
30. *Han shu* 94 II, chüan 64 II, "Account of the Hsiung-nu," II, 3a.
31. Yü Ying-shih, "Han . . . ", 436–446.
32. For information on Chi Yung, see the attached biography to the "Biography of Chi Tsun," *Hou Han shu*, 20, chüan 10.
33. *Hou Han shu* 90, chüan 80, "Account of the Hsien-pei," 9a. A lengthy note on the origins of the Hsien-pei can be found in the "Account of the Hsien-pei" in Chen Shou, *San-kuo chih* (reprinted Taipei, 1967), "Book of Wei," 30, 5b.
34. Yü Ying-shih, "Han . . . ", p. 443.
35. *Hou Han shu* 90, chüan 80, "Account of the Wu-huan," 4b–5a.
36. Ibid., 5a. For a more complete discussion of the significance of this event, see Yü Ying-shih, "Han . . . ", 438–440.
37. Ibid., 90, chüan 80, "Account of the Hsien-pei, 9b.
38. Ibid., 11a; Ibid., 90, chüan 80, "Account of the Wu-huan," 5b.
39. Ibid., 90, chüan 80, "Account of the Hsien-pei, 14a–b.
40. *San-kuo chih*, "Book of Wei," 30, "Account of the Hsien-pei," 6a.
41. Ibid., "Biography of K'o-pi-neng," 8b–9a.
42. Ibid., 8a.
43. Also known as Juan-juan. In Chinese Juan-juan means worm-like. Although this is the term most commonly used to designate these people, it demeans them and we choose not to use it.
44. The biography of Li Ch'ung is found in Wei Shou, *Wei shu* (reprinted Taipei, 1967) 66, chüan 54.

45. *Wei shu* 103, chüan 91, "Account of the Juan-juan," 20a–b.
46. Ibid., 1b.
47. It is unlikely that, being true nomads, the Jou-jan themselves planned to cultivate these seeds, but it is possible that there were Chinese among them who had fled the chaotic conditions in China who would grow crops for their nomadic lords. Another possible explanation for this unusual request might simply be that the Jou-jan planned to eat the seed grain just as they did the twenty thousand *tan* of non-seed grain provided them.
48. According to the Ch'ing scholar Chang Mu, Pai-lang shui is the present Ta-ling river. See Chang Mu's *Meng-ku yu-mu chi*, 1859. Reprinted in Taipei 1965, chüan 2, 14a–16a (89–91).
49. Li Yen-shou, *Pei shih* (reprinted Taipei, 1967) 94, chüan 82, "Account of the Khitan," 19b.
50. Ling-hu Te-fen, *Chou shu* (reprinted Taipei, 1967) 50, chüan 42, "Account of the Turks," 7b.
51. Wei Cheng, *Sui shu* (completed 644, reprinted Taipei, 1967) 84, chüan 49, "Account of the Turks," 3b–4a.
52. Ibid., 6b. For a thorough discussion of Sui intermarriage policies with Ishbara and other Turk leaders, see chapter five.
53. Ibid.
54. Ibid., 7a–8b.
55. Ibid.
56. Ibid.
57. Ibid., 12a–13a.
58. Ibid.
59. Ibid., 14b.
60. Ibid., 67, chüan 32, "Biography of P'ei Chu," 14a–b.
61. Ibid.
62. The writer of the *Hsin T'ang shu* makes it clear at the end of his "Biography of P'ei Chü" that he regarded him as a deceitful politician and not a far-sighted statesman. P'ei Chü's policies contributed to the Turk withdrawal of support for the Sui, and as a consequence, "the wickedness of P'ei Chü was sufficient to exterminate the Sui dynasty." See O-yang Hsiu, Sung Ch'i, et al., *Hsin T'ang shu* (reprinted Taipei, 1967) 100, chüan 25, 4a–b, 5b.
63. *Chiu T'ang shu* 57, chüan 7, "Biography of Liu Wen-ching," 5a.
64. Ibid., 194 I, chüan 144 I, "Account of the Turks," I, 4a.
65. Ibid.
66. Christopher I. Beckwith, *The Tibetan Empire in Central Asia* (Princeton, New Jersey, 1987), 85–86.
67. Ibid., 92.
68. Ibid., 92–93 citing Ssu-ma Kuang, *Tzu-chih t'ung ch'ien* (Peking, 1956, reprinted Taipei, 1979), 212, 6744.
69. *Chiu T'ang shu* 194 I, chüan 144 I, "Account of the Turks," I, 16b. Also see Beckwith, 102–103. About a century before Bilge Khan refused to join with the Tibetans to attack the T'ang, Koguryo (Korea) approached Chi-min Khan of the Turks to persuade him to form a Koguryo-Turk alliance against the Sui. The Turk khan exposed this conspiracy to Emperor Yang-ti, who gratefully lavished presents on the khan. See, *Sui shu* 84, chüan 49, "Account of the Turks," 14a.
70. *Hsin T'ang shu* 217 I, chüan 142 I, "Account of the Uighurs," I, 8b.
71. For additional discussion on Uighur-Turk interaction, see chapters two and five.
72. Hsüeh Chü-cheng and others, *Chiu Wu-tai shih* (completed 974, reprinted Taipei, 1967) 57, "Book of T'ang," 33, chüan 9, "Biography of Kuo T'ao," 1b.

73. Ibid., 43, "Book of T'ang," 19, "Annals of Ming-tsung," IX, 10a–b; Ibid., 89, "Book of Chin," 15, chüan 4, "Biography of Sang Wei-han," 3a–5b.
74. Toghto et al., *Sung shih* (completed 1346, reprinted Taipei, 1967) 186, chih 139, "Monograph on Economy," II, 8, entry on trade and navigation *(hu-shih po-fa)*, 22b–23b.
75. Ibid.
76. Ibid.
77. For a more complete discussion of these negotiations, see chapter four.
78. *Sung shih*, 186, chih 139, "Monograph on Economy," II, 8, entry on trade and navigation *(hu-shih po-fa)*, 22b–23b.
79. Ibid.
80. Ibid.
81. Ibid.
82. See Cheng Chü-chung's biography in *Sung shih* 351, chüan 110.
83. Ts'ai Ching's biography is in *Sung shih* 472, chüan 231.
84. Wa-ch'iao Gate was located in the area of present-day Hsiung-hsien in the central part of Hopei.
85. For a biography on Fu Pi, see *Sung shih* 313, chüan 72.
86. The Chinese text reads "sui-pi wu-shih-wan p'i-liang" which makes it impossible to discern whether this means five hundred thousand units of silk and silver altogether or five hundred thousand rolls of silk and also five hundred thousand taels of silver.
87. Hsü Meng-hsin, *San ch'ao pei-meng hui-pien* (completed by 1161, reprinted Taipei, 1982) vol. I, the entry of the fourth month of the eighth year of Cheng-ho [1118].
88. For a biography of T'ung Kuang, which, however, fails to mention his role in this debate, see *Sung shih* 468, chüan 227, the "Biographies of the Eunuchs," III.
89. For Wang Fu's biography, see *Sung shih* 470, chüan 229. There is only a brief discussion in this biography of Wang Fu's role in this debate.
90. *Sung shih* 351, chüan 110, "Biography of Cheng Chü-chung," 12b–13a.
91. These are the words of the Sung envoy Fu Pi found in Toghto et al., *Liao shih* (completed 1344, reprinted Taipei, 1967) 19, chi 19, "Annals of Hsing-tsung," II, 3a.
92 A rule of Mongolian pronunciation is that no "t" follows a vowel. However, because the last consonant in the word Oirad sometimes sounds more like a "t" than a "d" the variant spelling of Oirat has become quite common.
93. Chang T'ing-yü et al., *Ming shih* (completed 1736, reprinted Taipei, 1967) chüan 328, "Account of Wa-la [Oirads]," 7a.
94. Ibid., chüan 222, "Biography of Chang Hsueh-yen," 2b.
95. Ibid., 327, chüan 215, "Account of the Ta-tan," 9a.
96. Ibid.
97. *Chih-yüan* is an abbreviation drawn from the title *Chih Shu-mi-yüan shih*, the deputy director of *Shu-mi-yüan* (the general office for the mobilization of military force). It is a title that the Mongols brought back to their homeland after the collapse of the Yüan dynasty.
98. *Ming shih* 328, chüan 216, "Account of the Oirad," 5b.
99. A more complete discussion of Esen's struggle against the Ming is presented in chapter three.
100. *Ming shih* 327, chüan 215, "Account of the Ta-tan," 17a.
101. *Hsüan-lan-t'ang ts'ung-shu*, vol. 1, the entry of *Pei-ti Shun-i-wang An-ta teng kung-piao-wen*.

II. PEACE OR WAR

1. Pan Ku and Pan Chao, *Han shu* (reprinted Taipei, 1967) 94 II, chüan 64 I, "Account of the Hsiung-nu," II, 23b–25b.

2. Ibid.
3. Ibid.
4. Ssu-ma Ch'ien, *Shih chi* (reprinted Taipei, 1967) 100, chüan 40, "Biography of Chi Pu," 3a–b.
5. Hsüeh Chü-cheng and others, *Chiu Wu-tai shih* (completed 974, reprinted Taipei, 1967) 89, "Book of Chin," 15, chüan 4, "Biography of Sang Wei-han," 3a–5b.
6. Ibid.
7. *Han shu* 48, chüan 18, "Biography of Chia I," 12b–13b.
8. Ibid., 49, chüan 19, "Biography of Ch'ao Ts'o."
9. *Shih chi* 110, chüan 50, "Account of the Hsiung-nu," 3b–4a; *Shih chi* 4, chi 4, "Annals of Chou," 27a.
10. Li Ssu's biography is in *Shih chi* 87, chüan 27.
11. *Han shu* 64 I, chüan 34 I, "Biography of Chu-fu Yen," 17b–19a.
12. Ibid.
13. *Chung*—a measure of grain defined as sixty-four Chinese pecks, or *tou*.
14. *Tan*—a measure of grain defined as ten *tou*.
15. *Han shu* 64 I, chüan 34 I, "Biography of Chu-fu Yen," 17b–19a.
16. Ibid.
17. *Shih chi* 99, chüan 39, "Biography of Liu Ching," 12b–13a.
18. For further discussion on intermarriage relations, see chapter five.
19. *Shih chi* 110, chüan 50, "Biography of the Hsiung-nu," 18b–20a.
20. Ibid.
21. Ibid.
22. *Han shu* 53, chüan 22, "Biography of Han An-kuo," 15b–19a.
23. Ibid.
24. Ibid.
25. Ibid.
26. Ibid.
27. Ibid.
28. Ibid.
29. Duke Miu is commonly known as Duke Mu of Ch'in (d. 621 B.C.).
30. *Han shu* 53, chüan 22, "Biography of Han An-kuo," 15b–19a.
31. Ibid.
32. Ibid.
33. Ibid.
34. Ibid.
35. This document was translated by Esson M. Gale in 1931 and has since been reprinted under the title *Discourses on Salt and Iron*. Future citations for this document will be found under the name of the original author Huan K'uan.
36. Huan, 5.
37. Huan, 4–5.
38. *Han shu* 59, chüan 29, "Biography of Chang T'ang," 3b–4a.
39. Ibid.
40. *Shih chi* 30, shu 8, "Monograph on Economy," 3b–5a.
41. *Han shu* 94 II, chüan 64 II, "Account of the Hsiung-nu," II, 24a.
42. Ibid., 4a.
43. Fan Yeh, *Hou Han-shu* (reprinted Taipei, 1967) 18, chüan 8, "Biography of Tsang Kung," 23a–24b. A commandery was a standard unit of territorial administration. See Charles Hucker, *A Dictionary of Official Titles in Imperial China* (Stanford, 1985), 200.
44. *Hou Han-shu* 18, chüan 8, "Biography of Tsang Kung," 23b–24b.
45. Ibid., 24b.
46. Ibid., 89, chüan 79, "Account of the Southern Hsiung-nu," 9b, 12b–13a.

47. Ibid., 14b.
48. Ibid., 15a–16a.
49. Ibid., 24, chüan 15, "Biography of Lu Kung," 7b–9b.
50. Ibid., 41, chüan 31, "Biography of Sung I," that is attached to the "Biography of Sung Chun," 24a–25a.
51. The biography of Pan Ch'ao is in Hou Han shu 47, chüan 37.
52. Kan-ch'üan kung (palace) was located in the area of present-day Ch'ung-hua, Shensi.
53. At present, the term ti-kuo means an enemy country. In Han times it meant a rival country with equal powers and political status.
54. Han shu 78, chüan 48, "Biography of Hsiao Wang-chih," 9b–10a.
55. Ibid., 94 II, chüan 64 II, "Account of the Hsiung-nu," 2b.
56. Ibid., 20b–23b.
57. Hou Han shu 89, chüan 79, "Account of the Southern Hsiung-nu," 5b–6a.
58. Chen Shou, San-kuo chih (reprinted Taipei, 1967), "Book of Wei," 30, "Biography of K'o-pi-neng in the "Account of the Hsien-pei," 7b–8a.
59. Professor Jitsuzo Tamura suggested that this movement in Asian history is a historical event similar to the migration of the "barbarians" in European history. See Jitsuzo Tamura, "Higashi Ajia minzoku ido," Bongakubu Kenkyu kiyo, Kyoto University, no. 12, 1968.
60. Wei Shou, Wei shu (reprinted Taipei, 1967) 103, chüan 91, "Account of the Juan-juan," 14a–16b.
61. Li Po-yao, Pei Chi shu (reprinted in Taipei, 1967) 7, chi 7, "Annals of Wu-cheng-ti," 4a–b.
62. Ling-hu Te-fen, Chou shu (reprinted Taipei, 1967) 19, chüan 11, "Biography of Yang Chung," 21a–b; 50, chüan 42, "Account of Foreign Lands," II, "Account of the Turks," 6b.
63. Liu Hsü, Chiu T'ang shu (reprinted Taipei, 1967) 57, chüan 7, "Biography of Liu Wen-ching," 5a. For more information on Shih-pi Khan's relations with the Chinese during the early T'ang, see Ibid., 194 I, chüan 144 I, "Account of the Turks," I, 3a; Wei Cheng, Sui shu (completed 644, reprinted Taipei, 1967) 84, chüan 49, "Account of the Turks," 14b; O-yang Hsiu, Sung Ch'i and others, Hsin T'ang shu (reprinted Taipei, 1967) 215 I, chüan 140 I, "Account of the Turks," I, 3a; Ibid., 88, chüan 13, "Biography of Liu Wen-ching," 2a.
64. Chiu T'ang shu 55, chüan 5, "Biography of Liu Wu-chou," 6a–b; 194 I, chüan 144 I, "Account of the Turks," I, 1b.
65. Ibid., 56, chüan 6, "Biography of Liang Shih-tu," 11a–b.
66. Ibid.
67. Ibid., 67, chüan 17, "Biography of Li Ching," 4a.
68. Ibid., 194 I, chüan 144 I, "Account of the Turks," I, 2a.
69. Ibid., 194 II, chüan 144 II, "Account of the Turks," 5b–6a.
70. Hsin T'ang shu 217 II, chüan 142 II, "Account of Hsüeh-yen-t'o [Sir-Tartush]," which is attached to the "Account of the Uighur," II, 4a–b.
71. Ibid., 217 I, chüan 142 I, "Account of the Uighur," I, 1b–2a.
72. Ibid.
73. An Lu-shan was a T'ang general of non-Chinese origin. See his biography in Ibid., 225 I, chüan 150 I and Chiu T'ang shu 200 I, chüan 150 I.
74. Shih Ssu-ming's biography is found in Chiu T'ang shu 200 I, chüan 150 I, and Hsin T'ang shu 225 I, chüan 150 I.
75. Chiu T'ang shu 195, chüan 145, "Account of the Uighur," 4a–b; Hsin T'ang shu 217 II, chüan 142 II, "Account of the Uighur," II, 1b.

76. *Hsin T'ang shu* 217 I, chüan 142 I, "Account of the Uighur," I, 7b–8a.

77. Li Yü (later Emperor Tai-tsung), son of Emperor Su-tsung, was conferred the title of Prince Kuang-p'ing when he was fifteen. Cf. *Chiu T'ang shu* 11, chi 11, "Annals of Tai-tsung."

78. Ibid., 195, chüan 145, "Account of the Uighur," 3a–4a; *Hsin T'ang shu* 217 I, chüan 142 I, "Account of the Uighur," I, 4a, 7b–8a.

79. Shih Ch'ao-i's biographies are attached to the biographies of Shin Ssu-ming cited in note 74.

80. A fuller discussion of these intermarriage ties is presented in chapter five.

81. *Chiu T'ang shu* 195, chüan 145, "Account of the Uighur," 5b–6a; *Hsin T'ang shu* 217, chüan 142, "Account of the Uighur," 5a.

82. Hsüeh Chü-cheng and others, *Chiu Wu-tai shih* (completed 974, reprinted Taipei, 1967) "Book of T'ang," 15, "Annals of Ming-tsung," V, 4b.

83. *Hsin T'ang shu* 219, chüan 144, "Account of the Khitan," in "Account of the Northern Barbarians," 1b, 2b.

84. *Chiu Wu-tai shih* 137, "Account of Foreign Countries," "Account of the Khitan," 2a–b, 4b–6a; 4, "Book of Liang," "Annals of T'ai-tsu," 4, 3a.

85. Toghto et al., *Liao shih* (completed 1344, reprinted Taipei, 1967) 1, chi 1, "Annals of T'ai-tsu," I, 2a.

86. Shih Ching-t'ang was the son of Nieh-lieh-chi, a Sha-to Turk. It seems that both the father and the son were Sinicized nomadic persons.

87. "In the period of Ta-ting (1161–1189), the garrison stations were built from Tan-she in the west to Hu-lieh-kung in the east over [a distance of] about six hundred *li*." Toghto et al., *Chin shih* (completed 1344, reprinted Taipei, 1967) 93, chüan 31, "Biography of Tu-chi Ssu-chung," 8a. For more on the Khitan-Jurchen struggle, see Sechin Jagchid, "Kitan struggle against Jurchen oppression-nomadism versus Sinicization," *Zentralasiatische Studien* 16:165–186 (1982).

88. *The Secret History of the Mongols*, sect. 134. Although the meaning of *ja'ud khuri* is unclear, it is unquestionably a title for lower military officers.

89. After the reunification of the Mongols by Dayan Khan (1464–1524, r. 1487–1524?), he organized the Mongols into six *tümens* and divided them into right and left flanks. The three *tümens* in the east became the Left Flank Mongols, led personally by Dayan Khan, and the three *tümens* in the west became the Right Flank Mongols, led by his third son, Bars-bolod, with the title of *jinong*, the deputy khan. Altan Khan was the leader of one of the three *tümen* of the Right Flank. (There is much disagreement regarding when Dayan Khan was born and died. We have adopted the dates given by Okada Hidehiro, "Life and Work of Dayan Khan," in *Proceedings of the International Conference on China Border Area Studies* (Taipei, 1985), 491–505.

90. From 1620, the Ming court, in order to check the rising power of the Manchus, paid Lighdan Khan forty thousand taels of silver yearly, and from 1628, payments were increased to eighty-one thousand taels. The money was regarded as a military expenditure by the Ming, and no demands were made that Lighdan Khan subject himself to the Ming to obtain it.

91. For the submission of the Uriyangkha, see Chang Ting-yü et al., *Ming shih* 328, chüan 216, "Account of To-yen, Fu-yü and T'ai-ning," 8a–9a; for the surrender of the Chikin Mongols, see Ibid., 330, chüan 218, "Account of the Western Region," II, "Account of the Chigin Mongol Garrison," 18b–19a.

92. *The Secret History of the Mongols*, tr. Francis W. Cleaves (Cambridge, Mass., 1982), sect. 239, records that the Oirad people were a group of the *hoi-yin irgen*, "people of the woods". Chinggis Khan send his eldest son, Jochi, to subdue them. Khutukha, the tribal head of the Oirad, surrendered to Jochi without fighting. Chinggis Khan gave one of his

daughters to marry the son of Khutukha and put the whole tribe under the rule of Jochi. This suggests that even in the early 1200s the Oirad had already developed into a quite powerful people.

93. Lobsang-danjin, *Altan Tobchi* (Cambridge, Mass., 1952), part 2, 131; Saghang Sechen, *Erdeni-yin tobchi* (Hohehot, Inner Mongolia, 1981), 283. This event has been studied by Wada Sei, *Toashi Kenkyu, Mokohen* (Tokyo, 1959), 230.
94. *Ming shih* 328, chüan 216, "Account of the Oirad," 1a–b.
95. Ibid., 327, chüan 215, "Account of the Ta-tan," 6b–7a.
96. Ibid., 27b.
97. Ibid., 28a.
98. Ibid., 30b–31a.

III. FRONTIER MARKETS

1. Henry Serruys, "Trade Relations: The Horse Fairs, 1400–1600; Sino-Mongol Relations During the Ming III,"*Mélanges Chinois et Bouddhiques* 17:15–16 (1975).
2. *Ming shih-lu*, also known as *Huang-Ming shih-lu*, ed. and printed by Academia Sinica, (Taipei 1966) 19 II, "T'ai-tsung" entry of *Chi-wei* day of the fifth month of the first year of Yung-lo (1403). See *Min jitsuroku sho, Mokohen* (Kyoto, 1959) vol. I, 176.
3. Chang T'ing-yü and others, *Ming shih* 92, chih 68, "Monograph on Military Affairs," IV, entry on horse policy, 24a. According to this source, in the last year of T'ai-tsu's reign, 1398, only between ten thousand and thirteen thousand five hundred horses were acquired through these markets.
4. Ibid., 81, chih 57, "Monograph on Economy," V, entry on horse markets, 24a. A passage in this source, 92, chih 68, "Monograph on Military Affairs," IV, entry on horse policy, 24b–25a suggests that all three markets were located forty *li* from the cities.
5. Ibid., 144, chüan 32, "Biography of Ho Fu," 6b.
6. Ibid., 9, chi 9, "Annals of Hsüan-tsung," 5a.
7. Ibid., 328, chüan 216, "Account of To-yen, Fu-yü and T'ai-ning," 11a–b; 10, chi 10, "Annals of Ying-tsung, Earlier Section," 8a.
8. Ibid., 81, chih 57, "Monograph on Economy," V, entry on horse market, 24a.
9. Ibid., 328, chüan 216, "Account of the Oirad," 3b.
10. Wang Chen, see Ibid., 304. chüan 192, "Biographies of Eunuchs."
11. Ibid., 81, chih 57, "Monograph on Economy," V, entry on horse market, 24a–b.
12. Ibid., 328, chüan 216, "Account of the Oirad," 3b–4a. See another account of this event in Ibid., 10, chi 10, "Annals of Ying-tsung, Earlier Section," 10b.
13. Morris Rossabi, "Notes on Esen's Pride and Ming China's Prejudice," *The Mongolia Society Bulletin* 9:31 (1970).
14. *Ming shih* 171, chüan 59, "Biography of Yang Shan."
15. Frederick W. Mote, "The T'u-mu Incident of 1449," in Frank A. Kierman, Jr. and John K. Fairbank, eds., *Chinese Ways in Warfare* (Cambridge, Mass., 1974), 243–271.
16. *Ming shih* 12, chi 12, "Annals of Ying-tsung, The Later Section," 3a–6a; Ibid., 172, chüan 60, "Biography of Pai Kuei," 17b.
17. Morikhai Noyan was the leader of the Ongni'ud tribe. He was a descendant of Khachi'un, younger brother of Chinggis Khan.
18. *Ming shih* 14, chi 14, "Annals of Hsien-tsung," II, 2a–7a.
19. Ibid., 92, chih 68, "Monograph on Military Affairs," IV, the entry on horse policy, 19a.
20. Ibid., 382, chüan 216, "Account of To-yen, Fu-yü and T'ai-ning," 11a–b.
21. Ibid., 327, chüan 215, "Account of Ta-tan," 14a.
22. Ibid., 186, chüan 75, "Biography of Hsü Chin," 11b.

Notes for pages 85–89   201

23. Ibid., 15, chi 15, "Annals of Hsiao-tsung," 2a–12a.
24. L. Carrington Goodrich and Fang Chaoying, eds., *Dictionary of Ming Biography 1368–1644* (New York, 1976), 6.
25. *Ming shih* 15, chi 15, "Annals of Hsiao-tsung," 2a–12a.
26. Ibid., 16, chi 16, "Annals of Wu-tsung," 1a–2a.
27. Ibid., 327, chüan 215, "Account of the Ta-tan," 16a–b.
28. Ibid., 17, chi 17, "Annals of Shih-tsung," 1a.
29. Ibid., 327, chüan 215, "Account of the Ta-tan," 16b–17a.
30. Goodrich and Fang, eds., 6.
31. *Ming shih* 327, chüan 215, "Account of the Ta-tan," 18a.
32. Ibid., 198, chüan 86, "Biography of Weng Wan-ta," 24a–25b.
33. Ibid.
34. Ibid., 18, chi 18, "Annals of Shih-tsung," II, 1a–13a.
35. Ibid., 198, chuan 86, "Biography of Weng Wan-ta," 24a–25b. Yu-lin *wei*, or garrison, was located south of present-day Hohehot (Koke-khota), where Altan Khan's headquarters were located.
36. Ibid., 18, chi 18, "Annals of Shih-tsung," II, 1a–13a.
37. Ibid., 198, chuan 86, "Biography of Weng Wan-ta," 24a–25b. Weng Wan-ta frankly expressed his opposition to the continued killing of enemy emissaries, saying that these actions closed the door to peace. He advocated that the Mongols be allowed to pay tribute and warned that if tribute presentation was not allowed there might be a recurrence of decades of war.
38. Ibid.; *Ming shih-lu* 364, "Shih-tsung" entry of the *chia-shen* day, of the eighth month of the twenty-ninth year of Chia-ching (1550). *Min jitsuroku sho, Mokohen*, vol. VI, 636.
39. *Ming shih* 198, chüan 86, "Biography of Weng Wan-ta," 24a–25b.
40. Ibid., 18, chi 18, "Annals of Shih-tsung," II, 1a–13a.
41. *Ming shih-lu* 364, "Shih-tsung" entry of the *jen-wu* day, of the eighth month of the twenty-ninth year of Chia-ching (1550). *Min jitsuroku sho, Mokohen*, vol. VI, 632–633.
42. For Hsu Chieh's biography, see *Ming shih* 213, chüan 101.
43. *Ming shih-lu* 364, "Shih-tsung" entry of the *jen-wu* day, of the eighth month of the twenty-ninth year of Chia-ching (1550). *Min jitsuroku sho, Mokohen*, vol. VI, 632–633.
44. Ibid., 371, "Shih-tsung" entry of *jen-ch'en* day of the third month of the thirtieth year of Chia-ching (1551). *Min jitsuroku sho, Mokohen*, vol. VI, 664–668.
45. See Ch'ou Luan's biography attached to the "Biography of Ch'ou Yüeh," in *Ming shih* 175, chüan 63.
46. Ibid., 209, chüan 97, "Biography of Yang Chi-sheng," 24a.
47. The entire text of Yang Chi-sheng's memorial advocating war against the Mongols is found in *Ming shih-lu* 371, "Shih-tsung" entry of *kuei-mou* day of the third month of the thirtieth year of Chia-ching (1551). *Min jitsuroku sho, Mokohen*, vol. VI, 669–672:

> Last year [1550], the northern barbarians disobeyed the way of Heaven and committed great violence. The Lord Emperor was magnificently indignant and selected commanders and trained troops to vindicate the hatred of millions of beloved people and to avenge the humiliation of an invasion at the walls of our Capital. This was greatly appreciated by both gods and men. [I, your] vassal, have seen the letter from Altan rudely demanding that horse markets be opened. I had humbly thought that the Lord Emperor had determined to launch a northern campaign to carry out a war of punishment. However, the conference of Court officials has promised to temporarily open horse markets. [I, your] vassal, was unable to repress a sigh to Heaven. The Lord Emperor is brilliant and heroic. The kingdom flourishes, and

there are countless brave and strong men of low rank and position, so why is it impossible to capture the barbarian chieftain and exterminate the people and their seed, instead of formulating a worse policy leaving us without choice.

Here [I, your] vassal, list ten points of objection [to the pacifist policies of other advisors]. The first objection is: The horse market is another term for peace negotiations. Even if the barbarians are submissive, it still should not be discussed. Moreover, at present, the barbarians have insulted us. Why are we able to establish peace with them but unable to declare a war of punishment? How will we dissipate the anger of Imperial Ancestors above and dispel the hatred of the people below?

The second objection is: Recently, the Lord Emperor by ordinance has repeatedly declared [his commitment to] a northern campaign, and this was heard by both subjects and the barbarians. Everybody in the realm under Heaven anxiously anticipates that Royal troops will fight, not that peace negotiations will open. This will cause a great loss of faith in the realm under Heaven.

The third objection is: A dignified Celestial Court's disgracing itself by trading with dogs and sheep bears no difference from switching the positions of a hat and shoes. This will greatly impair the prestige of the Kingdom.

The fourth objection is: Hearing of the brutal disaster brought about by the barbarians, the heroes of the realm under Heaven were all highly indignant and desired to fight a decisive war of life and death against the rebellious renegades. Upon hearing of the opening of the horse markets, they will say that the court has no intention of punishing the barbarians. If our upright will collapses, it cannot be reinspired, and it will disappoint the voluntarily sacrificial spirit of the heroes.

The fifth objection is: After the barbarian incident of last year, military acts were emphasized and learned in the realm under Heaven. Because of the establishment of markets and peace, defenses will relax daily, and the morale of the generals and soldiers will decline daily; and this will diminish desire for learning military affairs.

The sixth objection is: Although officials and people of Hsüan-fu and Ta-t'ung are usually in collusion with the barbarians, still they are afraid of the law and dare not run wild. Now they will take the markets as encouragement, and who will be able to restrain those who make disturbances? In the future they will entice the enemy and create immeasureable disasters. This will open the door along the border and entice the barbarians.

The seventh objection is: The realm under Heaven is suffering from a flood, and the people suffer from heavy corvee duties. Everybody desires a rebellion but is intimidated and afraid. Now they will say that the military threat is insufficient to check the barbarians, and the masses will rise up as bandits. Who is able to pacify them? This will accelerate a disturbance by the people.

The eighth objection is: Last year the barbarians deeply intruded into our land. Because there was no battle, they thought that we were not prepared. Now, the troops have mobilized for a half year, but eventually markets will be allowed and peace established. It will thus encourage the northern barbarians to look down on the Middle Kingdom.

The ninth objection is: These dogs and sheep are untrustworthy and constantly changing. Now, when we send an important minister to carry gold and silk to the border, they may not abide by the agreement and may refuse to come. Or, because of the markets they may attack the customs area and invade. Or, they may come to the market to trade today but to invade tomorrow. Or, they may send their masses to invade and say that it was done by other tribes. Or, they may bring weak horses but ask for a high price. Or, because they sell horses, they may ask for excessive rewards. Or, they may demand something beyond what we can bear. As it is, we are unable to hobble them, but they are able to fool us. We will thus be trapped in a shrewd plot by the northern barbarians.

The tenth objection is: We will send several hundred thousand taels of silver to obtain tens of thousands of horses each year. If the markets continue, the barbarian horses will daily increase in number, and our finances will be exhausted. Then how can we handle them again? It is not a prudent long-range plan for the kingdom.

The opinion of those who try to deceive Your Majesty includes five erroneous theories. The first falsehood is: Some have said, "outwardly we should open the horse market to hobble them, but inwardly we can relax our defense preparations." The barbarians are extremely greedy. If it is impossible to satisfy their desires, the agreement will be broken. Then, the pretext for their invasion will be our unfaithfulness in failing to satisfy their needs. The horse trade offers little benefit. Has it been enough to hobble the enemy? If it be said that it is intended to strengthen military preparation for attack and defense, then we should not depend on this.

The second falsehood is: Someone has said, "at present, horses are needed badly, and we wish to buy them." The horses are purchased only for expeditions against the barbarians. If the markets lead to peace, then where are the horses to be used? Moreover, why should the barbarians give us good horses?

The third falsehood is: Someone has said, "allow them to establish a horse market to temporarily win their hearts and gradually carry out the payment of tribute. That will be beneficial for all." Is the so-called tribute today the same as that from subordinates who came to pay respects to the King in ancient days? It is nothing but a large bribe to the enemy to maintain an improper peace for a short time. Moreover, at the horse market we are still able to spend lesser sums to cover expenditures; but if we allow them to pay tribute, they will obtain valuable interests with an empty hand.

The fourth falsehood is: Again they have said, "because the barbarians look to us for profit they will not break the promise." These people do not know that the ugly villains increase daily, and their expenditures multiply daily. Is the profit from the horse trade sufficient to meet the needs of their multitude? If not, why should they observe words spoken in vain and harness themselves? Even if it is enough to hobble them, it will last for only two or three years.

The fifth falsehood is: "Military action is unpropitious and should not be carelessly carried out. It would be better to promise to temporarily open a horse market to rest the soldiers and people and to immediately reform internal administration rather than exercise the troops and disturb the masses to carry out an expedition offering no definite victory in a remote area thousands of miles away." Alas! Is it proper to avoid using medicine while the body of the man suffers from an ulcer? The destruction of national magnificience, nourishment of invading troops, and subversion of important affairs of the realm under Heaven will all begin at this point.

These ten objections and five errors are known by everybody, but why among court officials is there no one who dares identify them? Because they are worried about their personal profits and losses. The Lord Emperor is brilliant and heroic, but his vassals are foolish, weak and irresponsible. They are not trustworthy. What a great enmity exists if the heart wishes to move but the hands and feet are paralyzed? This is the turning point for the nation, after which it will flourish or decline. [I, your] vassal, cannot bear the silence that deceives Your Majesty.

48. Ibid.
49. Ibid.
50. Ibid.
51. Ibid.
52. Ibid.
53. Ibid.
54. Ibid.
55. Ibid.
56. Ibid.

57. *Ming shih-lu* 371, "Shih-tsung" entry of *jen-ch'en* day of the third month of the thirtieth year of Chia-ching (1551). *Min jitsuroku sho, Mokohen,* vol. VI, 664–668.

58. Ibid., entry of *kuei-mou* day of the third month of the thirtieth year of Chia-ching (1551). *Min jitsuroku sho, Mokohen,* vol. VI, 669–672.

59. *Ming shih* 92, chih 68, "Monograph on Military Affairs," IV, entry on horse policy, 19a.

60. Ibid., p. 20a.

61. *Ming shih-lu* 371, "Shih-tsung" entry of *kuei-mou* day of the third month of the thirtieth year of Chia-ching (1551). *Min jitsuroku sho, Mokohen,* vol. VI, 669–672.

62. Ibid.

63. Ibid.

64. *Ming shih* 327, chüan 215, "Account of the Ta-tan," 20a.

65. Ibid., 81, chih 57, "Monograph on Economy," V, entry on horse markets, 24b.

66. *Ming shih-lu* 371, "Shih-tsung" entry of *kuei-mou* day of the third month of the thirtieth year of Chia-ching (1551). *Min jitsuroku sho, Mokohen,* vol. VI, 669–672.

67. Ibid.

68. Ibid., 381, "Shih-tsung" entry of *ting-hai* day of the first month of the thirty-first year of Chia-ching (1551). *Min jitsuroku sho, Mokohen,* vol. VII, 2.

69. Ibid., 371, "Shih-tsung" entry of *jen-chen* day of the third month of the thirtieth year of Chia-ching (1551). *Min jitsuroku sho, Mokohen,* vol. VI, 664–668.

70. Ibid.

71. Ibid.

72. Ibid.

73. Ibid.

74. *Ming shih* 81, chih 57, "Monograph on Economy," V, entry on horse market, 24b; 18, chi 18, "Annals of Shih-tsung," II, 1a–13a.

75. *Ming shih-lu* 372, "Shih-tsung" entry of *ping wu* day of the fourth month of the thirtieth year of Chia-ching (1551). *Min jitsuroku sho, Mokohen,* vol. VI, 678.

76. *Ming shih* 81, chih 57, "Monograph on Economy," V, entry on horse market, 24b.

77. Ibid., 222, chüan 110, "Biography of Wang Ch'ung-ku," 9a–11a.

78. Ibid., 18, chi 18, "Annals of Shih-tsung," II, 1a–13a.

79. Ibid., 327, chüan 215, "Account of the Ta-tan," 21a–b.

80. *Ming shih-lu* 381, "Shih-tsung" entry of *ting-hai* day of the first month of the thirty-first year of Chia-ching (1551). *Min jitsuroku sho, Mokohen,* vol. VII, 1.

81. Goodrich and Fang, eds., 6–9.

82. *Ming shih-lu* 371, "Shih-tsung" entry of *kuei-mou* day of the third month of the thirtieth year of Chia-ching (1551). *Min jitsuroku sho, Mokohen,* vol. VI, 669–672.

83. *Ming shih* 222, chüan 110, "Biography of Wang Ch'ung-ku," 9a–11a.

84. Ibid., 19, chi 19, "Annals of Mu-tsung," 2a–3b; 327, chüan 215, "Account of the Ta-tan," 24a–b.

85. The best month-by-month chronicle of the unfolding of events at Ta-t'ung in this important year and the one that follows is found in Ibid., 19, chi 19, "Annals of Mu-tsung," 4a–5a. Henry Serruys has also written an illuminating essay on the events of 1570–71 entitled "Four Documents Relating to the Sino-Mongol Peace of 1570–71," *Monumenta Serica* 19:1–66 (1960).

86. Ibid., 3–8. Serruys provides an excellent discussion of the quarrel between Baghaachi and Altan Khan.

87. Ibid., 8–9.

88. *Ming shih* 222, chüan 110, "Biography of Wang Ch'ung-ku," 7a–9b.

89. Serruys, "Four . . .," 7–8, citing Kao Kung's *Fu-Jung chi-shih*, 21.

90. *Ming shih* 222, chüan 110, "Biography of Wang Ch'ung-ku," 7a–9b.

91. Ibid.
92. Bars-bolod was a son of Dayan Khan and was appointed by the khan to govern the three *tümen* of the Right Flank Mongols.
93. In the fall and winter when pastures were dry, Chinese strategists often burned the pastures along China's frontiers to deter the Mongols from approaching its borders.
94. *Ming shih* 222, chüan 110, "Biography of Wang Ch'ung-ku," 7a–9b.
95. Ibid.
96. Ibid., 327, chüan 215, "Account of the Ta-tan," 25b–27a.
97. Ibid., 222, chüan 110, "Biography of Wang Ch'ung-ku," 7a–9b.
98. Ibid.
99. Ibid.
100. Ibid.
101. Ibid.
102. Köndüleng, the younger brother of Altan, was also known as Ba'atur Köndüleng Khan or the Old Ba'atur (Lao Pa-tu in Chinese). He was the head of the Kharachin tribe.
103. *Ming shih* 327, chüan 215, "Account of the Ta-tan," 25b–27a.
104. Ibid., 22, chüan 110, "Biography of Wang Ch'ung-ku," 9a–11a.
105. Ibid.
106. Ibid., 327, chüan 215, "Account of the Ta-tan," 25b–27a.
107. Ibid.
108. Ibid.
109. Wang's proposal does not clarify how many one-month market periods were to be allowed each year, but a passage in the *Ming shih-lu* makes clear that an arrangement of 1551 with Altan Khan allowed for the opening of the markets at Ta-t'ung and Hsüan-fu twice annually. See, *Ming shih-lu* 371, "Shih-tsung" entry of *jen-ch'en* day of the third month of the thirtieth year of Chia-ching (1551). *Min jitsuroku sho*, Mokohen, vol. VI, 668.
110. The Japanese scholar Wada Sei, in an article entitled "Mingdaino hoppen boei" (Northern frontier defense of Ming China), in *Toashi Kenkyu*, Mokohen (Tokyo, 1959), 832, shows that the initial market framework was expanded to include a number of additional sites:

> In Liao-tung the markets were first established at Kuang-ning, K'ai-yüan, and such places as Fu-shun to trade with the three garrisons [of Uriyangkha] and the Jurchens. Later a lumber market was established for the three garrisons at I-chou. . . . Soon after these two markets were established outside the southern and northern gates of K'ai-yüan, markets were again opened outside the Hsin-an Gate of Ch'ing-yün, the Chen-an Gate of Kuang-ning, Ta-fu-pu, and Ta-k'ang-pu . . . in order to satisfy the three garrisons. . . . Along the western border, markets were established at Ta-t'ung from time to time. At Hsi-fen-k'ou a tribute custom was arranged for the three garrisons. During the Lung-ch'ing period [1571], after peace was concluded with Altan, horse markets, to carry out peaceful tribute and trade agreements, were set up at Hsi-fen-k'ou and Hei-yü-kuan of Chi-chen, Ta-shih-ch'ang of Chang-chai-k'ou of Hsüan-fu, Te-sheng-pu, Sha-hu-pu and Hsin-p'ing-pu of Ta-t'ung, Shuo-k'ou-pu of Yang-ho, Ying-hung-men of Shui-ch'üan of Shansi, Hung-shan of Yü-lin of Yen-sui, Ch'ing-shui-ying, Ping-lu-ch'ang and Chung-wei-ch'ang of Hsing-wu of Ning-hsia, and Pien-tu-k'ou of Kansu.

111. Serruys, "Four . . . ," 18.
112. Altan Khan's younger brother, Ba'atur (Köndüleng), and his eldest son, Sengge (*Khong Taiji*), were made *Tu-tu t'ung-chih* (deputy governor generals). Another of Altan's sons, Bintu *Taiji*, was named a *Chih-hui t'ung-chih* (deputy director). The title *Chih-hui*

ch'ien-shih (consulting director) was given to Altan's grandson, Namur *Taiji* (son of Sengge). The ranks of commander of a thousand, deputy commander of a thousand, and centurian were bestowed on Altan's relatives, Darkhan *Taiji*, Abai *Taiji*, and Kiya *Taiji* respectively. Except for the title of *Wang* (prince), the other ranks were among those customarily given to the leaders of the three Uriyangkha garrisons. See Wada Sei, 667–752.

113. *Ming shih-lu*, "Mu-tsung" entry of I-ch'ou day of the month of the fifth year of Lung-ch'ing (1571). *Min jitsuroku sho, Mokohen*, vol. VIII, 14–15.

114. The extent to which documents could be tampered with and even changed, with and without the knowledge of non-Chinese rulers, to make them suitable for presentation at a Chinese court is analyzed in Joseph F. Fletcher, "China and Central Asia, 1368–1884," in John K. Fairbank, ed., *The Chinese World Order* (Cambridge, Mass., 1968), 206–224.

115. *Hsüan-lan-t'ang ts-ung-shu* (reprinted in Taipei, 1986) vol. 1 (in the Central Library, Taipei). Part of the original memorial is also found at the front of Wada Sei, tablet 5–6.

116. *Hsüan-lan-t'ang ts'ung-shu*, vol. I.

117. As a supplement to the documents found in Serruys, "Four . . . ," and as an aid to those wishing to further analyze Altan Khan's position in these negotiations, the text found in the *Hsüan-lan-t'ang ts'ung-shu* of Altan Khan's memorial entitled "A Memorial for Tribute from Altan, Shun-i *Wang* of the Northern Barbarians," is cited in full:

> The newly installed Prince Shun-i, vassal of the northern barbarians, Altan, and others, bowed a hundred times to render grateful homage and have memorialized His Majesty, the Merciful Saintly Emperor of the Great Ming. The most honorable of all realms under Heaven is the Celestial Court of the Imperial Ming. He is truly the Son of Heaven above and legitimate lord of the Chinese and the Barbarians. All of the nine *i* [barbarians] and the eight *man* [barbarians] have received ranks and pay tribute individually. [We, your] vassals, have been raised in the northern foreign lands and know nothing about the rituals of vassalage. In earlier years, the Little Prince [the Khan] presented tribute and received bestowals from the Celestial Court. In recent years, the tribes have been drawn in by treasonous people and have forfeited the bestowals. [We, your] vassals, [have suffered] an increase of population and a shortage of clothing. The people of the *Jinong*, who is the nephew of [your] vassal, are scattered [over the lands] of the western bend of the Yellow river and the Great and Small Sung-shan west of the [Yellow] river; and the people of the younger brother of [your] vassal, Ba'atur, are spread [across the lands of] Chaghan Na'ur adjoining [the border of] the Three Garrisons of Doying, and on none of the borders were markets permitted to open. There was no way to satisfy our needs for clothing. Our felts and furs wear poorly in the summer heat, [but] it has been impossible to get even a piece of cloth. Incited and guided by Chao Ch'üan, we crossed the border and carried out the improper activities. Although [we] plundered the cities and met our needs, our people and horses were killed and wounded. In recent years, the border generals sent troops continually to destroy, kill, and kidnap our families and people, to loot our horses and set fire to our pastures outside the border. [Life] became difficult for both people and animals, [especially] during winter and spring. This was of course caused by the evil that we committed, which was caused also by Chao Ch'üan.
>
> Recently, Heaven assisted the Imperial Ming with its multitude of troops and generals and with its sympathy for the northern barbarians. Therefore, after the surrender of my grandson, Achi, the Celestial Mercy of Your Majesty dictated that he not be killed; [instead] he was received and nourished, and through the petitions from the governors-general, Achi received the official title, *Chih-hui-shih* [Director]. [I, your] vassal, my younger brothers, nephews, son, and grandsons, moved by this Celestial Mercy surrendered single-heartedly, swore not to violate any bor-

ders and willingly accepted ranks and titles as foreign subordinates forever. Consequently, [I, your] vassal, dispatched a *darkhan* [headman] with a document in barbarian language to be submitted to the governor-general and other officials. First, I sent Chang Wen-yen, then arrested and delivered the eight evil rebels, Chao Ch'üan and the others. The governor-general petitioned on my behalf, which [Your Majesty] accepted mercifully, then [you] bestowed on [my] grandson embroidered satin for facing and lining, along with other cloth, and returned him alive to [me, your] vassal. [I, your] vassal, and my grandson both bow to the south in gratitude for Heaven's mercy. But, [I, your] vassal of the northern barbarians, have neither the understanding of literature nor the document forms with which to petition for what is really needed. Again, in this, instructions came from the governor-general. [I, your] vassal, along with Ba'atur, the younger brother of [your] vassal, [your] vassal's nephew, the *Jinong*, and *Khong Taiji*, son of [your] vassal, have joined with the tribe of the relatives of [your] vassal, [such as] Yüngshiyebü, Dolo'on Tümed, Uushin, Bayod, and Uighurchin to swear single-heartedly not to transgress the borders. Only then was [the governor-general] allowed to memorialize on behalf of [your] vassal. Following this instruction, [I, your] vassal, gathered the leaders of all branches [to have each of them] send trustworthy members to be accompanied by the governor-general's interpreter, then [I, your vassal,] sent a *darkhan* and others to the office of the governor-general. After everything was translated and studied in detail, it was memorialized for [your] vassal.

[We, your vassals], have since received the Merciful Imperial Decree conferring the rank of Shun-i *wang* on [your] vassal . . . [and other ranks upon other relatives]. . . . [In addition] the titles of director commander of a thousand and centurion were bestowed on fifty-seven of [my, your] vassal's sons, grandsons and nephews. [I, your] vassal, have received the bestowal of one golden serpent, an official's coat of red embroidery and eight rolls of designed satin for facing and lining and [your] vassal's younger brothers, sons [and nephews] one red satin coat designed with the figure of a lion and four rolls of designed satin for facing and lining. [We, your] vassals, were allowed to present tribute and make exchanges at the markets. [We, your] vassals, are extremely appreciative of this Celestial Mercy.

[I, your] vassal, of the northern barbarians, knowing nothing of literature, also had no document forms. [I, your] vassal requested these forms and documentary papers from the office of the governor-general. [By your] vassal's order in the barbarian language was then written [my thoughts] in memorial form. All of these [communications] come sincerely from the heart of [your] vassal and from every other barbarian. [I] petition the Emperor, Your Majesty, to have pity on [me, your] vassal, who in his old age regrets [his] transgressions and is sincerely appreciative of the mercy extended to forgive the crime of border aggression that [your] vassal committed at the instigation of the traitors. [We, your] vassals, present tributary horses [to Your Majesty], so please accept them in your mercy and bestow rewards upon us.

The *Jinong* and [his relatives] are descendants of the [former] *Jinong*, who was an elderly relative of [your] vassal. [I, your] vassal, have already mutually agreed with them to surrender single-handedly. [We, your] vassals, have individually received official titles, but the *Jinong* and [his relatives] have not received titles or rank. [We, your] vassals, are fearful that [our] ancestors may condemn us, and [we] therefore petition for Sacred Mercy, that official titles might be bestowed on the *Jinong* and [his relatives] and that they be allowed to participate in the tributary markets.

Please permit [your] vassals to protect areas north of the desert and the bend area of the [Yellow] River and present tribute each year. [We] petition that the Imperial decree should be sent to those border officials, ordering them to establish markets and permitting the barbarians and Chinese to carry out trade once each year. This should occur in the spring of each year when barbarian envoys of [your] vassal pass through [border] customs, ending on the day [that they] return. Thus, both the Chinese and the barbarians may enjoy a peaceful life. [I, your] vassal, [together with my] brothers, nephews, sons, and grandsons will be grateful for this mercy from generation to generation and never rebel again. If [there be any] transgression let Heaven punish us. [I, your] vassal am extremely grateful for this mercy and conscientiously express the greatest thanks in this memorial. [I, your] vassal, and the barbarians of each branch present five hundred horses. All of this is reported through this memorial.

118. *Ong* means prince and *Sun* is a mispronunciation of Shun-i.
119. Saghang Sechen, *Erdeni-yin Tobchi*, Ulan Bator ed., p. 70a.
120. *Ming shih* 222, chüan 110, "Biography of Chang Hsüeh-yen," 2b.
121. The *Erdeni-yin Tobchi*, 67b, says, "Tümen Taiji . . . ruled together with [the leaders of] the Left Flank . . . and Right Flank. . . . The fame of Jasaghtu Khaghan [Tümen] was fulfilled in all directions and made the great nation enjoy the rule of tranquility."
122. *Altan Tobchi*, Harvard ed., part II, 180.
123. *Ming shih* 222, chüan 110, "Biography of Wang Ch'ung-ku," 11a.
124. Ibid., "Biography of Wu Tui," 17a.
125. Ibid., 18a.
126. Ibid., 327, chüan 215, "Account of the Ta-tan," 28b.
127. According to Hsiao Ta-heng's *Pei-lu shih-hsi* (completed 1594, published Peiping, 1930's), Bingtu was a grandson of Mergen *Jinong* of the Ordos tribe and a son of Baishingghur-Lang-*Taiji*, pasturing outside the border of Kan-chou and Chuang-lang. Bintu was a son of Altan, pasturing in the areas of Ho-chou of Shensi (present-day Linhsia, Kansu) and Hsi-hai (the Kökönor Lake) and marketing at Pien-tu k'ou in Kansu. See also Wada Sei, 699 and 727.
128. *Ming shih*, 327, chüan 215, "Account of the Ta-tan," 27b.
129. Ibid., 330, chüan 218, "Account of the Western Region," I, entry of *hsi-fan chu-wei* [the garrisons of the western barbarians], 8b–9a.
130. Ibid.
131. Ibid., 10a.
132. Ibid., 239, chüan 127, "Biography of Tung I-yüan," 11b.
133. Ibid., 222, chüan 110, "Biography of Fang Feng-shih," 14a–16a.
134. In Ibid., 91, chih 67, "Monograph on Military Affairs," III, entry on border defense, 1a–b; it suggests: "At first the four stationing quarters were established at Liao-tung, Hsüan-fu, Ta-t'ung, and Yen-sui, and, following this, the three stationing quarters were established at Ning-hsia, Kan-su, and Chi-chou. Besides, the commander of T'ai-yüan supervised P'ien-tou and the office of San-pien stationed at Ku-yüan. These are the 'nine borders.' "
135. Ibid., 222, chüan 110, "Biography of Fang Feng-shih," 14a–16a.
136. Ibid.
137. Ibid.
138. Emphasis is the authors.
139. *Ming shih*, 235, chüan 123, "Biography of Meng I-mai," 9b–10a.
140. Ibid., 81, chih 57, "Monograph on Economy," V, entry on horse markets, 24b–25a.
141. Ibid., 222, chüan 110, "Biography of Fang Feng-shih," 14a–16a.
142. Ibid.
143. Ibid.
144. Ibid., 81, chih 57, "Monograph on Economy," V, entry on horse markets, 24a–b.
145. Ibid.
146. Ibid.

147. Ibid., 92, chih 68, "Monograph on Military Affairs," IV, entry on horse policy, 24a.
148. Ibid., 222, chüan 110, "Biography of Wu Tui," 18a.
149. Ibid., 328, "Account of To-yen, Fu-yü and T'ai-ning," 10a; Ming shih-lu 371, "Shih-tsung" entry of jen-ch'en day of the third month of the thirtieth year of Chia-ching (1551). Min jitsuroku sho, Mokohen, vol. VI, 668.
150. Ming shih 327, chüan 215, "Account of the Ta-tan," 27b.
151. Ibid., 238, chüan 126, "Biography of [Li] Ju-sung," which is attached to the biography of his father, Li Ch'eng-liang.
152. Jongnon (or Chino'an) was a son of Engke, the noyan of Doyin (T'o-yen) of the Uriyangkha. See Wada Sei, Toashi, 617–618.
153. Ba'atur was a son of Subakhai Darkhan Noyan, the chief of the Ba'arin tribe. See Wada Sei, Toashi, 617–618.
154. Ming shih 238, chüan 126, "Biography of Li Ch'eng-liang," 9a–b.
155. He was only twelve years old in the Western way of considering age.
156. Ming shih 327, chüan 215, "Account of the Ta-tan," 31a.
157. Boshightu was recorded in Erdeni-yin tobchi as Boshigtu Jinong. He was the grandson of Noyandara Jinong.
158. Jongdolai was recorded in the Erdeni-yin tobchi as Jongdolai Uijeng Noyan of the Ordos. Ming shih 327, chüan 215, "Account of the Ta-tan," 28b, 31a; 20–21, chi 20–21, "Annals of Shen-tsung," I–II.
159. Ibid., 218, chüan 106 for the biography of Shen Shih-hsing. However, Shen's role in the debate about how to deal with Chürüge is not mentioned.
160. Ibid., 320, chüan 118, "Biography of Wan Kuo-ch'in," 4b–5a; 222, chüan 110, "Biography of Cheng Lo," 21b–22a; 20–21, chi 20–21, "Annals of Shen-tsung," I–II; "Account of the Ta-tan," 28a–b.
161. Mongkeshiri was a grandson of Noyandara Jinong and the son of Mingghan Noyan and was recorded in Erdeni-yin tobchi as Mongkeshiri Taiji.
162. The jinong by this time was Boshightu, grandson of Noyandara Jinong.
163. Sechen Taiji was recorded in Erdeni-yin tobchi as Khutughtu Sechen Khong Taiji. He invaded Tibet with Altan and finally persuaded Altan to convert to Buddhism.
164. Daiching was an honorable title of this period and it is difficult to identify who it refers to.
165. Shaji, a person unknown.
166. In the Ming shih 239, chüan 127, "Biography of Tu T'ung," 13a–b, it says: "In the winter of the twenty-ninth year of Wan-li [1601] . . . Mingghan [of the loop of the Yellow river], just after marketing, came to the border again and asked for a reward and threatened to invade the border. [Tu] T'ung . . . directed light cavalries and moved forward from Yü-lin [in north Shensi] in three columns . . . chopped off more than four hundred seventy heads of the enemy, beheaded Mingghan, and returned. Formerly, from the time when [Noyandara] Jinong presented tribute, there was peace along the border for twenty years, and now war broke out again. Bayantai, son of Mingghan tried to seek revenge day after day, and the invading and looting had no end."
167. Ibid., 327, chüan 215, "Account of the Ta-tan," 31a–b.
168. Ibid., 31b–32a.
169. Ibid., 31b–33b.
170. Ibid.
171. Ibid., 222, chüan 110, "Biography of Wang Ch'ung-ku," 12a.
172. Ibid., 317, chüan 215, "Account of the Ta-tan," 28a–b.
173. Ibid., p. 30a.

174. Ibid., 222, chüan 110, "Biography of Wang Ch'ung-ku," 9b.
175. Serruys, Trade Relations: The Horse, 15–16.

IV. TRIBUTE AND BESTOWALS

1. Henry Serruys, "Sino-Mongolian Relations during the Ming II: The Tribute System and Diplomatic Missions (1400–1600)," *Mélanges Chinois et Bouddhiques* 14:21 (1967).
2. Some of the significant monographic works on frontier markets and tribute presentation include: two edited works, John K. Fairbank, ed., *The Chinese World Order* (Cambridge, Mass., 1968), and Morris Rossabi, ed., *China Among Equals* (Berkeley, 1983); the studies of Henry Serruys, especially, "Sino-Mongolian Relations . . . , and "Sino-Mongolian Relations during the Ming III: Trade Relations: The Horse Fairs," *Mélanges Chinois et Bouddhiques* 17:1–288 (1975); Morris Rossabi, "Ming China's Relations with Hami and Central Asia, 1404–1513: A Reexamination of Traditional Chinese Foreign Policy" (diss., Columbia University, 1970); Yü Ying-shih, *Trade and Expansion in Han China* (Berkeley, 1967); Owen Lattimore, *Inner Asian Frontiers of China* (New York, 1951); Franz H. Michael, *The Origin of Manchu Rule in China* (Baltimore, 1942); Gertraude Roth-Li, "The Rise of the Early Manchu State: A Portrait Drawn from Manchu Sources to 1636" (diss., Harvard University, 1975).
3. Chang T'ing-yü and others, *Ming shih* 328, chüan 216, "Account of To-yen, Fu-yü and T'ai-ning," 13a–b; 317, chüan 215, "Account of the Ta-tan," 29b–30a.
4. Ibid., 239, chüan 127, "Biography of Kuan Ping-chung," 23b.
5. In the Mongolian material, Lobsang-danjin's *Altan Tobchi* (Cambridge, Mass., 1952), part 2, 150–51 records the events in Mongolia in 1449 after Esen captured the Ming emperor Ying-tsung and later released him:

> The six thousand Üchiyed people in the front of the mountain brought the Emperor Cheng-tung back and thereupon received *dayidu*. Because formerly they had given assistance to the Emperor Yung-lo and received three hundred *dayidu*, now they gave support to the Emperor Cheng-te and again received three hundred *dayidu*. This is the six hundred *dayidu* of the people in the front of the mountain. Someone said that the Mongols on the back of the mountain had brought Emperor Jingtei [Cheng-tung] back, and therefore three hundred *dayidu* were issued for [presentation to] them. Because the Mongols quarreled among themselves, payment was delayed and they did not get it. Thereupon, the six thousand Üchiyed people in the front of the mountain demanded and received it.

The *dayidu* were imperial orders and must have had some kind of relationship to "bestowals" and "tribute." Father Henry Serruys, in an article entitled "Ta-tu, Tai-tu, Day-idu," *Chinese Culture* 2.4 (1960) suggests that *dayidu* were documents or certificates entitling the holder to present tribute and accept bestowals.

6. Ssu-ma Ch'ien, *Shih chi* (reprinted Taipei, 1967) 110, chüan 50, "Account of the Hsiung-nu," 12b–13a.
7. See chapter one.
8. The more commonly used word for "to give," *tseng*, was rarely used in referring to gift exchange, except when expressing condolences.
9. Pan Ku and Pan Chao, *Han shu* (reprinted Taipei, 1967) 48, chüan 18, "Biography of Chia I," I, 28b.
10. *Shih chi* 110, chüan 50, "Account of the Hsiung-nu," 28b.
11. *Han shu* 94 II, chüan 64 II, "Account of the Hsiung-nu," II, 3b–4b.
12. Ibid.
13. Ibid., 7b.

Notes for pages 118–124

14. Ibid., 12a–b.
15. Ibid., 18a–b.
16. Ibid., 25b–26b.
17. Ibid., 28b.
18. Fan Yeh, Hou Han shu (reprinted Taipei, 1967) 89, chüan 79, "Account of the Southern Hsiung-nu," 5b–6b.
19. Ibid.
20. See chapter one.
21. For example, after his initial submission to the court, Pi received only ten thousand catties of lining silk while Hu-han-yeh acquired thirty thousand catties. Pi was given only 250,000 bushels of grain while Hu-han-yeh received 340,000 bushels. These figures are drawn from Hou Han shu 89, chüan 79, "Account of the Southern Hsiung-nu," 5b–6b.
22. Ibid., 5b–6b, 7a, 11b.
23. Ibid., 11b–12a.
24. Li Yen-shou, Nan shih (completed before 650, reprinted Taipei, 1967) 79, chüan 69, "Account of the Juan-juan," in the "Accounts of I-mo [Barbarians]," II, the "Northern Barbarians," sec. 17a–b; Ibid., 4, chi 4, "Annals of Ch'i," I, 15b; Ibid., 6, chi 6, "Annals of Liang," I, 26b; and Ibid., 7, chi 7, "Annals of Liang," II, 10b.
25. See chapter five.
26. Wei Shou, Wei shu (reprinted Taipei, 1967) 103, chüan 91, "Account of the Juan-juan," 12b–13b. See also, Li Yen-shou, Pei shih (reprinted Taipei, 1967) 98, chüan 86, "Account of the Juan-juan," 9a–10a. These two records are exactly the same except that the Pei shih refers to Emperor Shih-tsung as Hsüan-wu-ti and Su-tsung as Ming-ti.
27. Ibid.
28. Ling-hu Te-fen, Chou shu (reprinted Taipei, 1967) 50, chüan 42, "Account of the Turks," 7b.
29. Wei Cheng, Sui shu (completed 644, reprinted Taipei, 1967) 84, chüan 49, "Account of the Turks," 3b.
30. Ibid.
31. Ibid., 6a–b.
32. Ibid., 7a–b.
33. Ibid., 9b.
34. O-yang Hsiu, Sung Ch'i et al., Hsin T'ang shu (reprinted Taipei, 1967) 215, chüan 140 I, "Account of the Turks," 6b. The problem of T'ang Kao-tsu's subjugation to the Turks is discussed by Professor Li Shu-t'ung in his book T'ang shih k'ao-pien (Taipei, 1965), 214–246.
35. Hsin T'ang shu 215, chüan 140 I, "Account of the Turks," 3a.
36. Ibid., 4a.
37. Sui shu 84, chüan 46, "Account of the Turks," 8b.
38. Hsin T'ang shu 215 I, chüan 140 I, "Account of the Turks," I, 3b.
39. Sui shu 84, chüan 49, "Account of the Tieh-le," 19a.
40. Wei shu 103, chüan 91, "Account of the Kao-ch'e," 31b–32a.
41. Ibid., 31b–32a, 33a, 33b.
42. Hsin T'ang shu 217 I, chüan 142, "Account of the Uighur," 4a.
43. Hsüeh Chü-chang et al., Chiu Wu-tai shih (completed 974, reprinted Taipei, 1967) 138, "Account of the Uighur," in the Account of Foreign Countries," II, 3b–6a.
44. This concept is similar to that held by Ishbara Khan of the Turks towards Emperor Wen-ti of the Sui dynasty, which is discussed in chapter five. Ishbara had taken a princess of the Yü-wen family of the Chou dynasty as his wife, but he felt that his intermarriage ties with the Chinese court continued even after the Sui emperor usurped the throne of

Chou and created a new dynasty, bringing the Yü-wen dynastic rule to a close. Therefore, Ishbara called Emperor Wen-ti the father of his wife. Ishbara's views were tied to the nomadic practice of forming exogamous marriage ties.

45. *Chiu Wu-tai shih* 138, "Account of the Uighur," in the "Account of Foreign Countries," II, 3b–6a.

46. O-yang Hsiu, *Wu-tai shih-chi* (reprinted Taipei, 1967) 74, "Appendix of the Four Barbarians," III, "Account of Tang-hsiang," 4b–5a.

47. Ibid.

48. Toghto et al., *Sung shih* (completed 1346, reprinted Taipei 1967) 490, chüan 249, "Account of the Uighurs," in the "Accounts of the Foreign Countries," VI, 16a.

49. *Sui shu* 84, chüan 49, "Account of the Khitan," 20a.

50. *Hsin T'ang shu* 219, chüan 144, "Account of the Khitan," in the "Account of the Northern Barbarians," 4a.

51. Toghto and others, *Liao shih* (completed 1344, reprinted Taipei 1967) 1, chi 1, "Annals of T'ai-tsu," I, 2a.

52. *Chiu Wu-tai shih* 26, "Book of T'ang," 2, "Annals of Wu-huang," II, 13b.

53. *Liao shih* 1, chi 1, "Annals of T'ai-tsu," I, 2a.

54. *Chiu Wu-tai shih* 137, "Account of the Khitan," in the "Account of Foreign Countries," I, 5a.

55. Ibid., 34, "Book of T'ang," 8, "Annals of Chuang-tsung," 1b; 36, "Book of T'ang," 12, "Annals of Ming-tsung," 2, 7b; 39, "Book of T'ang, 15, "Annals of Ming-tsung," 5, 2a, 9b; 40, "Book of T'ang, 16, "Annals of Ming-tsung," 6, 3a; 43, "Book of T'ang, 19, "Annals of Ming-tsung," 9, 1a, 3a.

56. See Yao Ts'ung wu, "Shuo A-pao-chi shih-tai-ti Han-ch'eng," in *Tung-pei-shih luntsung* (Taipei, 1959) I, 91–188; and Sechin Jagchid, "The Kitans and Their Cities," *Central Asiatic Journal* 25 (1981).

57. *Chiu Wu-tai shih* 75, "Book of Chin," I, "Annals of Kao-tsu," I, 8b, 9b, 10b.

58. *Liao shih* 3, chi 3, "Annals of T'ai-tsung," I, 10b.

59. *Chiu Wu-tai shih* 137, "Account of the Khitan," in the "Account of Foreign Countries," 7b.

60. Liu Hsü and others, *Chiu T'ang shu* (reprinted Taipei, 1967) 57, chüan 7, "Biography of Liu Wen-ching," 5a.

61. *Wu-tai shih-chi* 72, "Account of the Khitan," in the Appendix of Four Barbarians," I, 13a.

62. *Chiu Wu-tai shih* 137, "Account of the Khitan," in the Account of the Foreign Countries," 8b.

63. Ibid., 8b–9a.

64. Ibid., 9b.

65. *Sung Hui-yao chi-kao*, 7682, cited by Wang Gungwu in "The Rhetoric of a Lesser Empire: Early Sung Relations with Its Neighbors," in Rossabi, ed. *China*, 53.

66. Ibid. Wang's article shows how the successor states to the T'ang dynasty, including the early Sung, attempted to maintain the rhetoric of imperial greatness even though their power vis-à-vis nomadic states markedly declined.

67. See his biographies in both *Sung shih* 279, chüan 38, and *Liao shih* 81, chüan 11. The *Liao shih* biography provides more detailed records on the peace negotiations between the Liao and the Sung.

68. *Liao shih* 14, chi 14, "Annals of Sheng-tsung," 6a.

69. Ibid.

70. *Sung shih* 281, chüan 40, "Biography of K'ou Chun," 20a–b.

71. Ibid.

72. Li T'ao, *Hsü Tzu-chih t'ung-chien ch'ang-pien* (Taipei, 1964), ch. 150, 16a; and T'ao Chin-sheng and Wang Min-hsin, eds., *Li T'ao Hsü Tzu-chih t'ung-chien ch'ang-pien*

Sung-Liao kuan-hsi shih-liao chi-lu (Taipei, 1974), 459 as cited by Tao Jing-shen in "Barbarians or Northerners: Northern Sung Images of the Khitans," in Rossabi, ed., *China*, 79.

73. *Sung shih* 281, chüan 40, "Biography of K'ou Chun," 20a–b.
74. For the biography of Liu Liu-fu see *Liao shih* 86, chüan 16, 2b. Liu Liu-fu's biography is recorded as that of Hsiao Te-mo (Temur?).
75. *Sung shih* 313, chüan 72, "Biography of Fu Pi," 2a–4b.
76. *Shih chi* 110, chüan 50, "Account of the Hsiung-nu," 11a.
77. *Liao shih* 19, chi 19, "Annals of Hsing-tsung," II, 3a.
78. *Sung shih* 313, chüan 72, "Biography of Fu Pi," 2a–4b.
79. *Liao shih* 19, chi 19, "Annals of Hsing-tsung," II, 3a.
80. Ibid., 86, chüan 16, "Biography of Liu Liu-fu," 2b–3a. Both in *Liao shih* and the *Sung shih* were written during the Yüan dynasty. The failure to agree on which terms were actually used simply reflects the fact that scholars were drawing from Liao sources to write one work and Chinese sources to write the other. Sung scribes were unwilling to admit Chinese subordination to the Khitan, and Liao scribes possibly inflated the Khitan position vis-à-vis the Chinese.
81. *Sung shih* 485, chüan 244, "Account of the Hsia State," I, in the "Account of Foreign Countries," I, 13a.
82. Ibid.
83. *Shih chi*, 110, chüan 50, "Account of the Hsiung-nu," 15b–16a.
84. *Chiu T'ang shu* 194 I, chüan 144 I, "Account of the Turks," I, 14b.
85. *Sung shih* 485, chüan 244, "Account of the Hsia State," I, in the "Account of Foreign Countries," I, 19b–20b; Ibid., 179, chih 132, "Monograph on Economy," II, 1, 6a–b.
86. *Sung shih* 485, chüan 244, "Account of the Hsia State," I, in the "Account of Foreign Countries," I, 19b–20b.
87. Herbert Franke, "Treaties Between Sung and Chin," *Études Song/Sung Studies*, series 1:60–68 (1970).
88. Franke, 68–76.
89. Both T'ang and Teng were located in the present-day Nan-yang area of Honan.
90. *Sung shih* 29, chi 29, "Annals of Kao-tsung," IV, 18b.
91. Franke, 76–82.
92. *Sung shih* 281, chüan 40, "Biography of K'ou Chun," 20a–b.
93. Ibid., 179, chih 132, "Monograph on Economy," II, 1, 6a–b.
94. Ibid., 33, chi 33, "Annals of Hsiao-tsung," I, 17b; Toghto and others, *Chin shih* (completed 1344, reprinted Taipei, 1967) 6, chi 6, "Annals of Shih-tsung," I, 15a–b.
95. *Chin shih* 12, chi 12, "Annals of Chang-tsung," 16a; *Sung shih* 39, chi 39, "Annals of Ning-tsung," III, 1a–b.
96. *Sung shih* 39, chi 39, "Annals of Ning-tsung," III, entry of the seventh year of Chia-ting [1214], 12a.
97. *Sung shih* 474, chüan 233, "Biography of Chia Ssu-tao," 14a.
98. See Hao Ching's biography in Sung Lien and others, *Yüan shih* (completed 1369, reprinted Taipei, 1967) 157, chüan 44.
99. *Sung shih* 474, chüan 233, "Biography of Chia Ssu-tao," 14a.
100. See Wada Sei, *Toashi Kenkyu, Mokohen* (Tokyo, 1959), 203–204.
101. *Ming shih* 327, chüan 215, "Account of the Ta-tan," 5b.
102. Bunyashiri is recorded in Mongolian sources as Öljei-temür khan.
103. *Ming shih* 328, chüan 216, "Account of the Oirad," 1b.
104. Mahmud is recorded in Mongolian sources as Batula Chingsang (prime minister).
105. *Ming shih* 328, chüan 216, "Account of the Oirad," 1a–b.
106. Ibid., 2a.

107. *Ming shih-lu*, ed., printed by Academia Sinica, (Taipei, 1966) 88, "T'ai-tsung" entry of *chi-yu* day of sixth month of the eleventh year of Yung-lo (1413). *Min jitsuroku sho*, Mokohen, vol. I, 426.

108. *Ming shih* 327, chüan 215, "Account of the Ta-tan," 7a.

109. L. Carrington Goodrich and Fang Chaoying, eds., *Dictionary of Ming Biography 1368–1644*, (New York, 1976), 416.

110. *Ming shih-lu* 96, "Ying-tsung" entry of *ken-ch'en* day of the ninth month of the seventh year of Cheng-t'ung (1442).

111. Ibid., 180, "Ying-tsung" entry of *chi-mo*, the first day of the seventh month of the autumn of the fourteenth year of Cheng-t'ung (1449). *Min jitsuroku sho*, vol. III, 211–212.

112. Ibid., 72, "Ying-tsung" entry of *ken-wu*, the first day of the tenth month of the winter of the first year of Cheng-t'ung (1440). *Min jitsuroku sho*, vol. II, 620.

113. Ibid., 88, "Ying-tsung" entry of *wu-yin* day of the first month of the seventh year of Cheng-t'ung (1442). *Min jitsuroku sho*, vol. III, 1.

114. Ibid.

115. Ibid., 96, "Ying-tsung" entry of *ken-ch'en* day of the ninth month of the seventh year of Cheng-t'ung (1442). *Min jitsuroku sho*, vol. III, 13.

116. In *Ming shih* 164, chüan 52, "Biography of I Ch'ien," 6a, there is a passage which suggests that the Ming court knew that merchants from the western regions of Central Eurasia were disguising themselves as official envoys to be allowed to enter China as members of tributary missions. Rather than deal with this problem, the Chinese chose to ignore it.

117. *Ming shih* 171, chüan 59, "Biography of Yang Shan," 12a–b.

118. Ibid.

V. INTERMARRIAGE

1. See, Sechin Jagchid, "Mongolian-Manchu Intermarriage in the Ch'ing Period," *Zentralasiatische Studien* 19:68–87 (1986).

2. Ssu-ma Ch'ien, *Shih chi* (reprinted Taipei, 1967) 99, chüan, 39, "Biography of Liu Ching," 4a–b.

3. Ibid.

4. Ibid., 94 I, chüan 64 I, "Account of the Hsiung-nu," I, 17a–b.

5. Ibid., 23b–24a.

6. Pan Ku and Pan Chao, *Han shu* (reprinted Taipei, 1967) 96 II, chüan 66 II, "Account of the Wu-sun of the western region," 2b–3b.

7. Ts'en-tsou was an official rank and the personal name of the grandson was Hsu-mi. See Ibid., 3a–b.

8. Ibid., 2b–3b.

9. Ibid.

10. Ibid.

11. See Pan Piao's biography in Fan Yeh, *Hou Han shu* (reprinted Taipei, 1967) 40, chüan 30.

12. Ibid., 89, chüan 79, "Account of the Southern Hsiung-nu," 9b–10a.

13. Wei Shou, *Wei shu* (reprinted Taipei, 1967) 4 I, chi 4 I, "Annals of Shih-tsu," 18b–19a.

14. Ibid., 103, chüan 91, "Account of the Juan-juan," 7b–8a.

15. Jennifer Holmgren, "*Wei-shu* Records on the Bestowal of Imperial Princesses During the Northern Wei Dynasty," *Papers on Far Eastern History* 27:21–97 (March 1983).

16. *Wei shu* 10, chi 10, "Annals of Ching-tsung," 5a; "Account of the Juan-juan," 21b.

17. Kao Huan was an influential court minister of the Eastern Wei dynasty, who laid

Notes for pages 146–152

the groundwork for the overthrow of the Eastern Wei by his son. After achieving power, his son posthumously designated Kao Huan to be Emperor Shen-wu of the Northern Ch'i dynasty.

18. Li Po-yao, *Pei Ch'i shu* (reprinted Taipei, 1967) 9, chüan 1, "Biography of Empress Lou of [Emperor] Shen-wu," 2a.

19. Ling-hu Te-fen, *Chou shu* (reprinted Taipei, 1967) 50, chüan 42, "Account of the Turks," 3a–b.

20. Ibid., 6b; 9, chüan 1, "Biographies of the Empresses," 3b–4b; 30, chüan 22, "Biography of Tou Chih," 7a–b; 33, chüan 25, "Biography of Wang Ch'ing," 9a.

21. Ibid., 50, chüan 42, "Account of the Turks," 7b–8a.

22. Ibid.

23. See Ho Jo-i's biography in Wei Cheng, *Sui shu* (completed 644, reprinted Taipei, 1967) 39, chüan 4. There is little recorded in his biography about this event.

24. *Pei Ch'i shu* 12, chüan 4, "Biographies of the Four Princes, [the sons] of the Emperor Wen-hsüan," 4a–b.

25. *Sui shu* 51, chüan 16, "Biography of Chang-sun Sheng," 6a.

26. Ibid., 84, chüan 49, "Account of the Turks," 8a–b.

27. *Sui shu* 51, chüan 16, "Biography of Chang-sun Sheng," 6a.

28. Ibid.

29. See chapter one.

30. *Sui shu* 84, chüan 49, "Account of the Turks," 9b; 51, chüan 16, "Biography of Chang-sun Sheng," that is attached to the "Biography of Chang-sun Lan," 6b–7a.

31. Ibid., 67, chüan 32, "Biography of P'ei Chü," 9b–10a.

32. Ibid., 51, chüan 16, "Biography of Chang-sun Sheng," that is attached to the "Biography of Chang-sun Lan," 6b–7a.

33. Ibid., 7a–b.

34. Ibid.; Ibid., 84, chüan 49, "Account of the Turks," 10a.

35. Ibid., 67, chüan 32, "Biography of P'ei Chü," 9b–10a.

36. Ibid., 84, chüan 49, "Account of the Turks," 9b–10a. Ming-chün was another title for Wang Chao-chün, who was also known as Ming Fei of the Han. Her personal name was Wang Ch'iang. She was a court lady of the Han emperor Hsüan-ti, and was given to the Hsiung-nu *Shan-yü* Hu-han-yeh during his visit to the Han court in 33 B.C.

37. Ibid., 10a–b.

38. Ibid., 51, chüan 16, "Biography of Chang-sun Sheng," that is attached to the "Biography of Chang-sun Lan," 7a–b.

39. For information on Yan Cheng-tao, see *Sui-shu* 59, chüan 24, "Biography of [Yang] Lan, Prince of Ch'i," in the "Biographies of the Three Sons of [Emperor] Yang," 9b.

40. Liu Hsü, *Chiu T'ang shu* (reprinted Taipei, 1967) 67, chuan 17, "Biography of Li Ching," 4a.

41. O-yang Hsiu, Sung Ch'i et al., *Hsin T'ang shu* (reprinted Taipei, 1967) 83, chüan 8, "Biographies of Princesses," entry of the nineteenth daughter of Emperor Kao-tsu, 2a. For further information on A-shih-na Tu-erh, see his biography in Ibid., 110, chüan 35, "Biographies of the Barbarian and Foreign Generals," 2b–3a.

42. Ibid., 100, chüan 25, "Biographies of Feng Lun and P'ei Chü," 5b–6a.

43. Ibid., 3a; *Chiu T'ang shu* 194 II, chüan 144 II, "Account of the Turks," II, 2a–b.

44. Ibid., 100, chüan 25, "Biographies of Feng Lun and P'ei Chu," 4b–5a.

45. *Chiu T'ang shu* 194 II, chüan 144 II, "Account of the Turks," II, 2a–b.

46. Ibid., 3a.

47. Ibid., 194 I, chüan 194 I, "Account of the Turks," I, 11a.

48. A *shuo* is a unit of measure for grain, which the *Hsin T'ang shu* 197, chüan 122, "Biography of T'ien Jen-hui," says is "thirty thousand *tan* of grain."

49. See his biography attached to that of Wu Ch'eng-ssu in *Chiu T'ang shu* 183, chüan 133.
50. Ibid., 194 I, chüan 144 I, "Account of the Turks," I, 11a.
51. Ibid.
52. Charles O. Hucker, *China's Imperial Past* (Stanford, 1975), 142.
53. *Chiu T'ang shu* 194 I, chüan 144 I, "Account of the Turks," I, 12a.
54. *Hsin T'ang shu* 215 II, chüan 140 II, "Account of the Turks," II, 1b–2a.
55. Ssu-ma Kuang, *Tzu-chih t'ung-chien* (reprinted Taipei, 1978) 212, "T'ang chi," (Chung-hua shu-chü edition), 28, 9b.
56. *Chiu T'ang shu* 199 II, chüan 149 II, "Account of the Khitan," in the "Account of the Northern Barbarians," 6a–7a; "Account of the Hsi," 8b–9a.
57. This characterization of Songtsan-gambo is Beckwith's. See Christopher I. Beckwith, *The Tibetan Empire in Central Asia*, (Princeton, New Jersey, 1987) 26.
58. For more information on the T'u-yü-hun, see *Hsin T'ang shu* 221 I, chüan 146 I, "Account of the Tu-yü-hun," in the "Account of the Western Regions," I, 6a–7b.
59. Ibid., 216 I, chüan 141 I, "Account of Tibet," 2a–3a, 7b.
60. Ibid.; Beckwith, 22–26.
61. Beckwith, 57–61.
62. Ibid., pp. 69–73. Beckwith suggests that it is not clear whether this princess married the Tibetan king Khridesungtsan or the dethroned "retired emperor," Lha.
63. *Hsin T'ang shu* 216 I, chüan 141 I, "Account of Tibet," 2a–3a, 7b.
64. Ibid., 9a–10a.
65. Ibid., 217 I, chüan 142 I, "Account of the Uighur," I, 3a–b; *Chiu T'ang shu* 195, chüan 145, "Account of the Uighur," 3a.
66. *Chiu T'ang shu* 195, chüan 145, "Account of the Uighur," 3a.
67. Ibid., 4a–5a. The same event is also recorded in *Hsin T'ang shu* 217 I, "Account of the Uighur," I, 4a–b.
68. For information on Li Yü, see *Chiu T'ang shu* 95, chüan 45, "Biography of the Yielded Emperor [Li] Hsien," in the "Biographies of the Sons of [Emperor] Jui Tsung," 4b.
69. See biographies on P'ei Mien in both the *Chiu T'ang shu* 113, chüan 63, and the *Hsin T'ang shu* 140, chüan 65. Both biographies fail to mention this event.
70. *Chiu T'ang shu* 195, chüan 145, "Account of the Uighur," 4a–5a. Also recorded in *Hsin T'ang shu* 217 I, chüan 142 I, "Account of the Uighur," I, 4a–b.
71. Ibid.
72. Ibid.
73. Ibid.
74. *Chiu T'ang shu* 195, chüan 145, "Account of the Uighur," 11b.
75. Ibid., pp. 4a–5a. Also recorded in *Hsin T'ang shu* 217 I, chüan 142 I, "Account of the Uighur," I, 4a–b.
76. According to Turkic tradition, the most beloved wives, concubines, trusted generals, and vassals killed themselves to honor their deceased khan. For instance, after Il Khan, who was captured by the T'ang court, died in captivity, a number of his subjects killed themselves. This loyalty was highly praised by Emperor T'ai-tsung of the T'ang. See *Chiu T'ang shu* 194, chüan 144, "Account of the Turks," I, 5b; and *Hsin T'ang shu* 215, chüan 140, "Account of the Turks," I, 7a. After Emperor T'ai-tsung died, his brother-in-law, A-shih-na Tu-erh, who was also a trusted general, petitioned to commit suicide, but his petition was rejected by T'ai-tsung's successor, Emperor Kao-tsung. (See *Chiu T'ang shu* 109, chüan 59, "Biography of A-shih-na Tu-erh," 2b; and *Hsin T'ang shu* 110, chüan 35, "Biography of A-shih-na Tu-erh," 3b.
77. *Chiu T'ang shu* 195, chüan 145, "Account of the Uighur," 5a–b.

78. Ibid., 10b.
79. Ibid., 10b–11a; *Hsin T'ang shu* 217 I, chüan 142 I, "Account of the Uighur," I, 10a.
80. See chapter two.
81. *Hsin T'ang shu* 224 I, chüan 149 I, "Biography of Pa-ku Huai-en," 2b, 5b.
82. Ibid., 217, chüan 142 I, "Account of the Uighur," I, 6b–7a.
83. Ibid., 4a–b; Also recorded in *Chiu T'ang shu* 195, chüan 145, "Account of the Uighur," 4a–5a.
84. Wang Ch'in-jo, Yang I, et al., *Tse-fu yüan-kuei* (completed 1005, reprinted Taipei) 979, (Shin-chieh shu-chü edition), p. 11505.
85. *Chiu T'ang shu* 195, chüan 145, "Account of the Uighur," 9b.
86. Ibid., 11b–12b; *Hsin T'ang shu* 217 II, chüan 142 I, "Account of the Uighur," II, 1a–b. Note that the figures cited are drawn from the entry in the *Hsin T'ang shu* which are higher than those suggested in the *Chiu T'ang shu*.
87. *Chiu T'ang shu* 195, chüan 145, "Account of the Uighur," 11b.
88. For Hu Cheng's biography, which also discusses this event, see *Hsin T'ang shu* 164, chüan 89.
89. Ibid., 217 II, chüan 142 I, "Account of the Uighur," II, 1a–b; *Chiu T'ang shu* 195, chüan 145, "Account of the Uighur," 12a–b.
90. *Chiu T'ang shu* 195, chüan 145, "Account of the Uighur," 12a–b.
91. Toghto et al., *Sung shih* (completed 1346, reprinted Taipei, 1967) 248, chüan 8, "Biographies of the Thirty-four Daughters of [Emperor] Hui-tsung," in the "Biographies of Princesses," 13b.
92. Toghto *et al.*, *Chin shih* (completed 1344, reprinted Taipei, 1967) 3, chi 3, "Annals of T'ai-tsung," 11b, 14a.
93. Sung Lien *et al.*, *Yüan shih* (completed 1369, reprinted Taipei, 1967) 1, chi 1, "Annals of T'ai-tsu," 15a–b, 17b–18a; *Chin shih* 14, chi 14, "Annals of Hsüan-tsung," I, 3b–4b; *The Secret History of the Mongols*, tr. Francis W. Cleaves (Cambridge, Mass., 1982), sect. 249.
94. Ong-gin seems to be a transliteration of the Jurchen family name Wan-yen, so that Prime Minister Ong-gin was probably the Chin Prime Minister Wan-yen Ch'eng-hui. Wan-yen Ch'eng-hui's biography is found in *Chin shih* 101, chüan 39.
95. *Secret History*, sect. 248.
96. *Hsin T'ang shu* 215 I, chüan 140 I, "Account of the Turks," 1a–b.
97. Ibid., "Account of the Uighur," I, 10b–11b.

VI. CONFLICT OR CALM

1. Ssu-ma Ch'ien, *Shih chi* (reprinted Taipei, 1967) 110, chüan 50, "Account of the Hsiung-nu," 1a–b.
2. Ibid., 129, chüan 69, "Monograph on Commodities and Trade," 1b. In this passage, north probably refers to parts of northern China as well as more distant regions of Central Eurasia. This explains the inclusion of copper and iron in this list of northern products.
3. Ibid., 6b.
4. Lo may not have been constrained by a regulated marketing structure. Scholars have been unable to determine whether or not there was an authorized marketing system between the nomadic and Chinese worlds before the Han formally opened border markets (*kuan-shih*) for the Hsiung-nu.
5. *Shih chi* 129, chüan 69, "Monograph on Commodities and Trade," 17a.

6. Pan Ku and Pan Chao, *Han shu* (reprinted Taipei, 1967) 91, chüan 61, "Monograph on Commodities and Trade," 7b.

7. Fan Yeh, *Hou Han shu* (reprinted Taipei, 1967) 89, chüan 79, "Account of the Southern Hsiung-nu," 9a–b.

8. Ibid., 90, chüan 80, "Account of the Wu-huan," 5a.

9. Ibid., "Account of the Hsien-pei," 8b.

10. Wei Shou, *Wei shu* (reprinted Taipei, 1967) 103, chüan 91, "Account of the Juan-juan," 1a–b. See also Li Yen-shou, *Pei shih* (reprinted Taipei, 1967) 98, chüan 86, "Account of the Juan-juan," 1a–b.

11. O-yang Hsiu, Sung Ch'i et al., *Hsin T'ang shu* (reprinted Taipei, 1967) 217 I, chüan 142 I, "Account of the Uighur," I, 2a.

12. Ibid., 219, chüan 144, "Account of the Northern Barbarians," 8b.

13. Known in Mongolian as *sarlagh*, this is a type of cattle better suited to work in mountainous, high-plateau areas.

14. Probably, the typical Mongolian wild horse, *khulan*.

15. The camel of Arabia rather than the two-humped variety normally found in Mongolia and Turkistan.

16. Probably another name for ermine, found in the T'ien-shan mountains of Central Asia.

17. A special Tibetan antelope whose horns were used as medicine.

18. Ammonium chloride.

19. Valued for medicinal qualities, they could only be obtained through trade with merchants having contact with peoples in Artic regions.

20. Probably obtained by the Uighur through trade with Arabian or Persian merchants.

21. Presumably produced in Jirantai-nor, the salt lake in the Alashan area of western Inner Mongolia.

22. The reason the Uighur were involved in raising crops relates to the conversion of the Uighur khan, Teng-li mo-yü, to Manichaeism. Early in 762 he campaigned in China to assist the T'ang dynasty in quelling the rebellion of Shih Ch'ao-yi. During the struggle, he met Manichaen priests in the city of Lo-yang and accepted Manichaeism, a faith committed to vegetarianism. After this, the Uighur began to plant crops and became a half-nomadic and half-agricultural people.

23. The release of these falcons suggests that the Sha-t'o Turkic leaders of the Later T'ang dynasty were already thoroughly Sinicized and has lost their interest in hunting.

24. O-yang Hsiu, *Wu-tai shih-chi* (reprinted Taipei, 1967) 74, "Appendix of the Four Barbarians," 3, "Account of the Uighur," 9a–10b. Jade was an especially prized item of tribute and trade. It was a symbol of luck and highly valued by the Chinese. One of the first Chinese adventurers in Central Asia, Chang Ch'ien, claimed that he "arrived at the origin of the [Yellow] river. The mountain is rich in jade. [The Han envoy] took [the jade] and brought it back." (See *Han shu* 61, chüan 31, "Biography of Chang Ch'ien," 7a.) However, the highest quality jade was produced in the Ho-t'ien district (present-day southern part of Sinkiang), not the Tibetan Kham and Amdo area (present-day Kökönor or Chinghai) where the headwaters of the Yellow river are found.

25. Hsüeh Chü-chang and others, *Chiu Wu-tai shih* (completed 974, reprinted Taipei, 1967) 76, "Book of Chin" 2, "Annals of Kao-tsu" 2, 13a. The wooden bowls mentioned in this passage were produced by Khitan craftsmen because the porcelain bowls of the Chinese were easily broken when used by the constantly moving nomads. Ginseng was a highly sought-after herb believed to have marvelous medicinal qualities. The plant grew in the Shang-tang region of the T'ai-hang Mountains of eastern Shansi and also in Manchu-

ria and Korea. During the Ch'ing period, the Manchu court monopolized the gathering and sale of the root and realized huge profits that were directed into the coffers of the imperial household. See Van Jay Symons, *Ch'ing Ginseng Management: Ch'ing Monopolies in Microcosm* (Tempe, Ariz., 1981), 1–121; and Imamura Tomo, *Ninjin shi* (Seoul, 1934–40), 7 vols.

26. Toghto et al., *Sung shih* (completed 1346, reprinted Taipei 1967) 186, chih 139, "Monograph on Economy" 8, entry on inter-marketing, 23b.

27. Hsiung-chou was controlled by the Sung who designated it as a place to trade with the Khitan.

28. Kao-ch'ang was originally an oasis state established in the area of present-day Turfan, Sinkiang. During the Yüan period, when the *Liao shih* was compiled, Kao-ch'ang was the name of a group of Uighur who migrated to the northwestern part of present-day Kansu. The Kao-ch'ang mentioned in this passage probably refers to a place where the Khitan and Uighur exchanged goods along their borders.

29. Po-hai or Parhae was a Tungusic state established in 713 in present-day southern Manchuria. It was occupied by the Khitan in 926, who changed its name to Tung-tan. It was from this spot that the Khitan conducted trade with the Tungusic Jurchens, the Koreans, and other northeast Asian peoples such as the Tieh-li, Mo-he, and Yü-chüeh.

30. Toghto et al., *Liao shih* (completed 1344, reprinted Taipai, 1967) 60, chih 29, "Monograph on Economy," 1a–b.

31. *Ming shih-lu*, ed. and printed by Academia Sinica, (Taipei 1966) 136, "Ying-tsung" entry of *ping-ch'en* day of the twelfth month of the tenth year of Cheng-t'ung (1449). *Min jitsuroku sho, Mokohen*, vol. III, 127.

32. *Shih chi* 110, chüan 50, "Account of the Hsiung-nu," 12a–b.

33. The excavation was done by the Russian archaeologist Kozlov. A part of his excavation is preserved in the museum of the Mongolian People's Republic at Ulan-bator.

34. *Han shu* 94 II, chüan 64 II, "Account of the Hsiung-nu," II, 4a–b.

35. *Hou Han shu* 89, chüan 79, "Account of the Southern Hsiung-nu," 6b. The complete list of items bestowed on the *shan-yü* included: "hats, belts, clothings, a golden seal, purple sashes, carts, canopies, adornments, ceremonial carts and pulling horses, precious knots, bows, arrows . . . gold, ten thousand pieces of embroidery, satins and silks, ten thousand catties of crude silk, musical instruments, drum-carts, ceremonial lances, weapons and arms, foodstuffs and other items. Besides, the Court ordered the officials of Ho-tung [present-day Shansi] to provide 25,000 *hu* of grain and 36,000 head of cattle and sheep for their needs."

36. Ibid., 11b.

37. Chen Shou, *San-kuo chih* (reprinted Taipei, 1967) "Book of Wei" 30, "Account of the Hsien-pei," 5a, 2a–b.

38. *Wei shu* 103, chüan 91, "Account of the Juan-juan," 17a–b.

39. Ibid., 20a–b. It is worthwhile to note that while the Jou-jan maintained relations with the Northern Wei court it also maintained ties with Chinese dynasties south of the Northern Wei. The "Account of the Jui-jui [Jou-jan]" in the *Nan-Ch'i shu* indicates that the Jou-jan requested from the Southern Ch'i court medical doctors, silk embroidery workers, a compass on a cart *(chih-nan che)*, and a water clock. The Southern Ch'i were unwilling to grant the Jou-jan their requests. See Li Yen-shou, *Nan-Ch'i shu* (completed by 650, reprinted Taipei, 1967) 59, chüan 40, "Account of the Jui-jui," 1a–3b.

40. Wei Cheng, *Sui shu* (completed 644, reprinted Taipei, 1967) 84, chüan 49, "Account of the Turks," 12a–13a.

41. Ssu-ma Kuang, *Tzu-chih t'ung-chien* (reprinted Taipei, 1978) 212, "T'ang chi," 28, 9b

42. *Ming shih-lu* 211, "Ying-tsung" entry of *ping-tzu* day of the twelfth month of the second year of Ching-tai (1451) in "The Appendix of the Abolished Emperor Ch'eng-li Wang," 29. *Min jitsuroko sho, Mokohen*, vol. III, 416.

43. Ibid., 47, "Tai-tsung" entry of *chia-yin* day of the twelfth month of the fourth year of Yung-lo (1406). *Min jitsuroku sho, Mokohen*, vol. I, 319–320.

44. Chang T'ing-yü and others, *Ming shih* (completed 1736, reprinted Taipei, 1967) 327, chüan 215, "Account of the Ta-tan," 20b.

45. Ibid., 222, chüan 110, "Biography of Wang Ch'ung-ku," 11a.

46. Ibid. See also, Henry Serruys, "Ta-tu, Tai-tu, Dayitu," *Chinese Culture* 2.4 (Taipei, 1960).

47. Henry Serruys, "Chinese in Southern Mongolia during the Sixteenth Century," *Monumenta Serica* 18:54–65 (1959). Though beyond the scope of this investigation, it has been suggested that widespread shortages of grain were a major catalyst for Manchu aggression in the early seventeenth century. In 1626, the Manchus were defeated by the Ming army, which blunted for a short period Manchu incorporation of new agricultural areas into their state, while at the same time, denying them rich booty. By this period, the population in Manchu-controlled areas was mushrooming due to the influx of captives and newly surrendered nomadic and Chinese allies. Because the Manchus' ties with Korea and China were chaotic, they could not depend on trade to secure grain to feed their people. As widespread famine broke out in 1627–28 and periodically thereafter, the Manchus became even more aggressive, seeking to secure booty and to acquire new lands to cultivate in order to feed their subjects. See Gertraude Roth, "The Manchu-Chinese Relationship, 1618–1636," in Jonathan D. Spence and John E. Wills, Jr., *From Ming to Ch'ing: Conquest, Region, and Continuity in Seventeenth-Century China* (New Haven, 1979), 26–31, and also Gertraude Roth-Li's thesis "The Rise of the Early Manchu State: A Portrait Drawn from Manchu Sources of 1636," (Diss., Harvard University, 1975).

48. *Han shu*, chüan 94, "Account of the Hsiung-nu," 32a, cited by Hsiao Ch'i-ch'ing, p. 610.

49. See p. 424 in the *Tso-chuan* as cited by Yang Lien-sheng, in John K. Fairbank, ed., *The Chinese World Order* (Cambridge, Mass., 1968), 25. Mary Ferenczy suggests that the image the Chinese have of nomadic people varied from time to time. By comparing writings about "barbarians" in the fourteenth-century *Sung shih* with those written in the sixteenth century in the *Sung shih hsin-pien*, she concludes that the sixteenth-century writer was more critical of the "barbarians" than his earlier counterpart. See Mary Ferenczy, "Chinese Historiographers' Views on Barbarian-Chinese Relations (14–16th C.)," *Acta Orientalia Academiae Scientiarum Hungaricae* 21.3:353–362 (1968).

50. For additional discussion of the perceptions of nomadic rulers of themselves as independent leaders of their peoples, see Hsiao Ch'i-ch'ing, "Pei-ya yu-mu-min-tsu nan-ch'in ko-chung yüan-yin ti chien-t'ao," *Shih-huo yüeh-k'an* 1.12:614–615 (March 1972).

51. The term *Kitad* is derived from the Khitan people who dwelled in North China during the tenth, eleventh, and part of the twelfth century, after establishing the Liao dynasty.

52. Cited in Mark Mancall, "The Ch'ing Tribute System: An Interpretive Essay," in Fairbank, ed., *The Chinese*, 71–72.

53. Huan K'uan, *Yen-t'ieh lun*, tr. Esson M. Gale (Leyden, 1931), 2–3.

54. See chapter one.

55. See chapter four.

56. Lo Jung-pang, "Policy Formulation and Decision-Making on Issues Respecting Peace and War," in Charles Hucker, ed., *Chinese Government in Ming Times* (New York, 1969), 56.

57. For Ssu-ma Ch'ien's personal view on why he was ordered castrated by Han Wu-ti,

see his "Letter to Jen An (Shao-ch'ing)," trans. by J. R. Hightower in Cyril Birch, comp. and ed., *Anthology of Chinese Literature from Early Times to the Fourteenth Century* (New York, 1965), 95–102.

58. *Ming shih* 304, chüan 191, "Biography of Wang Chih," 15b–16a. Further discussion of the military activities of these individuals can be found in Ibid., 327, chüan 215, "Account of the Ta-tan," 12b, 13b–14a.

59. Ibid., 171, chüan 59, "Biography of Yang Shan," 11a–b.

60. Ibid., 328, chüan 216, "Account of To-yen, Fu-yü and T'ai-ning," 10b.

61. Ibid., 177, chüan 65, "Biography of Li Ping," 13b.

62. Ibid., 328, chüan 216, "Account of To-yen, Fu-yü and T'ai-ning," 11b. Another example of the massacring of nomadic people who were peacefully coming to trade at frontier markets is evident in Ibid., 228, chüan 116, "Biography of Wei Hsüeh-tseng," 2a–b:

> [In the nineteenth year of Wan-li, 1591], the chieftain of the tribe in the bend of the [Yellow] river, Tümed Mingghan, after entering the market, requested an increase in rewards [to him]. [Wei] Hsüeh-tseng ordered the Commander, Tu T'ung, to kill [Tümed] Mingghan in a sudden attack. More than four hundred and ten persons were slain and an equal number of horses, animals, and equipment was captured. Because of this achievement [Wei] Hsüeh-tseng was promoted [to the post] Junior Protector of the Heir-Apparent. Then [Tümed] Mingghan's son, Bayantai, declared his intent to obtain revenge and notified all the tribes. In the next year [1592], Bobai rebelled and instigated other tribes to do the same.

63. Ibid., 328, chün 216, "Account of To-yen, Fu-yü and T'ai-ning," 11a.

64. Ibid., 81, chih 57, "Monograph on Economy," V, entry on horse markets, 24a.

65. In a study of the frontier policies of the Han dynasty towards the Ch'iang peoples in the upper reaches of the Yellow River, Rafe de Crespigny states that from 87 A.D., the Ch'iang people warred for a number of years with China because a Chinese commander induced their leader, Mi-wu, "to surrender and then killed him and several of his fellows by treachery, poisoning their wine at the ceremonial banquet, and then setting his soldiers to massacre their followers." Rafe de Crespigny, "The Ch'iang Barbarians and the Empire of Han A Study in Frontier Policy. Part II: Frontier Wars and the Great Rebellions 50–150 A.D.," *Papers on Far Eastern History* 18:198–199 (1978). See also Ibid., "Part I: The Establishment of Chinese Authority," *Papers on Far Eastern History* 16:1–25 (1977). In these two essays, de Crespigny suggests that the Han formulated an unrealistic, activist frontier policy, which included the forced colonization of the Northwest by Chinese peasants and the imposed removal of nomadic peoples from some areas. The author shows that the Ch'iang people were terribly mistreated by the Han because corrupt generals were asked to do impossible things.

66. *Ming shih* 279, chüan 167, "Biography of Lü Ta-ch'i," 1b.

67. See particularly the works of Henry Serruys on Mongol relations with the Ming.

68. *Ming shih* 222, chüan 110, "Biography of Wang Ch'ung-ku," 7a.

69. Owen Lattimore, *Inner Asian Frontiers of China*, (New York, 1951) 515.

70. Some excellent studies suggesting how interspersed the Mongols and the Chinese people became along the frontiers of China during the Mongol-Ming era have been published by Henry Serruys. See Henry Serruys, "Remains of Mongol Customs in China during the Early Ming Period," *Monumenta Serica* 16:137–90 (1957); "The Mongols in China During the Hung-wu Period (1368–1398)," *Mélanges Chinois et Bouddhiques* 11:1–328 (1959); "The Mongols in China 1400–1450," *Monumenta Serica* 27:233–305 (1968); "Landgrants to the Mongols in China: 1400–1460," *Monumenta Serica* 25:394–404 (1966); "Were the Ming against the Mongols' settling in North China," *Oriens Extremus* 6:131–

159 (1959–60); "Mongols Ennobled During the Early Ming," *Harvard Journal of Asiatic Studies* 22:209–260 (1959); "The Mongols of Kansu During the Ming," *Mélanges Chinois et Bouddhiques* 10:215–346 (1955); and "Chinese in Southern Mongolia During the Sixteenth Century," *Monumenta Serica* 18:1–95 (1959).

71. Yü Ying-shih, *Trade and Expansion in Han China* (Berkeley, 1967), 121–122.
72. Ibid., 129–130.
73. *Hou Han shu* 90, chüan 80, "Account of the Hsien-pei," 17a.
74. For information on Yü-wen T'ai, see Ling-hu Te-fen, *Chou shu* (reprinted Taipei, 1967) 1 and 2, chi 1 and 2.
75. *Chou shu* 50, chüan 42, "Account of the T'u-yü-hun," in the "Account of Foreign Regions," II, 9b–10a.
76. *Hsin T'ang shu* 217 I, chüan 142 I, "Account of the Uighur," I, 10b.
77. *Sung shih* 186, chih 139, "Monograph on Economy," 8 II, 23a.
78. Ibid., 24b.
79. Ibid., 23b–24a.
80. *Ming shih-lu* 3, "Ying-tsung" entry of *chi-hai* day of the twelfth month of the eighth year of Cheng-t'ung (1443). *Min jitsuroku sho, Mokohen*, vol. III, 56.
81. Ibid., entry of *ping-wu* day of the twelfth month of the eighth year of Cheng-t'ung (1443). *Min jitsuroku sho, Mokohen*, vol. III, 57.
82. Ibid.
83. *Ming shih* 304, chüan 192, "Biography of Wang Chen," in the "Account of the Eunuchs," 9b.
84. Ibid., 185, chüan 73, "Biography of Wu Shih-chung," 17b. Also see, Ibid., 175, chüan 63, "Biography of Shen Ying," 9a.
85. *Hsin T'ang shu* 215 I, chüan 140 I, "Account of the Turks," I, 7a.
86. Liu Hsü et al., *Chiu T'ang shu* (reprinted Taipei, 1967) 194 I, chüan 144 I, "Account of the Turks," I, 4a.
87. *Ming shih* 170, chüan 58, "Biography of Yü Ch'ien," 6b.
88. A representative document is translated in Fu Lo-shu, *A Documentary Chronicle of Sino-Western Relations* (Tucson, Ariz., 1966), 360–361:

> 10:10:17 (Dec. 7, 1805) The Emperor's Edict to the King of England
> The Emperor decreed to the King of England: "We reverently inherit the solemn mandate from Heaven and respectfully follow the great program of Our ancestors. We seek for peace and observe the regulations. The glory of Our Empire shines on this universe with brilliance. Therefore, We spread Our civilization through translations, and We appreciate the sincerity of those nations who submit to goodness. Strangers are awed by Our power, and receive Our hospitality which extends beyond the four seas, so that nations both near and far join Us in enjoying peace on this earth. Nobly they bring their tributes from remote distances and throng to do homage to Our Empire, even though they must scale mountains and sail seas on their journeying hither.
> Our mornings are usually devoted to consultation with Our ministers and Our afternoons to the disposal of state affairs. We handle the vast number of cases with great care, in order to achieve the unbounded happiness that renders great peace to all overseas.
> Your kingdom is far distant and separated from Us by the seas, yet you respectfully observe the duties of a vassal state. From a remote region, you manifest your loyalty toward the Sun. You have again respectfully dispatched messengers to pay homage to Our Court. We have read your memorial and found the language and sentiment expressed are reverent and respectful. Thereupon, We authorized the viceroy to accept the tribute which you present to Us, in order to fulfill your sincere wish.

Note for page 186

With regard to the subjects of your kingdom who have for years traded with us, the Celestial Empire has always looked upon them and all other nations with equal favor. Not one single person or country is excluded from Our kindness and benevolence. But we do not need the services of your kingdom.

Since you, the king, especially present to Us a memorial expressing your love and loyalty toward Us, and since you have ordered your local officials in India (Kang-chiao) to show their respect and veneration on meeting the soldiers and people of the Celestial Empire, you, the king, demonstrate vividly your admiration for Our justice and your leaning toward the civilization, that We deeply praise and appreciate.

Consequently, We send you an edict of praise and encouragement. We bestow upon you colorful silks and other gifts. We beg your Majesty to accept them. The Heavenly Grace is unbounded, and you will forever be honored with the favor of the Celestial Empire. If you continue to offer amity and friendship as an ally, if you can lead all your subjects to present tribute and serve Us as our vassals, then you will fulfill Our sublime principle of loving strangers and extending Our benevolence to them.

BIBLIOGRAPHY

Barfield, Thomas J. "The Hsiung-nu Imperial Confederacy: Organizations and Foreign Policy," *The Journal of Asian Studies* 41.1:45–61 (November 1981).

Beckwith, Christopher I. *The Tibetan Empire in Central Asia: A History of the Struggle for Great Power among Tibetans, Turks, Arabs, and Chinese during the Early Middle Ages.* Princeton, New Jersey: Princeton University Press, 1987.

"A Bibliography of the Publications of Joseph Fletcher," *Harvard Journal of Asiatic Studies* 46:7–10 (June 1986).

Birch, Cyril, comp. and ed. *Anthology of Chinese Literature from Early Times to the Fourteenth Century.* New York: Columbia University Press, 1965.

Burnham, Philip. "Spatial Mobility and Political Centralization in Pastoral Societies," in L'Equipe écologie et anthropologie des sociétés pastorales, ed., *Pastoral Production and Society.* Cambridge: Cambridge University Press, 1979.

Chang Mu 張穆 . *Meng-ku yu-mu chi* 蒙古游牧記 [The gazetteer of Mongolian pastures]. Completed 1859. Reprinted in Taipei, 1965.

Chang T'ing-yü 張廷玉 and others. *Ming shih* 明史 [The history of the Ming dynasty, 1368–1644]. Completed 1736. 332 chüan. Po-na edition 百納本. Reprinted in Taipei, 1967.

Ch'ang-ch'un chen-jen hsi-yu-chi 長春真人西遊記 [Ch'ang-ch'un chen-jen's travelogue in the Western region], by Li Chih-ch'ang 李志常 , in Wang Kuo-wei 王國維 ed., *Meng-ku shih-liao ssu-chung* 蒙古史料四種 . Reprinted in Taipei, 1962.

Chen Shou 陳壽 (d. 297 A.D.). *San-kuo chih* 三國志 [The history of the Three Kingdoms, Wei, Shu and Wu, 220–264]. 65 chüan. Po-na edition. Reprinted in Taipei, 1967.

Cohen, Paul. *Discovering History in China: American Historical Writing on the Recent Chinese Past.* New York: Columbia University Press, 1984.

Creel, H. G. "The Role of the Horse in Chinese History," *American Historical Review* 70.3:647–672 (April 1965).

de Crespigny, Rafe. "The Ch'iang Barbarians and the Empire of Han: A Study in Frontier Policy. Part I: The Establishment of Chinese Authority," *Papers on Far Eastern History* 16:1–25 (1977).

———. "The Ch'iang Barbarians and the Empire of Han: A Study in Frontier Policy.

Part II: Frontier Wars and the Great Rebellions 50–150 A.D.," *Papers on Far Eastern History* 18:193–245 (1978).
John K. Fairbank. "A Preliminary Framework," in John K. Fairbank, ed., *The Chinese World Order: Traditional China's Foreign Relations*. Cambridge, Mass.: Harvard University Press, 1968.
_____, ed. *The Chinese World Order: Traditional China's Foreign Relations*. Cambridge, Mass.: Harvard University Press, 1968.
Fan Yeh 范曄 (d. 446 A.D.?). *Hou Han shu* 後漢書 [The history of the Later Han dynasty, 25–220 A.D.]. 120 chüan. Po-na edition. Reprinted in Taipei, 1967.
Farquhar, David M. "The Origins of the Manchus' Mongolian Policy," in John K. Fairbank, ed., *The Chinese World Order: Traditional China's Foreign Relations*. Cambridge, Mass.: Harvard University Press, 1968.
Ferenczy, Mary. "Chinese Historiographers' Views on Barbarian-Chinese Relations (14–16th C.)," *Acta Orientalia Academiae Scientiarum Hungaricae* 21.3:353–362 (1968).
Fletcher, Joseph. "China and Central Asia, 1368–1884," in John K. Fairbank, ed., *The Chinese World Order: Traditional China's Foreign Relations*. Cambridge, Mass.: Harvard University Press, 1968.
_____. "The Mongols: Ecological and Social Perspectives," *Harvard Journal of Asiatic Studies* 6:11–50 (1986).
Franke, Herbert. "Treaties Between Sung and Chin," *Études Song/Sung Studies*. ser. 1:55–84 (1970).
_____. "Sung Embassies: Some General Observations," in Morris Rossabi, ed., *China Among Equals: The Middle Kingdom and its Neighbors 10th–14th Centuries*. Berkeley: University of California Press, 1985.
Fu Lo-shu. *A Documentary Chronicle of Sino-Western Relations (1644–1820)*. Tucson: The University of Arizona Press, 1966.
Gast, Marceau. "Pastoralisme Nomade et Pouvoir: La Societé Traditionnelle des Kel Ahaggar," in L'Equipe écologie et anthropologie des sociétés pastorales, ed., *Pastoral Production and Society*. Cambridge: Cambridge University Press, 1979.
Goldschmidt, Walter. "A General Model for Pastoral Social Systems," in L'Equipe écologie et anthropologie des sociétés pastorales, ed., *Pastoral Production and Society*. Cambridge: Cambridge University Press, 1979.
Goodrich, L. Carrington and Fang, Chaoying, eds. *Dictionary of Ming Biography, 1368–1644*. 2 vols. New York: Columbia University Press, 1976.
Holmgren, J. "*Wei-shu* Records on the Bestowal of Imperial Princesses During the Northern Wei Dynasty," *Papers on Far Eastern History* 27:21–97 (March 1983).
Hsiao Ch'i-ch'ing 蕭啟慶 . "Pei-ya yu-mu min-tsu nan-ch'in ko-chung yüan-yin ti

chien-tao" 北亞游牧民族南侵各種原因的檢討 [An analysis on the reasons for the southward invasions of the north-Asian nomadic peoples], *Shih-huo yüeh-k'an* 食貨月刊 1.12:609–619 (March 1972).

Hsiao Ta-heng 蕭大亨. *Pei-lu shih-hsi* 北虜世系 [The genealogy of the northern barbarians]. Attached to his book *Pei-lu Feng-su* 北虜風俗 (The customs of the northern barbarians). Completed 1594. Wen-tien-k'o 文殿閣 ed. Published in Peiping, 1930s.

Hsü Meng-hsin 徐夢莘. *San-ch'ao pei-meng hui-pien* 三朝北盟會編 [The records of the negotiations with the north during the reign period of the three emperors, Hui-tsung, Ch'in-tsung and Kao-ts'ung of the Sung dynasty]. Completed by 1161. Ssu-ku chen-pen 四庫珍本 ed. Reprinted in Taipei, 1982.

Hsüan-lan-t'ang tsung-shu 玄覽堂叢書 [The Hsüan-lan-t'ang collection]. Preserved in the Central Library, Taiwan. Reprinted in Taipei, 1986.

Hsüeh Chü-cheng 薛居正 and others. *Chiu Wu-tai shih* 舊五代史 [The old history of the Five Dynasties, Liang, T'ang, Chin, Han and Chou, 907–960]. Completed 974. 150 chüan. Po-na ed. Reprinted in Taipei, 1967.

Huan K'uan 桓寬. *Yen-t'ieh lun* 鹽鐵論 [Discourses on salt and iron]. Completed during the reign of Emperor Chao-ti (86–74 B.C.) of the Former Han dynasty. English trans. by Esson M. Gale. Leyden: E. J. Brill, 1931. Reprinted in Taipei, Ch'eng-wen, 1967.

Hucker, Charles O. *China's Imperial Past*. Stanford: Stanford University Press, 1973.

―――― . *A Dictionary of Official Titles in Imperial China*. Stanford: Stanford University Press, 1985.

Hudson, G. F. "Note by Mr. G. F. Hudson," in Arnold J. Toynbee, *A Study of History*. vol. 3. London: Oxford University Press, 1934.

Humphrey, Caroline. "Introduction," in Sevyan Vainshtein, *Nomads of South Siberia: the Pastoral Economies of Tuva*, tr. Michael Colenso. Cambridge: Cambridge University Press, 1980.

Huntington, Ellsworth. *The Pulse of Asia*. Boston: Houghton Mifflin Company, 1907.

―――― . *Mainsprings of Civilization*. New York: John Wiley and Sons, Inc., 1947.

Imamura, Tomo 今村鞆. *Ninjin shi* 人參史 [A history of ginseng]. 7 vols. Seoul: 1934–40.

Irons, William. "Political Stratification among Pastoral Nomads," in L'Equipe écologie et anthropologie des sociétés pastorales, ed., *Pastoral Production and Society*. Cambridge: Cambridge University Press, 1979.

Jagchid, Sechin 札奇斯欽. "Shintai Moko no chiho seijo seido 清代蒙古の地方政

洛制度 [The Mongolian local political institution during the Ch'ing period], Moko 蒙古 83 (April 1939).

———. Pei-Ya yu-mu min-tsu yü Chung-yüan nung-yeh min-tsu chien ti ho-p'ing chan-cheng yü mao-i chih kuan-hsi 北亞游牧民族與中原農業民族間的和平戰爭與貿易之關係 [Peace, War, and Trade Relationships between the Northern Asian Nomadic People and the Agricultural Chinese]. Taipei: Cheng-chung shu-chü, 1972.

———. "The Manchu-Ch'ing Policy towards Mongolian Religion," Walter Heissig, ed., in Tractata Altaica, Denis Sinor, Sexagenario Optime de Rebus Altaicis, Merito Dedicuta. Wiesbaden: Otto Harrassowitz, 1976.

———. "The Rise and Fall of Buddhism in Inner Mongolia," in A. K. Narain, ed., Studies in the History of Buddhism. New Delhi: B. R. Publishing Corporation, 1980.

———. "Kitan Struggle against Jurchen Oppression: Nomadism versus Sinicization," Zentralasiatische Studien 16 (1982).

———. "The Kitans and Their Cities," Central Asiatic Journal 25 (1981).

———. "Mongolian-Manchu Intermarriage in the Ch'ing Period," Zentralasiatisch Studien 19:68–87 (1986).

———. "The Uighur Horse Trade during the T'ang Period," in Walter Heissig and Klaus Sagaster, eds., Gedanke und Wirkung (Thought and Practice). Wiesbaden: Otto Harrassowitz, forthcoming.

——— and C. R. Bawden. "Some Notes on the Horse-Policy of the Yüan Dynasty," Central Asiatic Journal 10:246–268 (December 1965).

——— and Paul Hyer. Mongolia's Culture and Society. Boulder, Colo.: Westview Press, 1979.

Jenkins, Gareth. "A Note on Climatic Cycles and the Rise of Chinggis Khan," Central Asiatic Journal 18.4:217–226 (1974).

Khazanov, A. M. "Characteristic Features of Nomadic Communities in the Eurasian Steppes," in Wolfgang Weissleder, ed., The Nomadic Alternative. The Hague: Mouton Publishers, 1978.

———. Nomads and the Outside World, tr. Julia Crookenden. Cambridge: Cambridge University Press, 1984.

Kierman, Frank A. and John K. Fairbank, ed. Chinese Ways in Warfare. Cambridge, Mass.: Harvard University Press, 1968.

Lattimore, Owen. Inner Asian Frontiers of China. New York: American Geographical Society, 1951.

———. "The Geographical Factor in Mongol History," in Owen Lattimore, ed., Studies in *Frontier History: Collected Papers 1928–1958*. London: Oxford University Press, 1962.

Lee, Robert H. G. *The Manchurian Frontier in Ch'ing History*. Cambridge, Mass.: Harvard University Press, 1970.

Li Po-yao 李百藥 (d. 648). *Pei Ch'i shu* 北齊書 [The history of the Northern Ch'i dynasty, 550–577]. 50 chüan. Po-na ed. Reprinted in Taipei, 1967.

Li Shu-t'ung 李樹桐. *T'ang-shih k'ao-pien* 唐史考辨 [Studies and analysis of T'ang history]. Taipei: 1965.

Li Yen-shou 李延壽. *Nan-Ch'i shu* 南齊書 [The history of the Southern Ch'i dynasty, 479–502] in *Nan-shih* 南史 [The history of the Southern Dynasties, Sung, Ch'i, Liang and Ch'en, 420–589]. Completed before 650. 80 chüan. Po-na ed. Reprinted in Taipei, 1967.

———. *Nan-shih* 南史 [The history of the Southern Dynasties, Sung, Ch'i, Liang and Ch'en, 420–589]. Completed before 650. 80 chüan. Po-na ed. Reprinted in Taipei, 1967.

———. *Pei-shih* 北史 [The history of the Northern Dynasties, Wei, Ch'i, Chou and Sui, 386–618]. Completed before 650. 100 chüan. Po-na ed. Reprinted in Taipei, 1967.

Ling-hu Te-fen 令狐德棻 (d. 634). *Chou shu* 周書 [The history of the Northern Chou dynasty, 557–581]. 50 chüan. Po-na ed. Reprinted in Taipei, 1967.

Liu Hsü 劉昫 (d. 946?) and others. *Chiu T'ang shu* 舊唐書 [The old history of the T'ang dynasty, 618–907]. 200 chüan. Po-na ed. Reprinted in Taipei, 1967.

Lo Jung-peng. "Policy Formulations and Decision Making on Issues Respecting Peace and War," in Charles Hucker, ed., *Chinese Government in Ming Times*. New York: Columbia University Press, 1969.

Lobsang-danjin. *Altan Tobchi* [A brief history of the Mongols]. Scripta Mongolica I. Intro. by Antoine Mostaert. Reprinted in Cambridge, Mass.: Harvard University Press, 1952.

Mancall, Mark. "The Ch'ing Tribute System: An Interpretive Essay," in John K. Fairbank, ed., *The Chinese World Order: Traditional China's Foreign Relations*. Cambridge, Mass.: Harvard University Press, 1968.

Michael, Franz H. *The Origin of Manchu Rule in China*. Baltimore: John Hopkins University Press, 1942

Ming shih-lu 明實錄 also known as *Huang-Ming shih-lu* 皇明實錄 [The venerable records of the imperial Ming]. Ed. and printed by Academia Sinica, Taipei, 1966. *Min jitsuroku sho, Mokohen* 明實錄抄蒙古篇 [Selections from the Ming venerable records, Mongolian section]. Kyoto, 1959.

Mote, Frederick W. "The T'u-mu Incident of 1449," in Frank A. Kierman and John K. Fairbank, eds., *Chinese Ways in Warfare*. Cambridge, Mass.: Harvard University Press, 1968.

Okada Hidehiro. "Life and Work of Dayan Khan," in *Proceedings of the International Conference on China Border Area Studies*. Taipei, National Chengchi University, 1985.

O-yang Hsiu 歐陽修 (d. 1072), Sung Ch'i 宋祁, and others. *Hsin T'ang shu* 新唐書 [The new history of the T'ang dynasty, 618–907]. 255 chüan. Po-na ed. Reprinted in Taipei, 1967.

———. *Wu-tai shih-chi* 五代史記 [The historical record of the Five Dynasties, Liang, T'ang, Chin, Han and Chou, 907–960]. Po-na ed. Reprinted in Taipei, 1967.

Pan Ku 班固 (d. 92 A.D.) and sister Pan Chao 班昭 ,. *Han shu* 漢書 [The history of the Former Han dynasty, 206 B.C.-8 A.D.]. 120 chüan. Po-na ed. Reprinted in Taipei, 1967.

Rossabi, Morris. "Ming China's Relations with Hami and Central Asia, 1404–1513: A Re-examination of Traditional Chinese Foreign Policy" (Diss., Columbia University, 1970).

———. "Notes on Esen's Pride and Ming China's Prejudice," *The Mongolia Society Bulletin* 9:31–39 (1970).

———. "The Tea and Horse Trade with Inner Asia during the Ming," *Journal of Asian History* 42:136–168 (1970).

———. *China Among Equals: The Middle Kingdom and Its Neighbors, 10th–14th Centuries*. Berkeley: University of California Press, 1983.

Roth, Gertraude. "The Manchu-Chinese Relationship, 1618–1636," in Jonathan D. Spence and John E. Wills, Jr., *From Ming to Ch'ing: Conquest, Region, and Continuity in Seventeenth-Century China*. New Haven: Yale University Press, 1979.

Roth-Li, Gertraude. "The Rise of the Early Manchu State: A Portrait Drawn from Manchu Sources to 1636" (Diss., Harvard University, 1975).

Saghang Sechen. *Erdeni-yin tobchi* [Mongolian chronicle]. Hohehot, Inner Mongolia: Obor Mongghol-un arad-un keblel-un khoriya, 1981.

———. *Erdeni-yin tobchi* [Mongolian chronicle]. Scripta Mongolica II. Intro. by Antoine Mostaert. Reprinted in Cambridge, Mass.: Harvard University Press, 1956.

Schwartz, Benjamin. "The Chinese Perception of World Order, Past and Present," in John K. Fairbank, ed., *The Chinese World Order: Traditional China's Foreign Relations*. Cambridge, Mass.: Harvard University Press, 1968.

The Secret History of the Mongols, author unknown, completed 1240. English tr. Francis W. Cleaves. Cambridge, Mass.: Harvard University Press, 1982.

Serruys, Henry. "The Mongols of Kansu During the Ming," *Mélanges Chinois et Bouddhiques* 10:215–346 (1955).

———. "Remains of Mongol Customs in China during the Early Ming Period," *Monumenta Serica* 16:137–190 (1957).

———. "Chinese in Southern Mongolia During the Sixteenth Century," *Monumenta Serica* 18:1–95 (1959).

———. "Mongols Ennobled During the Early Ming," *Harvard Journal of Asiatic Studies* 22:209–260 (1959).

———. "The Mongols in China During the Hung-wu Period (1368–1398)," *Mélanges Chinois et Bouddhiques* 11:1–328 (1959).

———. "Were the Ming Against the Mongols' settling in North China," *Oriens Extremus* 6:131–159 (1959–1960).

———. "Four Documents Relating to the Sino-Mongol Peace of 1570–1571," *Monumenta Serica* 19:1–66 (1960).

———. "Ta-tu, Tai-tu, Dayidu," *Chinese Culture* 2.4 (May 1960).

———. "Landgrants to the Mongols in China: 1400–1460," *Monumenta Serica* 25:394–404 (1966).

———. "Sino-Mongolian Relations during the Ming II: The Tribute System and Diplomatic Missions (1400–1600)," *Mélanges Chinois et Bouddhiques* 14:1–650 (1967).

———. "The Mongols in China 1400–1450," *Monumenta Serica* 27:233–305 (1968).

———. "Sino-Mongolian Relations during the Ming III: Trade Relations: The Horse Fairs," *Mélanges Chinois et Bouddhiques* 17:1–288 (1975).

Sinor, Denis. *Inner Asia: A Syllabus*, 2nd ed. Bloomington: Indiana University Uralic and Altaic Series (vol. 96), 1971.

———. "Horse and Pasture in Inner Asian History," *Oriens Extremus* 19.1–2:171–183 (April 1972).

Ssu-ma Ch'ien 司馬遷 (d. 85 B.C.). *Shih chi* 史記 [Historical record, from the legendary period to the middle of the reign of the Emperor Wu-ti of the Han dynasty]. 130 chüan. Po-na ed. Reprinted in Taipei, 1967.

Ssu-ma Kuang 司馬光 (d. 1086) et al., *Tzu-chih t'ung ch'ien* 資治通鑑 [The historical chronology, from 403 B.C.-959 A.D.]. 294 chüan. Reprinted in Taipei, 1978.

Struve, Lynn A. *The Southern Ming 1644–1662*. New Haven: Yale University Press, 1984.
Sung Lien 宋濂 and others. *Yüan shih* 元史 [The history of the Yüan dynasty, from the beginning of the Mongol empire to the end of the Yüan dynasty, 1206–1368]. Completed 1369. 210 chüan. Po-na ed. Reprinted in Taipei, 1967.
Suzuki Chusei. "China's Relations with Inner Asia: The Hsiung-nu, Tibet," in John K. Fairbank, ed., *The Chinese World Order: Traditional China's Foreign Relations*. Cambridge, Mass.: Harvard University Press, 1968.
Symons, Van Jay. *Ch'ing Chinseng Management: Ch'ing Monopolies in Microcosm*. Tempe: Center for Asian Studies, Arizona State University, 1981.
Tamura, Jitsuzo 田村實造. "Higashi Ajia minzoku ido 東アジア民族移動 [The migration of the East Asian peoples]," *Bongakubu kenkyu kiyo* 文學部研究記要. Kyoto University, no. 12 (1968).
Tani, Mitsutaka. "A Study on Horse Administration in the Ming Period," *Acta Asiatica* 21:73–97 (1971).
Tao Jing-shen. *The Jurchen in Twelfth-Century China: A Study of Sinicization*. Seattle: University of Washington Press, 1976.
———. "Barbarians or Northerners: Northern Sung Images of the Khitans," in Morris Rossabi, ed., *China among Equals: The Middle Kingdom and Its Neighbors 10th–14th Centuries*. Berkeley: University of California Press, 1983.
Teggart, Frederick J. *Rome and China: A Study of Correlations in Historical Events*. Berkeley: University of California Press, 1939.
Toghto 托托 et al. *Chin shih* 金史 [The history of the Jurchen Chin dynasty, 1115–1234]. Completed 1344. 135 chüan. Po-na ed. Reprinted in Taipei, 1967.
———. *Liao shih* 遼史 [The history of the Khitan Liao dynasty, 907–1125]. Completed 1344. 160 chüan. Po-na ed. Reprinted in Taipei, 1967.
———. *Sung shih* 宋史 [The history of the Sung dynasty, 960–1276]. Completed 1346. 496 chüan. Po-na ed. Reprinted in Taipei, 1967.
Toyama Gunji. 外山軍治 *Kinchōshi kenkyu.* 金朝史研究 [Studies in the history of the Chin dynasty]. Kyoto, Toyoshi-kenkyu-kai, 1964.
Toynbee, Arnold J. *A Study of History*. 12 vols. London: Oxford University Press, 1946–1961.
Vainshtein, Sevyan. *Nomads of South Siberia: the Pastoral Economies of Tuva*. ed. and intro. Caroline Humphrey, tr. Michael Colenso. Cambridge: Cambridge University Press, 1980.
Wada, Sei 和田清. *Toashi Kenkyu, Mokohen* 東亞史研究蒙古篇 [Studies on the history of the Far East, Mongolia]. Tokyo, 1959.

Wakeman, Frederic Jr. *The Great Enterprise: The Manchu Reconstruction of Imperial Order in Seventeenth-Century China* 2 vol. Berkeley: University of California Press, 1985.

Wang Ch'in-jo 王欽若, Yang I 楊億 and others, ed. *Ts'e-fu yüan-küei* 冊府元龜 [The historical model, examples from the acts and records of the famous emperors and ministers]. 1000 chüan. Completed 1005. Reprinted in Taipei.

Wang Gungwu. "The Rhetoric of a Lesser Empire: Early Sung Relations with Its Neighbors," in Morris Rossabi, ed., *China among Equals: The Middle Kingdom and its Neighbors 10th–14th Centuries*. Berkeley: University of California Press, 1983.

Wei Cheng 魏徵 (d. 643) and others. *Sui shu* 隋書 [The history of the Sui dynasty, 581–618]. Completed 644. 85 chüan. Po-na ed. Reprinted in Taipei, 1967.

Wei Shou 魏收 (d. 571). *Wei shu* 魏書 [The history of the To-pa Wei dynasty, 386–557]. 140 chüan. Po-na ed. Reprinted in Taipei, 1967.

Weissleder, Wolfgang. "The Promotion of Suzerainty Between Sedentary and Nomadic Populations in Eastern Ethiopia," in Wolfgang Weissleder ed., *The Nomadic Alternative*. The Hague: Mouton Publishers, 1978.

———, ed. *The Nomadic Alternative*. The Hague: Mouton Publishers, 1978.

Yang Lien-sheng, "Historical Notes on the Chinese World Order," in John K. Fairbank, ed., *The Chinese World Order: Traditional China's Foreign Relations*. Cambridge, Mass.: Harvard University Press, 1968.

Yao Ts'ung-wu 姚從吾. *Tung-pei-shih lun-ts'ung* 東北史論叢 [A collection of the studies on the history of the Northeast]. 2 vols. Taipei: 1959.

Yü Ying-shih. *Trade and Expansion in Han China*. Berkeley: University of California Press, 1967.

———. "Han Foreign Relations," in Denis Twitchett and Michael Lowe eds., *The Cambridge History of China*. vol. 1. Cambridge: Cambridge University Press, 1986.

GLOSSARY

A-chu pn. 阿著
A-fu-chih-lo pn. Kao-ch'e 阿伏至羅
A-na-k'ui (Jou-jan khan, r. 518–552) 阿那瓌
A-shih-na Mi-she pn. Turk 阿史那彌射
A-shih-na Tu-erh pn. 阿史那杜尔
Abbisid (people)
Abughai (Abukhai) pn. Mongol
Alagh pn. Mongol
Alp Küchlüg Bilge Khan pn. 合骨咄祿毗伽可汗
Altan (Khan) (Mongolian leader, d. 1583)
An-i *kung-chu* (Sui princess) 安義公主
An Lu-shan pn. T'ang 安祿山
An-pa-chien pn. (See Yeh-lü A-pao-chi) 案巴堅
Arughtai pn. Mongol
Ayur-shiridara (Mongolian khan, r. 1370–1378)
Ba'atur (see Köngdüleng)
Bagha-achi pn. Mongol
Baisaugghur *Taiji* pn. Mongol
Bars-bolod pn. Mongol
Batu-möngke (see Dayan Khan)
Batula *Chingsang* (see Mahmud)
Bayantai pn. Mongol
Bilge Ch'ung-te Khan pn. Uighur 毗伽崇德可汗
Bilge Khan pn. Turk (r. 716–734) 毗伽可汗
Bintu pn. Mongol
Bingtu pn. Mongol
Bodi-alagh Khan (Mongolian khan, r. 1524–1547[?])
Bolai pn. Mongol
Börte pn. Mongol
Boshightu pn. Mongol

Bunyashiri Khan pn. Mongol
Buyan *Taiji* pn. Mongol
Chahar pl. 察哈尔
chang (stamp) 章
Chang Chao-yüan pn. Sung 張昭遠
Chang Ch'i pn. 張耆
Chang-chia k'ou pl. (see Kalgan) 張家口
Chang Chü-cheng pn. Ming 張居正
Chang Huan pn. Han 張奐
Chang-i pl. 張掖
Chang-sun Sheng pn. Sui 長孫晟
Chang-ti (Han emperor, r. 76–88 A.D., Liu Ta) 章帝
Chang Tuan-fu pn. Ming 張端甫
Ch'ang-an pl. 長安
Ch'ang-hsing (930–933) rp. Later T'ang 長興
Chao pl. 趙
Chao Chen (see Jen-tsung, Sung emperor) 趙禎
Chao Chi (see Hui-tsung, Sung emperor) 趙佶
Chao Ch'üan pn. Ming 趙全
Chao Heng (see Chen-tsung, Sung emperor) 趙恆
Chao Huan (see Ch'in-tsung, Sung emperor) 趙桓
Chao Kuang-i (see T'ai-tsung, Sung emperor) 趙匡義
Chao Kuang-yin (see T'ai-tsu, Sung emperor) 趙匡胤
Ch'ao Ts'o pn. Han 晁錯
Chen pl. 鎮
Chen-chou pl. 鎮州
Chen-fan pl. 鎮番
chen-fu ssu (office) 鎮撫司
Chen-tsung (Sung emperor, r. 997–1022, Chao Heng) 真宗
Ch'en Sheng pn. Han 陳勝
Ch'en Yüeh pn. Ming 陳鉞
Cheng-ch'iang-pu (castle) 鎮羌堡
Cheng Chü-chung pn. Sung 鄭居中
Cheng-kuang (520–524) rp. Wei 正光

Glossary

Cheng-ting pl. 正定
Cheng-t'ung (1436–1449) rp. Ming 正統
Ch'eng-hua (1464–1487) rp. Ming 成化
ch'eng-hsiang (prime minister) 丞相
Ch'eng-t'ien *tai-hou* (Liao empress dowager, 982–1009, Hsiao Ch'o) 聖天太后
Ch'eng-ts'ai (see Li Ch'eng-tsai) 承宷
Ch'eng-tsu (Ming emperor, also known as Yung-lo, r. 1403–1424, Chu Ti) 成祖
chi (gave) 給
Ch'i (dynasty, 479–502, also known as Southern Ch'i) 齊
Ch'i (dynasty, 550–577, also known as Northern Ch'i) 齊
Chi-hu (people) 稽胡
Chi-lien (mountains) 祁連
Chi-men pl. 薊門
Chi Pu pn. Han 季布
chi-wang-chüeh *K'o-han* (title) 繼往絕可汗
Chi Yung pn. Han 季肜
Ch'i-min (see Tölis Khan) 啟民
Chia-ching (1522–1566) rp. Ming 嘉靖
Chia I pn. Han 賈誼
Chia Ssu-tao pn. Sung 賈似道
Chia-yü pl. 嘉峪
chiang-chün (title) 將軍
Chiang-huai pl. 江淮
chiang-tu (princely title, see Liu Chien) 江都
ch'iang (Western barbarians, pejorative) 羌
chiao-tuan (animal) 角端
Chieh-li (see Il Khan) 頡利
Chieh-yu (Han princess) 解憂
Chien-chou Jurchen (people) 建州女真
Chien-te (572–577) rp. Northern Chou 建德
Chien-wu (25–55 A.D.) rp. Han 建武
Ch'ien-chin *kung-chu* (Chou princess) 千金公主

ch'ien-hu (title) 千户
Chih-chih (Hsiung-nu Shan-yü, r. 57–36 B.C.) 郅支
chih-hui (title) 指揮
chih-hui-shih (title) 指揮使
Chih-lien Khan (see Wu-t'i Khan) 赦連司汗
Ch'ih-shan pl. 赤山
chih-yüan (title) 知院
Chin (dynasty, 265–419) 晋
Chin (dynasty, 936–946, also known as Later Chin) 晋
Chin (Jurchen dynasty, 1115–1234) 金
chin (measurement) 斤
Ch'in (dynasty, 246–207 B.C.; state, 770–246 B.C.) 秦
Chin-ch'eng kung-chu (T'ang princess, d. 740) 金城公主
Chin-chou pl. 錦州
chin-i wei (Ming imperial guard) 錦衣衛
chin-kung (tribute) 進貢
Chin shih (history) 金史
Chin-yang pl. 晋陽
Ch'in-tsung (Sung emperor, r. 1126–1127, Chao Huan) 欽宗
Ching (Chin emperor) 璟
Ch'ing (dynasty, 1644–1911) 清
Ching-ba'atur pn. Mongol
Ching-chou pl 靜州
Ching-jung chün pl 靜戎軍
Ching-t'ai-ti (Ming emperor, r. 1450–1457, Chu Chi-yü) 景泰帝
Ching-te (1004–1008) rp. Sung 景德
Ching-ti (Han emperor, r. 156 B.C.–141 B.C., Liu Chi) 景帝
Ching-ti (See Ming emperor Ching-t'ai-ti) 景帝
Ching-tsung (Wei emperor, r. 528–530, T'o-pa Tzu-yu, also known as Chuang-ti) 敬宗
Ch'ing-chou pl. 青州

Ch'ing-li (1041–1048) rp. Sung 慶曆
Chikin (people) 赤斤
Chinggis Khan (Mongolian khan, r. 1206–1227)
chingsang (Mongolian transliteration of Chinese title ch'eng-hsiang)
chiu (father-in-law or uncle on the mother's side) 舅
Chiu T'ang shu (history) 舊唐書
Chiu Wu-tai shih (history) 舊五代史
Ch'iu Ch'u-chi pn. Chin 邱處機
Ch'o-chi-shih pn. Turk 咄吉世
Ch'o-lo Khan (Turk ruler, r. 618–620) 處羅可汗
Chokhor pn. Mongol
Chou (dynasty, 1122 B.C.–247 B.C.) 周
Chou (dynasty, 557–581, also known as Northern Chou) 周
Chou (dynasty, 684–705, established by Empress Wu) 周
Chou (dynasty, 951–959, also known as Later Chou) 周
Ch'ou Luan pn. Ming 仇鸞
chu (title) 主
Ch'u (a state) 楚
Chu Chan-chi (see Hsüan-Tsung, Ming emperor) 朱瞻基
Chu Ch'i-chen (see Ying-tsung, Ming emperor) 朱祁鎮
Chu Ch'i-yü (see Ching-t'ai-ti, Ming emperor) 朱祁鈺
Chu Chien-shen (see Hsien-tsung, Ming emperor) 朱見深
Chu-fu Yen pn. Han 主父偃
Chu Heng pn. Ming 朱衡
Chu Hou-chao (see Wu-tsung, Ming emperor) 朱厚照
Chu Hou-ts'ung (see Shih-tsung, Ming emperor) 朱厚熜
Chu I-chün (see Shen-tsung, Ming emperor) 朱翊鈞

Chu Ti (see Ch'eng-tsu, Ming emperor) 朱棣
Chu Wen (Liang emperor) 朱溫
Chu-wu-erh pn. Hei-shui Mo-ho 主兀兇
Chu Yüan-chang (see T'ai-tsu, Ming emperor) 朱元璋
Chu Yung pn. Ming 朱勇
Ch'u-ti (Chin emperor, 942–946, Shih Ch'ung-kuei) 出帝
Chü-ma (river) 拒馬
Chuang-tsung (Later T'ang emperor, r. 924–926, Li Tsun-hsü) 莊宗
chün (title) 君
Chün-ch'en (Hsiung-nu *Shan-yü*, r. 161–126 B.C.) 軍臣
chün-kung (title) 郡公
chung (measurement) 鐘
Chung-hang Yüeh pn. Han 中行說
Chung-shan pl. 中山
Chung-tu (Chin capital, Peking) 中都
Chung-yüan pl. 中原
ch'ung-hun *hou* (title) 重昏侯
Chürüge pn. Mongol 楮力克
Daiching pn. and title, Mongol
Daidu pl.
Daitsung Khan (see Toghto-bukha)
Dalad-Mingghantu pn.
Dayan Khan (Mongolian khan, r. 1487[?]–1524[?], Batu-Möngke)
Doying (Mongolian tribe, see To-yen)
dugha (Mongolian suffix)
Egami [Namio] (twentieth century Japanese historian) 江上波夫
Erdeni *Khong-taiji* pn. Mongol
Esen (Mongolian leader, d. 1454)
Fan-yang pl. 范陽
Fang Feng-shih pn. Ming 方逢時
feng (to present) 奉

Glossary

Feng-i *Wang* (title) 奉義王
Feng Lun pn. T'ang 封倫
fu (funeral gift, condolence) 賻
Fu-i *Wang* (title) 附義王
Fu-ning *hou* (title) 撫寧侯
Fu Pi pn. Sung 富弼
Fu-tang-chia pn. Mongol 伏當加
Fu-yü (people) 扶餘
Gobi pl.
Gün-bilig Mergen Jinong pn. Mongol (see Sayin-alagh)
Hai-hsi Jurchen (people) 海西女真
Hai-ling-ti (Chin emperor, r. 1149–1161, Wan-yen Ti-ku-nai, also known as Wan-yen Liang) 海陵帝
Hami pl. 哈密
Han (dynasty, 206 B.C.–220 A.D.) 漢
Han (dynasty, 947–950, also known as the Han of the Five Dynasties period) 漢
Han An-kuo pn. Han 韓安國
Han-chung *chün-wang* (title, see Li Yu) 漢中郡王
Han shu (history) 漢書
Han T'o-chou pn. Sung 韓侂冑
Hang-chou pl. 杭州
Hao Ching pn. Yüan 郝經
Hao-tan pn. Wu-huan 郝旦
Hei-shui Mo-ho (see Mo-ho) 黑水靺鞨
Ho-chien pl. 河間
Ho-chou pl. 河州
Ho Jo-i pn. Northern Chou 賀若誼
Ho-lan (Alashan mountains) 賀蘭
Ho-ning *Wang* (title) 和寧王
Ho-ti (Han emperor, r. 89–105, Lin Chao) 和帝
Hopei pl. 河北
Hou Han shu (history) 後漢書
hsi (imperial seal) 璽

Hsi-chün (Han princess) 細君
Hsi-yü chi (record) 西遊記
Hsia (kingdom of Tangut, 979[?]–1227) 夏
Hsiao-ching-ti (see Ching-ti, Han emperor) 孝景帝
Hsiao-ming-ti (see Su-tsung, Wei emperor) 孝明帝
hsiao-wang-tzu (title) 小王子
Hsiao-wen[-ti] (Wei emperor, r. 471–499, T'o-pa Hung) 孝文
Hsiao Ying pn. Khitan Liao 蕭英
Hsien-an kung-chu (T'ang princess) 咸安公主
Hsien-heng (670–673) rp. 咸亨
Hsien-ning po (title, see Ch'ou Luan) 咸寧伯
Hsien-pei (people) 鮮卑
Hsien-tsung (T'ang emperor, r. 806–820, Li Ch'un) 憲宗
Hsien-tsung (Ming emperor, r. 1465–1487, Chu Chien-shen) 憲宗
Hsien-yang (palace) 顯陽宮
Hsin (dynasty, 9 A.D.–23 A.D.) 新
Hsin-ch'eng pl. 新鄭
Hsin-chih-fen pn. Wu-huan 歆志賁
Hsin-chou pl. 忻州
hsin-ch'ou (lunar chronological terminology) 辛丑
Hsin T'ang shu (history) 新唐書
Hsingan (mountains) 興安
Hsing-ch'eng pl. (see Ning-yüan) 興城
Hsing-hsi-wang K'o-han (Uighur khan) 興昔亡可汗
Hsiung-chou pl. 雄州
Hsiung-hsien pl. 雄縣
Hsiung-nu (people) 匈奴
Hsü Chieh pn. Ming 徐階
Hsü Chin pn. 許進
Hsü-chou pl. 徐州
Hsü-shui-hsien pl. 徐水縣
Hsüan (Chou king, r. 827–782 B.C.) 宣王
Hsüan-fu pl. 宣府

Glossary

Hsüan-lan-tang tsung shu (record) — 玄覽堂叢書
Hsüan-ti (Han emperor, r. 73 B.C.–49 B.C., Liu Hsün, also known as Liu Ping-chi) — 宣帝
Hsüan-ti (Northern Chou emperor, r. 578–579, Yü-wen Pin) — 宣帝
Hsüan-tsung (T'ang emperor, r. 713–755, Li Lung-chi, also known as Emperor Ming-huang) — 玄宗
Hsüan-tsung (Chin emperor, r. 1213–1223, Wan-yan Hsün-chen) — 宣宗
Hsüan-tsung (Ming emperor, r. 1426–1435, Chu Chan-chi) — 宣宗
Hsüan-wu-ti (see Shih-tsung, Wei emperor) — 宣武帝
Hsüeh Chü pn. T'ang — 薛舉
hu (Northern barbarians, pejorative) — 胡
hu (measurement) — 斛
Hu Cheng pn. T'ang — 胡正
Hu-han-yeh (Hsiung-nu *Shan-yü*, r. 58–31 B.C.) — 呼韓邪
Hu-kuang pl. — 湖廣
Hu-lu-ku (Hsiung-nu *Shan-yü*) — 狐鹿姑
Hunan pl. — 湖南
Hupei pl. — 湖北
Hu-tu-erh-shih-tao-kao-jo-ti (Hsiung-nu *Shan-yü*) — 呼都而尸道皋若提單于
Huai (river) — 淮
Huai-jen *khaghan* (title) — 懷仁可汗
Huai-yang *Wang* (title, see Wu Yen-hsiu) — 淮陽王
Huan K'uan pn. Han — 桓寬
Huan-ti (Han emperor, r. 147–167, Liu Chih) — 桓帝
Huang-hua-yü (canyon) — 黃花峪
Huang-shih *kung* pn. (legendary Taoist) also (record) — 黃石公
Hui-chou pl. — 會州
Hui-tsung (Sung emperor, r. 1101–1125, Chao Chi) — 徽宗
hun-te kung (title) — 昏德公

Hung-chih (1488–1505) rp. Ming   弘治
Hung-shui tan pl.   紅水灘
Hung-ssu pu (castle)   弘賜堡
i (Eastern barbarians, pejorative)   夷
i (to send, to give)   遺
I-chen-tou Khan (see Tölis Khan)   意珍豆可汗
I-Ch'eng kung-chu (Sui princess)   義成公主
i-i chih-i (political idiom)   以夷制夷
i-i fa-i (political idiom)   以夷伐夷
I-mo barbarians   夷貊
I-nan (Sir-Tartush Turk leader)   夷男
Il Khan (Turk khan, r. 620–630)   頡利可汗
Ishbara Khan (Turk khan, r. 581–587, also known as Sha-po-lüeh and She-t'u)
Ismail pn. Mongol
Jan-kan pn. Turk (see Tölis khan)   梁干
ja'ud khuri (title)
Jen-tsung (Sung emperor, r. 1023–1063, Chao Chen)   仁宗
jinong (Mongolian title)
Jongdolai pn. Mongol
Jongnon pn. Mongol
Jou-jan (people)   柔然
ju-ju (Jou-jan people)   茹茹
ju-kung (tribute)   入貢
ju-k'uo (invasion)   入寇
Juan-juan (See Jou-jan)   蠕蠕
Jung (people)   戎
Jung-wang (princely title)   榮王
Jungdu (Chin capital, Chung-tu or Peking)   中都
Jurchen (people)   女真
K'ai-feng pl.   開封
K'ai-yüan pl.   開原
K'ai-yüan (713–741) rp. T'ang   開元
Kalgan (see Chang-chia k'ou)
Kan-chou pl.   甘州

Kan-ch'üan kung (palace) 甘泉宮
Kansu pl. 甘肅
Kao-ch'e (people) 高車
Kao Huan pn. Northern Ch'i 高歡
Kao Shao-i pn. Northern Ch'i 高紹義
Kao-ti (Han emperor, r. 206 B.C.–195 B.C., Liu Pang) 高帝
Kao-tsu (Northern Chou emperor, r. 561–577, Yü-wen Yung, also known as Emperor Wu-ti) 高祖
Kao-tsu (Later Chin emperor, r. 936–942, Shih Ching-t'ang) 高祖
Kao-tsu (T'ang emperor, r. 618–626, Li Yüan) 高祖
Kao-tsu of Han (see Kao-ti of Han) 高祖
Kao-tsung (T'ang emperor, r. 650–683, Li Chih) 高宗
Keng Ping pn. Han 耿秉
Kereyid (people)
Khalkha (people)
Khan Baligh pl.
Kharachin (people)
khara kitad (Chinese people, pejorative)
Khatagin (people)
khatun (Turkic-Mongol term for the queen or wife of a noble)
Khitan (people) 契丹
Kholochi Noyan pn. Mongol
khong taiji (title)
Khridesungtsan (Khri lde gtsug brtsan, Tibetan king, r. 704–755)
Khubilai Khan (Mongolian khan, r. 1260–1294)
khudal (Mongolian term meaning "to lie")
khudaldaa (Mongolian term for merchants, verbal form)
khudaldugha (Mongolian term for merchants, written form)

Khutughtu (see Lighdan Khan)
Kiangsu pl. 江蘇
Kirghiz (people)
Kitad *ulus* (China)
Ko-le Khan (Uighur khan, r. 745–759) 葛勒可汗
K'o-pi-neng pn. Hsien-pei, d. 229 A.D. 柯比能
Koguryu (country) 高駒麗
Kökönor (Ching-hai) pl.
Köndüleng pn. Mongol
körösü (skin)
körösü-ügei (skinless)
K'ou Chun pn. Sung 寇準
Ku-ch'e pl. 庫車
Ku-li-pei-lo (Uighur khan, r. 742–745) 骨力裴羅
Ku-pei k'ou (gate) 古北口
Kuang-ning pl. 廣寧
Kuang-p'ing (princely title, see Li Yü, later Emperor Tai-tsung of T'ang) 廣平
Kuang-wu-ti (Han emperor, r. 25–56 A.D., Liu Hsiu) 光武帝
Kuei-li-ch'ih pn. Mongol 鬼力赤
Kuei-tzu pl. 龜茲
kui-yu (lunar chronological terminology) 癸酉
k'un-ling *tu-hu* (title) 崑陵都護
K'un-mo (Wu-sun king) 昆莫
kung (tribute) 貢
kung-nu (title given to the Hsiung-nu during Wang Mang's reign) 恭奴
Kuo Ch'ien pn. Ming 郭乾
Kuo Ching pn. Ming 郭敬
k'uo-pien (border encroachment) 寇邊
Kutlug-Bilgä-Kül Khan (Uighur khan) 骨咄祿毗伽闕可汗
Kwangtung pl. 廣東
lai-hsiang (come to submit) 來降
Lan-chou pl. 蘭州
lang-chung (title) 郎中

Glossary

Lang *Taiji* pn. Mongol (see Baizangghur *Taiji*)
Lao-shang *Shan-yü* (Hsiung-nu *Shan-yü*, r. 174–161) 老上單于
Lao-tzu pn. Chou 老子
Lei Lu-chün pn. T'ang 雷盧俊
Lha (Tibetan ruler)
li (measurement, a Chinese mile) 里
Li pn. 李
Li Ch'eng-liang pn. Ming 李成梁
Li Ch'eng-ts'ai pn. T'ang 李承寀
Li Chiang pn. T'ang 李絳
Li Chih (See Kao-tsung, T'ang emperor) 李治
Li Ch'un pn. T'ang 李純
Li Ch'ung pn. Wei 李崇
Li Heng (see Su-tsung, T'ang emperor) 李亨
Li Heng (see Mu-tsung, T'ang emperor) 李恒
Li Hsün pn. T'ang 李巽
Li Ju-sung pn. Ming 李如松
Li K'o-yung pn. T'ang (Turk) 李克用
Li K'uo (see Te-tsung, T'ang emperor) 李适
Li Lung-chi (see Hsüan-tsung, T'ang emperor) 李隆基
Li Ping pn. Ming 李秉
Li Shih-min (see T'ai-tsung, T'ang emperor) 李世民
Li Shou-li pn. T'ang (see Yung, Prince) 李守禮
Li Ssu pn. Ch'in 李斯
Li Ssu-yüan (see Ming-tsung, Later T'ang emperor) 李嗣源
Li Ts'un-hsü (see Chuang-tsung, Later T'ang emperor) 李存勗
Li Yü (see Tai-tsung, T'ang emperor) 李豫
Li Yü pn. T'ang 李瑀
Li Yüan (see Kao-tsu, T'ang emperor) 李淵
Li Yüan-hao (Tangut-Hsia king, r. 1032–1048) 李元昊
Liang (dynasty, 502–556) 梁
Liang (dynasty, 907–923) 梁
Liang-chou pl. 涼州

Liang Shih-tu pn. T'ang	梁師都
Liao (Khitan dynasty, 907–1125)	遼
Liao (river)	遼河
Liao-ning pl.	遼寧
Liao shih (history)	遼史
Liao-tung pl.	遼東
Lighdan Khan (Mongolian khan, r. 1604–1634, also known as Khutughtu Khan)	
Lin-hsia pl.	臨夏
Lin Tse-hsü pn. Ch'ing	林則徐
Ling-wu pl.	靈武
Liu Ch'ang pn. Sui	劉昶
Liu Ch'e (see Wu-ti, Han emperor)	劉徹
Liu Ch'i (see Ching-ti, Han emperor)	劉啟
Liu Chien pn. Han	劉建
Liu Chih (see Huan-ti, Han emperor)	劉志
Liu Ching pn. Han	劉敬
Liu Han pn.	劉漢
Liu Heng (see Wen-ti, Han emperor)	劉恆
Liu Hsiu (see Kuang-wu-ti, Han emperor)	劉秀
Liu Hsün (see Hsüan-ti, Han emperor)	劉詢
Liu Liu-fu pn. Liao	劉六符
Liu Ping-chi (see Hsüan-ti, Han emperor)	劉病己
Liu Pang (see Kao-ti, Han emperor)	劉邦
Liu Ta (see Chang-ti, Han emperor)	劉炟
Liu Wen-ching pn. T'ang	劉文靜
Liu Wu-chou pn. T'ang	劉武周
Lo pn. Ch'in	傑
Lo-yang pl.	洛陽
Lu Kung pn. Han	魯恭
Lü (Han empress dowager, r. 187–180 B.C.)	呂后
Lü Ta-ch'i pn. Ming	呂大器
Luan-ch'eng pl.	欒城
lüeh-pien (looting border areas)	掠边
Lung Ta-yu pn. Ming	龍大有
Lung-ch'ing (1567–1572) rp. Ming	隆慶

Glossary

Lung-hsi pl. 隴西
Ma-i pl. 馬邑
Mahmud pn. Mongol, d. 1425[?]
maimai (buying and selling) 買賣
man (Southern barbarians, pejorative) 蠻
Mandughuli pn. Mongol
Mao-tun (Hsiung-nu *Shan-yü*, r. 209 B.C.–174 B.C.) 冒頓
meng-ch'ih *tu-hu* (title) 濛池都護
Meng I-mai pn. Ming 孟一脈
Meng T'ien pn. Ch'in 蒙恬
mergen jinong (title)
Ming (dynasty, 1368–1644) 明
Ming-chün pn. Han 明君
Ming-huang (see Hsüan-tsung, T'ang emperor) 明皇
Ming shih (history) 明史
Ming shih-lu (history) 明實錄
Ming-ti (Han emperor, r. 58–75 A.D., Liu Chuang) 明帝
Ming-tsung (Later T'ang emperor, r. 926–933, Li Ssu-yüan) 明宗
Miu (duke of Ch'in state during Chou dynasty) 繆公
Mo-chi-lien pn. Turk (Bilge Khan) 默棘連
Mo-ch'o (Turk khan, r. 691–716) 默啜
Mo-ho (people) 靺鞨
Mo-ni (Manichaen) 摩尼
Möngke Khan (Mongolian khan, r. 1251–1259)
Möngkeshiri pn. Mongol
Morikhai pn. Mongol
Mu-tsung (T'ang emperor, r. 821–824, Li Heng) 穆宗
Mu-tsung (Ming emperor, r. 1567–1572, Chu Tsai-hou) 穆宗
Mughan Khan (Turk khan, r. 553–572)
na (offering) 納
na (animal) 豽

naimai (Mongolian term for merchants)
Naiman (people)
Nanking pl. 南京
Nieh I pn. Han 聶一
Ning-hsia pl. 寧夏
Ning-kuo *kung-chu* (T'ang princess) 寧國公主
Ning-wu pl. 寧武
Ning-yüan pl. 寧遠
Ning-yüan pu pl. 寧遠堡
Noyan-uul pl.
Noyandara *jinong* pn. Mongol
Nurhachi (Manchu emperor, r. 1616–1626, also known as Ch'ing T'ai-tsu)
O-chou pl. (Wu-ch'ang) 鄂州
Ögödei (Mongolian khan, r. 1229–1241)
Oirad (people)
Old Ba'atur (see Ba'atur)
ong (the Mongolian pronunciation of the Chinese word *wang*, prince)
ong-jing pn. Mongol 王亨
Ong Khan (see To'oril)
Onggirad (people)
ou-shih (wife of a *Shan-yü*) 閼氏
Ordos pl.
Orkhon (river)
Pa-chou pl. 霸州
Pa-hsien pl. 霸縣
Pai-lang shui (river) 白狼水
Pai-lien (Buddhist sect) 白蓮
Pan Ch'ao pn. Han 班超
Pan Ku pn. Han 班固
Pan Piao pn. Han 班彪
pao-kuo *kung* (title, see Chu Yung) 保國公
Pao-ssu pn. Chou 褒姒
Parhae (see Po-hai)
Pei-chen pl. (see Kuang-ning) 北鎮

Glossary

Pei Ch'i shu (history) 北齊書
Pei shih (history) 北史
P'ei Chü pn. Sui and T'ang 斐矩
P'ei Mien pn. T'ang 斐冕
Peking pl. (Pei-ching)
P'eng pl. 彭
Pien-ching pl. (K'ai-feng) 汴京
Pien-liang (Sung capital, K'ai-feng) 汴梁
P'ien-ho pn. Hsien-pei 偏何
pin-*wang* (title, see Li Ch'eng-ts'ai) 邠王
Ping-chou pl. 并州
p'ing-chang (title) 平章
P'ing-ch'eng pl. 平城
p'ing-lu chiang-chün (title) 平虜將軍
Pir Mahamed pn. Oirad
Po-hai (country, Parhae) 渤海
Po-pai pn. Ming 哱拜
Pu-chen pn. Western Turk 步真
P'u-ku Huai-en pn. Turk 僕固懷恩
qatun (title) 可敦
Saghang Sechen pn. Mongol
Sai-na-la (see Sayin-alagh) 賽那剌
San-ch'ao pei-meng hui-pien (record) 三朝北盟會編
Sang Wei-han pn. Later Chin 桑維翰
Sayin-alagh (see Gün-bilig Mergen Jinong)
Salji'ud (people)
Sechen *Taiji* pn. Mongol
Sengge pn. Mongol
Sha-po-lo Tieh-li-shih pn. Turk 沙鉢羅咥利矢
Sha-po-lüeh (see Ishbara) 沙鉢畧
Sha-t'o (people) 沙陀
Shaji pn. Mongol
Shan-ku pl. 上谷
Shan-yü (Hsiung-nu title) 單于
shan-yü (title meaning "good man" adopted by Hsiung-nu rulers during Wang Mang's reign) 善于

Shan-yüan pl. (See also Treaty of Shan-yüan) 澶淵
Shang (dynasty, 1776 B.C.–1123 B.C.) 商
Shang-chün pl. 上郡
shang-tz'u (bestowal) 賞賜
Shansi pl. 山西
Shao-ti (Later Chin emperor, r. 943–946) 少帝
She-t'u (see Ishbara) 攝圖
Shen pl. 申
shen-ju (deep invasion) 深入
Shen Shih-hsing pn. Ming 申時行
Shen-tsung (I-chün, r. 1573–1620, Ming emperor) 神宗
Shen-yao (Kao-tsu, T'ang emperor) 神堯
Shen Ying pn. Ming 神英
sheng (sister's son) 甥
Sheng-tsung (Khitan Liao emperor, r. 983–1031, Yeh-lü Lung-hsü) 聖宗
Shensi pl. 陝西
Shih Ch'ao-i pn. T'ang 史朝義
Shih chi (history) 史記
Shih Ching-t'ang (Kao-tsu, Later Chin emperor) 石敬瑭
Shih Ch'ung-kuei (Ch'u-ti, Chin emperor) 石重貴
Shih Huang-ti (Ch'in emperor, r. 246–210 B.C., Ying Cheng) 始皇帝
Shih-pi Khan (Turk khan, r. 609–618) 始畢可汗
Shih-p'ing pl. 始平
shih-shang (market rewards) 市賞
Shih-shu-hu-hsi pn. Sui 史蜀胡悉
Shih Ssu-ming pn. T'ang 史思明
Shih Tao pn. Ming 史道
Shih T'ien-chüeh pn. Ming 石天爵
Shih-tsung (Wei emperor, r. 500–515, T'o-pa K'o, also known as Hsüan-wu-ti) 世宗
Shih-tsung (Chin emperor, r. 1161–1189, Wan-yen Wu-lu) 世宗

Glossary

Shih-tsung (Ming emperor, r. 1521–1567, Chu Hou-tsung) 世宗
Shou-hsiang ch'eng pl. 受降城
Shu-lü *huang-hou* (Khitan Liao empress, d. 953) 述律皇后
Shui-chüan ying pl. 水泉營
Shun-i *Wang* (title) 順義王
Shun-ning *Wang* (title) 順寧王
shuo (measurement) 碩
Shuo-chou pl. 朔州
Shuo-fang pl. 朔方
Shuo-fang chün pl. 朔方軍
Shuo-hsien pl. 朔縣
Sir-tartush (people) 薛延陀
Songtsan-gampo (Sron btsan sgampo, Tibetan king, d. 650)
Southern Sung (dynasty, 1127–1179) 南宋
Ssu-chin (see Mughan Khan) 俟斤
Ssu-ma Ch'ien pn. Han 司馬遷
Su-tsung (Wei emperor, r. 516–528, T'o-pa Hsü, also known as Hsiao-ming-ti) 肅宗
Su-tsung (T'ang emperor, r. 756–762, Li Heng) 肅宗
Sui (dynasty, 581–618) 隋
sui-pi (yearly payment) 歲幣
Sui shu (history) 隋書
Sun Ong (title)
Sung (dynasty, 960–1126) 宋
Sung Ching pn. Sung 宋京
Sung-chou pl. 松州
Sung I pn. Han 宋意
Sung-p'an pl. 松潘
Sung-shan pl. 松山
Sung shih (history) 宋史
Szechwan pl. 四川
ta-chü ju-k'uo (large-scale invasions) 大舉入寇
Ta-hsia (people) 大夏
Ta-hsi yang pl. 大西洋

Ta-i *kung-chu* (Chou princess) 大義公主
ta-jen (title) 大人
ta-ju (a great invasion) 大入
Ta-tan (people) 韃靼
Ta-t'ung pl. 大同
T'a-po (see Tapar Khan) 他鉢
Tai pl. 代
Tai-chou pl. 代州
Tai-hsien pl. 代縣
Tai-tsung (T'ang emperor, r. 763–779, Li Yü) 代宗
Tai-Yüan t'ien-sheng tai-k'o-han (title) 大元天盛可汗
T'ai-hang (mountains) 太行
T'ai-ho (477–499) rp. T'o-pa Wei 太和
T'ai-ho *kung-chu* (T'ang princess) 太和公主
t'ai-pu ssu (office) 太僕寺
t'ai-shih (title) 太師
T'ai-tsu (Sung emperor, r. 960–976, Chao K'uang-yin) 太祖
T'ai-tsu (Ming emperor, r. 1368–1398, Chu Yüan-chang) 太祖
T'ai-tsung (T'ang emperor, r. 626–649, Li Shih-min) 太宗
T'ai-tsung (Liao emperor, r. 927–947, Yeh-lü Te-kuang) 太宗
T'ai-tsung (Sung emperor, r. 976–997, Chao Kuang-i) 太宗
T'ai-yüan pl. 太原
taiji (Mongolian nobles)
taishi (title, Mongolian transliteration of Chinese term *t'ai-shih* or *t'ai-tzu*)
tan (measurement) 石
T'an-shih-huai (pn. Hsien-pei leader, d. 181) 檀石槐
T'ang (dynasty, 618–907) 唐
T'ang (Later T'ang dynasty, 923–934) 唐
T'ang pl. 唐
t'ang-mu (fief) 湯沐

Glossary

Tangut (people)
T'ao-chou pl. 洮州
t'ao-pien (robbing in border areas) 盜边
Tapar Khan (Turk khan, r. 527–581)
Tarim river basin pl. 塔里木河
Tarto (Turk khan, r. 575–603)
Tatar (people)
Te-tsung (T'ang emperor, r. 780–804, Li K'uo) 德宗
Temüjin (see *Chinggis Khan*)
Teng pl. 鄧
Teng-li mo-yü (Uighur khan, r. 759–788) 登里牟羽
Tebeg *Taiji* pn. Mongol
ti (Northern barbarians, pejorative) 狄
Ti Shan pn. Han 狄山
Ti-tao pl. 狄道
T'ieh-le (people) 鐵勒
T'ien Fen pn. Han 田蚡
T'ien Yin pn. Han 田銀
T'ien-fu (936–943) rp. 天福
T'ien-pao (713–755) rp. T'ang 天寶
T'ien-shan (mountain range) 天山
T'ien-shun (1457–1464) rp. Ming 天順
Ting pl. 定
Ting-chou pl. 定州
Ting-hsien pl. 定縣
Ting-ling (people) 丁零
To-yen (Ming garrison and Mongolian tribe, see Doying) 朶顏
T'o-pa pn. 拓跋
T'o-pa Hsü (see Su-tsung, Wei emperor) 拓跋詡
T'o-pa K'o (see Shih-tsung, Wei emperor) 拓跋恪
T'o-pa Tzu-yu (see Ching-tsung, Wei emperor) 拓跋子攸
Toghto-bukha pn. Mongol (see Daitsung Khan)
To'oril (Kereyid khan)
Toroghan pn. Mongol
Tölis (Turk khan, r. 559–609)

Tölös (see T'ieh-le)
Tou pn. Han 竇
Tou Hsien pn. Han 竇憲
Treaty of Shan-yüan (1005) 澶淵之盟
Tripitaka (Buddhist scriptures)
tsai-hsiang (title) 宰相
Ts'ai Ching pn. Sung 蔡京
Ts'ai Yung pn. Han 蔡邕
Ts'ang-chou (Ts'ang hsien) pl. 滄州
Ts'ao pn. 曹
Ts'ao Ts'ao (Han prime minister, founder of Wei dynasty d. 220) 曹操
Ts'en-tou pn. Wu-sun 岑陬
tseng (gift, to give, gift of condolence) 贈
tseng-lai (bestowals) 贈賚
tso hsiao-wei yüan-wai ta-chiang-chün (title) 左驍衛員外大將軍
Tu-chin pl. 度斤
tu-hu (title) 都護
Tu-lan (Turk khan, r. 588–600) 都蘭
tu-tu (title) 都督
Tu Wen-huan pn. Ming 杜文煥
T'u-chüeh (people) 突厥
T'u-mu pl. 土木
T'u-yü-hun (people) 吐谷渾
Tümed (people)
tümen (Mongolian political and military unit)
Tümen Khan (Turk khan, r. 1558–1592)
tung-ch'iang (plant) 東牆
tung-hu (general term for nomadic people, pejorative) 東胡
Tung I-yüan pn. Ming 董一元
T'ung-chou (T'ung hsien) pl. 通州
T'ung-hua (gate) 通化
T'ung Kuan pn. Sung 童貫
t'ung-kung (tribute) 通貢
T'ung-yeh-hu (Turk khan, r. 618–630) 統葉護

Glossary

Tunyukhukh pn. 暾欲谷
tzaisang (Mongolian transliteration of tsai-hsiang, Chinese term for prime minister)
tz'u (to bestow) 賜
Tz'u-men i (station) 磁門驛
tz'u-shih (title) 刺史
Ugechi-khashakha pn. Mongol
Uighur (people)
Ula'an-Khushi'un pl.
Uriyangkha (people)
Uushin (Mongolian tribe)
Wa-ch'iao (gate) 瓦橋
Wan-ch'üan pl. 萬全
Wan-li (1573–1620) rp. Ming 萬曆
Wan-yen Hsiang pn. Jurchen 完顏襄
wang (prince) 王
Wang Chen pn. Ming 王振
Wang Chi-chung pn. Liao 王繼忠
Wang Chih pn. Ming 王直
Wang Chih-hao pn. Ming 王之浩
Wang Ch'ung-ku pn. Ming 王崇古
Wang Fu pn. Sung 王黼
Wang Hui pn. Han 王恢
Wang Jing pn. Chin 王京
Wang Mang (Hsin emperor, r. 9 A.D.–23 A.D.) 王莽
Wang Yüeh pn. Ming 王越
Wei (state, 453–225 B.C.) 魏
Wei (dynasty, 220–264, also known as Ts'ao Wei) 魏
Wei (dynasty, 386–534, also known as T'o-pa Wei and Northern Wei) 魏
Wei, Eastern (dynasty, 534–550) 東魏
Wei, Western (dynasty, 534–557) 西魏
Wei Ch'ing pn. Han 衛青
Wei-ning po (title, see Ch'en Yüeh) 威寧伯
Wei shu (history) 魏書

Wei Wang (future Chin ruler Wei Hsiao-wang, r. 1208–1213, see Yün-chi) 衛王
Wei-yüan pu (castle) 威遠堡
Wen-ch'eng kung-chu (T'ang princess) 文成公主
Wen Ch'iu pn. Ming 文球
Wen-ti (Han emperor, r. 179–157 B.C., Liu Heng) 文帝
Wen-ti (Sui emperor, r. 581–604, Yang Chien) 文帝
Weng Wan-ta pn. Ming 翁萬達
Wu (Kiangsu) pl. 吳
Wu (T'ang empress dowager, r. 684–704, Tse-t'ien) 武后
Wu (Liang emperor, r. 907–922, Hsiao Yen) 武帝
Wu-ch'ang pl. 武昌
Wu Ch'eng-ssu pn. T'ang 武承嗣
Wu-chou pl. 武州
Wu-huan (people) 烏桓
Wu Kuang pn. Ming 吳廣
Wu-sun (people) 烏孫
Wu-tai shih-chi (history) 五代史記
Wu-ti (Han emperor, r. 140 B.C.–87 B.C., Liu Ch'e) 武帝
Wu-t'i (Jou-jan khan) 吳提
Wu-tsung (Ming emperor, r. 1506–1521, Chu Hou-chao) 武宗
Wu Yen-hsiu pn. T'ang 武延秀
Wu-yüan pl. 五原
yabkhu (pn. Uighur, also title)
Yang pn. 楊
Yang Cheng-tao pn. Sui 楊政道
Yang Chi-sheng pn. Ming 楊繼盛
Yang Chien (see Wen-ti, Sui emperor) 楊堅
Yang Hsin pn. Han 楊信
Yang Kuang (see Yang-ti, Sui emperor) 楊廣
Yang Shan pn. Ming 楊善
Yang-ti (Sui emperor, r. 605–618, Yang Kuang) 煬帝

Glossary

Yangtze (river)	楊子江
Yao An pn. Ming	姚安
Yeh-hu ling (mountain)	野狐嶺
Yeh-lü A-pao-chi (Khitan leader, 907–926)	耶律阿保機
Yeh-lü Ch'u-ts'ai pn. Yüan	耶律楚材
Yeh-lü Lung-hsü (see Sheng-tsung, Liao emperor)	耶律隆緒
Yeh-lü Te-kuang (see T'ai-tsung, Liao emperor)	耶律德光
Yen pl.	燕
Yen-an pl.	延安
Yen-ching (Peking) pl	燕京
Yen-men pl.	雁門
Yen-men-chai pl.	雁門砦
Yen-sui pl.	延綏
Yen-t'ieh lun (record)	鹽鐵論
Yen Yu pn. Han	嚴尤
Yen-yün (people)	獵犹
Yen-yung pl.	延永
Yi-li-bi (title) or pn. Khitan	夷離畢
Ying Cheng (see Shih Huang-ti, Chin emperor)	嬴政
Ying-chou pl.	營州
Ying-tsung (Ming emperor, r. 1436–1449 and 1457–1464, Chu Chi-chen)	英宗
Ying-wu wei yüan Bilge Khan (Uighur)	英武威遠毗伽可汗
Yu (Chou king, r. 781–771 B.C.)	幽王
yu-chien-men *ta-chiang-chün* (title)	右監門大將軍
Yu-chou pl.	幽州
yu tu-wei *chien-shih* (title)	右都衛簽事
yu-wei *ta-chiang-chün* (title)	右衛大將軍
Yü-chüeh (people)	于厥
Yü-lin wei (garrison)	榆林衛
yü-shih tai-fu (title)	御史大夫
Yü-wen pn. Chou	宇文
Yü-wen Pin (See Hsüan-ti, Northern Chou emperor)	宇文贇

Yü-wen T'ai (founder of the Northern Chou dynasty) 宇文泰
Yü-wen Yung (see Kao-tsu, Northern Chou emperor) 宇文邕
Yü-yang pl. 漁陽
Yüan (Mongolian dynasty, 1260–1368) 元
Yüan Chen pn. T'ang 袁振
Yüan Fu pn. Wei 元孚
yüeh (general term for non-Chinese from the South, pejorative) 越
Yüeh-chih (people) 月氏
yüeh-shang (monthly bestowals) 月賞
Yün pl. 雲
Yün-chi pn. Chin 允濟
Yün-chou pl. 雲州
Yung-lo (1402–1424) rp. Ming 永樂
Yung-lü pn. Sui 雍閭
Yung-p'ing (58 A.D.–75 A.D.) rp. Han 永平
yung-*wang* (princely title, see Li Shou-li) 雍王
Yung-yüan (89–104) rp. Han 永元
Yüngshiyebü (Mongolian tribe)

INDEX

A-chu. See Bars-bolod
A-fu-chih-lo: seeks alliance with Northern Wei, 123
A-na-k'ui: relations with Northern Wei, 38, 67–68, 121, 145; intermarries with Northern Ch'i, 145–146; rejects intermarriage with Tümen, 146; gifts received by, 170–171
A-shih-na Mi-she: titles given, 71
A-shih-na Tu-erh: intermarries with T'ang, 151
Abughai: Ming offers reward for, 86
Alagh: seeks peace with Ming, 49–50; fights with Esen, 83
Alp Küchlüg Bilge Khan: seeks intermarriage with T'ang, 160
Altan (Khan): and Tibetan Buddhism, 46, 175; family relations of, 48, 85, 97–98, 108; Right-Flank Mongol leader, 48, 199n89; titles granted, 49, 99, 102, 105n112; relations with Ming, 50–51, 76–78, 86–109, 114, 178, 191n50; overview of, 86; invades Tibet, 97; and Tümen Khan, 104; and trade, 105, 112, 113, 172–173, 181; death of, 107, 110; bestowals created for, 116; perceived differently by nomad than by Chinese, 174; memorial requesting tributary status, 206n117
An-i, Princess: intermarries with Tolis Khan, 150
An Lu-shan: rebellion of, 43, 72, 124, 156; non-Chinese general, 198n73
Annual payments: presented the Hsien-pei, 33; promised the Uighur, 72–73; presented the Khitan, 75; to Lighdan Khan, 199n90
Aridity: forces nomads to move, 5–6; as reason for nomadic aggression, 7–8
Arughtai: relations with Ming, 77, 81, 136–137, 178; vassal of Mongolian khan, 81
Ayur-shiridara; rejects Ming, 76

Ba'atur: receives title, 99–100, dies, 109
Bagha-achi: and Ming-Altan relations, 96–97, 102, 108
Baisangghur Taiji: relations with Ming, 87–88
Barbarians: Chinese perceptions of, 3, 55, 174; Western perceptions of, 4; weakened by drought and disease, 63
Bars-bolod: family relations of, 85–86, 97–98; leads Right-Flank Mongols, 85, 199n89, 204n92

Batu-möngke. See Dayan Khan
Batula Chingsang. See Mahmud
Bayantai: petitions for markets, 111; loots frontier, 209n166
Beans: trade in, 94–95, 172, 179
Bestowals: level of determined by relative power of participants, 14, 31, 108, 115–116, 118, 134–135, 138–139; as mechanism to promote peace, 16, 27, 53–54; presented to China's neighbors, 34, 55, 64, 111, 116, 120, 124, 133, 160; benefit nomadic rulers, 48, 115, 120, 131; when presented, 101, 116, 120; taxes collected to enable, 104; nature of, 115–116, 139–140; intermarriage a form of, 141
Bilge Ch'ung-te Khan: intermarries with T'ang, 160–162
Bilge Khan: and T'ang, 42, 153–154; and Tibet, 42, 154, 195n69; and Khitan, 154; and Sinicization, 193n7
Bingtu: and Ming, 105; and Tibet, 105; and Altan, 208n127
Bintu: and Ming, 105; and Tibet, 106; and Altan, 208n127
Bodi-alagh Khan, 50
Bolai: and Ming, 83–84
Books: Sung prohibits export of, 46
Booty: dispersed among Hsiung-nu, 25
Border markets. See Frontier markets
Börte: Chinggis Khan marries, 19
Boshightu: raids frontier, 110
Bows: made, 2, 167; presented to China, 34, 167; received by nomads, 169, 171
Britain: trade with China, 5, 185–186
Bronze: sale of forbidden, 108
Buddhism: Mongols convert to, 51, 81
Bunyashiri Khan: relations with Ming, 136–137
Buyan Taiji: successor to Tümen Khan, 109

Camels: exchanged, 27, 46, 122, 160, 166–171 passim; seized, 184
Cattle: exchanged, 34, 64, 94, 95, 119, 120, 166–172 passim, 179
Chai I: advocates aggressive nomadic policy, 55
Chang Chao-yüan: on frontier markets, 46
Chang Ch'i: proposes exchange, 129
Chang Chü-cheng: calls for harsh nomad policies, 3
Chang Huan: attacks the Hsien-pei, 35

259

Index

Chang-sun Sheng: accompanies Princess Ta-i, 148–149
Chang-ti, Emperor: borders well protected by, 33–34
Chang Tuan-fu: argues for military preparedness, 99
Chao Ch'üan: and Altan, 97, 103, 110
Ch'ao Ts'o: for aggressive policy against Hsiung-nu, 55
Chen-tsung, Emperor: and Khitan Liao, 47, 129–130
Ch'en Sheng: rebels against Ch'i, 53
Ch'en Yüeh: provokes war, 179
Cheng Chü-chung: against Southern Sung alliance with Jurchen, 47
Cheng-t'ung period: tribute relations during, 91, 100, 138, 168–169
Ch'eng-hua period: horse markets established during, 90–91
Ch'eng-t'ien, Empress: and Khitan-Sung relations, 45, 129
Ch'eng-tsu, Emperor: and Mongols, 77, 80–81, 102, 136–137, 178
Ch'i (Northern) dynasty: seeks alliance with Turks, 68, 121; struggle with Northern Chou, 68–69, 146–147; intermarries with Jou-jan, 145–146
Chi-hu: killed by Liang Shih-tu, 69
Chi Pu: argues against attacking Hsiung-nu, 53
Chi Yung: defeats Hsien-pei and Hsiung-nu, 33
Ch'i-min Khan. See Tölis Khan
Chia I: criticizes Han bestowals, 117
Chia Ssu-tao: deceives Mongols, 135
Chieh-yu, Princess: intermarries with Ts'en-tsou, 144
Ch'ien-chin, Princess: intermarries with Turks, 147–148; poem by, 149–150
Chih-chih, *Shan-yü*: defeated by Han-Southern Hsiung-nu alliance, 31
Chih-lien Khan. See Wu-t'i Khan
Chin (Later) dynasty: Khitan help establish, 75
Chin dynasty. See Jurchen Chin dynasty
Ch'in dynasty: Hsiung-nu role in fall of, 53
Chin-ch'eng, Princess: intermarries with Tibet, 156
Ch'in-tsung, Emperor: captured, 162
Ch'ing dynasty: seek tributaries, 11; relations with Britain, 185–186
Ching-ba'atur: attacks frontier, 105
Ching-te: period of Liao invasion, 47
Ching-ti, Emperor: promotes peace with Hsiung-nu, 26, 28, 55, 59, 142
Ching-ti, Emperor: occupies Ying-tsung's throne, 83
Ching-tsung, Emperor: relations with A-na-k'ui, 145

Chinggis Khan: successful rise of, 7–8, 12–13; and Jurchen, 19–20, 76, 135; and intermarriage, 162
Ch'o-lo Khan: friend and foe of T'ang, 69, 123, 150–151
Chokhor: Ming seeks alliance with, 111
Chou (Northern) dynasty: and Turks, 39, 68, 121; and Northern Ch'i, 68–69, 147; and intermarriage, 146–148; and contraband, 184
Ch'ou Luan: advocates trade with Altan, 89–92; executed, 94, 178
Chu-fu Yen: his arguments against Han dynasty going to war, 56–57, 59
Chu Heng: argues to accept tribute, confer rank, but not open markets, 99
Chu Ti. See Ch'eng-tsu, Emperor
Chu Wen: establishes Liang dynasty, 74
Chu Yung: provokes war during Ming, 84, 179
Chuang-tsung, Emperor: begins Later T'ang dynasty, 74; presents bestowals to Yeh-lü A-pao-chi, 43
Chung-hang Yüeh: warns against Sinicization, 25, 133, 169, 175
Chürüge: relations with Ming, 110–111
Climate: and nomadic aggression, 5–8, 18
Cloth: nomads depend on China for, 7, 13, 24, 25, 102–103; methods of securing, 27, 81; sought for by nomads, 30, 48, 50, 88, 148; acquired, 42, 75, 101, 104, 116–117, 138, 154, 160, 168–173 *passim*; exported by Khitan, 46; reward to market guards, 101
Confucianists: argue against war, 61–62
Contraband trade: 13, 15, 182–185
Cotton: traded, 104, 173
Crisis of 1541: 86–87

Daiching: seeks trade, 111
Dalad-Mingghannu: relations with Ming and Altan, 106
Dayan Khan: as forceful Mongol leader, 48, 49, 50, 85, 199n89; relations with Ming, 84–85
Defectors: among nomads, 43–44, 94–99 *passim*, 102–103, 173, 182–183, 221n70

Embroideries: exchanged, 55, 59, 72, 75, 107, 117, 133, 160, 169, 170
Envoys: quotas limiting number of, 82, 100–101, 108; mistreated, 135, 137, 139, 179–180
Erdeni *Khong Taiji*: followers poisoned, 181
Esen: leads Oirad Mongols, 48–49; reasons for war with China, 49, 82–83, 139, 179–80; and tribute system, 82, 100, 138–139, 172–173; captures Ying-tsung, 83, 210n5
Exchange: as alternative to war, 53, 165; nomads receive more than court, 161
Eyeballs of whales: offered as tribute, 167

Index

Famine: among nomads, 38, 171–172, 219n47
Fang Feng-shih: trade advocate, 106–108
Felt: produced, 2; uncomfortable for year-round wear, 50, 103
Feng Lun: proposes intermarriage, 151–152
Food: nomads depend on China for, 25, 31, 94–95, 116–117, 127, 169
Frontier: chaotic nature of, 182–183
Frontier markets: opened, 10–11, 14, 44–46, 84, 93–94, 122, 142, 160, 172, 205n110; advantages of, 16, 27–28, 50–55 passim, 90–91, 95, 98–99, 107; used to entrap nomads, 29, 35, 41, 176, 180, 220n62; and trade, 34, 42, 90–91, 168; Jurchen Chin do not rely on, 75–76; closed, 84, 106, 109; criticism of, 89–90, 107–108, 177–178; corruption at, 90, 95, 108–109; administration of, 101, 108–109, 205n109, 217n4
Fu Pi: counsels peace, 47, 130–132, 191n50
Furs: exchange of, 1, 34, 88, 101, 104, 166, 167, 173; suitable for nomad wear, 25; tiger, 34, 167; leopard, 34, 167; unsuitable for year-round wear, 50, 103; fox, 166; mink, 167; na, 167; ermine, 167, 168, 169; sable, 34, 124, 125, 160, 166–169 passim

Gifts: when presented, 128; exchange between Han and Hsiung-nu, 117–118
Ginseng: prized, 168, 218n25
Gold: offered nomads, 31, 55, 58, 60, 63, 69, 70, 75, 104, 116–118, 127, 130, 139, 152, 155, 160, 163, 168–175 passim
Grain: nomads secure from China, 1, 2, 7, 10–11, 13, 24–30 passim, 37–38, 48, 58, 61, 94–95, 104, 116, 118, 120, 169–173 passim, 179; shortage leads to Manchu invasion, 219n47
Great Wall: Wu-huan settle near, 32; built, 53; repair of suggested, 55; "robed-ones" inside, 58; "archers" outside, 58; Turks promote disunity south of, 69–70
Great Qatun: Altan intimidated by, 96–97

Hai-hsi Jurchen: horse trade of, 81, 90; ally with Tümen Khan, 104
Han, 1, 8, 10–11, 17, 25, 28, 30, 36, 47, 52–53, 55, 65, 124, 165, 169–170, 174, 194n25
Han An-kuo: position against war in Han debates, 59–61
Han T'o-chou: attacks Southern Sung, 135
Hao Ching: Khubilai sends envoys to, 135
Hao-tan: seeks exchange with Han, 34, 167
Hei-shui Mo-ho: offer tribute, 167
Hides: trade in, 1, 101, 104, 166, 173; suitable for nomads, 132–133
Ho Jo-i: seeks extradition of Kao Shao-i, 147

Ho-ti, Emperor: defeats Hsiung-nu, 34; Hsien-pei submit to, 34; dominated by Empress-Mother, 64
Horns: trade in, 166–167
Horses: exchange of, 1, 27, 34, 37, 40, 42, 46, 64, 74, 81, 88, 93, 95, 100–101, 104, 118–119, 122, 124, 125, 126, 153, 154, 160, 166–172 passim, 200n3; importance of, 80–81, 189n1; markets opened, 80, 84, 90; poor quality of Chinese, 83, 108–109, 183; scarcity in China, 84, 91; reduced prices for provokes war, 82, 139, 179–180; trade condemned, 90, 92, 99; tails of traded, 101, 173; skins of traded, 167; studies on, 189n1
Hostages, 30, 34, 50, 117, 118, 119–120, 134, 136
Hsi-chun, Princess: intermarries with King of Wu-sun, 142–144
Hsia. See Tangut Hsia
Hsiao Ying: negotiates with Sung, 130
Hsien-an, Princess: intermarries, 160
Hsien-pei: consolidation of power, 32–36, 63–65; and Wei, 67; description of, 167, 170; acquire contraband, 183
Hsien-tsung, Emperor: unstable frontier under, 84; supports intermarriage, 158; father of Princess T'ai-ho, 161
Hsin dynasty: 52, 63, 66
Hsin-chih-fen: leader of Wu-huan, 33
Hsiung-nu, 8, 10–11, 25–36 passim, 53, 55, 64–67, 116–119 passim, 131, 133, 143–144, 165–169 passim, 174, 180, 183, 193n5, 194n25
Hsü Chieh: recommends gifts to Mongols, 88
Hsüan-fu: market at, 86, 88, 90, 94, 100–113 passim, 184
Hsüan-ti, Emperor: and Southern Hsiung-nu, 30, 66, 118–119, 169
Hsüan-tsung, Emperor: and Turks, 42, 153–154, 171; and Uighur, 72; and Khitan, 74
Hsüeh Chu: Turks negotiate with, 70
Hu Cheng: escorts Princess T'ai-ho, 161–162
Hu-han-yeh: relations with Han, 30–32, 66–67, 118–119, 169–170, 174, 210n21
Hu-lu-ku Shan-yü: seeks exchange, 30
Hu-tu-erh-shih-tao-kao-jo-ti Shan-yü: desires Han recognition as equal, 119
Hui-tsung, Emperor: daughter's fate, 162

I-chen-tou Khan. See Tölis Khan
I-Ch'eng, Princess: marries four khans, 150, 152
i-i chih-i: "use barbarians to check barbarians," 56, 70, 80, 136
i-i fa-i: "use barbarians to attack barbarians," 56, 64, 80, 137
I-nan: relations with T'ang, 71

Il Khan: relations with T'ang, 42, 69–70, 131, 150, 151, 152
Intermarriage: factors determining, 14, 151, 154; to promote peace, 16, 53–54; during Han, 26–30, 55–65 passim, 116–117, 142–143, 167, 169; during Northern Wei, 37, 145; with Turks, 39, 121, 154, 171; with Jung, 56; with Ti, 56; Uighur-T'ang, 72–73, 124, 157–162 passim; Esen's son falsely assured of, 82; seen as disgraceful, 107; with Khitan, 129–132 passim; between Mongols during Ming, 137, 199n92; to obtain commodities, 141; for political objectives, 141, 151; little relied upon by Sung, Southern Sung, and Ming, 141, 162; Yüan and Ch'ing not traditional, 142–143; when practiced, 141, 144–145; princesses seldom emperor's daughters, 154; imposed by Mongols, 162; suffering of princesses, 163; relations sustained through dynastic change, 211n44
Iron: government managed, 61; sale to nomads forbidden, 108, 183; acquired by nomads, 166, 183
Ishbara: Sui controls through trade and intermarriage, 39, 121–123, 147–149, 158
Ismail: conflict with Ming, 84, 179

Jade: exchange of, 1, 42, 43, 72, 88, 118, 124, 127, 168, 218n24
Jan-kan. See Tölis khan
Jen-tsung, Emperor: relations with Khitan, 46–47, 130
Jongdolai: raids frontier, 110
Jou-jan: famine among, 171; unsuitability of term Juan-juan, 194n43
—relations with: Wei, 37; Liang, 120; Sung, 120; Southern Ch'i, 120; Northern Wei, 120–121, 144–145, 170–171; Kao-ch'e, 123; Khitan, 126; Northern Ch'i, 145–146; Turks, 146; dynasties south of Northern Wei, 219n39
Jung: intermarriage and trade of, 56, 166
Jurchin Chin dynasty: adopts Chinese pattern of governing, 17–19; and Sung, 44, 47, 75–76, 87, 133–135, 162, 191n51; and Khitan, 47–48, 54, 168; and Ming, 80–81; similar to later Manchus, 112, 192n57; and Mongols, 163

Kao Huan: founder of Northern Ch'i dynasty, 145–146, 214n17
Kao Shao-i: extradited by Tapar Khan, 147
Kao-ti, Emperor: establishes Han dynasty, 26; and Wu-ti, 29, 60; and Mao-tun, 57, 60, 116, 142; promotes exchange, 55, 65, 169

Kao-tsu, Emperor: establishes Later Chin dynasty, 44, 54; seeks alliance with Khitan, 74, 127; a Sha-to Turk, 199n86
Kao-tsu, Emperor: T'ang vassal to Turks, 41, 43, 54, 69–70, 122, 131–132, 151
Khitan Liao dynasty: relations with others, 37, 43, 75, 125–126; emergence of, 43–44, 74–75, 128, 133; relations with Sung, 45, 47, 48, 124, 125, 128–134, 162, 168, 184, 191n50, 191n51; with Chin, 54, 127–128; with T'ang, 125–126, 154–155; Chinese refugees among, 127; trading network of, 168
Kholochi Noyan: seeks markets, 110–111
Khridesungtsan: emergence of, 155–156
Khubilai Khan: bestows titles, 76; and legitimist successors, 76; invades China, 135
Khutughtu. See Lighdan Khan
Kidnapping, 103, 185
Kirghiz: relations with sedentarists, 74; with Uighur, 124, 167; with Khitan, 43
Ko-le Khan: allies with T'ang, 72–73; marries Emperor Su-tsung's daughter, 157–160
K'o-pi-neng: secures plunder, 35–36; relations with Wei dynasty, 36–37; titles given, 67
Koguryo: and Han, 63; and Khitan, 168; and Turks, 195n69
Köndüleng: and Altan, 97–98, 205n102; and Tümen, 105
K'ou Chun: reluctant to grant concessions to Khitan, 129–130
Ku-li-pei-lo: relations with T'ang, 72
Kuang-p'ing. See Tai-tsung, Emperor
Kuang-wu-ti, Emperor: promotes exchange, 31, 63, 65, 144; allies with Wu-huan and Hsien-pei, 33–34
Kuei-li-ch'ih: relations with Ming, 136
K'un-mo: marries Princess Hsi-chun and also Hsiung-nu bride, 143
Kuo Ch'ien: against opening markets, 99
Kuo Ching: trades arrowheads for horses, 185

Lacquer: acquired by nomads, 46, 168, 171
Lang Taiji: relations with Ming, 87–88
Lao-shang Shan-yü: cautioned against Sinicization, 25, 169; and Han, 58
Legalists: argue for war, 61–62
Lei Lu-chün: eunuch, 158
Li Ch'eng-liang: stabilizes frontier, 109
Li Ch'eng-ts'ai: marries Ko-le Khan's surrogate daughter, 157
Li Chiang: prefers intermarriage to war, 163
Li Hsün: accompanies Princess Ning-kuo, 157
Li Ju-sung: killed, 109
Li K'o-yung: seeks Khitan alliance, 126
Li Ping: criticizes random killing of nomads, 180
Li Ssu: against war with nomads, 56

Li Ts'un-hsü. *See* Chuang-tsung, Emperor
Li Yü. *See* Tai-tsung, Emperor
Li Yü: accompanies Princess Ning-kuo, 157–158
Li Yüan. *See* Kao-tsu, Emperor
Li Yüan-hao: warns against Sinicization, 132–133
Liang dynasty: and Khitan, 43, 74–75; and Jou-jan, 120; and Uighur, 124
Liang Shih-tu: establishes Liang dynasty, 69
Liao. *See* Khitan Liao dynasty
Liao-tung: 33, 49, 81, 90, 99, 112, 179
Lighdan Khan: and Ming-Mongol-Manchu relations, 76, 109–112, 199n90
Lin Tse-hsü: seized Western opium, 186
Liu Ching: counsels Kao-ti to marry own daughter to Mao-tun, 57, 142
Liu Liu-fu: negotiates with Sung, 130
Liu Pang. *See* Kao-ti, Emperor
Liu Wen-ching: negotiates with Turks, 69
Liu Wu-chou: assisted by Turks, 69
Lo: frontier trader, 166
Lu Kung: against war with Hsiung-nu, 64
Lü, Empress: will not intermarry own daughter to Mao-tun, 26–27, 53, 142
Lü Ta-ch'i: poisons Mongols, 181
Lung Ta-yu: beheads Altan's envoy, 87

Ma-i: Hsiung-nu entrapped at, 28–29, 41, 59–61, 65, 117, 180, 183
MacCartney, Lord: seeks concessions from Ch'ing, 186
Mahmud: relations with Ming, 77, 136–137
Maladministration: deception of bureaucrats, 82–83; mismanagement cause of war, 94–95; contributes to discord, 176–182; of Canton trade, 186; leads to Ch'iang revolt, 221n65
Manchus: nomadic policies, 11, 17, 20–21; emergence of, 111–112, 192n57; and British, 186
Mandughuli: Uriyangkha reluctant to follow, 84
Manichaeism: Teng-li mo-yü converts to, 184, 218n4; priests smuggle, 184
Manufactured goods: nomads depend upon China for, 7, 11, 13, 27, 123–124
Mao-tun: stabilizes relations with Han, 26, 27, 29; and intermarriage, 26–27, 53, 57, 60, 116, 142; conquers Tung-hu, 32; exchanges goods, 54, 169; wars with Kao-ti, 57, 60
Meng I-mai: critic of markets, 107
Meng T'ien: consolidates Ch'in power, 60
Ming: fruitful for study, 17; and Mongols, 48–49, 76, 81, 111, 115, 136–139, 191n50; and frontier markets, 79–113
Ming-ti, Emperor: borders secured by, 33–34
Ming-tsung, Emperor: lavishly entertains nomads, 125, 177

Miu: Duke of Ch'in attacks Western Jung, 60
Mo-chi-lien. *See* Bilge Khan
Mo-ch'o: rejects intermarriage with family of Empress Wu, 152–153
Möngke Khan: invades Szechwan, 135
Mongkeshiri: defeated by Ming, 111
Mongols: establish Yuan dynasty, 18, 20, 48; Right-Flank, 48, 76–78, 85–87, 97–98, 110, 112, 199n89; Left-Flank, 49, 85–86, 109–110, 112, 199n89; relations with others, 75–76, 110–111, 115, 136–137, 162; and markets, 79–113, 173, 184, 192n63, 220n62; and raids, 172, 179
Morikhai: seeks control of Mongolia, 84
Mu-tsung: relations with Mongols, 96; confers titles, 101, 102, 161
Mughan Khan: allies with Northern Chou, 68, 146, 151

Naiman: offer tribute to Ming, 109–110
Nieh I: seeks to entrap Hsiung-nu, 28–29, 59
Ning-kuo, Princess: intermarries, 157–159
Ning-kuo, Little Princess: intermarries, 159
Nomadic aggression: caused by, 5–8, 13–15, 25, 68; nature of, 24; cyclical, 6
Nomadic states: characteristics of, 13; grow in response to sedentarist power, 190n28; "states on horseback," 193n5
Nomads: and agriculture 2, 175–176; and herding, 2, 166; and hunting, 166, 170; viewed as aggressor, 4, 68, 181; looked down upon, 89, 90, 93, 99; perception of Chinese, 174, 175; seldom studied in West, 189n11; interdependent with sedentarists, 191n37
Noyandara Jinong: heads Ordos Mongols, 97–98; receives title, 100; presents tribute, 209n166
Nurhachi: declares himself khan of Manchu, 111

Ogödei Khan: moderates Yüan excesses, 20
Oirad: led by Esen, 48; relations with Ming, 77, 80–82; and Yüan, 77, 199n92; and Altan, 97; collapse, 135–136; and Eastern Mongols, 137; exchange with Ming, 138–139, 168–169, 172, 184–185
Ong-jing: presents terms of surrender, 163
Onggirad: intermarries with Chinggis Khan, 19
Ordos Mongols: and Ming, 87–88, 97–98, 110–111; invade Tibet, 97
Oxen: exchange of, 37, 80, 101, 122, 126

Pan Ch'ao: secures silk routes, 65
Pan Ku: writes about Hsiung-nu, 3, 17, 27, 119
Pan Piao: advocates increased bestowals, 144
Paper currency: nomads' disinterest in, 81
Peace of 1571: 77

P'ei Chü: T'ang authority on Turks, 41, 105n62, 151–152
P'ei Mein: accompanies Princess Ning-kuo, 157
Pi: submits, 31, 119; humiliated, 31–32; receives smaller gifts, 120, 210n21
P'ien-ho: attacks Wu-huan and Northern Hsiung-nu, 33
Pir Mahamed: presents tribute, 168–169
Plunder: distribution of, 35–36; promised by T'ang, 73–74; to secure goods, 103
Po-hai: relations with Khitan, 43
Po-pai: rebels, 110
Pots: nomads acquire, 101, 171, 173
Prejudice: in nomadic-sedentarist relations, 3, 173–177, 186, 220n49, 222n88
Provisioning troops: difficulty of, 53
P'u-ku Huai-en: daughters wed Teng-li-muo-yü, 159–160

Quilts: received by nomads, 169, 171

Relative power: impact on nomadic-Chinese relationship, 53, 114, 122, 124–126, 129, 134–135, 212n66
Rhinoceros horn: exported by Khitan, 46
Rice: nomads seek, 30, 46, 116–117, 168, 169, 171

Saddles: acquired by nomads, 2, 169
Sai-na-la. See Bars-bolod
Saghang Sechen: glorifies Altan's achievements, 103
Sang Wei-han: opposes war with Khitan, 54, 75
Satin: exchanged, 27, 40, 41, 55, 93, 101, 117, 121, 138, 169, 171, 172, 173
Sayin-alagh: appointed to rule Right-Flank Mongols, 85
Seal testicles: nomads trade, 167
Sechin Taiji: petitions for markets, 111; invades Tibet, 209n163; persuades Altan to accept Buddhism, 209n163
Seeds: nomads acquire, 38, 170, 195n47, 152
Sengge: supports Tümen Khan, 105
Sha-po-lüeh. See Ishbara
Sha-t'o Turks: relations with Khitan, 43; led by Li K'o-yung, 126; establish Later T'ang, 74
Shaji: petitions for markets, 111
Shan-yüan, Treaty of: between Khitan Liao and Sung, 45–46, 129–130, 133
Sheep: exchanged, 42, 46, 94, 95, 120, 122, 126, 154, 166–171 passim, 179
Shen Shih-hsing: argues for markets, 110
Shen-tsung, Emperor: and Tümen Khan, 109; and Manchus, 111
Sheng-tsung, Emperor: relations with Sung, 45
Shih Ch'ao-i: struggle against T'ang, 73, 159, 160

Shih Ching-t'ang. See Kao-tsu, Later Chin emperor
Shih Ch'ung-kuei: as Emperor Ch'u-ti willing to call himself grandson but not vassal, 128
Shih Huang-ti, Emperor: criticized for nomadic policy, 53, 57, 60
Shih-pi Khan: and T'ang, 41, 69, 122, 123, 150–151, 198n63
Shih-shu-hu-hsi: entrapped by Sui, 41
Shih Ssu-ming: rebellion against T'ang, 43, 72–73, 156
Shih Tao: and Altan, 86, 93–95
Shih T'ien-chüeh: Altan's envoy, 86–87
Shih-tsung, Emperor: insists Jou-jan subordinate selves to Northern Wei, 120–121
Shih-tsung, Emperor: considers peace or war with nomads, 85, 89–96 passim
Shu-lü, Princess: regards nomads as catalyst for sedentarist-nomad interaction, 128
Silk: highly coveted, 1, 9, 25–31 passim, 42, 47, 55, 58, 59, 63, 75, 81, 93, 101, 107, 116–143 passim, 148, 152, 154, 160, 163, 166–173 passim, 175, 184, 185; trade routes contested for by Han and Hsiung-nu, 8, 30, 65; not suitable apparel for Hsiung-nu, 25; promised nomads for military help, 69, 70, 72, 73; disfigured, 82, 139, 179, 180
Silver: presented as yearly payment, 116
—received by: Southern Hsiung-nu, 31; Uighur, 43, 160; Khitan, 46–47, 129, 132; Tangut, 133; Jurchen, 134–135; Mongols, 136, 163, 172; Chinese, 168, 175
Sinicization: of nomads, 4, 25, 40–41, 65, 67, 112, 133, 155, 169, 193n7
Sir-tartush: relations with T'ang and Hsiung-nu, 70–71
Slaves: 25, 34, 131, 167, 171
Smuggling: a problem for many dynasties, 45, 80, 108–109, 182–185
Soldiers: guard markets, 101; salaries reduced to maintain markets, 108
Songtsan-gampo: forces T'ang to intermarry with Tibetan court, 155
Southern Sung dynasty: established, 44, 47, 134; debate Khitan alliance, 47, 168; decline of, 76; reliance on yearly payments, 162
Spying: Chinese fear nomads', 4, 45, 93, 109
Ssu-chin. See Mughan Khan
Ssu-ma Ch'ien: on nomads, 2–3, 17, 25–27, 62, 165–166; on his being castrated, 178, 220n57
Su-tsung, Emperor: and Northern Wei relations with Jou-jan, 37, 67, 120–121
Su-tsung, Emperor: and T'ang relations with Uighur, 43, 72, 124; and T'ang intermarriage with Ko-le Khan, 157–159

Index

Sui: 17, 41, 69, 121–123, 126, 146–150, 171, 184–185
Sung: 11–12, 44, 45, 48, 80, 120, 124–125, 128–134, 162, 191n50, 191n51
Sung Ching: deceives Mongols, 135
Sung I: argues against war, 64

Ta-hsia: Wu-ti seeks alliance with, 142
Ta-i, Princess: intermarries, 148–149, 158
Ta-tan: led by Toghto-bukha, 49
Ta-t'ung: market at, 49, 81–113 passim, 126, 179, 184–185
Tai-tsung, Emperor: nomads aid him to consolidate T'ang power, 72–73, 159, 199n77
T'ai-ho, Princess: intermarries, 160–162
T'ai-tsung, Emperor: on T'ang relations with nomads, 70, 74; admits Kao-tsu gave tribute to Turks, 122; husband of Empress Wu
T'ai-tsung, Emperor; on Liao foreign policies, 42, 44–45, 75, 127–128
T'ai-tsung, Emperor: on Sung-Khitan relations, 129; captures Il Khan, 131
T'an-shih-huai: attacks Han, 35–36
T'ang: 9, 17, 41, 54, 70, 74, 124–127, 151–161, 171, 185
T'ang, Later: 43–44, 74–75, 124–127
Tangut Hsia: 124–125, 132–134, 162, 184
Tapar Khan: and Northern Ch'i, 69, 147; presents horses, 121; seeks intermarriage, 147
Tarto Khan: challenges Sha-po-lüeh, 40
Te-tsung, Emperor: intermarries with Uighur, 160; served by Li Chiang, 163
Tea: exchange of, 46, 80–81, 133, 185
Teng-li mo-yü: alliances sought with, 73; intermarries with T'ang, 159–160; converted to Manichaeism, 184, 218n22
Third Dalai Lama: Altan visits, 105
Ti Shan: counsels intermarriage, 62
Tibet: and Uighur, 17–18, 124; and Bilge Khan, 42, 195n68; and tea-horse trade, 80; and Altan, 97; and Bingtu, 105; and Bintu, 106; and China, 154–157, 192n56; and T'u-yü-hun, 155
T'ieh-le: predecessors of Uighur, 123; trade with Khitan Liao, 168
Ting-ling: and Hsiung-nu, 26, 30, 32; and Hsien-pei, 35
T'o-pa: found Northern Wei dynasty, 37, 67
Toghto-bukha: on Esen and his war with Ming, 49–50, 83; and Ming tributary system, 49, 88, 94, 100, 138–139, 172
Tölis Khan: relations with Sui, 40–41, 171; intermarriage, 149–150; relations with Koguryo, 195n69
Tonyukhukh: warns against Sinicization, 132, 193n7

Tou family: dominates Han court, 64–65
Treaty of 1042: between Liao and Sung, 45–46; territory sought, 130
Treaty of 1123: between Sung and Jurchen, 133–134
Tribute system: Chinese assumptions regarding, 4, 15–16; rhetoric of kinship used in, 14–15, 44, 57, 117, 118, 124, 127, 134–135, 142; to promote peace, 16, 53–55, 79, 89, 107, 113, 201n37; exchange through, 30, 37, 38, 55, 100, 106, 109, 122, 138–139, 160, 167–169, 172, 180, 190n31, 192n55; advantageous to nomads, 13–15, 31, 55, 87, 89, 90, 107, 114–116, 117; ten objections to establishing, 89–90; Wang Ch'ung-ku's program regarding, 100–101; mechanisms used for exchange, 114–115; unruly nomads in, 137–139; Altan's memorial seeking, 206n117; merchants disguised as envoys, 214n116
Ts'ai Ching: argues for alliance with Jurchen against Khitan, 47
Ts'ai Yung: warns against attacking Hsien-pei, 183
Ts'ao Ts'ao: relations with Hsien-pei, 36–37
Tu-lan Khan: marries and kills Ta-i, 149
Tu Wen-huan: defeats Ordos Mongols, 111
T'u-mu: Ming Ying-tsung captured at, 50, 139
T'u-yü-hun: Tibet attacks, 155; Yu-wen T'ai campaigns against, 155
Tümen Khan: wars with Altan and Ming, 48–50, 96–98, 103–105, 109–110, 208n121
T'ung Kuan: for Sung alliance with Jurchen against Khitan, 47–48
T'ung-yeh-hu: seeks intermarriage, 152
Turk: relations, with Wei, 37; T'ang, 42, 54, 69–71, 122, 127, 132, 151, 155, 171; Northern Ch'i and Northern Chou, 68, 121, 146–147; Khitan, 126; Jou-jan, 146; Sui, 147–150, 171; Tibet, 155; Koguryo, 195n69; warned against Sinicization, 133, 175; traditions when ruler dies, 216n76

Uighur: relations with, T'ang, 43, 71, 124–127, 156–162; Sir-tartush, 71; Kirghiz, 74; the Five Dynasties, 74, 124–126; Manichaeism, 167, 184, 218n4
Uriyangkha: and Ming, 77, 80–81, 84, 90, 104, 109, 172, 199n91; and Tümen Khan, 80, 104; reasons for invading China, 180–181

Vassal: title adopted by nomad and sedentarist alike, 14–15, 70, 102, 117, 119, 120, 123, 127, 129, 130, 133, 134, 145, 174

Wan-li: Tümen Khan wars with, 109
Wan-yen Hsiang: offers titles to nomads, 76
Wang Chen: provokes war, 82, 179–180, 185

Wang Chi-chung: offers concessions to nomads, 129
Wang Chih: provokes war, 179
Wang Chih-hao: debates title granting, 100
Wang Ch'ung-ku: Viceroy of Hsüan-fu and Ta-t'ung, 96; eight-point program of, 99–101; negotiates peace with Altan, 96–105; continues Fang Feng-shih's policies, 105–106; criticizes frontier officials, 181
Wang Fu: wants war with Khitan, 48
Wang Hui: wants war against Hsiung-nu, 59–61
Wang Jing: presents titles to nomads, 76
Wang Mang: an activist in nomad policies, 31, 63, 65–66; establishes Hsin dynasty, 52, 119; T'ang T'ai-tsung adopts his title-granting policies, 71; leads Hsiung-nu to seek new relations with China, 119; weakens Han, 174
Wang Yüeh: investigates corruption, 181
War: traditional arguments against, 53–57, 59–64, 90–92; arguments for, 54, 59–60, 89–90, 201n47; reasons for outbreak of, 94–96, 102–103, 179–181, 189n6; carnage of, 62, 107, 178; enriches soldiers, 48, 191n50; disadvantageous to nomadic rulers, 131; breaks out on margins of society, 182
Wei dynasty: relation of Ts'ao Ts'ao Wei with nomads, 36, 65, 67
Wei, Northern: relations with nomads, 37, 120–121, 123, 125–126, 170–171; established, 67; breaks up, 68, 121; title-granting policies, 71; intermarry defectors to integrate into state, 145
Wei, Eastern: established, 68, 121
Wei, Western: established, 39, 68, 121
Wei Ch'ing: attacks Hsiung-nu, 62
Wen-ch'eng, Princess: intermarries, 155–156
Wen Ch'iu: offers rewards to Lighdan Khan, 111
Wen-ti, Emperor: relations with Hsiung-nu, 26–27, 58, 60; war and peace debated, 55
Wen-ti, Emperor: relations with Turks, 39–40, 121–122; and bestowals, 117; and intermarriage, 148–149; consolidates Sui, 147; and markets, 177
Weng Wan-ta: advocates peace, 87, 191n50; opposes killing envoys, 201n37; calls for tribute relations, 201n37
Wine: exchanged, 25, 26, 30, 116–117, 169
Wooden bowls: offered as tribute, 168, 218n25
Wool: suitable apparel for nomads, 25, 132–133; nomads rely upon, 1, 166–170 passim
Wu, Emperor: presents bestowals to Yeh-lü A-pao-chi, 43
Wu, Empress: establishes Chou dynasty, 152–153, 156
Wu-huan: and Hsiung-nu, 30, 32, 34, 63–64; and Hsien-pei, 32–35; description of, 32, 170; and Han, 34, 36; and Ts'ao Ts'ao, 37; offer tribute, 167
Wu Kuang: seeks bribes from Uriyangkha, 180
Wu-sun: and Hsiung-nu, 30, 143; and Hsien-pei, 35; and Wu-ti, 142–143
Wu-ti, Emperor: frontier markets of, 28, 183; and intermarriage, 28, 117, 142–144; wars of, 29, 51; entraps Hsiung-nu at Ma-i market, 29, 61, 65, 117, 180, 183; relations with other states, 32, 142, 144; debate on peace or war, 52, 56–57, 59–63
Wu-tsung, Emperor: chaotic relations with Mongols, 85
Wu Yen-hsiu: sent to marry daughter of Mo-ch'o, 152–153

Yabkhu: early T'ang ally, 72–73, 159
Yak tails: Uighur trade with China, 124, 125
Yang Cheng-tao: I-Ch'eng supports, 150
Yang Chi-sheng: lists ten objections to trade, 89–90; punished, 92, 178; suggests profits of horse trade adequate, 95; memorial advocates war against Mongols, 201n47
Yang Hsin: negotiates with Hsiung-nu, 117
Yang Shan: negotiates with Esen, 139
Yang-ti, Emperor: relations with Turks, 40–41, 195n69
Yao An: disrupts frontier, 180–181
Yearly payments: to provide goods and promote peace, 27, 53–55; to Hsiung-nu, 28, 47, 120; to Khitan, 44, 46, 47, 127, 129–132, 162, 172; benefit nomadic courts, 48, 131, 191n50; mandated by nomads, 115–116; to Uighur, 124; to Tangut, 132–133, 162; to Jurchen, 134–135, 162, 172; conclusions regarding, 139; to Mongols, 179–180
Yeh-lü A-pao-chi: unifies Khitan, 43; alliances sought, 74–75, 126
Yeh-lü Ch'u-ts'ai: counsels against plundering China, 20
Yeh-lü Te-kuang. See T'ai-tsung (Liao emperor)
Yen Yu: argues against war, 52–53, 57
Yi-li-bi: presents tribute, 168
Ying-tsung, Emperor: captured at T'u-mu, 50, 83; closes horse markets, 81; regains throne, 83; and tribute missions, 139; events in Mongolia after capture, 210n5
Yüan Chen: against intermarriage, 153–154
Yüan dynasty: 48, 76–77
Yüeh-chih: attacked by Hsiung-nu, 26; Wu-ti seeks alliance with, 142
Yung-lo: and Mongols, 77; and boundaries, 80; and horse markets, 90
Yung-lü: denied intermarriage, 149; rebels, 150
Yüngshiyebu: attacked by Ming, 84